MW01088733

Journal of the American Revolution

EDITORIAL BOARD

TODD ANDRLIK, EDITOR-IN-CHIEF

DON N. HAGIST, EDITOR

HUGH T. HARRINGTON, EDITOR EMERITUS

J. L. BELL, ASSOCIATE EDITOR

JIM PIECUCH, ASSOCIATE EDITOR

RAY RAPHAEL, ASSOCIATE EDITOR

JOURNAL

OF THE

AMERICAN REVOLUTION

Annual Volume 2016

WESTHOLME
Yardley

Compilation © 2016 The Journal of the American Revolution

All articles © 2016 by their respective authors

Images are from the Library of Congress unless otherwise indicated.

All rights reserved under International and Pan-American Copyright Conventions. No part of this book may be reproduced in any form or by any electronic or mechanical means, including information storage and retrieval systems, without permission in writing from the publisher, except by a reviewer who may quote brief passages in a review.

Westholme Publishing, LLC
904 Edgewood Road
Yardley, Pennsylvania 19067
Visit our Web site at www.westholmepublishing.com

First Printing April 2016
10 9 8 7 6 5 4 3 2 1
ISBN: 978-1-59416-253-4
Also available as an eBook.

Printed in the United States of America.

CONTENTS

EDITORS' INTRODUCTION

It has been 250 years since the series of political events that led to the American Revolution. A lot has been written about the era since then, and rightfully so: not only did the rebellion, war, and Constitution create a great nation, they established a new form of democratic government that has been emulated, to some degree, around the globe. With so much already written, one might wonder how it is that there is still more to write. And yet, *Journal of the American Revolution* has completed its third year of providing fresh, insightful, and important content.

Two major factors have made this possible. First, it so happens that much of what was written in the past about America's founding era is wrong, having been biased, exaggerated, and sometimes even invented to put a positive and righteous spin on what was in reality a troubled and turbulent era. Second, modern technology has made an unprecedented quantity of primary sources readily accessible; research that once required expensive journeys to far-away archives can now be done at home during free time. Only a fraction of the era's manuscript information is available in digital form, but that has already made an enormous difference in the depth and fidelity of information available to researchers. Rather than relying on the retold folklore and mythology that has shaped public perception of the American Revolution, it is now easier than ever to read the words of the participants, from the statesmen and generals to the common soldiers and citizens.

This combination of inaccurate early historiography and widely available source material has allowed the *Journal of the American Revolution* to thrive. It would not be possible, of course, without the outstanding efforts of intelligent, motivated contributors who recognize the journal as the ideal forum to correct misconceptions and present exciting new information. The third annual volume presents a selection of *Journal* articles published in 2015. Far from running out of new things to say, it's clear the contributors are just getting started.

The Seed from which the
Sons of Liberty Grew

❀❧ BOB RUPPERT ❧❀

On March 9, 1764, George Grenville proposed a stamp tax in a speech to Parliament; its purpose was to reduce the cost of maintaining 10,000 garrisoned soldiers in North America. Grenville claimed it would be similar to the one administered in England in 1694.[1]

Eleven months later, on February 17, the Act was passed in the House of Commons by a vote of 205 to 49; on March 8, it passed in the House of Lords unanimously; and on March 22, it was given Royal assent. It was to become effective November 1.[2]

The Stamp Act caused both anger and resentment in the colonies – not so much because of its imposition of a tax, but rather because of its manner of enactment and means of enforcement. The colonists believed that it violated their rights as Englishmen.

In Boston a group of men formed a "social club." Their purpose, however, was more than social, it was to formulate and organize a response to the Stamp Act when news of its passage reached Massachusetts.

They called themselves the "Loyal Nine." They were respectable merchants and tradesmen; but not the most prominent citizens of the city. They were unassuming, avoided undue publicity, and operated in complete secrecy. They were John Avery, a distiller; Henry Bass, a merchant and Samuel Adams' cousin; Thomas Chase, a distiller; Stephen Cleverly, a brazier (a person who worked with brass); Thomas Crafts, a painter; Benjamin Edes, owner of the *Boston Gazette*; John Smith, a brazier; George Trott, a jeweler; and Henry Welles, a

---

1. "5 & 6 William III & Mary II c. 21," in *Acts of the Parliament of England, prior to 1707.*
2. Carl Becker, *The Eve of the Revolution* (New Haven, CT: Yale University Press, 1918), 48.

ship owner.[3] Some records show Joseph Field, a shipmaster, as a member, but there is some question.

The Loyal Nine met in one of two locations; either in "a small compting Room in Chase and Speakman's Distillery"[4] or under the foliage of a large elm tree in nearby Hanover Square. The tree would soon become known as the "Liberty Tree." It would serve for the next ten years as a meeting place for speeches and a staging area for protests and demonstrations.

News the Act's passage reached Boston in May. Knowing they were going to need help organizing a resistance movement, the Loyal Nine turned to Ebenezer Mackintosh and his mob of rabble-rousers, known as the South Enders. They "managed" most activities in the south part of the city. Inciting public disturbance was not foreign to them. Somehow the Loyal Nine convinced Mackintosh to put aside his local quarrels with Henry Swift and the North Enders and direct their strength against the Stamp Act. It may have been related to an incident that occurred on August 12. Samuel Adams, one of the city's tax collectors and strongly associated with the Loyal Nine, had sworn out a warrant for unpaid taxes against Mackintosh and then suddenly dropped the matter. Was "an arrangement" arrived at?

As the sun rose on August 14, the citizens of Boston were greeted by

> something so Rair as to draw the attention of almost the whole Town—it was no less than the Effigie of the Honourable Stamp Master of [the] Province hanging on one of the great Trees at the south end directly over the main street—behind him was a Boot hung up with the Devil Crawling out, with the Pitchfork in his hand, on the Effigie's Right arm was writ and sew'd on the letters AO [Andrew Oliver]—On his left arm was wrote these words 'It's a glorious sight to See a stamp-man hanging on a Tree' . . . This Effigie hung in this manner alday . . . the mob . . . took the Image down, after the performance of some Cerimonies. It was brought through the main street to near Olivers Dock, and in less than half an hour laid it even with the ground then took timbers of the house and caryd 'em up on Fort Hill where they stamped the Image & timber & made a bonfire—the fuel faild.—they Immediately fell upon the stamp Masters Garden fence, took it up, stampd it and

3. L. H. Butterfield ed., *Diary and Autobiography of John Adams*, Vol. I, *Diary 1755-1770* (Cambridge, MA: The Belknap Press of Harvard University Press, 1961), 294.
4. Ibid.

burnt it . . . Not contented with this they proceeded to his Coach house took off the doars, stampd 'em & burnt 'em.—While they was doing this, the Sheriff began to read the proclamation for the mob to withdraw.[5]

This was the first, large-scale action in Boston against the Stamp Act and, more specifically, a Stamp Master. It was well planned, directed at a specific target and executed accordingly. The Loyal Nine's rationale was simple: without Stamp Masters, the Act could not go into effect. John Dickinson said it was "the most effectual and most decent Method of preventing the Execution of a Statute, that strikes the Axe into the Root of the Tree."[6]

Unfortunately, on August 26, "persons disguised and armed with clubs and sticks collect[ed] in King Street . . . they hurr[ied] away to [Lt. Governor Thomas] Hutchinson's house with the rage of mad-men. He sen[t] off his children; bar[red] his doors and windows, and meant to remain but [was] soon under the necessity of withdrawing, first to one house, then to another, where he continued till four in the morning."[7] One of the best houses in the province was completely in ruins, nothing remaining but the bare walls and floors. The plate, family pictures, most of the furniture, and wearing apparel, about £900 sterling in money, and the manuscripts and books which Governor Hutchinson had been 30 years collecting, beside many public papers in his custody, were either carried off or destroyed.[8] The evening's destruction was not directed by the Loyal Nine. They had set strict boundaries regarding how far violence could go and on this evening, those boundaries had been crossed. They repudiated the ransacking of Hutchinson's house. In an article in the *Boston Gazette* on September 2, it was stated, "In some extraordinary Cases the Cause of Liberty requires an extraordinary Spirit to support it . . . [the actions of the two evenings proceeded] from different Motives, as their conduct was evidently different . . . The pulling down Houses and robbing Persons . . . when any suppos'd Injuries can be redress'd by Law [was]

5. "Letter from Cyrus Baldwin to Laommi Baldwin, 15 August 1765," Massachusetts Historical Society, Miscellaneous Bound Manuscripts.

6. Paul Leicester Ford, ed., "John Dickinson's Anti-Stamp Broadside," November 1765, in "The Writings of John Dickinson: I, Political Writings, 1764-1774," *Memoirs of the Historical Society of Pennsylvania*, XIV (Philadelphia, 1895), 201-205.

7. William Gordon, *The History of the Rise, Progress and Establishment of the Independence of the United States of America*, Vol. I (London: Charles Dilly Co., 1787), 175-177.

8. Abiel Holmes, *Annals of America* (Cambridge, MA, 1829), II, 135-136.

utterly inconsistent with the first Principles of Government, and subversive of the glorious Cause."[9] Bernard Bailyn believes it was on this night that "Force had been introduced into the Revolutionary movement in a form long familiar but now newly empowered to widely shared principles and beliefs. It would never thereafter be absent."[10] This is not to say that incidents of protest had not been occurring in other cities and towns from Halifax to Charleston, but now force had been introduced as a tool of the masses.

On August 26, Andrew Oliver informed his fellow Stamp Master, Jared Ingersoll of Connecticut, his intention to resign from his office,

> Sir: The News Papers will sufficiently inform you of the Abuse I have met with. I am therefore only to acquaint you in short, that after having stood the attack for 36 hours—a single man against a whole People, the Government not being able to afford me any help during that whole time, I was persuaded to yield, in order to prevent what was coming in the night; and as I happened to give out in writing the terms of Capitulation, I send you a copy of them.[11]

Four days later, Hutchinson wrote to Richard Jackson, "The encouragers of the first mob never intended matters should go to this length and the people in general express the utmost detestation of this unparalled outrage."[12]

On November 1, the day that enforcement of the Stamp Act was to begin, there appeared in a Boston newspaper a caricature by John Singleton Copley, entitled, "The Deplorable State of America." The "cartoon" expressed the emotions of the citizens of Boston who felt threatened by the revenue measure. Some of the actors in it were Minerva, Britannia, Mercury, an American Indian Princess, and Liberty; some of the images were a

> Flying Britannia, leaving behind fragments of Magna Charta, holding out Pandora's Box to America, saying, 'Take it Daughter its

9. *Boston Gazette*, September 2, 1765; Eliot to Hollis, August 27, 1765, *Collections of the Massachusetts Historical Society*, 4th Series, Vol. IV, 406-407.

10. Bernard Bailyn, *Pamphlets of the American Revolution 1750-1776*, Vol. I (Cambridge, MA: Belknap Press of Harvard University Press, 1965), 585.

11. Andrew Oliver to Jared Ingersoll, Esq., 26 August 1765, in *Papers of the New Haven Colony Historical Society* Vol. IX (New Haven, 1918), 328.

12. Quoted by Edmund S. Morgan in his useful collection of documents, *Prologue to Revolution—Sources and Documents on the Stamp Act Crisis, 1764-1766* (Chapel Hill, 1959), 109.

"The Deplorable State of America or Sc[otc]h Government." (*John Carter Brown Library at Brown University*)

only the S–p A–t'; America, appealing to Minerva, Goddess of Wisdom, begs her to shield her, as Liberty lies dying at America's feet; the asp that stings Liberty creeps out of a thistle, symbolic of Scotland and the Scotch influence around the throne; Loyalty, holding the crown and leaning against the Tree of Liberty, sighs that she fears she will lose her support; above them flies a figure representing France, who uses gold to influence Lord Bute, a boot in the sky whose rays seem like marionette strings holding Britannia; in the left background one well-dressed gentleman remarks that they will lose 500 pounds per year, and another comments, 'Who would not sell their country for so large a sum'; in their vicinity are . . . gallows labeled 'Fit Entertainment for St–p M–n'; and one man leaning over the grave asks, 'Will you resign,' and a voice answers from within the grave, 'Yes, yes, I will.'[13]

On November 5, the citizens of Boston were greeted by an unusual scene—Ebenezer Mackintosh, Captain of the South Enders, and Henry Swift, Captain of the North Enders, two bitter rivals, were leading their men side-by-side down the streets of Boston. These were two mobs that had gone at each other with clubs and knives on Guy Fawkes Day for as long as anyone could remember. The citizens were

13. John Adams, *Papers of John Adams*, Vol. I (Cambridge, MA: Harvard University Press, 2003), xi.

amazed and confused—what had happened? The answer is the "Union Feast." Samuel Adams with the assistance of John Hancock organized a series of dinners the night before and encouraged "all classes of men," meaning the two mobs, to share a meal together. Some of he Loyal Nine were present and "with Heart and Hands in flowing Bowls and bumping Glasses,"[14] the Sons of Liberty were born!

In the evening of December 16, Andrew Oliver received a notice from the Sons of Liberty that his presence was requested at the Liberty Tree the next day to publicly resign his office of Stamp Master. The letter ended with the following caveat: "Provided you comply with the above, you shall be treated with the greatest Politeness and Humanity. If not . . . " The next morning he sent for his friend, John Avery; he hoped that he would act as an intermediary between himself and the Sons of Liberty. Avery told him that it was too late—that the effigies were already prepared. Oliver then offered to resign at the courthouse, but was told that would not be acceptable. Shortly before noon Ebenezer Mackintosh appeared at his door; his charge was to escort Oliver through the streets of Boston to the Liberty Tree. Because there was a heavy rain, Oliver was permitted to read his resignation from an upper window of a house next to the Liberty Tree. Henry Bass described the Loyal Nine's involvement in the day:

> On seeing Messrs. Edes & Gill in last mondays Paper, the Loyall Nine repair'd the same Evg. [December 16] to Liberty Hall, in order to Consult what further should be done respecting Mr. Oliver's Resignation, as what had been done heretofore, we tho't not Conclusive & upon some little time debating we apprehended it would be most Satisfactory to the Publick to send a Letter to desire him to appear under Liberty Tree at 12 oClock on Tuesday, to make a publick Resignation under Oath: the Copy of which the advertisement, his Message, Resignation & Oath you have Inclos'd. The whole affair transacted by the Loyall Nine in writing the Letter, getting the Advertisements Printed, which were all done after 12 oClock Monday night, the advertisements Pasted up to the amount of a hundred was all done from 9 to 3 oClock.[15]

Messrs. Crafts and Chase gave John Adams a similar account:

14. "Francis Bernard to Thomas Pownall, November 6, 1765," in *Bernard Papers* (Cambridge, MA: Houghton Library, Harvard University).

15. Henry Bass to Samuel P. Savage, 19 December 1765, "Savage Papers," *Proceedings of the Massachusetts Historical Society*, 44 (Boston, 1910-1911), 888-889.

[They] gave me a particular Account of the Proceedings of the Sons of Liberty on Tuesday last in prevailing on Mr. Oliver to renounce his office of Distributor of Stamps, by a Declaration under his Hand, and under the very Tree of Liberty, nay under the very Limb where he had been hanged in Effigy, Aug. 14, 1765. Their absolute Requisition of an Oath, and under that Tree, were Circumstances, extremely humiliating and mortifying, as Punishment for his receiving a Deputation to be a Distributor after his pretended Resignation, and for his faint and indirect Declaration in the News Papers last Monday.[16]

On the evening of January 15, 1766, John Adams was invited by Crafts and Trott to spend an evening with them and the rest of the Loyal Nine at the distillery.

I went, and was civilly and respectfully treated, by all Present. We had Punch, Wine, Pipes and Tobacco, Bisquit and Cheese etc . . . I heard nothing but such Conversation as passes at all Clubs among Gentlemen about the Times. No Plots, no Machinations. They chose a Committee to make Preparations for grand Rejoicings upon the Arrival of the News of a Repeal of the Stamp Act, and I heard afterwards they are to have such Illuminations, Bonfires, Piramids, Obelisks, such grand Exhibitions, and such Fireworks, as were never before seen in America.[17]

One month later, Adams was again invited by Thomas Crafts to attend the Monday gathering, but this time instead of writing "with the Loyal Nine" he wrote "the Sons of Liberty."

Yesterday I wrote you a few lines, by Dr Tufts, informing you the Sons of Liberty desired your company at Boston . . . on Monday next, because they want you to write those inscriptions that I mentioned to you when last at Boston; one in favor of Liberty, not forgetting the true-born sons, and another with encomiums on King George, expressive of our loyalty . . . P.S. Destroy this after reading it.[18]

On March 18, 1766, Parliament repealed the Stamp Act. "In this present Parliament assembled, and by the authority of the same, that

16. Butterfield ed., *Diary and Autobiography of John Adams*, 265.
17. Butterfield ed., *Diary and Autobiography of John Adams*, 294.
18. Charles Francis Adams, ed., *The Works of John Adams*, Col. II (Boston: Charles C. Little and James Brown, 1850), 185-186.

from and after the first day of May, one thousand seven hundred and sixty-six, the above-mentioned Act, and the several matters and things therein contained, shall be, and is and are hereby repealed and made void to all intents and purposes whatsoever."[19] The Loyal Nine had fulfilled their purpose.

Three years later the group, less Joseph Field and Henry Welles, would attend the largest social gathering held by the Sons of Liberty. At 11:00 a.m. they met at the Liberty Tree and offered 14 toasts, then repaired to Dorchester where they

> dined with 350 Sons of Liberty at [Lemuel] Robinsons, the Sign of Liberty Tree . . . We had two Tables laid in the open Field by the Barn, with between 300 and 400 Plates, and an Awing of Sail Cloth overhead, and should have spent a most agreeable Day had not the Rain made some Abatement in our Pleasures. . . . After Dinner was over and the Toasts drunk . . . we [sang] the Liberty Song. . . . This is cultivating the Sensations of Freedom. There was a large Collection of good Company. Otis and Adams are politick, in promoting these Festivals, for they tinge the Minds of the People, they impregnate them with the sentiments of Liberty. They render the People fond of their Leaders in the Cause, and averse and bitter against all opposers.[20]

The account in the *Boston Gazette* of August 21 gave the final toast as "*Strong Halters, Firm Blocks, and Sharp Axes* to all such as deserve either."[21]

On November 27, 1773, the first of three ships carrying chests of tea arrived in Boston harbor. The North-End Caucus met at the Green Dragon Tavern and organized night patrols along the wharf to keep watch of the ships; others organized a series of meetings in the Old South Meetinghouse to discuss what to do with the tea. The patrols were in existence for nineteen days. Among those on duty on November 29 were Henry Bass, Thomas Chase, and Benjamin Edes.[22]

19. avalon.law.yale.edu/18th_century/repeal_stamp_act_1766.asp.

20. William Palfrey, "An Alphabetical List of the Sons of Liberty who din'd at Liberty Tree [Tavern], Dorchester," *Massachusetts Historical Society Online Collections*; Butterfield ed., *Diary and Autobiography of John Adams*, 341.

21. *The Boston Gazette and Country Journal*, Monday, August 21, 1769, in the Annotated Newspapers of Harbottle Door (Boston: Massachusetts Historical Society).

22. Francis S. Drake, *Tea Leaves: Being a Collection of Letters and Documents Relating to the Shipment of Tea to the American Colonies in the Year 1773 . . . , An Introduction* (Boston: A. O. Crane, 1884), 46.

Sixty-three years later, Peter Edes, the son of Benjamin Edes, wrote the following in a letter to his grandson:

> I recollect perfectly well that, in the afternoon preceding . . . the destruction of the tea, a number of gentlemen met in the parlor of my father's house, how many I cannot say . . . I was not admitted into their presence . . . They remained in the house till dark, I suppose to disguise themselves like Indians, when they left the house and proceeded to the wharves where the vessels lay. After they left the room I went into it, but my father was not there.[23]

Benjamin Edes (and Thomas Chase) had left to participate in the Boston Tea Party.[24]

---

23. Letter from Peter Edes to his grandson, Benjamin C. Edes, dated February 16, 1836, in the *Proceedings of the Massachusetts Historical Society 1871-1873*, Vol. 12 (Boston: Massachusetts Historical Society, 1873), 174-175.
24. Benjamin J. Carp, *Defiance of the Patriots: The Boston Tea Party and the Making of America* (New Haven, CT: Yale University Press, 2010), Appendix.

Newton Prince and the Struggle for Liberty

❧ J. L. BELL ☙

On the 5th of March 1770, Newton Prince heard Boston's church bells start to ring. He ran to the door of his house and heard "the cry of fire." Putting on his shoes, Prince went out to help fight the blaze, as town inhabitants were supposed to do. On the streets he asked other men where the fire was. According to his later testimony, "they said it was something better than fire."[1]

As he pressed on to the center of Boston, Newton Prince moved into the struggle for liberty in British North America. But his experience of liberty differed from most of his neighbors'. Newton Prince was a black man, born in 1733. When he married in 1761, town records listed him as a "negro servant"—i.e., slave—of John Gould, Jr. By March 1767, when he married his second wife, Phillis Binn, Prince was a free man and a member of Boston's Old South Meeting.[2]

According to the merchant Gilbert Deblois, the Princes "Supported themselves . . . with Reputation in the Pastrycook branch by attending & Cooking at most of the Public Entertainments &c." Prince himself wrote that he "supported himself & family in a decent

---

1. Newton Prince's descriptions of what he saw on 5 March 1770 are collected in *Legal Papers of John Adams*, L. Kinvin Roth and Hiller B. Zobel, editors (Cambridge, MA: Harvard University Press, 1965), 3:77, 201.

2. *Boston Town Records*, 30:39, 327. Prince's first wife was Martha Barnaby, a free black woman. Prince's master Gould died before 1765; *Colonial Society of Massachusetts Publications*, 20:14-15. To the British government Prince identified himself as "a native of Boston in America." In 1770 Robert Treat Paine wrote in his trial notes that Prince came "from [blank] in the WI," interpreted as the West Indies; *Legal Papers of John Adams*, 3:77. Prince might actually have said he came from Boston's West End since his route to the center of town went past "the Chapple," most likely King's Chapel.

& comfortable way" for years.[3] He might have catered dances and concerts at the building on Hanover Street called Concert-Hall, which the Deblois family owned in the 1760s.

In March 1770, Boston had been occupied by British army regiments for almost a year and a half. As soon as those soldiers arrived, there had been friction between them and locals: over using public buildings for barracks, over whether town watchmen could give orders to army officers, over the use of the streets. In those months Concert-Hall stayed busy with musical performances, but even those were political fodder: local Whigs happily reported about a concert on January 25, 1769, that some "noisy and clamorous" officers had "turned topsy turvy."[4]

Turmoil waxed and waned, but as that winter ended Boston was roiled by several conflicts. The town's Whigs were promoting a boycott of goods from Britain to protest the Townshend duties, and putting harsh pressure on the small number of shopkeepers still selling imports. A demonstration outside one storefront on 22 February had ended with a Customs employee fatally shooting a young boy. In early March an insult that one ropemaker threw at one soldier had grown into days of running brawls.[5]

In that atmosphere, word that the army sentry guarding the Customs house had clubbed a barber's apprentice with his musket was incendiary. The apprentice's friends spread the news and rang the bells of a nearby church to summon more people. Some of the men who arrived had already been fighting soldiers outside their barracks.

As Newton Prince headed to the center of town, he met some people carrying fire-fighting equipment and others with "clubs" and "sticks in their hands." He reached the Town House, seat of the provincial legislature. An angry crowd surrounded Pvt. Hugh White, the sentry in front of the Customs office a block away down King Street. As Prince watched, Cpl. William Wemms led a squad of six grenadiers from the 29th Regiment from the main guardhouse through the crowd "with their guns and bayonets fixed."

---

3. Deblois's 10 March 1781 letter to the Loyalists Commission and Prince's undated petition from about the same time are in the Newton Prince file, Audit Office 13/75, 282-7, National Archives, Great Britain.

4. O.M. Dickerson, compiler, *Boston Under Military Rule, 1768-1769* (Boston: Chapman & Grimes, 1936), 55.

5. The most thorough treatment of this period appears in Hiller B. Zobel, *The Boston Massacre* (New York: W. W. Norton, 1970).

Prince was standing at the west door of the Town House. He listened to the people around him argue about attacking the main guard. "For God's sake, do not meddle with them," said some. "By God we will go," said others.[6] In the end, nobody made a move in that direction. Instead, it appears, those men "huzzaed and went down *King-street*" toward the Customs office. More people joined the crowd from other directions, and Prince followed them.

He recalled, "The soldiers were all placed round in a circle with their guns breast high. I stood on the right wing." Capt. Thomas Preston, officer of the day, joined the soldiers from the main guard. Prince recalled that locals thronged around the captain to speak to him, and he moved with those men "next to the *Custom-house* door."

By this point men were crowded only "three or four feet" from the soldiers' bayonets. Some were shouting, "Fire, damn you, fire!" "Fire, you lobsters!" "You dare not fire!" Prince stated:

> I saw people with sticks striking on their guns at the right wing. I apprehended danger and that the guns might go off accidentally. I went to get to the upper end towards the Town house, I had not got to the center of the party, before the guns went off; as they went off I run, and did not stop till I got to the upper end of the Town-house.

Three men lay dead in the street. Two more had been fatally wounded, and six more suffered lesser wounds. Prince said he "saw the bodies carried away."

Whigs named that event the Boston Massacre. Prince was called to testify at two of the trials that followed, of Capt. Thomas Preston and of the enlisted men. In both cases, he was a defense witness. His testimony was not entirely damning for the townspeople—he said, for example, that he had not seen anything thrown at the soldiers "but snow balls, flung by some youngsters." But, in contrast to some prosecution witnesses, he described the crowd as aggressive.

Suffolk County juries acquitted Capt. Preston and all but two of the soldiers. Pvts. Edward Montgomery and Mathew Kilroy were convicted of manslaughter, a crime punished at the first offense by branding instead of hanging. Locals continued to argue the justice of those verdicts.

---

6. Words quoted from Prince's testimony with modern punctuation for clarity.

Newton Prince reappears in the record of Boston politics in the spring of 1773 when the Massachusetts legislature debated a petition from four men. Peter Bestes, Sambo Freeman, Felix Holbrook, and Chester Joie identified themselves as slaves and asked for their liberty in the same spirit that the province was demanding its political liberties from the Crown.

That petition was not a spontaneous plea. It was an organized campaign by the town's African-Americans, supported by some anti-slavery whites. The four men's letter, dated "Boston, April 20th, 1773," was printed for distribution to the legislators, with an address line printed on the front: "For the Representative of the town of [blank]."[7]

The four slaves had neither liberty nor legal standing, but Newton Prince spoke for them. Years later Samuel Dexter, then a member of the Council or upper house of the legislature, recalled how he had received the petition:

> I was called out of the Council Chamber, and very politely presented with the pamphlet by Newton, who, after making his best bow, said that the negroes had been informed that I was against the slave-trade, and was their friend. He had several more to give to particular members of the House of Representatives. Upon my returning into the chamber, I boasted, as I have since, that I was distinguished from all the other members of council by this mark of respect.

Dexter wrote on his copy of the pamphlet that "it was given to me by Mr. Newton Prince, lemon merchant, in the name and at the desire of a number of negroes."[8] Boston's representatives in the lower house also received a copy of the young merchant James Swan's essay, "A Dissuasive to Great-Britain and Her Colonies from the Slave-Trade."[9] Prince was thus acting as what we would now call a civil-rights lobbyist.

---

7. The New-York Historical Society owns a copy of the leaflet marked for a representative from Thompson, Massachusetts. This petition followed one signed by Felix [Holbrook?] alone.

8. Samuel Dexter to the Rev. Dr. Jeremy Belknap, February 26, 1795, Weston, quoted in *Massachusetts Historical Society Collections*, 5th Series, 3:387. Note that Dexter referred to Prince in his letter by his first name—not out of closeness but reflecting how Massachusetts society still did not treat the former slave in the same way as a white man.

9. John Allen, *An Oration on the Beauties of Liberty, or The Essential Rights of the Americans*, 4th edition (Boston: E. Russell, 1773), 78.

According to their letter, after becoming free those four men planned

> to leave the province, which we determine to do as soon as we can, from our joynt labours procure money to transport ourselves to some part of the Coast of Africa, where we propose a settlement.

This was a presage of American abolitionism's colonization movement as blacks sought any route to liberty that the dominant society would allow.[10]

That year the Massachusetts legislature voted to bar people from importing new slaves from Africa, but it did nothing to end slavery within the province. And then the royal governor vetoed that law anyway. It took another ten years and a war before Massachusetts's highest court ruled that the new constitution of 1780 had made slavery unenforceable within the state.[11]

According to Prince, his testimony in the Massacre trials had already made him unpopular with Bostonians who were "not attach'd to Government"—i.e., supporters of the Crown. Some neighbors "deserted him" while others even "Enter'd into associations, *to utterly destroy him*, by Tarring & Feathering him." There is no evidence those men ever succeeded in carrying out that plan, but the threat drove Prince closer to the friends of the royal government.[12]

When the Revolutionary War began in 1775, Newton and Phillis Prince stayed inside Boston. In March 1776, they joined the evacuation of Loyalists to Halifax, leaving behind their shop, goods, and debts they would never be able to collect. In Nova Scotia the Princes supported themselves by working for Gilbert Deblois, probably as cooks or other house servants.

Later Newton and Phillis Prince sailed to London, capital of the British Empire. By the early 1780s, he was running a coal and chandler's shop there. The word "chandler" can mean either "candlemaker" or "retailer of provisions and supplies," usually for ships, and Prince was probably the latter.

10. Petition quoted in Gary B. Nash, *Race and Revolution* (Lanham, MD: Rowman & Littlefield, 1990), 174. Peter Bestes appeared (as Peter Bess) as one of seven men signing a 1777 anti-slavery petition and (as Peter Best) as a founding member of Boston's African Lodge of Freemasons.

11. For a précis of that historical change, see: www.masshist.org/endofslavery/index.php.

12. In *Rough Crossings: Britain, the Slaves, and the American Revolution* (London: BBC Books, 2005), Simon Schama wrote that Prince "was tarred and feathered by infuriated Patriots," but neither Prince nor the witnesses supporting his requests for support described such an attack, and there is no contemporaneous report of one. Tarring and feathering in a crowded town was meant to be a public humiliation, widely viewed.

In 1781 Prince applied to the British government to reward him as a Loyalist. Gilbert Deblois and the Massachusetts-born baronet Sir William Pepperell wrote to support his claim. In 1783 Prince petitioned again, saying that his wife was in poor health.[13]

Recognizing his adherence to the Crown, the Loyalists Commission granted Newton Prince an annual government pension of £10. That was not a large amount, as those grants went, but it was a steady supplemental income for a working man. Newton Prince thus found his liberty in the heart of the British Empire, collecting his pension until he died in 1819.[14]

13. The file does not state Mrs. Prince's given name, but Deblois's mention of the couple as having supported themselves for years in Boston suggests this was Phillis.
14. Gregory Palmer, *Biographical Sketches of Loyalists of the American Revolution* (Westport, CT: Meckler, 1984), 704. E. Alfred Jones, *The Loyalists of Massachusetts: Their Memorials, Petitions, and Claims* (London: Saint Catherine Press, 1930), 239.

Why Did George Washington Become a Revolutionary?

RAY RAPHAEL

In 1758, just before returning home from the French and Indian War, George Washington ran for a seat in Virginia's House of Burgesses. Given his social standing and renown, the office was his for the taking, and on the day of the election he treated the 397 men who showed up at the poll to 46 gallons of beer, 35 gallons of wine, 2 gallons of hard cider, 3 1/2 pints of brandy, 40 gallons of "Rum Punch," and "1hhd [hogshead] & 1 Barrell of Punch, consisting of 26 Gals. best Barbados Rum & 12 1/2 Pds S. Refd. Sugar."[1] As a Burgess, Washington was expected to represent his constituents' interests, dole out patronage, and help the colony govern itself in local matters; in return for his services, he would earn respect, deference, and some degree of power. Certainly, when he entered the political arena, the returning war hero did not expect to engage in heated disputes with the British Parliament or challenge the status quo in any other way.

How, then, did George Washington, one of America's elite 1 percent, become its leading revolutionary? His evolution came in stages.

STAGE I: ACCRUING DEBT

Early the following year, George Washington married the wealthy

---

1. George Washington, *The Papers of George Washington*, W. W. Abbot and Dorothy Twohig, eds., (Charlottesville: University Press of Virginia, 1983-), Colonial Series. 5:323, 331-343, 374. Each voter cast ballots for two of the four candidates, and Washington was the top vote getter—by different tallies, he received 307, 309, or 310 votes. He was not present on election day, but he thanked those who put on the party on his behalf. "I am extreme thankly to you & my other friends for entertaining the Freeholders in my name—I hope no exception were taken to any that voted against me but that all were alike treated, and all had enough it is what I much desired—my only fear is that you spent with too sparing a hand." (Washington to James Wood, July c. 28, 1758, Washington, *Papers*, Colonial Series, 5:349.)

widow, Martha Custis, and by combining their fortunes—primarily in land and slaves—George and Martha created one of Virginia's most impressive estates.[2] Buying out his neighbors, Washington more than doubled his Mount Vernon plantation, expanded his mansion, and purchased all the finest clothing and home furnishings that his factor in London, Robert Cary, could procure.[3] By the fall of 1760, less than two years into his spending spree, Washington noticed a serious discrepancy between the money he made (the season's yield from tobacco, his main source of income, had been very low due to a wet summer) and the money he spent (the fall shopping list he sent to Cary included hundreds of items, ranging from "1 pair crimson velvet breeches" to "1 dozn stone chamber pots").[4] Despite the expense, Washington grumbled that the clothes Cary sent him didn't fit, and worse yet, they were dated. "Instead of getting things good and fashionable . . . we often have articles sent us that coud only have been used by our forefathers in the days of yore," he wrote to Cary. "'Tis a custom . . . with many shop keepers, and tradesmen in London when they know goods are bespoke for exportation to palm sometimes old, and sometimes very slight and indifferent goods upon us, taking care at the same time to advance 10, 15 or perhaps 20 prct upon them."[5]

By 1763, Washington reported to a friend that after "some purchases of lands and Negroes I was necessitated to make adjoining me— (in order to support the expences of a large family)," his expenditures had "swallowed up before I well knew where I was, all the money I got by marriage nay more." Years of free spending had "brought me in debt," he admitted.[6]

As yet, Washington perceived no link between his financial troubles and British imperial policies, but he was clearly upset by his dependent relationship with London merchants in general and with Robert Cary in particular.

2. Since a married woman at that time could not possess her own property, one-third of Martha's wealth passed to George for the duration of his life, and the other two-thirds went in trust to her son John, with George as the administrator.

3. George Washington, *The Diaries of George Washington*, Donald Jackson, ed., (Charlottesville: University Press of Virginia, 1976-1979), 1:241.

4. Invoice to Robert Cary, September 28, 1760, Washington, *Papers*, Colonial Series, 6:461-464.

5. Washington to Charles Lawrence and Washington to Robert Cary, September 28, 1760, Washington, *Papers*, Colonial Series 6:458-460.

6. Washington to Robert Stewart, April 27, 1763, Washington, *Papers*, Colonial Series 7:206.

STAGE 2: SEEKING WESTERN LANDS

It did not take Washington long to realize that tobacco and the slaves who produced it—the mainstays of Virginia's economy—would not get him out of debt. In fact, tobacco had helped plunge him into it; through the early 1760s the crop was poor and the market just as bad. Because he depended on a single cash crop, his economic well being was determined by two things beyond his control: the market price for tobacco and the savvy of Robert Cary. Repeatedly, Washington protested that Cary was selling his tobacco at too low a price while charging too much for the wide variety of goods he was shipping to Mount Vernon.[7]

Since his days as a surveyor for the Ohio Company of Virginia, Washington had understood that the wealth of America lay in development of her western lands. At the close of the French and Indian War, he and other investors formed the Mississippi Land Company, which petitioned King George III for rights to 2,500,000 acres on the east shore of the Mississippi, land just acquired from France. The Crown turned them down; instead, it issued its sweeping Proclamation of 1763, which prohibited settlement past the Appalachian Divide. This thwarted the hopes of the Ohio Company and the Mississippi Land Company, and it placed on hold Washington's access to bounty land that was his due as a veteran of the war.[8]

In 1767, however, Washington heard that upcoming negotiations with Iroquois Indians would soon open up sections of the West for white settlement. Seizing the moment, he contacted William Crawford, a former officer in his regiment during the French and

7. Washington to Robert Cary & Co., August 10, 1764, Washington, *Papers*, Colonial Series 7:323.
8. For the Mississippi Land Company, see Washington, *Papers*, Colonial Series 7:242-246. See also 7:219-225, 415-417, and 511-513. Blocked from the West, Washington invested in a scheme to the southeast: 40,000 acres of wet, uninhabited terrain near the North Carolina border. After gaining title from the legislature, each of the ten "Adventurers for Draining the Dismal Swamp"(as the Dismal Swamp Land Company was initially called) agreed to contribute five slaves, who were to be charged with emptying out the water. They would log the swamp as they drained it, and then start farming. Washington himself surveyed the land, and he dutifully purchased new slaves to fulfill his commitment, but the project literally got bogged down, for the draining proved more difficult than anticipated, and Washington lost more money than he made. (Washington, *Papers*, Colonial Series 7:269-276, 300, 314; Washington, *Diaries*, 1:319-326.) For the complete story of this venture, see Charles Royster, *The Fabulous History of the Dismal Swamp Company: A Story of George Washington's Times* (New York: Alfred A. Knopf, 1999).

Indian War who had moved illegally with his family across the Appalachians. "I can never look upon that Proclamation [of 1763] in any other light (but this I say between ourselves) than as a temporary expedient to quiet the minds of the Indians & must fall of course in a few years," he wrote. "Any person therefore who neglects the present opportunity of hunting ou[t] good lands & in some measure marking & distinguishing them for their own (in order to keep others from settling them) will never regain it." He then asked Crawford, who knew the region well, to locate the best lands that they each might claim. Speed and secrecy were key to the enterprise, he cautioned: "If the scheme I am now proposing to you was known it might give alarm to others & by putting them upon a plan of the same nature (before we coud lay a proper foundation for success ourselves) set different Interests a clashing and very probably overturn the whole." To keep the matter under "silent management," Washington suggested that Crawford travel "under the pretence of hunting other game which you may I presume effectually do at the same time you are in pursuit of land."⁹

Crawford liked Washington's idea. Indeed, he had already entertained "the same sceem in my head," including the "hunting sceem, which I intend befor you wrote me."¹⁰

On his end, Washington petitioned the Virginia Council to deed the 200,000 acres promised to himself and his soldiers, and when the Council approved their petition, he ventured a visit to the lands Crawford had located, confident of his claims. This would not be the end of the matter, however.

STAGE 3: OPPOSING IMPERIAL TAXATION

Although Washington sat out the Stamp Act controversy of 1765, the furor over the Townshend Duties in the late 1760s captured his attention. In 1769, after receiving a copy of the Philadelphia merchants' nonimportation agreement, he teamed up with George Mason to fashion a similar document suited for the particular exigencies of Virginia. While he, like others, was upset about taxation without representation, the idea of shunning British imports resonated with him personally. There were "private as well as public advantages" to adopting a nonimportation agreement that Virginia gentry like himself

9. Washington to William Crawford, September 17, 1767, Washington, *Papers,* Colonial Series 8:26-29.

10. Crawford to Washington, September 29, 1767, Washington, *Papers,* Colonial Series 8:39.

might sign, Washington told Mason. Many were "considerably indebted to Great Britain," and "a scheme of this sort will contribute more effectually than any other I can devise" to relieve that burden. Speaking in the third person instead of the first, he elucidated the benefits that would accrue to people who had wrung up large tabs with British merchants, as he had done:

> The extravagant & expensive man . . . is thereby furnished with a pretext to live within his bounds, and embraces it.–Prudence dictated economy to him before, but his resolution was too weak to put it in practice; for how can I, says he, who have lived in such a manner change my method? I am ashamed to do it: and besides, such an alteration in the system of my living, will create suspicions of a decay in my fortune, & such a thought the World must not harbour.[11]

A nonimportation agreement, in other words, would allow indebted planters, without being viewed as parsimonious, to cut their expenses in the name of patriotism.

Washington's proactive role in the nonimportation movement brought him into the mainstream of political protest in the colonies. Henceforth, if imperial land policies thwarted his western enterprises, he would do more than stew over his dependent relationship with the mother country. Working with others, he would endeavor to change it.

STAGE 4: LANDS DENIED: LORD HILLSBOROUGH'S BOMBSHELL

Early in 1774, Washington flew into a rage at Lord Hillsborough, recently Secretary of State for the Colonies, who suddenly maintained that when the Proclamation of 1763 promised land to veterans of the French and Indian War, it had meant to reward only British Regulars, not Americans. Having failed during that war to gain a commission as a British officer, and having spent a great deal of energy for a decade trying to gain title to land he thought he had been promised, Washington fumed obsessively about "his Lordships malignant disposition towards us poor Americans; founded equally in Malice, absurdity, & error." Aside from the danger such a view presented to the patents Washington was trying to secure, Hillsborough's declaration insulted all Americans. Bombastically, Washington asked "why Americans (who have serv'd his Majesty in the late war with as much

11. Washington to George Mason, April 5, 1769, Washington, *Papers*, Colonial Series 8:177-180.

fidelity, & without presumption, with as much success, as his British troops) should be stigmatiz'd."12

Fortuitously, as Washington stewed at this latest threat to his acquisition of western lands, Parliament struck back at the perpetrators of the Boston Tea Party by shutting its port and revoking key provisions of the Massachusetts Charter. Suddenly he "connected the dots," as we say today, or to use terms more appropriate to Washington's time and vocation, he meted the line between terminal points. Past politics and resentments, however disparate, fell into a pattern: Parliament's continuing insistence on taxation without representation, the preferential treatment given to British land speculators, his financial dependence on Robert Cary, his indebtedness to other British merchants, and perhaps even his rejection by Lord Loudoun, the British commander who had passed over his request for a commission almost two decades past. From his new perspective, this was all of a piece, and the vindictive, mean-spirited punishment of Boston proved the point once and for all: there was a "regular, systematick plan" to curtail American rights. Again and again in his letters during the summer of 1774, he seethed about the deliberate designs of the British ministry, which was attempting to impose "the most despotick system of tyranny that ever was practiced in a free government."13

Since British officials had already made up their minds to repress American colonists, there was no longer any point in petitioning them for their favors. The time for pleading had passed. "Shall we after this whine & cry for relief, when we have already tried it in vain?" he asked rhetorically. "Shall we supinely sit, and see one Provence after another fall a sacrifice to despotism?" Certainly not. "The crisis is arrivd when we must assert our rights, or submit to every imposition that can be heap'd upon us; till custom and use, will make us as tame, & abject slaves, as the Blacks we rule over with such arbitrary sway."14

STAGE 5: THE FINAL INSULT: AMERICAN SURVEYS NULL AND VOID

As aggravating as it was, Lord Hillsborough's pronouncement was

---

12. Washington to James Wood, February 20, 1774, and Washington to William Preston, February 28, 1774, Washington, *Papers*, Colonial Series 9:490 and 501. See also letters of February 17 and 28 (483 and 501).
13. Washington to Bryan Fairfax, July 20 and August 24, 1774, Washington, *Papers*, Colonial Series 10:130 and 156.
14. Washington to Bryan Fairfax, July 20 and August 24, 1774, Washington, *Papers*, Colonial Series 10:130 and 155. These words, penned to an aristocratic neighbor who had been siding with British policies, signal Washington's cognizance of the ironic use of the term "slavery" in the colonists' complaints.

not yet official policy. All glimmer of hope disappeared the following spring, however, when Washington heard that surveys of the 200,000 acres of bounty land had just been declared illegal—the ostensive reason being that William Crawford, the surveyor, did not possess the proper credentials. Initially, Washington treated the news as too "incredible" to believe; at worst, he thought, it was a trick of professional surveyors "to filch a little more money from us." But when the rumors continued, he wrote an impassioned letter to Virginia's Governor Lord Dunmore, begging him to intervene. Five years earlier, after going through all the proper channels, Crawford had been assigned to survey the 200,000 acres "with all possible expedition," Washington explained, and since that time, many of Crawford's patents had been officially granted "under your Lordships signature & the seal of the colony." How could all this be reversed at so late a date, and *why*? "It appears in so uncommon a light to me, that I hardly know yet how to persuade myself into a belief of the reality of it," he concluded.[15]

To this letter, over one thousand words long, Dunmore penned a perfunctory reply: the reason for declaring the surveys "null and void" was "a report that the surveyor who surveyed those lands did not qualify agreeable to the Act of Assembly directing the duty and qualification of surveyors." That's all he said. Dunmore's token response was penned on April 18, the day British Regulars set out from Boston toward Lexington and Concord.[16]

Such a piece of bureaucratic chicanery pushed George Washington completely over the edge. William Crawford was his good friend, business associate, and indispensable agent in the West. With many years of experience and unsurpassed knowledge of the lands he surveyed, Crawford was certainly better qualified than any quill-pushing official three thousand miles away, and besides, he had been pre-approved. In fact, Crawford knew the land so well that countless others had asked him to survey it, and Lord Dunmore himself had just relied on him to lead a dangerous expedition into Indian country. The move was so blatantly illogical that only one explanation remained: British authorities would stoop to any level to keep colonials from receiving legitimate title to lands across the mountains.

15. Washington to Lord Dunmore, April 3, 1775, Washington, *Papers*, Colonial Series 10:320-322.
16. Lord Dunmore to Washington, April 18, 1775, Washington, *Papers*, Colonial Series 10:337-338.

Washington concluded there was no way for Americans to expand into the West without addressing the arrogant abuses of governmental authority coming from the East. Two months later, when the Continental Congress asked him to command a rebel army, he readily agreed.

This is not to say that George Washington went to war simply to acquire western lands for himself. His mission was broader than that. From the beginning, he envisioned an expansive nation—at first a *British* nation—extending into the fertile interior of the North American continent. When British officials, rather than encouraging such an endeavor, did everything in their power to hinder colonial subjects from developing the West, he vowed to fight for liberty and the right to realize that nationalist vision. Then, following independence and a successful conclusion to the Revolutionary War, he devoted his energies to establishing a Potomac Canal that would connect the Atlantic seaboard with the interior. Viewed through Washington's lens, the Revolutionary War becomes not only a war of liberation but also a war of expansion, the way Native people saw it. Our identity as a nation, like the Revolutionary War, encompasses both dimensions.

Tides and Tonnage: A Different Take on the Boston Tea Party

❦ HUGH T. HARRINGTON ❦

The story of the Boston Tea Party has been told and retold endlessly. It has become a part of American mythos. On the evening of December 16, 1773, in Boston a group of 100 to 150 citizens, dressed like Indians, descended on three ships loaded with tea from England. Politely, but firmly, they demanded the captains open the holds of their ships. The citizens brought chests of tea on deck where the chests were broken open and the tea dumped over the side into Boston harbor. Afterwards the men wandered off into the night having made their very public statement about the Tea Act. Yet, there is more to the tale, and some of it is unexpectedly comical.

The disguises, of course, were not worn to make anyone think they actually were Indians. The idea was to protect the identities of the tea party participants. Joshua Wyeth, one of the participants, wrote, "We agreed to wear ragged clothes and disfigure ourselves, dressing to resemble Indians as much as possible, smearing our faces with grease and lamp black or soot, and should not have known each other except by our voices. Our most intimate friends among the spectators had not the least knowledge of us. We surely resembled devils from the bottomless pit rather than men."[1] Another participant described his companions as being "fantastically arrayed in old frocks, red woolen caps or gowns, and all manner of like habiliments."[2] However, some did not wear any sort of disguise as they were spur of the moment volunteers or citizens of such minor status that they felt safe.

---

1. Francis S. Drake, *Tea Leaves: Being a Collection of Letters and Documents Relating to the Shipment of Tea to the American Colonies in the Year 1773, by the East India Tea Company* (Boston: A.O. Crane, 1884), LXXI. See also Edward Everett Hale, ed., *Old and New*, Vol. 9, January 1874-July 1874 (Boston: Roberts Brothers, 1874), 104-106.
2. Drake, *Tea Leaves*, LXXIII.

The ringleaders, however, were careful to keep their war-painted faces well covered with blankets and other camouflage. In addition, these "Chiefs" did not want to take the chance of their voices being recognized so they spoke in "Indian jargon" as they gave directions to a Commander or "interpreter" who would then issue orders to the ships' captain, crew, or to the men working on the destruction of the tea.[3]

The job of dumping the tea into the harbor was far easier said than done. In fact, it is probable that the organizers of the tea party had not comprehended what a huge undertaking was involved. The tea was aboard three ships carrying a total of 342 tea chests. Each chest weighed about 400 pounds. The chests had to be taken from the hold by block and tackle. On deck the chests were broken up with axes and crowbars. The broken chests and the tea were thrown and shoveled over the side. Even breaking open the chests was difficult as they were covered with canvas. Joshua Wyeth wrote years later that he had "never worked harder in my life."[4]

To put this project into proper perspective one must consider that 342 chests at 400 pounds apiece works out to 136,800 pounds, which is over 68 tons, that had to be hauled on deck and then dumped overboard. The block and tackle on the ship derricks helped getting the tea out of the holds. However, putting the broken chests and tea over the side was done by hand and with a great deal of shoveling of tea leaves. The tea on one ship was stowed beneath other cargo. That cargo had to be carefully removed without damaging it and then put back into place after the tea chests were removed.[5] While the cubic volume of the loose tea leaves cannot be determined, it was enormous.

Ideally, the tea ought to have been dumped on an outgoing tide which would clear the tea away from the ships as it was pitched over the side, moving it into the harbor and out to sea. However, the tea party took place between 6 and 9 p.m. and low tide was 7:23 pm. Not only was it low tide but it was an exceptionally low tide.

Tidal experts Donald W. Olsen and Russell L. Doescher have calculated the tides for the evening of December 16, 1773. They found that "in Boston harbor the mean range of the tides is about 9.5 feet. Spring tides are those of increased range occurring twice monthly as

---

3. "A Bostonian," *Traits of the Tea Party, Being a Memoir of George R.T. Hewes, One of the Last of its Survivors* (New York: Harper & Brothers, 1835), 180-186.

4. Hale, *Old*, 104-106.

5. Drake, *Tea Leaves*, 195.

a result of the Moon being in syzygy (that is, either new or full), when the tide-raising forces of the Moon and Sun combine for a greater net effect. At Boston, the Spring range averages about 11.0 feet. Perigean tides of increased range also occur monthly when the Moon is at perigee (nearest Earth) and the lunar tide-raising force is greatest. If the time of lunar perigee falls near a syzygy, then perigean spring tides of unusually large range can occur. This is exactly what happened in the middle of December 1773 . . . results indicate that the tidal range in Boston harbor exceeded 14 feet during the four day period beginning December 13th."[6]

In other words the tide was exceptionally low that evening. At least two of the ships, while tied to the wharf, were resting on the bottom of the harbor in two feet of water. Many of the tea party men were given the undesirable task of tromping through the frigid water and mud alongside the ships where they "beat up more thoroughly the fragments of boxes and masses of tea, which were thrown over in too great haste."[7] It wasn't long before this became a very tiring job as the tea leaves, water, and mud became thick, much like wet oatmeal. As they worked even more tea cascaded down upon them.

The tea piled up against the sides of the ships as the bottom of the tea pile was resting on the bottom of the harbor despite the efforts of the men working alongside the ships in the water. Benjamin Simpson, one of the tea party men, recorded that "the tea was so high by the side of [the ships] as to fall in; which was shoveled down more than once."[8] Another participant wrote that the men trampling the tea in the water and mud "found their return upon deck a good deal facilitated by the immense pile which accumulated beneath and around them."[9] It takes a great deal of tea to make a pile so high and so dense that men could climb it. It also must be kept in mind that the ships were tied to Griffin's wharf so only one side of each ship was available for tea-dumping.

The *Massachusetts Gazette and Boston Weekly News-Letter* reported that "when the tide rose it floated the broken chests and the tea insomuch that the surface of the water was filled therewith a considerable

6. Donald W. Olson and Russell L. Doescher, "The Boston Tea Party," *Sky & Telescope*, 86 (December 1993), 83-86. Texas State University, Faculty Publications-Physics. Paper 10. digital.library.txstate.edu/handle/10877/4029.
7. "A Bostonian," *Traits*, 262-265.
8. George Folsom, *History of Saco and Biddeford* (Saco, ME: Alex. C. Putnam, 1830), 287-288.
9. "A Bostonian," *Traits*, 180-186.

An early nineteenth-century illustration of the Boston Tea Party. (*Library of Congress*)

way from the south part of the town to Dorchester Neck, and lodged on the shores."[10] Some of the tea that floated to Dorchester, over a mile away, was salvaged as it was still dry. The morning after the party an island of floating tea was seen in the harbor. A group of volunteers set out in small boats and worked at stirring it into the water.[11]

While the tea party was in progress a crowd of between 1,000 and 2,000 people gathered to watch. They stood in silence. In fact, the tea party men worked in silence as much as possible as well. Joshua Wyeth commented that, "We were merry, in an undertone, at the idea of making so large a cup of tea for the fishes, but were as still as the nature of the case would admit, using no more words than were absolutely necessary. Our most intimate acquaintances among the spectators had not the least knowledge of us."[12]

A couple of men attempted to steal tea by hiding it in their clothes, another man came in a rowboat. The men were handled roughly, the rowboat was sunk by those working with the tea in the water.

After all the tea had been dumped into the harbor the men swept the decks of any remaining tea and returned everything as they had found it. A mate or ship's officer was then called on deck to confirm that no cargo, other than the tea, had been damaged and there was

10. *Massachusetts Gazette and Boston Weekly News-Letter*, December 23, 1773.
11. Drake, *Tea Leaves*, LXXVII.
12. Drake, *Tea Leaves*, LXXII, also in Hale, *Old*, 104-106.

no damage to the ship. On one ship a padlock was replaced for one that had been broken.[13]

When the job was finished all the men involved were lined up and ordered to remove their shoes and empty out any tea that had accumulated in them. Then, the men formed into ranks and shouldered their axes, crowbars, hatchets, and other implements. While a fife struck up a lively tune they marched from the wharfs for a few blocks then quietly went to their own homes.[14]

Many would-be hosts dread having a party because of the effort needed in the morning to clean up after the party-goers have gone home. The aftermath of the Boston Tea Party had some similarities to a house party. However, unlike a house party the tea party took place in relative silence. Also, the site of the party, the ships, was left neat and tidy after the party was over. However, that does not mean there wasn't a horrific mess afterward. There is no way the tea could be stamped into the freezing water by the men working at the sides of the ships. There was far too much tea to disperse. After the tea was dumped and the decks cleaned up the party was over. The men struggling in knee-deep water with the tea piles had done all they could and doubtless were glad to go home.

To many the tea party aftermath is visualized as broken tea chests, and tea leaves, floating around the tea ships. The reality is far less picturesque. The tea was in great heaps mixed with mud. In any case, the final cleanup was left to the tides. In a few hours the tide, higher than normal, would lift the debris and carry it off.

13. Hale, *Old*, 104-106.
14. "A Bostonian," *Traits*, 180-186.

Thomas Gage Reconsidered: When Law Interferes with War

❦ GARY SHATTUCK ❦

You have sent General Gage, who is a man of great abilities, to quell the disturbances in that country, which I am sure he never will do, unless, at the same time that you give him the sword in one hand, you give him the olive branch in the other; and I think you will gain more by the olive branch being properly used, according to the temper of those people, than you will by striking a severe blow with the sword.—*Colonel Isaac Barré, House of Commons, concerning Gage's assignment to Boston April 15, 1774*[1]

I have repeatedly given the strongest assurances that I intended nothing hostile against the Town [Boston] or Country, and therefore desire you to ease the minds of the people against any reports that may have been industriously spread amongst them to the contrary; my wish is to preserve peace and tranquility.—*General/Royal Governor Thomas Gage, responding to a Worcester County grievance October 1774*[2]

But it is more than evident that you cannot force [the Americans], united as they are, to your unworthy terms of submission–it is impossible: and when I hear General Gage censored for inactivity, I must retort with indignation on those whose intemperate meas-

---

1. *Essex Gazette* (Salem, MA), May 31 to June 7, 1774.
2. *The Journals of Each Provincial Congress of Massachusetts in 1774 and 1775* (Boston: Dutton and Wentworth, 1838), 869.

ures and improvident councils have betrayed him into his present
situation.—*William Pitt, Earl of Chatham, debating a House of Lords' effort
to withdraw Gage's troops from Boston January 20, 1775*[3]

For over two hundred years, Revolutionary War historiography has
repeatedly excoriated Gen. Thomas Gage, seeking to assign him virtually sole responsibility for the early reverses suffered by British policy in 1774-1775 intended to quell colonial discord. Assuming the
opprobrium heaped upon him by contemporaries, one calling him "a
lukewarm coward" and his own soldiers describing him as "Tommy,
the old woman," modern day historians unsympathetically pass a similar judgment.[4] For the discriminating John Shy, Gage was "a weak
link," "surprisingly feeble" in understanding the challenges he faced,
warranting blame for advocating a misplaced legal resolution to the
conflict when, rather, the "practical" military option should have been
employed.[5] While constituting a convenient, shorthand dismissal of
Gage's actions, these myopic assessments wholly fail to acknowledge
the very real, and persistently looming, constraints imposed on him by
the titanic changes then taking place within the complex British
Empire's constitutional system. When those important legal consider-
ations, ones designed for peace over war, are factored into the military
context of the times, an entirely different perspective emerges that
seriously calls into question those condemnations of purported inep-
titude.

The early martial education of Thomas Gage (1721-1787), the second son of Irish peer Viscount Thomas Gage, is first noted with his
enlistment in the army in 1741 as a lieutenant. Following a period of
service in Europe, as a lieutenant colonel he accompanied General
Edward Braddock to North America in 1754 at the opening of the
Seven Years' War. Surviving the debacle on the Monongahela River
the following year, Gage went on to serve in various capacities at

3. Henry Steele Commager and Richard B. Morris, eds., *The Spirit of Seventy-Six: The
Story of the American Revolution as Told by Its Participants* (Edison, NJ: Castle Books,
1958), 230.
4. John Fisk, *The American Revolution*, vol. 1 (Boston: Houghton, Mifflin and Co.,
1891), 112; Richard M. Ketchum, *Decisive Day: The Battle for Bunker Hill* (New York:
Henry Holt and Company, 1962), 15. Ketchum graciously describes Gage as "an
even-tempered, persistent man who saw his duty and followed it to the best of his
ability." Ibid., 14.
5. John Shy, *A People Numerous and Armed: Reflections on the Military Struggle for
American Independence* (Ann Arbor: University of Michigan Press, 1990), 114.

Ticonderoga, Lake Ontario, and Quebec. He was named governor of Montreal in 1760, instituting a welcomed period of "mild rule" over a population that had experienced oppression under his predecessor. With the arrival of peace in 1763, Gage had attained such respect that he was promoted to major-general and then was named commander-in-chief of all British forces upon Gen. Jeffrey Amherst's return to England.[6]

Thomas Gage (1721–1787), captain-general and royal governor of Massacusetts colony between 1774 and 1775. (*Yale University*)

To understand the myriad of challenges that Gage faced in the next several years, it is necessary to consider the effects of huge philosophical changes taking place within the vast British Empire as they concerned relations between London and its many colonies. It had actually started some years earlier upon the conclusion of King George's War in 1748, when Parliament decided the times were ripe to exert its authority outwards. Up until then, the profitable benefits of a robust trading network, further enhanced by various navigation acts passed in the homeland's favor, precluded the need for close supervision over the colonies. But this unintentionally fostered the appearance of unacceptable notions of independence in their midst, in the form of a dizzying number of some twenty-five separate constitutions on the eve of the Revolution, each the product of widespread assemblies with differing constituencies advocating differing needs and which were not always in accord with each other. While there was never a single body of law emanating from London that tried to reconcile their numerous differences, attempts were made by the Privy Council and Board of Trade to administer the challenges they posed in a consistent manner. As a result, a complex legal situation presented itself in the form of no less than three distinct kinds of constitutions: the British constitution applicable to "the central state and its immediate dependencies" (Cornwall, Wales, and Scotland); separate provincial constitutions for

---

6. Leslie Stephen, ed., *Dictionary of National Biography*, vol. 20 (New York: Macmillan and Co., 1889), 355. While on the Monongahela, Gage struck up a friendship with George Washington, who later solicited his assistance in obtaining future employment with the British army. George Washington's Mount Vernon, "Thomas Gage," accessed July 16, 2015, www.mountvernon.org/research-collections/digital-encyclopedia/article/thomas-gage/.

Ireland and each of the colonies; and, "an undefined . . . unacknowl-
edged, imperial constitution—the constitution of the British Empire."
These allowed for the simultaneous rule by Parliament over general
affairs as the colonies attended to their respective local needs.[7]

Making the situation even more difficult to administer, there was
also a profound transition taking place concerning the many participants' perception of the location of the center of power. By the 1760s
an aggressive Parliament, no doubt emboldened by the war's successes, unashamedly, and earnestly, began flexing its muscle on multiple
levels, much to the detriment of the royal prerogative, itself in slow
decline following the Glorious Revolution of 1688. While this was the
moment when "parliamentary omnipotence" was becoming
entrenched within the country's constitutional order, it was hardly a
universally accepted notion for the colonies. Consistent with their
particular constitutions, they argued that their interests had to also be
acknowledged and addressed within the larger umbrella of the British
constitution.[8] As a result, as one legal historian describes, there were
diametrically opposed, and irreconcilable, concepts at issue:

> The dynamics of the eighteenth-century British constitution had
> produced a constitutional dilemma. American liberty–the right to
> be free of arbitrary power–could not be secured under parliamen-
> tary supremacy. British liberty–the representative legislature over
> the crown–could not be secured without parliamentary suprema-
> cy.[9]

In sum, a developing constitutional scheme played out on a world-
wide stage, together with rising internal conflicts over the questioned
supremacy of Parliament and representation of far-off colonies. These
tensions were well understood by politicians and military men alike,

---

7. Jack P. Greene, *The Constitutional Origins of the American Revolution* (Cambridge:
Cambridge University Press, 2011), 13-18, 53-54. Subsumed within this constitutional hierarchy was the all important aspect concerning the legitimacy of colonial laws
passed by the various assemblies which were, in turn, subject to Privy Council review
to determine their repugnancy to established law, a concept one legal scholar recently termed the "Transatlantic Constitution." Mary Sarah Bilder, *The Transatlantic
Constitution: Colonial Legal Culture and the Empire* (Cambridge: Harvard University
Press, 2004), 1.
8. Greene, *The Constitutional Origins*, 46; see also, Greene, *Peripheries and Center:
Constitutional Development in the Extended Polities of the British Empire and the United
States, 1607-1788* (Athens: University of Georgia Press, 1986).
9. John Phillip Reid, *Constitutional History of the American Revolution: The Authority of
Law* (Madison: University of Wisconsin Press, 1993), 173.

including Thomas Gage, as critical issues that had to be acknowledged in the execution of their duties.

Notwithstanding, there were basic concepts that all shared and which were at the root of those larger differences. Fundamentally, the importance of a constitution for the protection of individuals' property interests was manifest. In fact, it was that specific issue justifying its very existence, with one Member of Parliament describing in 1647: "The law of God doth not give me property, nor the Law of Nature, but property is of human constitution. I have a property and this I shall enjoy. Constitution founds property."[10] And there was no more important aspect of the right to pursue property (to include personalty, realty, and office holding) than to uphold one's liberty in doing so, for if that was infringed, then one was deprived of a fundamental aspect of an Englishman's prerogative. Finally, protecting all of this was the unspoken power of the rule of law, the fence that guarded all from trespassing intruders.[11]

The times were becoming even more complex for those involved with military matters. Concepts of equity and fair play between warring contestants were no longer disregarded and began to enter into the minds of both British and American commanders, instilled in them by such important works as Swiss philosopher and diplomat Emer de Vattel's 1758 *Law of Nations*.[12] In fact, Vattel's highly influential tome describing the rights and obligations of nations in their interactions with each other on the international stage drew the attention and set the expectations of many, remaining today one of the most important works of its kind. Discerning the existence of some semblance of order even within a state of nature, de Vattel prescribed appropriate avenues of conduct that a nation was obligated to pursue, to a sympathetic public, itself already appreciative of the fact that "the rationality of the universe provided a source of obligation governing all human conduct."[13]

10. John Phillip Reid, *Constitutional History of the American Revolution: The Authority of Rights* (Madison: University of Wisconsin Press, 1986), 30-31.

11. Ibid.

12. Emer de Vattel, *The Law of Nations; or, Principles of the Law of Nature applied to the Conduct and Affairs of Nations and Sovereigns* (London: G.G. and J. Robinson, 1797), *passim.* For additional information regarding the effect of Vattel's work as applied to Revolutionary War prisoners of war, see this writer's article "Christopher French, Prisoner of War," *Journal of the American Revolution*, May 5, 2015, allthingsliberty.com /2015/05/major-christopher-french-prisoner-of-war/.

13. Henry J. Bourguignon, "Incorporation of the Law of Nations during the American Revolution—The Case of the San Antonio," *American Journal of International Law* 71, no. 2 (April 1977): 281.

While there was no statutory body of law mandating the conduct of military officials when a civil war arose, such as the one taking place in North America, de Vattel provided appropriate guidance, telling them "it is very evident that the common laws of war—those of humanity, moderation, and honor . . . ought to be observed by both parties . . . ."[14] With these several overarching concerns, those of complex constitutional dimension, the overriding need to protect Englishmen's fundamental right to property and liberty, each protected in turn by the rule of law, and internationally recognized expectations of conduct in a time of war, all coming together at one time as they did when Gage assumed command of North American British interests, it is now possible to view the challenges he faced, and the decisions he made, with much heightened appreciation.

Between 1763 and 1772, Gage administered to the varying demands of British policy from his New York City headquarters where he received and sent out many dispatches from and to military and civilian correspondents.[15] Revealing a discerning intellect, adapting to many thorny complaints which often required an understanding of the law in their resolution, Gage worked through delicate issues monitoring the empire's western frontier as voracious traders and settlers sought to work around the prohibitions imposed on them by the Proclamation of 1763 that limited their ability to exploit Indian lands.

On occasion, Gage raised legal concerns that might affect the way a particular matter was resolved. One instance occurred in 1766 when he invoked the teachings of de Vattel concerning questionable French conduct, writing, " . . . but I don't conceive that it is consistent with the Law of Nations . . . ."[16] Three years later, he cautioned another, "You are doing everything you can that some sort of Justice may be carried on in the settlements . . . But I would have you avoid giving any handle to litigious people, who might hereafter endeavor to hamper you with tricks of law."[17] That concern was further evident in 1768

14. De Vattel, *The Law of Nations*, 425.
15. See, e.g., Thomas Gage, "Some Letters and Papers of General Thomas Gage," *The John P. Branch Historical Papers of Randolph-Macon College* 4, no. 2 (June 1913): 86-111.
16. Gage to General Conway, June 24, 1766; Charles H. Metzger, "Sebastien Louis Meurin: The Last of the Illinois Jesuit Indian Missionaries," *Illinois Catholic Historical Review* 3, no. 1 (July 1920): 258.
17. Gage to Commanding Officer, March 24, 1769, "Some Letters," 96. On another occasion, Gage wrote to Indian superintendent Sir William Johnson lamenting the "irregular behavior of the traders," a situation he explained he had forwarded on to London superiors counseling that "they must be restrained by law, and a judicial power invested in the officers commanding at the posts, to see such law put in force." Gage to Johnson, January 25, 1767, E.B. O'Callaghan, ed., *The Documentary History of the State of New York*, vol. 2 (Albany: Weed, Parsons & Co., 1849), 836.

when British troops arrived in Boston requiring accommodations that local inhabitants refused to provide because of a local law requiring they be housed at nearby Castle Island. When Gage arrived on the scene to help resolve the standoff he found himself similarly frustrated in acquiring quarters for the troops, mindful that he could be cashiered from the service should the civil authorities find him guilty of disobeying the law.[18] Further, his frustration with the law interfering with his work was made evident when he described to London the challenge that a pernicious presence of lawyers presented during the Stamp Act protests: "The lawyers are the source from whence the clamors have flowed in every province."[19] Clearly, Gage fully understood the important role that law played in the minds of the colonists and it was a factor never far from any consideration he made in a military context.

At the time of the Boston Tea Party in December 1773, Gage was in Britain having relinquished his duties in New York City. It is true that he viewed the event with great disdain, arguing to George III that force be used against the colonists; his view contributed to Parliament's passing the several so-called Coercive Acts. However, with his subsequent appointment as both captain-general and governor to Massachusetts in order to see to the implementation of those acts, he also appreciated the legal conundrum he faced. With his occupying both military and civil positions, he wisely chose to clarify the authority the government was allowing him, ultimately receiving permission to employ military resources in support of the civil law.[20]

However, the delegation of such expansive authority was not without limitation. As directed by the American secretary of state, Lord Dartmouth, while his use of force was permitted, it came with conditions:

> The King trusts, however, that such necessity will not occur, and commands me to say, that it will be your duty to use every endeavor to avoid it; to quiet the minds of the people, to remove their prejudices, and, by mild and gentle persuasion, to induce such a submission on their part, to this law.[21]

18. Fisk, *The American Revolution,* 59.
19. Milton M. Klein, "Prelude to Revolution in New York: Jury Trials and Judicial Tenure," *William and Mary Quarterly* 17, no. 4 (Oct. 1960): 440.
20. Shy, *A People Numerous and Armed,* 103.
21. Dartmouth to Gage, April 9, 1774, *The Parliamentary History of England, from the earliest period to the year 1803,* vol. 18 (London: T.C. Hansard, 1813), 75-76.

Even so, it was a monumental challenge that Gage faced, having assessed it on a plane far exceeding forcing mere compliance with law by a recalcitrant population, telling his superiors that their grievances were of constitutional magnitude:

> There are three fundamentals on which the people of this country endeavor to establish the political doctrines they have promulgated within these few years. These are Charter Rights, British Constitution, and the Laws of God and Nature.[22]

Notwithstanding, armed with both direct and indirect authority, Gage then set off in an effort to execute his difficult assignment with the same degree of tact and understanding, consistent with Dartmouth's guidance to use "mild and gentle persuasion," as he had in the past.

While Gage had been warmly received upon his arrival in Boston in May 1774, greeted by a population that appreciated his past conduct towards them, things changed quickly with the closing of the all-important harbor and institution of the remaining onerous acts. It was no mean feat on his part to then navigate the following difficult months in a peaceful manner as colonists assembled both provincial and continental congresses to address the acts' meaning and impact. However, as the summer unfolded it became obvious that more troops were needed to quell increasing protests leading Gage, in a display of "realism," to not only petition for more, but to also recommend rescinding the laws he had been sent to enforce, causing his London overseers to seriously question his resolve.[23]

Meanwhile, confined in Boston with his men awaiting the arrival of reinforcements, Gage was forced to assume a non-confrontational approach which allowed for many displays of untoward conduct by the local inhabitants challenging his authority, essentially daring him to take action. Declining to impose martial law on the city, Gage allowed the residents "almost complete freedom," refusing to censor the press, allowing troublemakers to attend and conduct their meetings, and watching as those in the countryside assembled their militia and collected their tools of war.[24] At the same time, he severely constrained his soldiers, refusing to allow them to carry side arms and bringing them up on charges when they ran afoul of the local population, even allowing for their public flogging when found at fault.

22. Reid, *Constitutional History: The Authority of Rights*, 214.
23. Robert Middlekauff, *The Glorious Cause: The American Revolution, 1763-1789* (New York: Oxford University Press, 1982), 262.
24. Ketchum, *Decisive Day*, 15.

By early 1775, the situation had developed to such a degree that both British and Americans realized it was only a matter of time before hostilities broke out. The colonists had refused to back off of their confrontational approach and Gage's troops were becoming increasingly frustrated at being restrained. Word that Gage had allowed the militia to assemble and train was met with disdain by Dartmouth, writing to the commander in January of his incredulity on this point while also revealing British continued reliance on the primacy of law to justify their actions. Now, he suggested to Gage a convenient opening allowing the application of additional authority, a move that had been approved by both the attorney and solicitor generals: "In reviewing the charter of Massachusetts," he wrote, "I observe there is a clause that empowers the governor to use and execute the law martial in time of actual war, invasion, and *rebellion.*"[25] From London's point of view, the line had been crossed by the colonists and now an "actual and open rebellion" existed inviting the imposition of martial law. However, refusing to be held responsible at a later time for such a dire act, Dartmouth predictably cautioned that "the expediency and propriety of adopting such a measure must depend upon your own discretion."[26]

Meanwhile, with Gage's inclination towards caution and hesitancy in handling the rising discord becoming more evident, and the naming of three generals to act as his replacements (William Howe, Henry Clinton, and John Burgoyne), the tenor at home calling for the shedding of blood became even shriller. As Burgoyne rhetorically, and tellingly, inquired of Parliament that February, while also invoking his own interpretation of the legal issues at stake, "Is there a man in England—I am sure there is not an officer or soldier in the king's service—who does not think the Parliamentary rights of Great Britain a cause to fight for—to bleed and die for?"[27] Clearly Gage was alone in his isolated predicament, delaying imposition of martial law while weighing the costs and benefits of unleashing his troops at a time when, to his mind at least, all legal avenues had not been exhausted, while some in England recognized that that time had long passed.

As these others weighed in and evaluated his actions, Gage began to shrug off his solicitous attitude towards the unappreciative colonists and assumed a calculated approach, reluctantly invoking the

25. Dartmouth to Gage, January 27, 1775, Jared Sparks, *The Writings of George Washington,* vol. 3 (Boston: American Stationers' Company, 1837), 508.
26. Ibid.
27. Richard Frothingham, *History of the Siege of Boston, and of the Battles of Lexington, Concord, and Bunker Hill* (Boston: Little, Brown, and Company, 1903), 52-53.

use of the military to fulfill his difficult mandate, an effort he intended to protect those under his care. Lamenting the protestors' failure to adhere to existing law by sending their complaints to Parliament for resolution as they had done in the past, he later justified his recent actions to Connecticut governor Jonathan Trumbull:

> I have commenced no operations of war but defensive. Such you cannot wish me to suspend, while I am surrounded by an armed country . . . But it must quiet the minds of all reasonable people when I assure you that I have no disposition to injure or molest quiet and peaceable subjects, but on the contrary shall esteem it my greatest happiness to defend and protect them against every species of violence and oppression.28

Unfortunately, that effort to disarm the rebelling colonists on April 19, 1775, resulting in the debacle of Lexington and Concord followed by his subsequent encirclement in Boston by a horde of angry farmers, met with wholesale failure. However, even in that instance Gage refused to abandon a peaceful approach as he then agreed with selectmen to grant the requests of scared residents seeking permission to leave the town. At the same time, some two hundred local merchants and traders rallied to his assistance and formed a Loyalist contingency to aid him in his troubles.29

A short distance away within the rebel ranks evidence that not all of them were opposed to his presence became clear, identifying themselves as "King's Troops," ones standing in opposition to what they called the "Parliaments," demonstrating that even they appreciated the legal aspects of what they were doing.30 With both outright support coming to his side and the presence of a disruptive rebel faction, itself in search of an appropriate identity, it is not difficult to understand Gage's plight as he wrestled with further thoughts of having to use his military powers to enforce the law.

Yet, it did indeed become more complex following the arrival of the three generals and only days before the Pyrrhic victory at Bunker Hill. On June 12 Gage found it necessary to take more forceful action

28. Gage to Trumbull, May 3, 1775, Trumbull Papers, *Collections of the Massachusetts Historical Society*, vol. 10, Fifth Series (Boston: Published by the Society, 1888), 298-301.

29. Ibid., 93-96. At the same time, the provincial congress made clear its disdain for Gage, ordering no further obedience be given and declaring him "an unnatural and inveterate enemy of the country." Benson John Lossing, *Washington: A Biography*, vol. 3 (New York: Virtue, Emmins Co., 1856-1860), 551.

30. Reid, *Constitutional History: The Authority of Law*, 173.

to demonstrate that events had not spiraled entirely out of his control. Now, as he explained to Dartmouth, there was in fact a rebellion, one so "open and manifest [as not] to need the opinion of the law officers."[31] Consistent with his past cautious approach, however, he was only willing to incrementally increase the pressure on the population by issuing "A Proclamation" addressing "the present unnatural rebellion" standing in opposition to "the constitutional authority of the state."[32] Recognizing that under the circumstances "justice cannot be administered by the common law of the land," its terms provided for the issuance of pardons, excepting certain leaders, to anyone laying down arms and returning to their peaceable ways. It ended with the imposition of martial law. Of course, only days later the confrontation that took place on the Charlestown Peninsula changed everything and any future thought of control Gage might have had over the population was absolutely lost.

As stalemate continued to surround the helpless soldiers in the following months, and up until the time of his departure in October, Gage remained steeped within legal constructs, including those provided by de Vattel's *Law of Nations*. When captured American officers removed into Boston following Bunker Hill experienced rough handling by Gage's men, Washington angrily wrote to him echoing the legal scholar's dictates to treat his opponents with "humanity, moderation, and honor," while also reminding the British commander that "the obligations arising from the rights of humanity . . . are universally binding and extensive."[33] Not needing any lecture from a rebel acting contrary to established law, Gage responded two days later telling him "To the glory of civilized nations, humanity and war have been compatible, and compassion to the subdued is become almost a general system."[34] Continuing, he told Washington that "your prisoners, whose lives, by the law of the land, are *destined to the cord* [emphasis in original], have hitherto been treated with care and kindness, and

31. Gage to Dartmouth, June 12, 1775, Sparks, *The Writings of George Washington,* 510.
32. Library of Congress, "By his Excellency The Hon. Thomas Gage, Esq. . . . A Proclamation," accessed July 18, 2015, memory.loc.gov/cgi-bin/ampage?collId =rbpe&fileName=rbpe03/rbpe038/03801700/rbpe03801700.db&recNum=0&itemLi nk=r?ammem/rbpebib:@field(NUMBER+@band(rbpe+03801700)):&linkText=0.
33. Washington to Gage, August 11, 1775, Peter Force, ed., *American Archives, Fourth Series,* vol. 3 (Washington: M. St. Clair Clark and Peter Force, 1837), 245.
34. Gage to Washington, August 13, 1775, *The London Magazine or Gentleman's Monthly Intelligencer for the Year 1775,* vol. 44 (London: By His Majesty's Authority, 1775), 519-520.

more comfortably lodged, than the king's troops in the hospitals; indiscriminately it is true, for I acknowledge no rank that is not derived from the king."

Gage then took Washington to task for his own treatment of British prisoners before expressing hope he would treat them with "sentiments of liberality." In ending, he then referred to the war's illegality before describing what he expected from his men, and their own devotion to the law:

> I trust, that British soldiers, asserting the rights of the state, the laws of the land, the being of the constitution, will meet all events with becoming fortitude. They will court victory with the spirit their cause inspires, and from the same motive will find the patience of martyrs under misfortunes.[35]

Clearly, even on the issue of prisoners, and as he had consistently done in the past, Gage never abandoned a position on the side of law and order.

In October, Gage took sail for England leaving his troubles under the care of William Howe. During the course of his trip he penned his thoughts, giving vent in a retrospective review of what led to his misfortune. From this late perspective much became clear to him as he determined that the recent upheavals had long been in the minds of the colonists and, inferring that he was himself a victim, that many well-intentioned people had been lulled into believing their protestations of loyalty to the Crown. Writing once again to Dartmouth, he opined that, "I am convinced, that the promoters of the rebellion have no real desire of peace, unless they have a *carte blanche*. Their whole conduct has been one scene of fallacy, duplicity, and dissimulation, by which they have duped many well inclined people."[36] His protestations and the subsequent fallout that ensued upon his arrival home notwithstanding, Thomas Gage remained within the military for the next several years, finally being named a full general in 1782.

The American Revolution constituted a seismic event in the legal arena for both the British and the Americans. With the Declaration of Independence in July 1776, the colonists formally announced their separation not from English legal precedents, but in rejection of the interpretations that London had put those precedents to the detriment of those in North America. Even with the split, during the war the Americans continued to utilize their rich English past, incorporat-

---

35. Ibid.
36. Gage to Dartmouth, October 15, 1775, Sparks, *Writings of George Washington*, 514.

ing its common law into their decisions; they continued to do so after the peace in 1783 when they established their own legal framework.

That very perception of the importance and needed continuity that the law represented was something that Thomas Gage never abandoned in the years leading up to the outbreak of war. Some may argue that it was a misplaced, misdirected attention he allowed to overcome him when he should have simply struck out in militaristic form at an earlier point in time. As a result of such simplistic thinking, history has subsequently been unkind to this unfortunate man, one placed into an unwinnable situation from which few, if any, could have extracted themselves in honorable fashion. In the end, revealing just how much he actually did appreciate and understand the fine line separating peace and war, Gage delayed in implementing aggressive action knowing that once unleashed, it could never be recalled. And for that, can he truly be faulted?

Visiting Boston's Liberty Tree Site

❀ JOHN L. SMITH, JR. ❀

"For it's a tall old tree and a strong old tree. And we are the sons, yes, we are the sons . . . the sons of liberty."[1] So went the catchy song that the tea-dumping Sons of Liberty sang loudly in the streets that night, all in perfect harmony and accompanied by mysterious instruments that came out of nowhere, in the 1957 Walt Disney film, *Johnny Tremain*.

The Liberty Tree still holds a revered place in many Americans' hearts, and it should. For ten years it had been the unofficial meeting place of the rebellious Bostonians, "collective activity by ordinary people"[2] chafing against their perceived British injustice. Its symbolism still abounds in American culture. Consider Jefferson's famous quote: "The tree of liberty must be refreshed from time to time with the

---

1. "The Liberty Tree" (Wonderland Music, BMI, 1956) music by George Bruns with lyrics by Tom Blackburn for the soundtrack to Disney's film *Johnny Tremain*. Disney trivia controversy exists over whether the mob sings the lyrics as an "oak tree" or an "old tree." Since the original Liberty Tree was an elm tree and known to be an elm tree when Disney's writers were researching the script story, perhaps the proponents of "old tree" win out. Esther Forbes never states in her popular 1943 book of the same name whether the tree was an oak or elm. The Disney trivia "oak tree" proponents would counter that the large living Liberty Tree in Liberty Square at the Magic Kingdom in Walt Disney World Resort is a Southern live oak tree. But then, that large oak tree was on the Disney Kissimmee land when they bought it and was simply uprooted and moved to its Liberty Square location. The controversy rages on. There is no controversy however of the goof in the film: the Liberty Tree built in the studio soundstage is shown with leaves. Since the real tea dumping event was in December, the tree would have no leaves. But it's just more dramatic with leaves.

2. Alfred F. Young, *Liberty Tree: Ordinary People and the American Revolution* (New York: NYU Press, 2006), 4.

blood of patriots & tyrants."[3] And Samuel Adams talking of the "Fruit from the fair Tree of Liberty, planted by our worthy Predecessors, at the expense of their treasure."[4]

Today, however, if you want to visit the Liberty Tree site in Boston, you have to go to the Registry of Motor Vehicles or dodge Chinatown traffic in a busy intersection. But it wasn't always like that . . . .

THE LIBERTY TREE STORY

"Liberty Tree" was part of a grove of elm trees said to have been planted in 1646 by property owner and innkeeper Garrett Bourne.[5] It was described in a 1765 poem as a "stately elm . . . whose lofty branches seem'd to touch the skies."[6] In 1765 the tree was closest to the street of two old elm trees behind a fence "enclosure"[7] in the front yard of Deacon John Elliott, who lived far down on Orange Street (now Washington Street) toward the Boston neck.

The open space at the four corners of Washington, Essex, and Boylston Streets was once known as Hanover Square, from the royal house of Hanover, and sometimes as the Elm Neighborhood, from the magnificent elms with which it was environed. It was one of the finest of these that obtained the name of Liberty Tree.[8]

3. Thomas Jefferson to William S, Smith, Nov. 13, 1787, Paris; in Jean M. Yarbrough, *The Essential Jefferson* (Cambridge, MA: Hackett Publishing, 2006), 167.
4. Harry Alonzo Cushing, ed., *The Writings of Samuel Adams: 1770-1773* (New York: G.P. Putnam's Sons, 1906), 2:372.
5. Thomas J. Campanella, *Republic of Shade: New England and the American Elm* (New Haven, CT: Yale University Press, 2003), 34.
6. Oscar Wegelin, ed. *Early American Poetry: A Compilation of the Titles of Volumes of Verse and Broadsides Written by Writers Born or Residing in North America, and Issued During the Seventeenth and Eighteenth Centuries*, Vol. 1 (1903), 69; "Liberty, Property and No Excise: A Poem Compos'd On Occasion of the Sight seen on the Great Trees, (so called) in Boston, New-England, on the 14th of August, 1765. Printed in the Year, 1765. (Price 6 Cop.) 12mo. Pp. 2 4-8." books.google.com/books?id=jPIUAA AAIAAJ &pg=PA69&dq=Liberty,+Property+and+No+Excise:+A+Poem&hl=en&sa=X&ei= m6YVVc3zDYyogwSe5oE4&ved=0CC0Q6AEwAw#v=onepage&q=Liberty%20tree &f=false (accessed March 27, 2015).
7. Samuel Adams Drake, *Old Landmarks and Historic Parsonages of Boston* (Boston: James R. Osgood and Company, 1873), 397. (Drake wrote comments about Liberty Tree over a century past the actual events, so the words were not a contemporary memory of Drake; just romantic musing on his part.)
8. Samuel Adams Drake, *Old Landmarks*, 396. (See cautionary comment in end note 7.)

On the morning of August 14, 1765, Bostonians passing by "Deacon Elliott's tree"[9] noticed a body hanging in effigy from one of the limbs. The body had a sign hanging from it with the simple initials "A.O." People pretty much knew it meant Andrew Oliver, the new Stamp Tax collector in Boston. However, next to Oliver's effigy, was a large boot. This not-so-veiled reference was to the earl of Bute who colonists (incorrectly) thought had pushed the hated Stamp Tax through Parliament. But the best part yet was an image of the Devil sticking his head up out of Bute's boot. Being displayed in the same company as the Devil and the earl of Bute was not good for Oliver that morning. The crowds continued to grow at the tree throughout the day, so Massachusetts lieutenant governor Thomas Hutchinson sent the sheriff of Suffolk County to cut the offending images down. The sheriff delegated it to his deputies, who reported back that they "could not do it without imminent danger to their lives."[10] The Loyall Nine,[11] a small group of Boston Whigs and a precursor to the Sons of Liberty, had planned this effigy hanging the night before across the street from the tree at Thomas Chase's distillery.[12] So alcohol (specifically rum punch) may have been involved in the creation of what would become known as the Liberty Tree. But more significantly, the first organized show of opposition against British rule took place that day at the Liberty Tree.

By the evening of that first day, the now-really-worked-up crowd left the Liberty Tree and went to Oliver's Stamp Tax office on Kilby Street and completely dismantled it. Then the mob went to Oliver's home and pretty much destroyed that also. Oliver got the message and decided to resign his new job. "The next day he made it known that he would not serve."[13] Oliver had wanted to quit at the Towne-House, the central office for official British doings, but the Loyall Nine insisted it be done at their home office—the Liberty Tree.

About a month after that encounter with Oliver, in fact on September 11, 1765, hundreds of Bostonians met under the branches of their new symbol for fighting tyranny. They nailed a copper plate

9. John Rowe, Diary, August 14, 1766, Massachusetts Historical Society; David Hackett Fischer, *Liberty and Freedom* (New York: Oxford University Press, 2005), 21.
10. Fischer, *Liberty and Freedom*, 20.
11. Ira Stoll, *Samuel Adams—A Life* (New York: Free Press, 2008), 41.
12. "The distillery and the elm that became known as the Liberty Tree were both in Hanover Square." Stoll, *Samuel Adams*, 41.
13. Arthur M. Schlesinger, "Liberty Tree: A Genealogy," *The New England Quarterly*, December 1952, 437.

to the tree trunk that bore the words, "Tree of Liberty."[14] The meeting area under the Liberty Tree also had a name. According to Massachusetts governor Francis Bernard in an intelligence letter to Lord Hillsborough, the area beneath the tree limbs of the Liberty Tree was called "Liberty-Hall"[15] by the insolent provincials. An additional cause for Tory alarm was that other New England towns, and even cities as far away as Savannah, Georgia, were starting to adopt their own trees—with Boston's Liberty Tree as their inspiration.

By 1768, the Liberty Tree and Liberty Hall were getting noticed with a level of curiosity even over in London. In the "Late Proceedings at Boston" section of *The London Magazine, Or, Gentleman's Monthly Intelligencer*, the column pronounced "A notification was posted up in diverse parts of the town, requesting the sons of liberty to meet at Liberty-Hall on Tuesday the 14th, at ten o'clock in the forenoon . . . Early on Tuesday morning the colours were flying on liberty-tree."[16]

On that particular day, August 14, 1768, Samuel Adams planned a third-anniversary celebration of Bostonians' first protest against the Stamp Act. Never mind that the Stamp Act had been repealed in 1766.

---

14. Fischer, *Liberty and Freedom*, 22.
15. Governor Bernard to the Earl of Hillsborough, June 16, 1768 (on page 25) at books.google.com/books?id=hJYBAAAAQAAJ&printsec=frontcover&dq=Liberty+Tree&hl=en&sa=X&ei=MGTZVO78NMTqgwT814HQBg&ved=0CGAQ6AEwCThG#v=onepage&q=Liberty%20Tree&f=false. The letter speaks of the Sons of Liberty who were called to assemble at Liberty-Hall under the Liberty-Tree. Bernard specifically says, " . . . has obtained the Name of Liberty-Tree, as the Ground under it has that of Liberty-Hall." Adding to that assumption is this statement, "The ground around the tree had become sacred soil, and was designated as Liberty Hall." Frederick Fitch Hassam, *Liberty tree, Liberty hall, 1775, Lafayette and loyalty!* (Boston, 1891), 1; Google-digitized, Public Domain; original resides at University of Michigan. There is some speculation however that "Liberty Hall" was actually a tavern next to the Liberty Tree property. Consider this issue of the *Boston Gazette* of August 18, 1766: "At the Hour of XII they convened at the sacred Tree of Liberty, every Bosom dilating with Joy, and every Eye sparkling with Satisfaction . . . The Company then retired to the Hall of Liberty, adjacent to the Tree, and drank the following loyal Toasts." The *Boston-Gazette and Country Journal*, No. 594, August 18, 1766, bottom of third column of page 2; The Annotated Newspapers of Harbottle Dorr; www.masshist.org/dorr/volume/1/sequence/482 (accessed March 6, 2015). In yet another reference, Thomas Chase's distillery, across the street from Liberty Tree, was referred to as Liberty Hall.
16. Isaac Kimber, Edward Kimber, ed's., *The London Magazine, Or, Gentleman's Monthly Intelligencer*, Volume 37 for the Year 1768, 422. This article was a pick-up from the June 20, 1768, issue of *The Boston Gazette*.

In 1768, Adams still wanted to keep the party alive, so guess where ground zero was for the events? "The day's festivities began at the Liberty Tree, with the discharge of fourteen cannon at dawn, and escalated at noon with the singing of 'The Liberty Song.'"[17] No surprise, the next year a *fourth* anniversary of the Stamp Act protests was scheduled on August 14, 1769, by Sam Adams at—where else?—the Liberty Tree. Only this time, the revelers left the real tree and joined up with about 355 Sons of Liberty for some serious celebrating up on Dorchester at a new drinking location—the Liberty-Tree Tavern.

By 1770, the "venerable Liberty-elm"[18] became the communication center for the early Boston rebels, much like a message board on a college campus. Commercial advertisements were even nailed to the tree trunk and the tree became a destination point for sales. William Billings noted on the title page of his *New-England Psalm-Singer* that additional copies of the hymnal could be purchased from "Deacon Elliott, under Liberty-Tree."[19] The Liberty Tree was also the designated gathering spot as, "The North and South End gangs paraded together to the Liberty Tree with effigies,"[20] advertising their "abhorrence of POPERY,"[21] a perceived connection between "the Pope [and the] Devil."[22]

But more than anything, the Liberty Tree remained the central point of assembly for angry American colonists. Simply said, "The rituals at the Liberty Tree were devices for maintaining continuity and preserving unity."[23] As late as November 1773, it was still being listed as an established meeting spot, as this news clip from the *Boston Gazette* indicates: "Boston November 3; Wednesday there was a numerous assembly of inhabitants of this and neighbouring towns, at Liberty Tree."[24]

It was also where Bostonians gathered to mourn their own. The funeral procession for eleven-year-old Christopher Seider, shot to

17. Stoll, *Samuel Adams*, 69.

18. *Boston Chronicle*, 22 May 1769; Fischer, *Liberty and Freedom*, 23.

19. "The New-England Psalm-Singer, 1770," American Antiquarian Society, www. americanantiquarian.org/Inventories/Revere/psalmsinger.pdf (accessed March 25, 2015).

20. Stoll, *Samuel Adams*, 49.

21. Stoll, *Samuel Adams*, 49; *The Boston Post-Boy and Advertiser*, November 11, 1765.

22. Stoll, *Samuel Adams*, 49.

23. Fischer, *Liberty and Freedom*, 27.

24. *Boston Gazette and Country Journal*, No. 970, Monday, November 8, 1773, top left column of page 2; The Annotated Newspapers of Harbottle Dorr; www. masshist. org/dorr/volume/4/sequence/472 (accessed March 6, 2015).

death by customs service informer Ebenezer Richardson, is described in the March 5, 1770, issue of the *Boston Gazette,* "The little Corpse was set down under the Tree of Liberty, from whence the procession began."[25] Following that event, a board was nailed to the Liberty Tree containing verses from the Bible describing that the wicked should be punished.

Then just a few weeks later, the funeral procession for the four victims of what would become known as the Boston Massacre followed a route that was sure to include the famous tree: from Faneuil Hall, south to circle the Liberty Tree, and then up to the Granary Burial Grounds. So, as the flames of the oncoming Revolutionary War were getting hot, the Liberty Tree in south Boston remained the headquarters and communications center for "the body of the people."[26]

Sometimes the people also sat in judgement of their own and the Liberty Tree served as the location of an ad hoc court. In a desperate letter to Lord Hillsborough from Governor Bernard, he exclaimed in astonishment about rebel courts, "We have seen justices attending at Liberty Tree."[27] In 1774, British customs officer John Malcolm was tarred, feathered, and dragged "through the main street into King street, from thence to Liberty Tree."[28] At the Liberty Tree, he was forced to drink a tea toast to every Parliamentary politician and royal family member who could be thought of in an effort to encourage Malcolm to rethink his career path. The torturous process began to be known by Loyalists as undergoing "the Tree Ordeal."[29]

It appears that sometimes the Sons of Liberty had parade entourages swing out of the way south of town to loop around the Liberty Tree. That appeared to have established a parade route that both sides of the conflict used as needed for their purposes. John Trumbull describes the British army's punishment parade route that was parodying the Sons of Liberty's Liberty Tree loop:

25. Stoll, *Samuel Adams,* 81.
26. Cushing, ed., *The Writings of Samuel Adams,* 150.
27. Governor Bernard to the Earl of Hillsborough, Nov. 14, 1768, at books.google. com/books?id=j3NbAAAAQAAJ&pg=PA23&dq=Liberty+Tree&hl=en&sa=X&ei= 0mzZVIWAFbSSsQTcpILQAQ&ved=0CDoQ6AEwAjiqAQ#v=onepage&q=Libert y%20Tree&f=false.
28. John Almon, *A Collection of Interesting, Authentic Papers—Relative to the Dispute between Great Britain and America* (London: J. Almon, 1777; reprint Bedford, MA: Applewood Books), 254.
29. Peter Oliver, "Origins and Progress of the American Rebellion to the Year 1776," Gay Transcripts, Massachusetts Historical Society; Schlesinger, "Liberty Tree," 438; Fischer, *Liberty and Freedom,* 28.

In 1765, the "Liberty Tree" was the tree closest to the street of two old elm trees behind a fence ("enclosure") in the front yard of Deacon John Ellicott, as shown in this 1825 engraving. (*Houghton Library, Harvard University*)

Early next morning they stripped him entirely naked, covered him with warm tar, and then with feathers, placed him on a cart, conducted him to the north end of town, then back to the south end, as far as Liberty-Tree; where the people began to collect in vast numbers.[30]

Finally in 1775, when British troops were besieged in Boston after their disastrous skirmishes out in Lexington and Concord, Liberty Tree pay-back time had arrived. A group of British regulars aided by some remaining Tories cut the offending tree down. The *New-England Chronicle* covered the dastardly deed with all the Yankee verbal flourishes of the time:

> Cambridge August 31–The Enemies to Liberty and America, headed by Tom Gage, lately gave a notable Specimen of their Hatred of the very Name of Liberty. A Party of them, of whom one Job Williams was the Ringleader, a few Days since, repaired to a Tree at the South End of Boston, known by the Name of Liberty Tree, and, armed with Axes, etc. made a furious Attack upon it.

30. John Trumbull, *The Political Works of John Trumbull, LL. D. and Memoir* (Hartford: Samuel G. Goodrich, 1820), 56. Passage is from Trumbull's poem "M'Fingal" published within this compilation. The infraction Trumbull was describing was "a parade by the 47th Regiment punishing a man from Billerica for trying to buy soldiers' muskets in early 1775." Per. J. L. Bell, March 27, 2015.

After a long Spell of laughing and grinning, sweating, swearing and foaming, with Malice diabolical, they cut down a Tree because it bore the Name of Liberty.³¹

It was reported that the Liberty Tree was so large that it yielded fourteen cords of firewood. It was also reported that since tree cutting safety procedures were not so stringent back then, a helper of the "foaming" Tory faction was killed by a huge falling limb from the Liberty Tree. Another version reported that the helper fell out of the tree and was killed. The victim's name was never reported, which seems suspicious, but Patriots ran with the story regardless that it was a divine sign that the tree went down fighting. No one could argue the fact however that the only thing remaining after the hatchet job was just a stump.³²

But hey, after the war, industrious Patriots did what they could to honor the former Liberty Tree with what they now proudly called "the Liberty Stump,"³³ but it lacked the punch of the earlier name. A 1782 broadside advertised goods "to be sold near Liberty Stump."³⁴ On Marquis de Lafayette's 1825 tour of the new United States, he stopped in Boston to lay the cornerstone of the Bunker Hill monument and was taken to the Liberty Stump. He reportedly was underwhelmed, but still uttered some memorable words. "La Fayette was much affected . . . in front of the stump of the Liberty Tree."³⁵ It just wasn't working. Eventually urban sprawl enveloped what had been Deacon Elliott's property and the Liberty Stump. Unlike sites like the Old State House, Faneuil Hall, or the Old South Church, it was felt that the stump just wasn't worth saving.

---

31. *The New-England Chronicle or the Essex Gazette*, Number 370, August 24-31, 1775; middle column of page 3; The Annotated Newspapers of Harbottle Dorr; www.masshist.org/dorr/volume/4/sequence/878. In the precise index annotations that Harbottle Dorr made on almost all of his newspapers, he has inscribed a "(1)" to both listings of the noun "Liberty Tree" in this story. At the far lower right of this newspaper page, he has written: "(1) see index, Vol. 1. under Liberty Tree." Dorr was really organized.

32. Jerome V.C. Smith, M.D., ed., *The Boston News-letter: And City Record*, Volume 1, (Jan.-July 1826), 19. Regarding the death from chopping down the tree, "Suspiciously, no sources inside the besieged town reported this death, and no name is attached to the story." Per. J. L. Bell, March 27, 2015.

33. Dirk Hoerder, *Crowd Action in Revolutionary Massachusetts, 1765-80—Studies in Social Discontinuity* (New York: Academic Press, 1977), 209; Smith, *Boston News-letter*, 19.

34. Hoerder, *Crowd Action*, 209.

35. Hassam, *Liberty tree*, 3.

THE LIBERTY TREE SITE TODAY

If you would like to visit the site of the Liberty Tree in today's Boston, you won't find it on the popular Freedom Trail. Its location, even if there was a tree stump to see, would be off the beaten path as it sits a couple blocks east of the most southern tip of modern day Boston Common. The site of Deacon Elliott's yard and fabled tree is in (of all places) Chinatown. One would take the Orange Line of the "T" (MBTA), get off at the "Chinatown" stop and walk up the stairs to the Washington Street entrance. Once outside, if you literally turn and look up the front of the building, you'll see that the premises (630 Washington Street) is part of the Commonwealth of Massachusetts Registry of Motor Vehicles. In the front third floor window, you'll see a bas-relief plaque of a tree . . . the Liberty Tree. The words below the tree say, "Sons of Liberty 1766; Independence of their Country 1776." You're standing at the corner where the Liberty Tree stood behind the fence of Deacon Elliott and where so much of the early part of the American Revolution took place; now just a busy intersection in downtown Boston with little notice to say what happened there.

The brick building at the corner of Washington and Essex streets you're looking at was built in 1850, and today comprises a small historic district called The Liberty Tree District. The area and Liberty Tree Building have been on the National Register of Historic Places for thirty-five years. But that was following some civic and political intervention.

In 1966, a history-loving rookie reporter for the *Boston Herald* named Ronald Kessler[36] walked to the Liberty Tree site and found the same bas-relief plaque, originally commissioned by Sears, in the same window as it appears today. But he found the brick building in much the same shape as the neighborhood—seedy, run down, and dangerous. In October 1966, he began a series of articles about the Liberty Tree and its importance in those early days of unrest in Boston. He appealed to Massachusetts governor John Volpe to get involved. After visiting the site, Governor Volpe "promised to create a park with monuments to let Americans know about the history of the Liberty Tree."[37] However, reportedly because of so many buried utilities in that area, the park idea had to be scrapped. Instead a marker was

36. In 2015, "Ronald Kessler is the New York Times bestselling author of 20 non-fiction books." From: www.ronaldkessler.com/bio.html (accessed March 22, 2015).
37. "America Must Remember Boston's Liberty Tree" www.newsmax.com/Ronald Kessler/America-Boston-Liberty-Tree/2011/10/03/id/413067/ (accessed March 19, 2015).

embedded into the brickwork in the traffic island across from the Liberty Tree window.[38] But now a seedling of hope has again been planted by the City of Boston, and "Liberty Tree Plaza" may break ground by fall 2015 or spring 2016[39]—weather permitting, of course!

National historic sites are often in danger of destruction. But a living entity, such as an elm tree, is particularly vulnerable to forces such as, well, Dutch elm disease, droughts, ice-snow-wind storms, insects, root starvation from urban growth, and just plain age-related collapse. So the fact that no tree can be found on the site of Boston's Liberty Tree shouldn't alarm history lovers. But completely forgetting about the Liberty Tree's story would be its worst epitaph. As the Marquis de Lafayette said in 1825 standing in front of the Liberty Stump, "the world should never forget the spot where once stood Liberty Tree, so famous in your annals."[40] But watch out for that car, Marquis!

38. According to J.L. Bell's April 8, 2007, blog article "Adding Liberty Tree Site to the Freedom Trail?": "Plans for expanding Liberty Tree Park have been in the air since 1974 . . . " boston1775.blogspot.com/2007/04/adding-liberty-tree-site-to-freedom .html (accessed March 22, 2015).
39. In an email to this author on March 25, 2015, Allison Perlman, project manager for Boston Parks and Recreation Department gave this very promising status report, "Improvements to Liberty Tree Plaza are currently in the Construction Documents phase. Parks anticipates the project will start construction Fall 2015/Spring 2016." She cautioned, however, that all things are weather dependent! But it does indeed sound hopeful.
40. The Freedom Trail Foundation, "Liberty Tree, by Matthew Wilding," www.the-freedomtrail.org/educational-resources/article-liberty-tree. shtml (accessed March 22, 2015).

Prelude to Rebellion: Dunmore's Raid on the Williamsburg Magazine

❧ NORMAN FUSS ❧

April in Virginia is regarded by many as the best month of the year. Sandwiched between the chilly bluster of March and the growing heat and humidity of May and June, April is characterized by warm but not hot days, cool but not cold nights, gentle breezes and gentle rains. There are, of course, exceptions. And the night of April 20–21, 1775, was one of them. Winds gusting to over 40 miles per hour shook the newly leafed trees. Clouds threatening rain scudded across the sky, intermittently plunging the land into almost total darkness as they blotted out the light from the silvery half moon.[1] Altogether, it was a night on which most people would choose to be at home in their beds and not tramping the roads through the countryside.

Most, but not all.

At about 4:00 a.m. on the morning of April 21, 1775 a body of men might have been observed moving along the road from Burwell's

---

1. The description of weather conditions at Williamsburg on the night of April 21, 1775 is based on the following: Astronomical conditions U. S. Naval Observatory, Astronomical Applications Department, Sun and Moon Data for One Day, Williamsburg, VA (Longitude W76° 43′, Latitude N37° 17′), April 21, 1775 Eastern Standard Time, aa.usno.navy.mil/rstt/onedaytable?form=1&ID=AA&year= 1775& month=4&day=21&state=VA&place=Williamsburg, (accessed January 7, 2015). "Phase of the Moon Waning Gibbous with 63% of the Moon's visible disk illuminated." Atmospheric weather conditions *A Log for His Majesty's Ship Fowey, from Decr 6th, 1774 to Decr 6th 1775 by James Kellie, Master*. (PRO ADM 52/1749 in Virginia Colonial Records Project Microfilm Reel M945, Rockefeller Library, Colonial Williamsburg Foundation, Williamsburg, VA), entry for Thursday, 20th April, 1775: "Fresh Gales & cloudy." (NOTE: The day on board ship begins and ends at 12:00 noon. The entry for April 20 covers from 12:00 noon, April 20 to 12:00 noon April 21, land time.) On April 20/21, 1775 *HMS Fowey* was moored in the James River near Newport News, about 15 miles from Williamsburg.

Ferry on the James River toward Virginia's capitol of Williamsburg. As they neared, an observer (had there been one) would have noted that they were about twenty in number. As they came even nearer he would have seen that they were led by a young man in the uniform of a lieutenant of His Majesty's Navy, that some wore the red faced white uniforms of His Majesty's Marines,[2] while others wore common seaman's garb,[3] and that all were armed.[4] Following closely behind were two men in a wagon.[5]

They came on with the steady, purposeful stride of men on a mission. For men on a mission is what they were. They had been ordered to remove from the Williamsburg Magazine the gunpowder that was stored there. They did not know why, nor did they care. They were merely doing their duty; just following orders. They did not know— nor could they have known—that in carrying out those orders they would set alight a fuse which would ignite a series of events that would culminate in the expulsion of Royal Authority and the elimination of any organized British influence in Virginia for the next five years.

Trouble had been brewing between the colonists and the royal governor, John Murray, Fourth Earl Dunmore, for some time. In response

2. Purdie, *Virginia Gazette Supplement* (April 21, 1775), 3. "This morning, between 3 and 4 o'clock, all the gunpowder in the magazine, to the amount, as we hear, of about 20 barrels, was carried off in his Excellency the Governor's wagon, escorted by a detachment of marines from the armed schooner Magdalen, now lying at Burwell's ferry, and lodged on board that vessel."

3. Dunmore mentions only seamen in his report to Lord Dartmouth; Dunmore to Dartmouth (No. 26), Williamsburg 1st May 1775 (PRO CO 5/1353) in William Bell Clark, *Naval Documents of the American Revolution* (Washington: U.S. Navy Department, 1964) 1:259-61 (hereafter cited as Clark, *NDAR*). "I accordingly requested of Lieut. [Henry] Collins commanding His Majesty's armed Schooner the *Magdalen*, to convey the powder on board the *Foway* [sic!] Man of War now on this station, which that Officer, with a party of his Seamen Diligently executed."

4. *A Journal of the proceedings of His Majesty's Schooner Magdalen under my Command Commencing 17th April 1775 & ending the 8th Septr 1775 by Henry Collins*. (PRO ADM 51/3894 in Virginia Colonial Records Project Microfilm Reel M942, Rockefeller Library, Colonial Williamsburg Foundation, Williamsburg, VA) (hereafter cited as *Journal, HMS Magdalen*), entry for Thursday, 20th April, 1775, "At 3 AM landed 20 men Armed to take some Gunpowder out of the Magazine at Williamsburg."

5. Dunmore provided the wagon used to transport the almost half ton of gunpowder from the Magazine to the *Magdalen*; Purdie, *Virginia Gazette Supplement* (April 21, 1775), 3, op. cit. The two men in the wagon would have been Captain Edward Foy and a servant driver.

to what the colonists perceived as the increasingly coercive actions of Parliament and the growing restrictions being placed on their rights as Englishmen, resistance had been building for years. When Lord Dunmore arrived as royal governor for Virginia in 1771, he had been warmly welcomed. But tensions between Parliament and the people were already at a high level. They continued to increase during the next four years.

Dunmore was Scottish aristocrat. An earl and a member of the House of Lords, he moved among the wealthiest and most powerful people of British society. But there were shadows.

In 1745 his father had supported Charles Stuart (Bonnie Prince Charlie) in his attempt to wrest the British crown from King George II. At age 15, John had served as a page in the Prince's court. When the uprising failed at the Battle of Culloden, English retribution had been swift and harsh. Dunmore's father was arrested, tried, convicted of treason, and sentenced to hang. It was only through the intervention of Dunmore's uncle, John Murray, 2nd Earl of Dunmore, who was held in high regard by the king, that William Murray was pardoned on condition that he remain " . . . a Prisoner during his Life in such Place or Places as We, Our Heirs and Successors should be pleased from Time to Time . . . to direct."[6] Thus, almost miraculously, the Dunmore titles were preserved to be passed on to young John, albeit accompanied by a cloud of suspicion that never entirely dissipated.

Although he rubbed elbows with the mighty and influential in British society and government, he was never really one of the important personages in that circle. Keenly aware of his relatively low status among the movers and shakers of his time, he spent much of his life attempting to improve the family fortune and his position in British society.

His chance came in 1770 when he was appointed to the governorship of New York. He was making some progress toward his goal of acquiring vast tracts of land in New York when, in 1771, he learned that he had been replaced as governor of New York and was to assume the governorship of Virginia (which he viewed as a consolation prize).

Convivial, fun loving, and personally courageous, he was also characterized by contemporaries as arrogant, impetuous, egocentric, combative, highly sensitive to perceived slights or disrespect, possessed of a capable but not formidable intellect, and lacking in judgment, self

6. Newcastle to William Murray, November 30, 1747, Dunmore Papers, Earl Greg Swem Library, College of William & Mary, Williamsburg, VA, box 2, folder 71.

control, diplomatic dexterity, and finesse.[7] After two weeks of inter-
acting with Dunmore at Pittsburgh during Dunmore's 1774 expedition
against the Shawnee, Augustine Prevost[8] wrote this concise character-
ization of him:

> His L[ordshi]p in a private character is by no means a bad man.
> On the contrary, he is a jolly, hearty companion, hospitable and
> polite at his own table, but as G[overno]r or the com[mande]r of a
> military expedition [he is] the most unfit, the most trifling and most
> uncalculated person living.[9]

This, then, was the man into whose hands the king and Parliament
had entrusted British interest and influence in Virginia, its wealthiest
and most populous colony in America.[10]

Dunmore found himself increasingly in conflict with the growing
aspirations of the people and the independent spirit of Virginia's colonial leaders. Accustomed to and expecting unquestioning obedience,

7. For brief biographies of Dunmore see: H. C. G. Matthew and Brian Harrison (eds.),
Oxford Dictionary of National Biography (Oxford: Oxford University Press, 2004), 39:
955-56; Mark M. Boatner III, *Encyclopedia of the American Revolution*, (New York:
David McKay, 1974) 340-41; _____, *Encyclopedia Virginia*, (Virginia Foundation for
the Humanities and the Library of Virginia); and Sidney Lee (ed.), *Dictionary of
National Biography* (London: Smith, Elder & Co., 1894), 39: 388. For fuller treatments
of Dunmore, see James Corbett David, *Dunmore's New World* (Charlottesville:
University of Virginia Press, 2013); John E. Selby & Edward M. Riley, *Dunmore*
(Williamsburg: Virginia Independence Bicentennial Commission, 1977), and James A.
Hagemann, *Lord Dunmore: Last Royal Governor of Virginia, 1771-1776* (Hampton:
Wayfarer, 1974).

8. Augustine Prevost was the son of Major General Augustine Prevost who, as commander of British forces in East Florida, played an important role in the capture of
Savannah in 1778 and its successful defense in 1779. The younger Prevost served in his
father's regiment, attaining the rank of major before leaving British service at the end
of the Revolution. Nicholas B. Wainwright, "Turmoil in Pittsburgh: Diary of
Augustine Prevost," *Pennsylvania Magazine of History and Biography*, 85 (Philadelphia:
Historical Society of Pennsylvania, 1961), 111-62. (hereafter cited as Wainwright,
Turmoil in Pittsburgh).

9. Wainwright, *Turmoil in Pittsburgh*, 143.

10. Estimated population in 1775: Virginia = 400,000. Massachusetts (the next most
populous colony) = 358,000. Evarts B. Greene, *American Population Before the Federal
Census of 1790* (1981; repr. Baltimore: Genealogical Publishing Co., 1997), 7. Value of
exports in 1763: Virginia = £1,040,000. Pennsylvania (the next colony in value of
exports) = £705,500. John Mitchell or Arthur Young, *American Husbandry. Containing
an account of the soil, climate, production and agriculture of the British colonies in North-
America and the West-Indies; with observations on the advantages and disadvantages of settling in them, compared with Great Britain and Ireland.* (London: J. Bew, 1775), 1: 124-
25, 256-57.

he grew frustrated and angry when those colonial leaders were so bold (and in Dunmore's view, disrespectful) as to act in opposition to his wishes. His response to rising colonial concerns and to the growing militancy of the Virginia General Assembly was to twice dissolve that body, thereby effectively shutting down civil government in Virginia.

"... about the middle of April ..." (probably about April 9–10), at Dunmore's request, Hugh Miller, the Keeper of the Magazine, had "... delivered up the keys to the Magazine to the Governor ...." According to Miller, there were in the Magazine at that time "... twenty one barrels and a half of Powder, including the three unfitted [i.e., unfit for use, needing reconstitution], three hundred and forty two new Muskets, lately cleaned and in complete order, others that wanted but small repairs ..." and a number of old guns and other articles "... almost useless ..."[11]

Several days later, Miller reported to Mayor John Dixon and the Williamsburg Common Hall that he had received information to the effect that agents of the governor had been entering the magazine by night and had removed the locks from the 342 new muskets that were stored within, thereby rendering them inoperable. Additionally he reported that there were credible reports that the governor was planning to remove the colonies supply of gunpowder that was also stored in the magazine.[12]

This was alarming news. The Williamsburg Magazine was the central repository for the arms, ammunition, and equipment needed for defense against Indian raids, slave revolts, riots, and insurrections. If Miller's information was true, Virginia would be rendered virtually defenseless.

Lacking access to the magazine (the keys were in Dunmore's hands) the town authorities could not verify Miller's information regarding the musket locks. They also could not verify the allegation that "... the Governor was planning to carry off the stock of powder," for any effort to do so, should it become known to the governor, would undoubtedly be viewed by Dunmore as an outrageous affront and precipitate a confrontation for which they were not prepared.

11. "The Complete Report of the Commotion Committee appointed to inspect the contents of the Public Magazine" presented 13 June 1775 in H. R. McIlwaine & J. P. Kennedy, eds., *Journals of the House of Burgesses of Virginia: 1619-1776* (Richmond: Virginia State Library, 1905-1915), 13:223-24.
12. John Burk, *The History of Virginia from its Settlement to the Present Day* (Petersburg: Dunnavant, 1805), 2: 409 (hereafter cited as Burk, *History of Virginia*).

The powder magazine at Williamsburg, Virginia. (*Albert Herring*)

They did what they could, which was to set a watch on the magazine to observe who, if anyone, was going in and out during the hours of darkness. Beginning on Easter Sunday, April 16, citizen volunteers mounted watch on the magazine from sunset to sunrise.

The information that Dunmore planned to seize the colony's gunpowder was all too true. Days earlier he had ordered Lt. Henry Collins, commander of His Majesty's Schooner *Magdalen*,[13] then moored in the James River off Burwell's Ferry, to organize a shore party to seize the gunpowder in the magazine. Lieutenant Collins was to hold the party in readiness to act immediately upon notification from Dunmore that the coast was clear, inasmuch as Dunmore

13. HMS *Magdalen* was a small schooner measuring just over 60 feet long and about 19 feet wide. She mounted six light 3 pounder carriage guns and had a crew of about 30. For specifications of HMS *Magdalen* see David Lyon, *The Sailing Navy List, All The Ships of the Royal Navy, Built, Purchased and Captured, 1688-1860* (London: Conway Maritime Press, 1993), 212. For the number of guns and crew see: *Disposition of the Squadron under Vice Admiral Samuel Graves, List of the North American Squadron on the 1st January 1775*, Graves Conduct, I, 40, 41, MassHS Transcript in Clark, *NDAR* 1:47 and *Disposition of the [British] Fleet on the 30th of June 1775*, Graves Conduct, I, 132, MassHS Transcript in Clark, *NDAR* 1: 785. For the size of the *Magdalen*'s guns see *Journal, HMS Magdalen*, entry for Thursday, 15th June 1775, " . . . lost overboard in getting the stores out of the Vessel 1, 3 pound and swivel grape Shot occasion by the lanyard of the Bow giving way at 2 PM."

wished the removal to be done "privately."[14] Dunmore also undertook to provide a small wagon from the palace to transport the almost half ton of purloined powder.[15]

Through the nights of Sunday, Monday, Tuesday, and Wednesday the watchers watched. And saw nothing. Between 1:00 to 2:00 on the morning of April 21, perhaps out of extreme boredom, perhaps because of the blustery weather, perhaps a combination of both, the volunteers on watch that night left their stations.[16]

That was just what Dunmore had been waiting for. For while the volunteers had been watching the magazine, Dunmore's servants had been watching the watchers. When they departed that night, Dunmore was immediately informed.

Summoning his personal secretary and advisor, Navy captain Edward Foy, Dunmore gave him the key to the magazine, instructed him to take one of the wagons in the palace stables and notify Lieutenant Collins. This he did. With one of the servants as a driver, he set off for Burwell's Ferry.[17]

Captain Foy arrived at Burwell's Ferry around 2:30 a.m. He alerted Lieutenant Collins who alerted the men designated for the landing party. It took perhaps 20 minutes to wake the men, arm and accouter them, inspect them, and prepare them for the mission which they were about to undertake. At 3:00 a.m., twenty armed men came ashore.[18] A handful of these men were marines—no more than six or seven[19]—who formed the core of the landing party. The rest were sea-

14. *Dunmore to Dartmouth (No. 26) Williamsburg 1st May 1775* in Clark, *NDAR,* 1:259. Op. cit. "I accordingly requested of Lieut. [Henry] Collins of His Majesty's armed Schooner *Magdalen, to convey the powder on board the* Foway [sic] Man of War now on this station . . . it was intended to be done privately . . . "

15. Purdie, *Virginia Gazette Supplement,* April 21, 1775, 3. Op. cit.

16. Burk, *History of Virginia,* 2: 410-11.

17. Dunmore needed to send a messenger to HMS *Magdalen* with notification that the way was clear. He also needed to supply a wagon to transport the powder. The most efficient and secure way to accomplish both would have been to send the messenger with the wagon. The messenger would have been someone highly trusted by Dunmore. The most trusted member of his "family" was (Navy) Captain Edward Foy, Dunmore's long time private secretary and personal advisor. Foy, as a gentleman and a captain in His Majesty's Navy would almost certainly not have driven the wagon himself.

18. *Journal,* HMS *Magdalen,* entry for Thursday, April 20, 1775, "At 3 AM landed 20 men Armed to take some Gunpowder out of the Magazine at Williamsburg."

19. The number of marines on board Royal Navy ships in the eighteenth century was roughly equal to the number of guns. Personal correspondence, National Museum, Royal Navy, December 17, 2014. At six guns, HMS *Magdeline* would have had about a half-dozen marines on board. The rest of the "20 men Armed" would have been seamen.

men. Among them, as the only men present with the training and knowledge to properly and safely handle large quantities of gunpowder, were the *Magdalen's* gunner and gunner's mate.[20]

Led by the marines and followed by the Governor's wagon, the party marched at a steady pace along the four mile road between Burwell's Ferry and Williamsburg. It took them a little more than an hour. As they approached the city, they advanced cautiously, conscious of Dunmore's desire for "privacy." Passing to the left of the Capitol Building, they went along South Street (now Francis Street) rather than Main Street (now Duke of Gloucester Street) because it had fewer houses, fewer people, and hence offered less chance of being discovered.[21] Shortly after 4:00 a.m. they reached the rear of the magazine.[22]

The Williamsburg Magazine was the central repository for the arms, ammunition, and equipment for the colony. Built in 1715, it was a two-story octagon building with thick walls of fired brick. Arms, accouterments, and other military equipment were stored on the second floor. Gunpowder was stored on the first floor in a room that was accessible only by a separate door in the rear of the building. During the course of the French and Indian War, a 10 foot high perimeter wall and guardhouse had been added to accommodate the influx of munitions occasioned by that conflict. The heavy oak gate through the perimeter wall and the doors to the magazine itself were secured by strong locks.[23]

To enter the magazine, the party had to move to the front gate. No sooner had they done so than an alarm was sounded. It is not known who sounded the alarm—perhaps some citizen suffering from insomnia, perhaps a watcher who had sheltered from the weather in the

---

20. Every Royal Navy ship had a gunner and one or more gunner's mates in its crew. Trained, examined, and accountable to the Board of Ordnance, they were responsible for insuring that the ship's armaments, especially its store of gunpowder, were kept in safe and sound condition. *National Museum of the Royal Navy*, www.royal-navalmuseum.org/info_sheets_nav_rankings.htm (accessed January 21, 2015). Common prudence would have dictated that these men be included in the party sent to remove the gunpowder from the Williamsburg Magazine.

21. *Plan de la Citie et environs du Williamsburg en Virginie, America au 11 Mai 1786.* On display in the Rockefeller Library, Colonial Williamsburg Foundation, Williamsburg, VA.

22. This scenario is speculative, but appears to make the most sense from a logistical and tactical point of view.

23. John F. Lowe, *The Magazine Historical Report*, Block 12, Building 9, Lot 00, Originally Entitled: *"Manual for the Public Magazine"* (Williamsburg: Colonial Williamsburg Foundation, 1990), 4-7.

courthouse just across Main Street. No matter who sounded the alarm, "privacy" was no longer possible.

Lieutenant Collins acted quickly. Detailing a couple of marines to guard the wagon, he unlocked the front gate, entered the courtyard, led the rest of his party to the rear of the building and unlocked the door to the powder room.

Entering first with the double-shielded lantern that he used when working in the *Magdalen*'s powder room, the Gunner looked about. Stacked against one wall were eighteen half-barrels, each containing 50 pounds of gunpowder and weighing in total about 65 pounds each.[24] Off to one side were three other full half barrels and one more only partially full. He quickly recognized that the three half-barrels setting apart contained damaged powder waiting to be reconstituted, and that all the good powder was in the other eighteen half-barrels.

At an order from Lieutenant Collins, each of the men slung his musket, picked up a half-barrel of powder, hurried through the front gate, and deposited it in the wagon.

There was not time for more—the alarm was spreading rapidly. Locking the door to the powder room and the gate behind him, Lieutenant Collins and his party set off the way they had come—at a far faster pace than they had employed on their approach.

By the time enough citizens had been roused from their beds to make a crowd of appreciable size, the raiding party was too far away to be overtaken. And no one present was prepared to confront an armed party of His Majesty's Marines—even a small one.

At about 6:00 a.m. the party arrived back at its starting point at Burrell's Ferry.[25] The powder was transferred to the *Magdalen*. The wagon departed and the men returned on board, their mission accomplished.

They had no way of knowing of the attempt to seize colonist's arms and ammunition that had taken place some 600 miles to the north at Lexington and Concord in the colony of Massachusetts Bay less than 48 hours earlier, and of the violent and bloody reaction that

24. Military barrels for gunpowder were made of 3/4 inch thick oak, hooped with heavy (3/16 inch thick) copper bands. A half-barrel for gunpowder measured 13 1/2 inches diameter by 20 inches high and weighed approximately 15 pounds. Total weight for a full half-barrel of gunpowder was about 65 pounds, not difficult for a man to carry for short to intermediate distances. Cooper's Shop, Colonial Williamsburg, private conversation, January 5, 2015 (information confirmed during a 2013 visit by the cooper to The Historic Dockyard, Chatham, UK).
25. *Journal*, HMS *Magdalen*, entry for Thursday, April 20, 1775 "At 6 the people returned with 15 half Barrs . . . ."

it had precipitated. Nor had they any reason to anticipate the angry reactions and the disastrous chain of events that would follow from this night's work. They had merely done their duty.

But in doing so, they had lit the fuse to a chain of events that culminated in the disastrous British defeat at the Battle of Great Bridge and the eradication of British authority in Virginia, leaving the wealthiest and most populous state of the fledgling United States free of any organized British presence for the next five years.

Patrick Henry's "Liberty or Death": Granddaddy of Revolution Mythologies

RAY RAPHAEL

I first encountered Patrick Henry in fifth grade. He was the patriot of "Give me liberty, or give me death!" fame—not to be confused with that other "H" patriot, Nathan Hale, who was disappointed because he had only one life to give for his country. More than half a century later, students are still asked to couple "liberty or death" with Patrick Henry on multiple choice tests, never suspecting that the quotation originated with William Wirt, a man they've never heard of. More is at stake than attribution. Hidden within this most pervasive mythology of the Revolution is a distortion of the Revolutionary experience.

WILLIAM WIRT'S TRICKY TASK

In 1805, while practicing law in Virginia at the age of 32, Wirt embarked on an ambitious project: a biography of the legendary orator Patrick Henry, who died shortly before the turn of the century. Although Wirt had neither met Henry nor heard him speak, he assumed he could find sufficient material by consulting newspaper accounts, combing through Henry's private papers, and communicating with Henry's contemporaries.[1] But in 1815, ten years into his quest, he confessed to a friend he had come up empty:

> It was all speaking, speaking, speaking. 'Tis true he could talk– 'Gods how he could talk!' but there is no acting 'the while.' . . . And

1. William Wirt to Betsy Wirt, April 14, 1805, referenced in Judy Hample, "The Textual and Cultural Authenticity of Patrick Henry's 'Liberty or Death' Speech," *Quarterly Journal of Speech* 63 (1977): 299. The original is in the William Wirt Papers, Maryland Historical Society.

then, to make the matter worse, from 1763 to 1789, covering all the bloom and pride of his life, not one of his speeches lives in print, writing or memory. All that is told me is, that on such and such an occasion, he made a distinguished speech . . . . [T]here are some ugly traits in H's character, and some pretty nearly as ugly blanks. He was a blank military commander, a blank governor, and a blank politician, in all those useful points which depend on composition and detail. In short, it is, verily, as hopeless a subject as man could well desire.[2]

Hamlet-like, Wirt questioned his ability to continue. "Then, surely, you mean to give it up?" he asked himself, but he could not abandon the project: "I have stept in so deep that I am determined, like Macbeth, to go on." And so he did, but it wasn't easy. "Fettered by a scrupulous regard to real facts," he confessed, felt "like attempting to run, tied up in a bag. My pen wants perpetually to career and frolic it away."[3]

Yet Wirt's pen *needed* room to roam. He knew he could not say that Henry "made a distinguished speech" and "keep saying this over, and over, and over again, without being able to give any account of what the speech was." To celebrate Henry's oratory, he would have to put it on display—and that meant placing words in his subject's mouth. This gave him further cause for doubt: wouldn't that be "making too free with the sanctity of history?" Yet there was no other way. Based only on distant memories of aging men, he imagined what his subject might have said—or perhaps what he wished Henry had said—despite his pledge to tell "the truth, the *whole* truth, and *nothing but the truth*, at least in this book."[4]

In 1816 the editors of *Port Folio* magazine asked Wirt to publish a sample of his forthcoming book, and the author selected the alleged text of the speech Patrick Henry delivered in Richmond's Henrico Church on March 23, 1775, more than four decades earlier. The final work, *Sketches of the Life and Character of Patrick Henry*, came out the following year. An instant bestseller, it was reprinted twenty-five times in the next half-century.[5]

---

2. Wirt to Dabney Carr, August 20, 1815, John P. Kennedy, *Memoirs in the Life of William Wirt: Attorney-General of the United States* (Philadelphia: Blanchard and Lea, 1856), 1:345.

3. Ibid., 346, 344.

4. Ibid., 345, 347.

5. Hample, "Textual Authenticity," 302, 299.

How accurate is Wirt's rendition of Henry's most famous speech?

Wirt did correspond with men who had heard the speech firsthand and others who were acquainted with those present. All agreed that the speech had produced a profound effect on the listeners, but it seems that only one of Wirt's informants, Judge St. George Tucker, tried to render an actual text.[6] By his own admission, however, Tucker's account of the speech was based on "recollections," not recorded notes. "In vain should I attempt to give any idea of his speech," he admitted to Wirt.[7] Further, Tucker's attempt at a reconstruction amounted to only one section, less than one-fifth of the speech that Wirt set forth. Here is Tucker's version:

> Let us not, I beseech you, sir, deceive ourselves longer. Sir, we have done every thing that could have been done, to avert the storm which is now coming on. We have petitioned—we have remonstrated—we have supplicated—we have prostrated ourselves before the throne, and have implored its interposition to arrest the tyrannical hands of the ministry and parliament. Our petitions have been slighted; our remonstrances have produced additional violence and insult, our supplications have been disregarded; and we have been spurned, with contempt, from the foot of the throne. In vain, after these things, may we indulge the fond hope of peace and reconciliation. There is no longer any room for hope. If we wish to be free—if we mean to preserve inviolate those inestimable privileges for which we have been so long contending—if we mean not basely to abandon the noble struggle in which we have been so long engaged, and which we have pledged ourselves never to abandon, until the glorious object of our contest shall be obtained—we must fight!—I repeat it sir, we must fight!! An appeal to arms and to the God of Hosts is all that is left us![8]

Wirt wrote back, thanking Tucker for his contribution: "I have taken almost entirely Mr. Henry's speech in the Convention of '75 from you, as well as your description of its effect on you verbatim."[9] Wirt did adopt one other phrase, "peace when there was no peace,"

---

6. Ibid., 300-2.

7. Tucker to Wirt, undated and now lost, quoted in Moses Coit Tyler, *Patrick Henry* (Boston: Houghton, Mifflin, 1898; first published in 1887), 143.

8. Tyler, *Patrick Henry*, 142-43.

9. Wirt to Tucker, August 16, 1815, *William and Mary Quarterly*, First Series, 22 [1914], 252. Unfortunately, the term "verbatim" in this sentence is unclear: does it refer to the speech itself, or merely to the effect it had on Tucker, which Wirt diligently reported in a footnote? In either case, Wirt acknowledged that Tucker was his main source.

from an article that Edmund Randolph, a firsthand witness, published in 1815 in the *Richmond Enquirer*.[10] That was all. More than one thousand of the 1,217 words in the speech we think of as Henry's—including the stirring last paragraph—were conjured by William Wirt.

Undoubtedly, Wirt's reconstruction included words that Henry could have said. The phrase "liberty or death," for instance, was common currency; Christopher Gadsden used the Latin form, "aut mors aut libertas," as a masthead for a newspaper column ten years earlier during the Stamp Act protests.[11] But the diction, cadence, and structure were Wirt's. It should come as no surprise that William Wirt created such a masterpiece, for he was one of the great orators of *his* day. He gained prominence as lead prosecutor in Aaron Burr's trial for treason, went on to become attorney general under President Madison, and delivered the memorial speech to Congress when both John Adams and Thomas Jefferson died on July 4, 1826, the nation's jubilee anniversary, an unlikely coincidence seen by many as an act of God.[12]

THE REVOLUTION IN RETROSPECT: WHITEWASHED HISTORY

In fact, at least one person who heard Henry's speech gave a report just two weeks afterward, and this account differs substantially from Wirt's rendition. In a letter dated April 6, 1775, James Parker, a Scottish merchant residing in Virginia, wrote to Charles Stewart, a former Surveyor General of Customs in North America who had returned to Great Britain in 1769:

> You never heard anything more infamously insolent than P. Henry's speech: he called the K—— a Tyrant, a fool, a puppet, and a tool to the ministry. Said there was no Englishmen, no Scots, no Britons, but a set of wretches sunk in Luxury, that they had lost their native courage and (were) unable to look the brave Americans in the face . . . . This Creature is so infatuated, that he goes about I am told, praying and preaching amongst the common people.[13]

Even allowing for the bias of an unsympathetic observer, Parker's account is plausible. As in any era, hawkish patriots during the

10. Hample, "Textual Authenticity," 301.
11. *South-Carolina Gazette and Country Journal*, February 11, 1766.
12. An excellent short biography of Wirt appears on the website for the William Wirt Papers at the Maryland Historical Society: www.mdhs.org/findingaid/ william-wirt-papers-1784-1864-ms-1011.
13. *Magazine of History*, March 1906, 158: play.google.com/books/reader?id= YyY2A QAAMAAJ&printsec=frontcover&output=reader&hl=en&pg=GBS.PA158.

American Revolution probably questioned their adversaries' courage and descended to name-calling. Demagoguery is the underbelly of oratory, yet "wretches sunk in Luxury" did not make a showing in Wirt's speech.

Henry might also have pandered to his audience by playing the "slave card." Although we have no direct evidence for this, we can build a strong circumstantial case.

In 1772 Lord Mansfield, chief justice of the King's Bench, determined that James Somerset, who had been purchased in Virginia, taken to England, and then escaped, could not be forcibly returned to his master because there was no "positive law" permitting slavery in England. This caused great concern for slave-owning Virginians. A runaway ad in the *Virginia Gazette* stated that an escaped couple might be trying to board a ship for England "where they imagine they will be free (a Notion now too prevalent among Negroes, greatly to the Vexation and Prejudice of their Masters)." Another announced that a man named Bacchus would probably try "to board a vessel for Great Britain . . . from the knowledge he has of the late Determination of Somerset's Case."[14]

As tensions mounted in the wake of the Coercive Acts and armed conflict became a distinct possibility, white Virginians worried that Crown officials would actually encourage slaves to revolt against their masters. "If america & Britain should come to an hostile rupture," James Madison wrote in November 1774, "I am afraid an Insurrection among the slaves may & will be promoted. In one of our Counties lately a few of those unhappy wretches met together & chose a leader who was to conduct them when the English troops should arrive— which they foolishly thought would be very soon & by revolting to them they should be rewarded with their freedom."[15] Four months later, when Patrick Henry delivered his rousing speech, armed conflict seemed imminent and it was no longer "foolish" to expect English troops would arrive "very soon." Since Henry's aim was to mobilize a military resistance, he would have been foolish *not* to play on fears of a British-inspired slave insurrection.

The following month, Governor Dunmore seized gunpowder from the Williamsburg Magazine and warned that if colonials harmed a single British official in response, he would "declare Freedom to the

14. Gerald Mullin, *Flight and Rebellion: Slave Resistance in Eighteenth-Century Virginia* (New York: Oxford University Press, 1972), 131.
15. Madison to William Bradford, November 26, 1774, at Founders Online: founders.archives.gov/documents/Madison/01-01-02-0037.

Slaves, and reduce the City of Williamsburg to Ashes."[16] As independent military companies from seven counties prepared to march on Williamsburg, one, from Albemarle, resolved "to demand satisfaction of Dunmore for the powder, and his threatening to fix his standard and call over the negroes."[17] Eventually the incipient rebels all turned back, but the company from Hanover, under the leadership of Patrick Henry, was the last to disband.

Six months later, when Dunmore actually did declare freedom for all slaves willing to join British forces, Patrick Henry, on nobody's authority but his own, dispatched a circular letter:

> As the Committee of Safety is not sitting, I take the Liberty to enclose you a Copy of the Proclamation issued by Lord Dunmore; the Design and Tendency of which, you will observe, is fatal to the publick Safety. An early and unremitting Attention to the Government of the SLAVES may, I hope, counteract this dangerous Attempt. Constant, and well directed Patrols, seem indispensably necessary.[18]

Wirt's account reflected none of this. He used the word "slavery" three times, each with rhetorical flourish. Witness the dramatic conclusion: "Is life so dear, or peace so sweet, as to be purchased at the price of chains and slavery? Forbid it, Almighty God! I know not what course others may take; but as for me, give me liberty or give me death!"[19]

16. William J. Van Schreeven, Robert L. Scribner, and Brent Tarter, eds., *Revolutionary Virginia: The Road to Independence, a Documentary Record* (Charlottesville: University Press of Virginia, 1973–1983), 3:6.

17. Ibid., 3:52, 69–70, cited in Woody Holton, "Rebel Against Rebel: Enslaved Virginians and the Coming of the American Revolution," *Virginia Magazine of History and Biography* 105 (1997):174.

18. Henry's broadside can be viewed on the Library of Congress's American Memory, American Time Capsule: Three Centuries of Broadsides and Other Printed Ephemera: loc.gov/loc.rbc/rbpe.1780180a. It is also reprinted in Richard R. Beeman, *Patrick Henry: A Biography* (New York: McGraw-Hill, 1974), insert between pp. 57 and 59.

19. Patrick Henry, "Give Me Liberty Or Give Me Death." Avalon Project, Lillian Goldman Law Library, Yale Law School: avalon.law.yale.edu/18th_century/ patrick. asp. Apparently an authoritative source, the editors of the Avalon Project include Wirt's rendition of Henry's speech in a section called "18th Century Documents," along with various treaties, Acts of Parliament and Congress, nonimportation agreements, the Articles of Confederation, state constitutions, notes on the Federal (Constitutional) Convention by Madison and others, state ratifications of the federal Constitution, and inaugural addresses. As with other renditions based on Wirt, they

"CAESAR HAD HIS BRUTUS": ANOTHER DOCTORED SPEECH

"Liberty or death" was not the only speech to receive a touch-up. Ten years earlier, in his first term as a representative to Virginia's House of Burgesses, Henry had stepped forth to denounce the Stamp Act. Here is Wirt's version of that story:

> It was in the midst of this magnificent debate, while he was descanting on the tyranny of the obnoxious act, that he exclaimed, in a voice of thunder, and with the look of a god, "Caesar had his Brutus–Charles the first, his Cromwell–and George the third– ('Treason,' cried the speaker [Speaker of the House]–'treason, treason,' echoed from every part of the house.–It was one of those trying moments which is decisive of character.–Henry faltered not for an instant; but rising to a loftier attitude, and fixing on the speaker an eye of the most determined fire, he finished his sentence with the firmest emphasis)–may profit by their example. If this be treason, make the most of it."[20]

In this folkloric rendition, which Wirt heard and repeated half-a-century after the fact, Patrick Henry dramatically defied his detractors. At the time, however, a French traveler who observed the event first-hand noted that Henry responded to the charge of "treason" quite differently:

> Shortly after I Came in one of the members stood up and said he had read that in former times tarquin and Julius had their Brutus, Charles had his Cromwell, and he Did not Doubt but some good american would stand up, in favour of his Country, but (says he) in a more moderate manner, and was going to Continue, when the speaker of the house rose and Said, he, the last that stood up had spoke treason, and was sorey to see that not one of the members of the house was loyal Enough to stop him, before he had gone so far. upon which the Same member stood up again (his name is henery) and said that if he had affronted the speaker, or the house, he was ready to ask pardon, and he would shew his loyalty to his majesty King G. the third, at the Expence of the last Drop of his blood, but what he had said must be attributed to the Interest of his

take the further liberty of changing Wirt's third person reporting to the first person. (Wirt: "'No man,' he said, 'thought more highly than he did, of the patriotism, as well as abilities, of the very worthy gentlemen who had just addressed the house'" Avalon: "No man thinks more highly than I do of the patriotism, as well as abilities, of the very worthy gentlemen who have just addressed the House.")
20. Wirt, *Patrick Henry*, 65.

Country's Dying liberty which he had at heart, and the heat of passion might have lead him to have said something more than he intended, but, again, if he said anything wrong, he begged the speaker and the houses pardon. Some other Members stood up and backed him, on which that afaire was droped.[21]

While nineteenth-century Romantics depicted Henry as bold and defiant in the face of numerous adversaries, the firsthand witness shows Henry apologizing profusely to his lone critic, the Speaker of the House. He backpeddled, as an up-and-coming political figure might be expected to do when accused of excess. Indeed, the notion that *anybody* in 1765 would actually embrace the charge of treason could only be conjured in retrospect, once "treason" against British rule had become fashionable. It's a classic case of reading history backwards.

William Wirt of course had no access to the French traveler's private journal or James Parker's letter. He did not cover up evidence; instead, he perpetuated an oral tradition that had evolved over decades, adding his own embellishments. By then Henry had become a larger-than-life hero, and that is precisely why Wirt chose him for the subject of a biography. Dedicating his book "TO THE YOUNG MEN OF VIRGINIA," Wirt hoped to inspire youthful Americans to defend liberty, much as Henry had. "The present and future generations of our country can never be better employed than in studying the models set

21. "Journal of a French Traveller in the Colonies, 1765," *American Historical Review* 26 (October 1920-July 1921), 745. An interesting account of printed renditions of this speech prior to Wirt's is on pp. 727-29. Initially, even Wirt had his doubts about the folkloric account he passed on: "I had frequently heard the above anecdote of the cry of treason but with such variations of the concluding words, that I began to doubt whether the whole might be fiction. With a view to ascertain the truth, therefore, I submitted it to Mr. Jefferson as it had been given to me by Judge Tyler, and this is his answer:—'I well remember the cry of treason, the pause of Mr. Henry at the name of George III, and the presence of mind with which he closed his sentence, and baffled the charge vociferated.' The incident, therefore, becomes authentic history." (Wirt, *Patrick Henry*, 65.) Such was the standard of evidence in Wirt's time: confirmation by one witness half-a-century later. But Jefferson by that time had allowed other accounts to influence his memory—he even imagined that the ceremonial signing of the Declaration of Independence, his signature document, had occurred on July 4 when all contemporaneous evidence indicates otherwise.

before them by the fathers of the Revolution," Wirt wrote to John Adams shortly after the book's publication.[22]

Wirt achieved his goal. His "liberty or death" speech became an instant classic. Students in the nineteenth century memorized it and competed with each other for the most dramatic delivery. Today, it remains a cornerstone of grade-school textbooks, an iconic representation of the American Revolution that encapsulates the military mobilization of 1775.

The phenomenal appeal of Wirt's speech reveals how Americans in the nineteenth century were drawn to a glorified "memory" of the Revolution, one that masked the myriad complexities of eighteenth century history. Further, we, like Wirt and his contemporaries, *want* Henry to have made that immortal speech. While Englishmen sunk in luxury and the perils of British-inspired slave insurrections can no longer stir our patriotism, such oratory continues to inspire.

22. Wirt to Adams, January 12, 1818, John P. Kennedy, *Memoirs in the Life of William Wirt: Attorney-General of the United States* (New York: G. P. Putnam, 1872), 2:46, quoted in Andrew Burstein, *America's Jubilee* (New York: Alfred A. Knopf, 2001), 46. Adams had presented Wirt with a number of names of patriots from Massachusetts who figured prominently in the revolutionary ferment, and Wirt suggested that more could and should be written about all of them.

A Fast Ship from Salem: Carrying News of the War

✸ BOB RUPPERT ✸

On April 24, General Gage sent his account of the confrontations at Lexington and Concord aboard the 200-ton, cargo-laden *Sukey* to Lord Barrington, the Secretary of War and to the Earl of Dartmouth, the Secretary of State for the Colonies.[1] His letter to Lord Barrington, written on the 22nd, began with an understated opening sentence: "I have now nothing to trouble your Lordship with, but of an affair that happened here on the 19th instant." Something must have quickly changed his perception of the confrontations because the next day he sent a dispatch to Admiral Graves asking that

> Captn [John] Bishop to examine every letter on board her those directed for Docr [Benjamin] Franklin, [Arthur] Lee, [William Bollan] Borland &c to be sent to Boston; any other Suspicious letters to be put under Cover to the Secretary of State, and given to Lieut [Joseph] Nun, Capn Bishop telling his Lordship, that he was directed in this Critical Juncture, to send him the Inclosed for his perusal, as they might contain some Intelligence of the Rebels here— [2]

Determined to get the colony's version of the confrontations to England first, on April 22 the Second Provincial Congress of Massachusetts appointed a committee of nine to take depositions, "from which a full account of the Transactions of the Troops under

---

1. Edwin Carter, ed., "Gage to Barrington, April 22, 1775," *The Correspondence of General Thomas Gage with the Secretaries of State, and with the War Office and the Treasury, 1763-1775* (Hamden, CT: Archon Books, 1969), 2:673-74; "Gage to Dartmouth," Ibid., 1:396.

2. "Gage to Admiral Graves, 23 April 1775," *Naval Documents of The American Revolution* (Washington, DC: G.P.O., 1964), 1:211.

General Gage, in their route to and from Concord, etc . . . on Wednesday last, may be collected."[3] The committee interviewed 97 people in three days and secured signed, sworn statements from all of them. Each person deposed was administered an oath by a justice of the peace whose "good faith" was certified by a notary public. The main point of all the depositions was that no provincial at either Lexington or Concord fired until the British had fired first. On April 25, the Provincial Congress rushed to have the depositions included in *"A Narrative, of the Excursions and Ravages of the King's Troops Under the Command of General Gage, on the nineteenth of April, 1777: Together with the Depositions taken by order of Congress."* The account was written by Benjamin Church, Elbridge Gerry, and Thomas Cushing;[4] it was printed by Isaiah Thomas of Worcester.[5]

Needing the fastest vessel they could find, Richard Derby, Jr., a member of the Congress, agreed to outfit one of his vessels, the *Quero*, and his younger brother, John Derby, Esq., would command her. On April 27, General (Dr.) Joseph Warren gave him his orders:

> Resolved, That Capt. Derby be directed and he hereby is directed to make for Dublin or any other good port in Ireland, and from thence to cross to Scotland or England and hasten to London. This direction is given so that he may escape all enemies that may be in the chops of the channel, to stop the communication of the Provincial intelligence to the agent. He will forthwith deliver his papers to the agent on reaching London.[6]

The papers were a "letter of instruction" for Benjamin Franklin,[7] a copy of the depositions, a letter from Dr. Joseph Warren titled "To the Inhabitants of Great Britain"[8] and copies of the *Essex Gazette* that contained the colonists' account of the confrontations.[9]

3. Peter Force, ed., *American Archives,* 4th Series, 2:765.
4. *Naval Documents,* 1:212.
5. www.masshist.org/revolution/docviewer.php?old=1&mode=nav&item_id =667.
6. "Committee of Safety Resolution, 27 April 1775," *Journals of each Provincial Congress of Massachusetts in 1774 and 1775, and of the Committee of Safety* (Boston: Dutton and Wentworth, 1838), 159.
7. William B. Willcox, ed., *The Papers of Benjamin Franklin* (New Haven and London: Yale University Press, 1982), 22:29–30.
8. "Provincial Congress to the Inhabitants of Great Britain." April 26, 1775, Force, *American Archives,* Series 4, 2:487-88.
9. Ralph D. Paine, *The Ships and Sailors of Old Salem* (New York: Outing Publications Co., 1909), 191.

On the night of April 28, Capt. John Derby and the *Quero* set sail from Salem. The *Quero* was a fast, 62-ton schooner. On this trip it would carry no cargo, only ballast. In the postscript to his instructions from Dr. Warren, Capt. Derby was told "You are to keep this order a profound secret from every person on earth." In fact, "the crew [did not] know their destination 'till they were on the banks of Newfoundland."[10]

Disregarding Warren's instructions, Derby sailed directly to the Isle of Wight in the English Channel, secured transportation to Southampton and then made his way to London where he arrived on May 29. His entire trip took four weeks.

He delivered the papers to Arthur Lee, Franklin's successor, because Franklin had recently sailed for Philadelphia. Copies of the depositions were made and the originals were placed in the custody of John Wilkes, a radical who espoused the American cause, who also happened to be the Lord Mayor of London.[11] The next day the depositions and the *Essex Gazette* account appeared in the *London Evening Post*. Other newspapers picked up the story and within a few days the entire country knew of the confrontations. It caused a sensation among those sympathetic to the colonies, but caught the ministry by surprise.

The former governor of Massachusetts, Thomas Hutchinson, who was now serving as an "advisor" to the Secretary of State for the American Colonies, "carried the news to Lord Dartmouth, who was much struck [by] it. The first accounts were very unfavorable, it not being known that they all came from one side. The alarm abated before night, and we wait with a greater degree of calmness for the accounts from the other side."[12] The next day, May 30, Dartmouth published the following bulletin in a government gazette:

> A report having been spread, and an account having been printed and published, of a skirmish between some of the people in the Province of Massachusetts Bay and a detachment of His Majesty's troops, it is proper to inform the publick that no advices have as yet been received in the American Department of any such event.

10. Robert S. Rantoul, "The Cruise of the 'Quero': How We Carried the News To the King," *Essex Institute Historical Collections*, 36#1 (1900), 8.

11. Fred J. Hinkhouse, *The Preliminaries of the American Revolution as Seen in the English Press, 1763-1775* (New York: Columbia University Press, 1926), 183-97.

12. Thomas Hutchinson, *The Diary and Letters of His Excellency Thomas Hutchinson*, Peter Orlando Hutchinson, ed. (London: Sampson Low, Marston, Searle & Rivington, 1883), 1:455.

There is reason to believe that there are dispatches from General Gage on board the *Sukey*, Captain Brown, which, though she sailed four days before the vessel that brought the printed accounts, is not arrived.[13]

Arthur Lee responded by publishing the following notice: "All those who wish to see the original affidavits which affirm the account are deposited in the Mansion House with the Right Lord Honorable Mayor for their inspection."[14]

On May 31, Hutchinson wrote to Gen. Gage,

> The arrival of Captain Darby from Salem on the 28th with dispatches from the Congress at Watertown, immediately published in the papers, caused a general anxiety in the minds of all who wish the happiness of Britain and her Colonies. I have known the former interesting events have been partially represented: I therefore believe with discretion the representation now received. It is unfortunate to have the first impression made from that quarter . . . It is said your dispatches are on board Cap. Brown, who sailed some days before Derby. I hope they are at hand and will afford us some relief.[15]

While the ministry was waiting for the arrival of the *Sukey*, every effort was made to locate Derby and his ship. The harbor and nearby waterways of Southampton were searched but with no success.

Dartmouth was frustrated. Three times he had summoned John Derby to appear before him and three times he failed to show up.[16] Little did he know that on June 1, Capt. Derby had left London. The *Quero* was no longer in an inlet on the Isle of Wight but rather in the harbor at Falmouth. When he arrived he paid the custom inspection and clearance fees and prepared his ship for departure.

On June 3, Hutchinson recorded the following in his diary:

> Went to Lane and Fraser's . . . the London correspondents of the Derby family. Found that Captain Darby had not been seen since the first instant; that he had a letter of credit from Lane on some house in Spain. Afterwards I saw Mr. Pownall [assistant Secretary of State under Lord Dartmouth] at Lord Dartmouth's office, where

13. Rantoul, "The Cruise of the 'Quero,'" 6.
14. Ibid., 6-7.
15. Hutchinson, *The Diary and Letters*, 456-57.
16. Benjamin Franklin Stevens, "John Pownall to Lord Dartmouth, dated 29 May 1775," *British Accounts of the American Revolution*, Vol. VII, *American Revolutionary War Series* (Great Britain: Historical Manuscripts Commission, 1887), 304.

I . . . and Pownall was of opinion Darby was gone to Spain to purchase ammunition, arms, &c. We are still in a state of uncertainty concerning the action in Massachusetts. Vessels are arrived at Bristol, which met with other vessels on their passage, and received as news that there had been a battle, but could tell no particulars.[17]

On June 9, the *Sukey* arrived in Southampton; unaware of the urgency that awaited his arrival, Captain Brown did not deliver the dispatches to Lord Dartmouth until the next day. Hutchinson's diary contains this entry for June 10:

A lieutenant in the navy [Joseph Nunn] arrived about noon at Lord Dartmouth's office. Mr. Pownall gave me notice, knowing my anxiety; but though relieved from suspense, yet received but little comfort, from the accounts themselves being much the same with what Darby brought. The material difference is the declaration by Smith, who was the commander of the first party though not present at the first action, that the inhabitants fired first, and returns show only 63 were killed outright, yet 157 were wounded, and 24 missing; which upon the whole is a greater number than Darby reported.[18]

The dispatches confirmed what the newspapers had been saying, with the exception of Gen. Gage's claim that the colonists had fired first. Dr. Warren had hoped that the account of the confrontations, the depositions, and his letter would lead to an end to any further bloodshed. He wrote, "Lord Chatham and our friends must make up the breach immediately or never. The next news from England must be conciliatory, or the connection between us ends, however fatal the consequences may be." When Dartmouth presented the dispatches to the King, he reacted angrily. He had no intention of entering into talks with his subjects who were now engaged in a rebellion.

Three weeks later, Lord Dartmouth sent the following dispatch to General Gage:

Sir: On the 10th of last month in the morning, Lieutenant Nunn arrived at my office with your despatch containing an account of the transaction on the 19th of April of which the public had before received intelligence by a schooner, to all appearances sent by the enemies of government, on purpose to make an impression here by representing the affair between the King's troops and the rebel

---

17. Hutchinson, *The Diary and Letters,* 463-64.
18. Ibid., 466.

Provincials in a light the most favorable to their own view. Their industry on this occasion had its effect, in leaving for some days a false impression upon people's minds, and I mention it to you with a hope that, in any future event of importance, it will be thought proper . . . to send your dispatches by one of the light vessels of the fleet.[19]

On July 19, the *Quero* arrived in Salem, however Derby was not on board. He had gone ashore earlier and left William Carlton, his sailing master, in command. He was already making his report to General Washington and the provincial Congress.[20]

On August 1, the Provincial Congress of Massachusetts approved Capt. Derby's personal expense report. He submitted charges totaling 57 pounds, 8 pence; he did not submit an expense for his services.[21]

19. Robert S. Rantoul. *A Collection of Historical and Biographical Pamphlets* (Salem, 1881), 240.
20. "George Washington to John Hancock, 21 July 1775," *The Papers of George Washington*, Revolutionary War Series, Vol. 1, Philander D. Chase, ed. (Charlottesville: University of Virginia Press, 1985), 143-44; "James Warren to John Adams, 20 July 1775," *The Adams Papers*, Robert J. Taylor, ed. (Cambridge: Harvard University Press, 1979), 3:82-85.
21. Peter Force, *American Archives*, Series 4, Vol. 3, 298.

How Paul Revere's Ride was Published and Censored in 1775

TODD ANDRLIK

Because of Henry Wadsworth Longfellow's famous poem, "Paul Revere's Ride," most people think that Revere was critical to the start of the Revolutionary War. In trying to dispel Longfellow's myth of a lone hero, modern scholars have portrayed Revere as just one rider among dozens on April 18–19, 1775, and argued that his previous rides for the Patriot cause might have been more important. A survey of newspapers from 1774 and 1775 shows that in fact those earlier rides had made Revere prominent enough that he did stand out in reports of the fighting at Lexington and Concord, even as Massachusetts authorities kept the extent of his activities quiet.[1]

1. Edmund S. Morgan, ed., *Paul Revere's Three Accounts of His Famous Ride* (Boston: Massachusetts Historical Society, 1961). See Morgan's introduction. Morgan highlighted early American Revolution books for their lack of Revere references. "In the early histories of the Revolution the part played by Paul Revere was scanted, and his name was not even mentioned," wrote Morgan based on his study of works by William Gordon, David Ramsay, Hannah Adams, and Mercy Warren. Morgan explained that "this neglect of the messengers could not have been wholly the result of ignorance. Paul Revere, though he did not belong to what was then called the 'better sort,' was well-known in Boston, not only as a silversmith and engraver but also as the principal messenger of the patriot leaders."

Ray Raphael, *Founding Myths: Stories That Hide Our Patriotic Past* (New York: New Press, 2004), 14-15. Raphael succinctly summarized Morgan by stating "all the early historians of the Revolution agreed: Revere was not a major player in the outbreak of hostilities." Raphael took a closer look at Roxbury, Massachusetts, minister William Gordon, who conducted his own interviews with eyewitnesses and first published his account of the hostilities in colonial newspapers. "Gordon did not feature Paul Revere's ride in his detailed account of the events of Lexington and Concord," wrote Raphael. "Gordon expanded his treatment in the full-length history he published thirteen years later, but he still made no mention of any heroic exploits by Paul Revere."

Paul Revere was a man who wore many hats. He was well known throughout New England for his engravings, his silver work, his Masonic fellowship and his political activity. Plus, in 1774 and early 1775, Revere worked as an express rider for the Boston Committee of Correspondence and the Massachusetts Committee of Safety. He frequently carried letters, newspapers, and other important communication between cities, including Boston, Hartford, New York, and Philadelphia. Revere's early dispatches related to some of the biggest American events of the eighteenth century, including the destruction of the tea, the Boston Port Bill, and the Suffolk Resolves. In December 1774, at the age of 39, he rode to Portsmouth to alert local Patriot leaders that the Royal Navy was on its way to seize gunpowder and arms from Fort William and Mary. Newspaper printers would eagerly print Revere's tidings, frequently attributing the particular intelligence to being delivered by "Mr. Paul Revere," and often emphasizing his name in all capital letters. At least 33 New England newspaper issues (from 10 different New England titles) prominently plugged Paul Revere, the express, during the ten-month window between May 9, 1774, and March 12, 1775. Even newspapers in the middle and southern

[*note 1, continued*] Reading Morgan and Raphael, one might think Revere's name was absent from all contemporary retellings of Lexington and Concord. Morgan and Raphael were clearly referencing the first full books about the American Revolution, but I would argue that "early histories" should include 1775 correspondence and newspapers, both of which featured some elements, albeit sparse ones, of Revere's ride. In fact, it is important to note that Gordon's newspaper version of Lexington and Concord, which first appeared in the June 7, 1775, *Pennsylvania Gazette*, did prominently feature Revere's story with one full paragraph dedicated to it.

David Hackett Fischer, *Paul Revere's Ride* (New York: Oxford University Press, 1994). Fischer plays up Revere's role in the months before the outbreak of war.

The historically correct and iconic moments of Revere's ride vary in depth and breadth based on your source but typically include:

Revere and William Dawes being sent express by Joseph Warren
Revere coordinating lantern signals
Revere rowing past the British warship *Somerset*
Revere evading patrols near Cambridge
Revere alarming militia officers in the countryside
Revere alerting John Hancock and Samuel Adams in Lexington
British officers capturing Revere, Dawes, and Samuel Prescott on the road to Concord, but Prescott and Dawes escaping, and Prescott being the only one to reach Concord
British officers escorting Revere back to Lexington until they heard gunshots and freed Revere
Revere assisting Hancock and his family escape with a trunk of Hancock's papers
Revere witnessing some of the battle on Lexington Green

colonies, as well as overseas, frequently re-attributed content from Philadelphia, New York, and Boston to Paul Revere's dispatches. This extraordinary volume of newspaper coverage certainly cemented Revere's popular status as the principal Patriot messenger.[2]

Revere's name also appeared in the newspaper reports of the Battle of Lexington and Concord, but in notably different ways. Among the frenzy of private correspondence racing across the American countryside in late April 1775, at least two letters originating from the Hartford area mentioned Paul Revere by name. Being the seat of Connecticut government and the middle point between New York and Boston, Hartford was a stopping point during Revere's rides in

2. The thirty-three known New England newspapers naming Paul Revere with his earlier rides: *Essex Journal* (Newburyport, MA), May 18, 1774; *Essex Journal* (Newburyport, MA), June 1, 1774; *Boston Post-Boy*, May 9, 1774; *Boston Post-Boy*, May 23, 1774; *Boston Post-Boy*, September 19, 1774; *Providence Gazette*, May 21, 1774; *Providence Gazette*, June 4, 1774; *Providence Gazette*, September 24, 1774; *Essex Gazette* (Salem, MA), May 31, 1774; *Essex Gazette* (Salem, MA), September 27, 1774; *Essex Gazette* (Salem, MA), October 18, 1774; *Essex Gazette* (Salem, MA), February 7, 1775; *Connecticut Courant* (Hartford), May 24, 1774; *Connecticut Courant* (Hartford), June 7, 1774; *Connecticut Courant* (Hartford), September 26, 1774; *Connecticut Courant* (Hartford), October 17, 1774; *Connecticut Courant* (Hartford), March 13, 1775; *Newport Mercury*, May 23, 1774; *Newport Mercury*, May 30, 1774; *Newport Mercury*, June 6, 1774; *Newport Mercury*, June 20, 1774; *Boston Evening-Post*, May 16, 1774; *Boston Evening-Post*, May 30, 1774; *Boston Evening-Post*, October 17, 1774; *New-Hampshire Gazette* (Portsmouth), May 20, 1774; *New-Hampshire Gazette* (Portsmouth), June 3, 1774; *New-Hampshire Gazette* (Portsmouth), September 30, 1774; *Boston News-Letter*, June 2, 1774; *Boston News-Letter*, October 20, 1774; *Connecticut Journal* (New Haven), June 3, 1774; *Connecticut Journal* (New Haven), September 23, 1774; *Connecticut Gazette* (New London), June 3, 1774; *Boston Gazette*, May 30, 1774.

Many more newspapers outside New England, and even overseas, also re-attributed Paul Revere as the source of key dispatches in 1774, including Clementina Rind's *Virginia Gazette* (Williamsburg), June 9, 1774, and June 23, 1774; and October 27, 1774 (the latter being "printed by John Pinkney, for the benefit of Clementina Rind's children"). Though Readex's digital newspaper archive doesn't include Revolution-era newspapers from Georgia, South Carolina, or North Carolina, it is known that they reprinted extracts from the *Virginia Gazettes* and other papers in Philadelphia, New York, etc. At least nine British newspapers re-attributed content to Paul Revere in 1774: *Derby Mercury*, July 15, 1774; *Shrewsbury Chronicle*, July 23, 1774; *Caledonian Mercury*, November 16, 1774; *Northampton Mercury*, November 14, 1774; *Caledonian Mercury*, July 20, 1774; *Shrewsbury Chronicle*, November 19, 1774; *Kentish Gazette*, July 20, 1774; *Hibernian Journal*, July 25, 1774; *Hampshire Chronicle*, November 14, 1774. In virtually every instance of the above newspaper mentions, Paul Revere's name introduced the content he delivered, such as "By Mr. PAUL REVERE, who returned Express from Philadelphia last Friday Evening, we have the following Important Intelligence" (*New-Hampshire Gazette*, September 30, 1774).

1774 and Hartford-area Patriots knew him well.[3] Printers in New York and Philadelphia read and typeset portions of the Connecticut letters as they hurried to piece together bits of oral, manuscript, and printed intelligence to corroborate accounts of Lexington and Concord. As a result, the Revere-related intelligence differs per city.

An extract of one letter from Wethersfield, Connecticut, to a gentleman in New York, dated April 23, 1775, speculated that Revere was murdered. The following is part of that letter as it was printed in the April 27 *New-York Journal* and May 1 *New-York Gazette*.

> The late frequent marchings and countermarchings into the country, were calculated to conceal the most cruel and inhuman design, and imagining they had laid suspicion asleep, they pitched upon Wednesday night for the execution. A hint being got, two expresses were sent to alarm the Congress; one of them had the good fortune to arrive, the other (Mr. Revere) is missing, supposed to be way-laid and slain.[4]

A second Connecticut letter, also dated April 23, presumably credited Revere with delivering "secret and speedy intelligence" to John Hancock and Samuel Adams in Lexington, but the letter was reprinted with enough variation by the *New-York Journal* (alongside the Wethersfield article) to prevent Revere from getting credit in print. John Holt printed the "secret and speedy intelligence" letter this way in his April 27 *New-York Journal*:

> Extract of another letter of the same date [April 23],
> On Tuesday night the 18th instant, as secretly as possible, General Gage draughted out about 1000 or 1200 of his best troops, which he embarked on a transport, and landed that night at Cambridge. –Wednesday morning by day break they marched up to Lexington, where before breakfast, as usual, about 30 of the inhabitants were practising the material exercise. –Upon these, without the least

---

3. At least five times between May 24, 1774, and March 13, 1775, the Hartford-based *Connecticut Courant* prominently named Paul Revere in conjunction with his messenger rides. Paul Revere's name typically introduced the content he delivered, such as "Saturday last passed through this Town on his return to Boston, from the General Congress, Mr. Paul Revere—Nothing has yet transpired from that grand and important Assembly." (*Connecticut Courant*, October 17, 1774). In addition to at least five Hartford newspaper mentions, Revere's name also appeared in at least one New London and two New Haven newspapers between June and October 1774.
4. *New-York Journal*, April 27, 1775; *New-York Gazette and Weekly Mercury*, May 1, 1775.

provocation, they fired about 15 minutes killed six men, and wounded several, without a single shot from our men, who retreated as fast as possible. –Hence they proceeded to Concord; on the road thither, they fired at, and killed a man on horseback, –went to the House where Mr. Hancock lodged, who, with Mr. Samuel Adams, luckily got out of their way, by the means of secret and speedy intelligence. The House was searched for them, but when they could not be found, the inhuman soldiery killed the woman of the house and all the children, and set fire to the house. Mr. Paul Revere was missing when the express came away in their way to Concord, the Regulars fired at and killed hogs, geese, cattle, and every thing that came in their way, and burnt several houses. . . .[5]

This version of the letter, with Revere not being tied directly to the secret and speedy intelligence, was republished in the May 1, 1775, *New-York Gazette,* and copies of the *Gazette* soon sailed across the Atlantic where the same account was printed in at least three British newspapers.[6]

Another version of the "secret and speedy intelligence" letter was published in the April 28 *Pennsylvania Mercury.* Thanks to Philadelphia printers Enoch Story and Daniel Humphreys, Revere was properly credited this time with delivering the intelligence. Story and Humphreys' version of the letter appeared this way:

on the road thither, they fired at, and killed a man on horseback, went to the house of Samuel Adams, luckily got out of their way by secret and speedy intelligence from Paul Revere, who is now missing, and nothing heard of him since; when they searched the house for Mr. Hancock, and Adams, and not finding them there, killed the woman of the house and all the children, and set fire to the house.[7]

This version of the letter, crediting Revere, was reprinted in the April 29 *Pennsylvania Ledger* and again in the May 1 *Pennsylvania Packet.* And on the same page of the May 1 *Pennsylvania Packet* a paragraph of apparent oral intelligence summarizing the Connecticut letters includes this line:

5. *New-York Journal,* April 27, 1775; *New-York Gazette and Weekly Mercury,* May 1, 1775.
6. *Ipswich Journal,* June 17, 1775; *Chester Chronicle,* June 17, 1775; *Kentish Gazette,* June 17, 1775.
7. *Pennsylvania Mercury,* April 28, 1775; *Pennsylvania Ledger,* April 29, 1775; *Pennsylvania Packet,* May 1, 1775.

Mr. Paul Revere, who left Boston to acquaint Messrs. Hancock and Adams of the design against them, was taken prisoner, but got clear again by a stratagem.[8]

This printed oral intelligence, with explicit information about Revere's mission, was republished in the May 3 *Pennsylvania Journal* and then again in the May 9 *Maryland Gazette*. So, within three weeks of Lexington and Concord, Revere's name was printed in conjunction with Lexington and Concord in two of three New York newspapers, four of seven Philadelphia newspapers, and one of two Baltimore newspapers. Although Revere was one of many involved in the New England Patriot alarm system, he was the only rider mentioned because people already knew of him as an express rider. Still, while these letters and newspapers mention Revere, he's lost in a dense fog of sensational, unfounded accusations. British troops never went to the house where Hancock and Adams were staying, they never killed women and children there, and they didn't shoot a local on horseback while marching west.

In late April and early May 1775, newspapers were loaded with eyewitness accounts about the battles, which primarily consisted of gossip and skewed depositions collected by the Massachusetts Provincial Congress to shape the Whig version of events (much like what happened after the Boston Massacre). The accounts and depositions included scores of false statements and exaggerated claims about atrocities committed by royal troops. Revere's own deposition failed to make the Provincial Congress' official report and was noticeably absent from New England newspapers that were publishing many one-sided testimonies.[9]

It wasn't until early June that a more comprehensive and somewhat balanced account of Lexington and Concord was published. The account came in the form of a lengthy letter, dated May 17, 1775, which was titled "An Account of the Commencement of Hostilities between Great-Britain and America, in the Province of Massachusetts-Bay, by the Rev. Mr. William Gordon, of Roxbury, in a

8. *Pennsylvania Packet*, May 1, 1775; *Pennsylvania Journal*, May 3, 1775; *Dunlap's Maryland Gazette*, May 9, 1775.

9. The title of the official report is *A Narrative of the Excursion and Ravages of the King's Troops Under the Command of General Gage, On the nineteenth of April, 1775* (Worcester, printed by Isaiah Thomas, by order of the Provincial Congress). Available online: www.masshist.org/database/viewer.php?item_id=627. Newspapers that printed other depositions include: *Pennsylvania Ledger* (Philadelphia), May 13, 1775; Dixon and Hunter's *Virginia Gazette* (Williamsburg), June 3, 1775.

Letter to a Gentleman in England." Gordon was unique in that he was an English clergyman developing his account based on on-site interviews he conducted in the weeks following the battle. Gordon's letter was first "Published with the Consent of the Author" in the June 7 *Pennsylvania Gazette* and spans the entire first page and half of the fourth. That means the *Pennsylvania Gazette* gave Paul Revere his first front-page feature treatment:

> Mr. Paul Revere, who was sent express, was taken and detained some time by the officers, being afterwards upon the spot, and finding the regulars at hand, pass thro' the Lexington company with another, having between them a box of papers belonging to Mr. Hancock, and went down across road, till there was a house so between him and the company, as that he could not see the latter; he told me likewise, that he had not got half a gun shot from them before the regulars appeared; that they halted about three seconds; that upon hearing the report of a pistol or gun, he looked round, and saw the smoke in front of the regulars, our people being out of view because of the house; then the regulars huzza'd and fired, first two more guns, then the advanced guard, and so the whole body; the bullets flying thick about him, and he having nothing to defend himself, ran into a wood, where he halted and heard the firing for about a quarter of an hour.

Gordon's version of Lexington and Concord, which dedicates the most attention to Revere's story of any previous accounts, is still partial to the Americans, leaving out details that British officers' accounts emphasized, like provincials firing alarm guns and the first shot. However, Gordon was apparently writing "to a Gentleman in England," and attempting to play the role of a reliable chronicler, not a propagandist, so he included some information that the Massachusetts Provincial Congress had buried or neglected, such as Revere's official statement. David Hackett Fischer's meticulous and acclaimed volume, *Paul Revere's Ride*, has this to say about Gordon's account and treatment of Revere:

> By early June, the first report of Paul Revere's ride appeared in print. Its author was William Gordon, Roxbury's English-born Congregationalist minister, who appointed himself the first historian of the American Revolution. After the battle, Gordon rode to Concord and interviewed many participants, including Paul Revere himself. In the first week of June, he published an account of the battle which mentioned Revere by name, and briefly described the

midnight ride, the capture, the rescue of John Hancock's trunk and Revere's presence at the battle of Lexington. Gordon's essay was very short, but remarkably full and accurate. . . .

While Gordon was publishing the first account, the Whig leaders themselves kept silent. Many had sworn a vow of secrecy about their activities, and were guarded even in conversation with one another. . . .

The elaborate preparations that lay behind the midnight ride did not fit well with the Whig image of Lexington and Concord as an unprovoked attack upon an unresisting people. Here was the first of many myths that came to encrust the subject–the myth of injured American innocence, which the Whigs themselves actively propagated as an instrument of their cause.

To maintain that interpretation, the earliest written account of the midnight ride by Paul Revere himself appears to have been suppressed by Whig leaders. In the aftermath of the battles Revere and many other eyewitnesses were asked to draft a deposition about the first shot at Lexington. He produced a document that was doubly displeasing to those who requested it. Revere refused to testify unequivocally that the Regulars had fired first at Lexington Common. He also added an account of the midnight ride that suggested something of the American preparations that preceded the event.

Other depositions were rushed into print by the Massachusetts Provincial Congress, and circulated widely in Britain and America, but Revere's testimony was not among them. It did not support the American claim that the Regulars had started the fighting, and revealed more about the revolutionary movement than Whig leaders wished to be known. Paul Revere's deposition was returned to him. It remained among his private papers unpublished until 1891.[10]

Although Revere's deposition was returned to him, it was prominently featured in Gordon's account, which was first published in the June 7 *Pennsylvania Gazette*, and republished with the Revere paragraph in at least two more newspapers: the June 10 *Supplement to the Pennsylvania Ledger* and June 15 *Supplement to the New-York Journal*. To recap, below is a list of Paul Revere's American newspaper coverage in the aftermath of April 19, 1775.

10. David Hackett Fischer, *Paul Revere's Ride* (New York: Oxford University Press, 1994), 327.

1. April 27 *New-York Journal*
2. April 28 *Pennsylvania Mercury* (Philadelphia)
3. April 29 *Pennsylvania Ledger* (Philadelphia)
4. May 1 *Pennsylvania Packet* (Philadelphia)
5. May 1 *New-York Gazette and Weekly Mercury*
6. May 3 *Pennsylvania Journal* (Philadelphia)
7. May 9 *Maryland Gazette* (Baltimore)
8. June 7 *Pennsylvania Gazette* (Philadelphia)—Gordon's account
9. June 10 *Supplement to the Pennsylvania Ledger* (Philadelphia)—Gordon's account
10. June 15 *Supplement to the New-York Journal*—Gordon's account

It is peculiar that Revere's involvement in Lexington and Concord was reported in so many Philadelphia and New York newspapers, but not one New England newspaper (after thirty-three New England newspaper issues gushed about Revere's previous rides, earning him celebrity status throughout the colonies). However, Patriot leaders in New England had obvious reasons not to reveal their hair-trigger alarm system for militia in the region, the most important of which was they wanted to be perceived as innocent respondents to royal aggression. Despite the apparent efforts by New England Patriot governments and organizers to suppress the Revere story, it was widely published in the only mass media of the era. Then, several decades later, Peter Force published Gordon's newspaper version, including the Revere paragraph, in *American Archives*, making it visible to historians from the mid-1800s on. As such, Gordon's newspaper account of Lexington and Concord, featuring the earliest published version of Revere's own deposition and thus the most substantial details of Revere's ride available at the time, is hugely significant in the early shaping and understanding of the opening battles of the Revolutionary War.[11]

11. See note 2 for list of thirty-three New England newspaper issues mentioning Paul Revere in 1774 and early 1775. According to Richard Frothingham, *History of the Siege of Boston: And of the Battles of Lexington, Concord and Bunker Hill* (Boston: Charles C. Little and James Brown, 1849), 31, "[William Gordon's] account, substantially, appeared in several almanacs of 1776, and, with additions and much abridgment, it was incorporated in his history." As far as I can tell, none of the almanac versions of Gordon's account include the Revere paragraph, which is also omitted from Gordon's 1788 history book about the Revolution. For almanac examples, see *The North-American Almanac, And Gentleman's and Lady's Diary, for the Year of our Lord Christ 1776 by Samuel Stearns* (Worcester, Watertown, and Cambridge, 1775); *An Astronomical Diary, or Almanack, for the Year of Christian Aera, 1776* (Boston, 1775). William Gordon, *The History of the Rise, Progress, and Establishment of the Independence of the University States of America* (London: 1788).

Another reason to believe the Provincial Congress' scheme to censor any deposition that didn't fit its preferred version of events is the amount of effort they took to win the battle for public opinion in London. It took Whig leaders 47 days to get their report of the Boston Massacre to London in 1770. By then, the Crown side of the story was already widely circulated. Losing that earlier battle of public opinion may have made Patriots work faster and harder to win the propaganda battle (in New England and Great Britain) over Lexington and Concord. The Provincial Congress swiftly gathered depositions and influenced the local and regional press about the battles. Then, the legislature commissioned a Salem schooner, *Derby*, to sail with no cargo except three copies of the *Essex Gazette* (Salem, MA), which contained Congress' battle report. *Derby* was under sail by April 29 and arrived in London on the evening of May 28 with the first Patriot-controlled European reports of the battle published soon after. General Thomas Gage's official account didn't arrive until two weeks later, appearing in the *London Chronicle* on June 13.[12]

While the *Derby* was preparing to push off from Salem with the Patriot-approved newspapers about Lexington and Concord, New York printer John Holt was typesetting his next weekly edition of the *New-York Journal*, the first American newspaper that didn't hesitate to print Paul Revere's name in conjunction with the battle. Holt, who apparently felt no pressure to keep a lid on evidence of the New England alarm system, was a Patriot supporter and one of Revere's contacts during his previous rides back and forth to Philadelphia. Revere delivered newspapers and other intelligence directly to Holt's New York print shop, and Holt's *Journal* printed Revere's name in conjunction with other rides at least four times in mid-1774. More so, as a trusted Patriot messenger throughout the northern colonies, Revere delivered additional perspective and insight with his intelligence, which was certainly welcomed by distant printers and associates. For instance, following Revere's ride to a Philadelphia meeting about the Boston Port Bill, several newspapers published this context:

12. For Derby departure date, see Robert Samuel Rantoul, *The Cruise of the "Quero": How We Carried the News to the King* (Essex Institute, 1900), 6. For arrival dates and content related to the early arrival of American reports about Lexington and Concord, see *London Chronicle*, May 30, 1775; *London Chronicle*, June 1, 1775; *London Chronicle*, June 13, 1775.

"It was noticed by Mr. Revere, that in this Meeting Mr. [John] Dickinson spoke longer and with more Life and Energy than ever he had done on any former Occasion."[13]

Modern historians who have emphasized the absence of Revere's name in early history books may have overlooked the abundance of Revere newspaper publicity in 1774 and 1775. Shortly after hostilities commenced, private correspondence and newspapers promoted parts of Revere's iconic ride. So, long before Longfellow's poem so heavily influenced American culture, while news of Lexington and Concord was still fresh, sprinkles of the Revere story appeared in print and reached thousands of tables in American homes and businesses. And considering his existing celebrity status, it is safe to assume that many more heard the Paul Revere story in mid-1775 as it was chattered about in taverns and other public places.[14]

13. For the first mention of Paul Revere in conjunction with Lexington and Concord, see *New-York Journal*, April 27, 1775. For an example of Revere's newspaper delivery, see *New-York Journal*, September 22, 1774, "Mr. Paul Revere, by whom we received Mr. Dunlap's *Pennsylvania Packet*." *New-York Journal* Revere mentions in 1774: *New-York Journal*, May 19, 1774; *New-York Journal*, May 26, 1774; *New-York Journal*, September 22, 1774; *New-York Journal*, October 6, 1774. For examples of Revere's perspective and insight, see *Essex Gazette* (Salem, MA), May 31, 1774; *Essex Journal* (Newburyport, MA), June 1, 1774; *Boston News-Letter*, June 2, 1774; *Connecticut Gazette* (New London), June 3, 1774; *Connecticut Journal* (New Haven), June 3, 1774; *New-Hampshire Gazette* (Portsmouth), June 3, 1774; *Providence Gazette*, June 4, 1774.

14. For modern historians emphasizing the absence of Revere's name in early history books, see note 1. To calculate the reach of Revere's newspaper coverage: The printers of two of the largest newspapers in Boston, the *Boston Gazette* and *Massachusetts Spy*, boasted circulations of 2000 and 3500 during the Revolution, respectively (*Boston Gazette*, January 2, 1797; *Massachusetts Spy*, December 21, 1780). According to James Rivington (*New-York Gazetteer*, October 31, 1774), he had a weekly impression of 3600. Taking that into consideration and assuming 2750 for the average circulation of New York and Philadelphia newspapers, where most of the ten Revere newspaper mentions were made in the weeks following April 17, 1775, Revere's name had approximately 27,500 impressions with the potential for far greater reach since newspapers were often shared or read aloud in public places.

Richard Williams Maps the Siege of Boston

❧ ALLISON K. LANGE ❧

British lieutenant Richard Williams was one of the few artists to document the siege of Boston from 1775 through 1776. He created maps, sketches, and watercolors of the places he visited. Today, this collection of imagery is in high demand by museums and private collectors because it gives us a rare glimpse of the war. In addition to his artwork, he kept a diary filled with his thoughts and drawings. The journal gives insights into how he made his art and the daily lives of British soldiers.[1] The items Williams left behind offer us a unique perspective on Boston and its residents during the siege.

Before Williams made maps and views of the colonies, he traveled in Europe. His diary, begun in January 1774, recounts his adventures and features sketches of things that caught his eye: architectural details, a German count, and elaborate clocks. Williams honed his artistic skills under the direction of Paul Sandby, who was also a mapmaker and landscape artist, at the Royal Military Academy at Woolwich.

In late April 1775, twenty-five-year-old Williams left for Boston to join his regiment that had already been in America for two years, the 23rd Regiment of Foot, the Royal Welch Fusiliers. He declared the coffee on board his ship to be "very good" and recounted attempts to catch sharks and porpoises, perhaps for some fresh sustenance.[2] While Williams's trip across the Atlantic probably resembled that of many

---

1. The Grosvenor Rare Book Room at the Buffalo and Erie County Public Library houses the original diary. Parts of it were transcribed and published as Jane Van Arsdale, ed., *Discord and Civil Wars: Being a Portion of the Journal Kept by Lieutenant Williams* (Buffalo: Easy Hill Press, 1954).
2. Diary of Richard Williams, May 18-19, 1775, 67 and June 5, 1775, 71-72.

other soldiers, his diary has left us with impressions of these everyday experiences.

The journal allows us to see Williams as a person rather than a nameless soldier. On June 2, his ship neared Nova Scotia. A wounded bird flew on board and he welcomed it. He wrote:

> Wellcome to our hospitable care my little featherd friend. Wellcome, for know that Pity & soft compassion dwell within a Soldier's breast, driven from thy native shore by some rude blast, thy feeble wings could not long withhold thee from the threatening waves when that kind providence which or'elooks the world, and often frees us from the mouth of danger brought thee to our Vessel.

Williams's sentiment for the small creature is poignant. His words might have reflected his own concerns about the wind carrying him away from his own "native shore." Later he noted that a fellow soldier put the bird in a box to keep it warm, but it was found dead the next day. Williams lamented the death and sketched a memorial portrait of the bird, which suggests it was a chestnut-sided warbler.[3]

On June 7, as the ship neared Massachusetts, the soldiers encountered fishermen and learned about the battles of Lexington and Concord. Williams recalled that they said "we shou'd none of us live to return again," which "brought a hearty damning on the poor fisherman" from his fellow soldiers.[4] Even before Williams landed, he experienced the colonists' animosity.

By the time Williams arrived in Boston on June 11, the British had been confined to the city after their retreat following the action at Lexington and Concord in April. Williams entered a city surrounded by Gen. George Washington's American soldiers. He reflected on the scene: "what a country are we come to, Discord, & civil wars began, & peace & plenty turn'd out of doors." Despite his dismay about the continued conflict, Williams was glad to be in Boston. He declared "the Land was a pleasing object after six weeks of absence from it."[5]

Williams was glad to leave the ship because his duties were tied to the land. As a cartographer and artist, he mapped the Boston area for local military leaders and London officials soon after his arrival. Williams took stock of the city from Beacon Hill, where he had a better view of the rebellious colonists across the Charles River in

3. Williams, May 18-19, 1775, 69-71.
4. Williams, June 7, 1775, 72-73.
5. Williams, June 11, 1775, 74-76.

Cambridge. Of the city, Williams concluded that "Boston is large & well built, tho' not a regular laid out town. it has several good streets, the generality of houses are built of timber & mostly with their gabel ends to the street." He thought, however, the area had seen better days "before the present unhappy affairs" when "it was livly and flurishing."[6]

Williams used the view from Beacon Hill to draw his maps and panoramic sketches. He likely drew the *Plan of Boston and its Environs Shewing the True Situation of His Majesty's Troops* (overleaf) from this vantage point. The manuscript map depicts the American and British positions in October 1775. Williams noted that he "went so far as our advanced post at a house in the road towards Roxbury," which is southwest of Boston, but he never ventured beyond the British lines.[7] His map, therefore, reflects his view from the hill along with information he gathered from others. Fortifications were colored yellow for the rebels, and green for the British. Camps, like the one for British soldiers on the Boston Common, are red.[8]

Williams's map demonstrates the geography that made the siege possible for the newly organized American troops. In the eighteenth century, the city of Boston was practically an island. Only one thin strip of land—referred to as the Boston Neck—connected the city to the rest of Massachusetts. This geography facilitated a large harbor, which helped make the city one of the busiest colonial ports. Over the course of the nineteenth century, Bostonians filled in much of the bay. Today the city barely resembles the outline on Williams's map.

British military and political leaders had commissioned Williams to make maps and sketches so that they could best formulate their strategies. Williams sent this map of Boston to London, possibly in a group that he noted sending on July 28, 1775.[9] The map was engraved and printed less than two weeks before the British army evacuated the city on March 17, 1776. By the time the maps could be widely consulted, they practically became irrelevant. The delay between Williams's initial sketches and their publication illustrates the challenges the British government faced as they orchestrated a war across the Atlantic Ocean.

6. Williams, June 12, 1775, 76-79.
7. Williams, June 15, 1776, 80.
8. [Richard Williams], "*A Plan of Boston and its Environs Shewing the True Situation of His Majesty's Troops and Also Those of the Rebels, Likewise All the Forts, Redoubts and Entrenchments Erected by Both Armies,*" 1775, Manuscript, pen and ink and watercolor, 18 x 26 inches, British Library, Additional Mss. 15535.5.
9. Williams, July 28, 1775, 117.

As Williams learned more about the conflict, he wrote about his impressions of its origins. He noted, "The immediate and pretended cause of all these troubles now broke out in N. America is assigned by the artful leaders of this people, to the usurpd authority of the Britis[h] Parliament."[10] Rather than a sincere desire for liberty, Williams believed the leaders of the revolution wanted more power. He thought the colonists had "not in the least deviated from the steps of their ancestors, allways grumbling & unwilling to acknowledge the authority of any power but what originated amongst them."[11]

In addition to mapping Boston, Williams painted panoramic watercolors of the landscape. The pictures are aesthetically pleasing even as they offer important details about fortifications and encampments. From his perch on Beacon Hill, he created *A View of the Country Round Boston, Taken from Beacon Hill* with sketches of the city's churches, homes, and British encampments.[12] At the bottom of the scene, Williams included a key to identify fortifications like Castle William and the "Redoubts of the Rebels."

Sometimes Williams made multiple impressions of the same scene. This watercolor offers a view of the Boston neck and house of John Hancock, a merchant and signer of the Declaration of Independence who would later become the first governor of Massachusetts.[13] Two British officers stand in the foreground and point to the colonists' encampments. The scene appears more like a bucolic landscape rather than a portrait of war. In contrast, a second watercolor of the same view labels the details that officials needed to know: the rebels' lines on the other side of the Charles River, British encampments, and the road to Cambridge.[14]

The landscape views that Williams labeled with crucial details were sent to London and became part of the collection of King George III,

10. Williams, June 15, 1775, 81.
11. Williams, June 15, 1775, 82.
12. Richard Williams, "*A View of the Country Round Boston, Taken from Beacon Hill . . . Shewing the Lines, Redoubts, & Different Encampments of the Rebels Also Those of His Majesty's Troops under the Command of His Excellency Lieut. General Gage, Governor of Massachuset's* [sic] *Bay,*" 1775. Manuscript, ink, and watercolor, each 7 x 19 inches, British Library, King George III Topographical Collection, 120.38.
13. Richard Williams [Boston Neck, with the British lines and John Hancock's house], 1775, watercolor, 17 x 47 cm, Richard H. Brown Revolutionary War Map Collection.
14. Richard Williams [View of the country round Boston taken from Beacon Hill], 1775, watercolor, 17 x 47.6 cm, British Library, King George III Topographical Collection 120.38.c. Find out more about Williams and the mapping of the American Revolution in: *Revolution: Mapping the Road to American Independence, 1755-1783.* New York: W. W. Norton & Company, 2015.

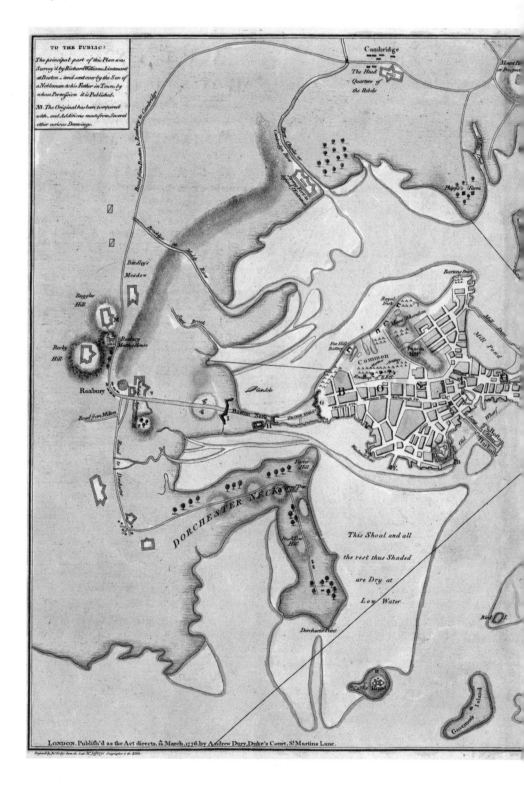

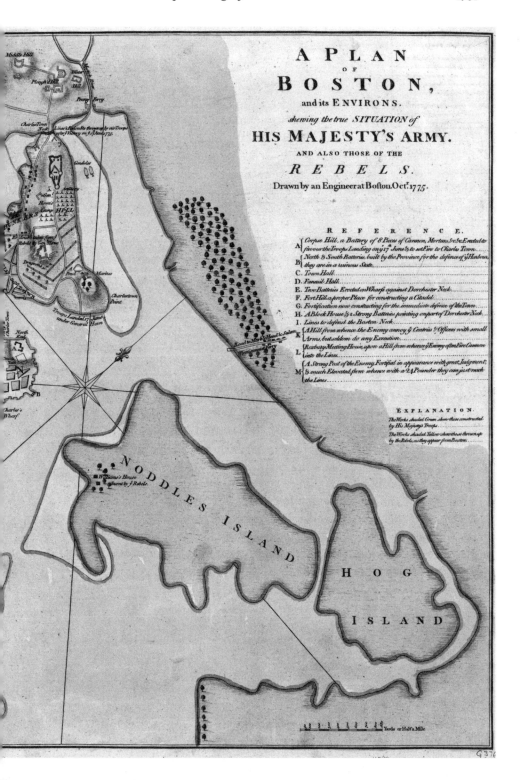

who reigned from 1760 to 1820. In addition to using maps to influence the course of the American war, the king was an avid collector of maps and views. The British Library now houses these pieces as part of King George III's Topographical Collection.

For the first time, the British Library has loaned Williams's work for display in the city that Williams captured on paper. The Norman B. Leventhal Map Center at the Boston Public Library features the map and watercolors in their 2015 exhibition *We Are One: Mapping America's Road from Revolution to Independence*.[15] More maps and views by Williams can also be viewed online in the American Revolution Portal database, funded by the National Endowment for the Humanities.

One reason why Williams's images are so valued is that we have very few images of the Revolutionary War. Today we have instant access to photographs and videos of conflicts, but the first few war photographs were not taken until the Crimean War (1853–1856). By the time the Civil War began in 1861, a corps of photographers took war views to sell to the public.

Eighteenth-century public imagery, in contrast, often consisted of engravings. Because colonists had limited access to engraving supplies and trained artists, most of the imagery that circulated in the colonies and early republic was created in Europe.

Lt. Richard Williams's diary ends mid-sentence during his September 4, 1775, entry. He evacuated Boston in March of 1776 with the rest of the British troops and sailed for Nova Scotia, where he continued to capture the landscape with his watercolors. Shortly after his arrival, he became ill and went back to Britain. A death announcement from London's *Morning Post & Daily Advertiser* for May 8, 1776, tells us that he arrived but died in Cornwall on April 30.

Although Williams died young, the unique maps, views, and diary he left behind offer valuable insights into life during the siege of Boston. Besides the few Boston and Cambridge residents who remained, soldiers like Williams were the only ones who could document experiences of the siege. These now treasured maps and views have helped thrust Williams and his impressions of the siege into the spotlight.

---

15. The exhibit travels to Colonial Williamsburg in 2016 and the New-York Historical Society in 2017.

The Bermuda Powder Raids of 1775

❄ HUGH T. HARRINGTON ❄

In 1775, the tension between the American colonies and Great Britain escalated into armed conflict at then-little-known places such as Lexington, Concord, and Bunker Hill. As a result, throughout the spring and into the summer American colonial legislatures and the military were scrambling to secure supplies of every kind.

Until that time much of the arms, clothing, lead, flints, and gunpowder had come from abroad. Now, facing the might of the Royal Navy, the colonists would find it difficult to obtain supplies from overseas. It was essential that time not be lost in acquiring war materiel wherever it might be located.

George Washington, in command of the colonial forces laying siege to Boston, faced an extraordinary crisis. He had only 36 barrels of powder for the 14,000 men fit for duty in his army. That worked out to "not more than 9 cartridges a Man."[1]

Washington convened a council of war on August 3. The council agreed to send a detachment of 300 men to make an attempt to capture the British powder magazine at Halifax, Nova Scotia.[2]

In addition, Washington wrote letters to the governors of the colonies requesting immediate assistance. He begged Governor Jonathan Trumbull of Connecticut "in strict confidence" for "every ounce [of powder] in the Province." Washington added that "the case calls loudly for the warmest and most strenuous exertions of every

---

1. Washington to President of Congress, August 4, 1775, George Washington Papers, Library of Congress, memory.loc.gov/ammem/gwhtml/gwhome. html (hereinafter cited as GWP).
2. Peter Force, *American Archives*, Series IV, Vol. 3, minutes of Council of War held at Cambridge, Headquarters, August 3, 1775, 36, dig.lib.niu.edu/amarch/.

friend to his country, and does not admit of the least delay; no quantity however small is beneath notice."[3]

In his letter to Governor Nicholas Cooke of Rhode Island Washington said his

> . . . necessities in the articles of powder and lead are so great as to require an immediate supply . . . forward every pound of each in the colony which can possibly be spared . . . no quantity, however small, is beneath notice and should any arrive I beg it may be forwarded as soon as possible.[4]

Meanwhile, Washington proposed a bold plan to Governor Cooke:

> I have resolved in my mind every other possible chance and listened to every proposition on the subject which could give the smallest Hope; Among others I have had one mentioned which has some Weight with me, as well as the General Officers to whom I have proposed it, one Harris is lately come from Bermuda, where there is a very considerable Magazine of Powder in a remote Part of the Island and the Inhabitants well disposed not only to our Cause in General, but to assist in this Enterprize in particular; we understand there are two armed Vessels in your Province commanded by Men of known Activity and Spirit; one of which it is proposed to dispatch on this Errand, with such other assistance as may be required; Harris is to go along as the Conductor of the Enterprize and to avail ourselves of his knowledge of the Island, but without any Command. I am very sensible that at first view the project may appear hazardous and its Success must depend on the Concurrence of many Circumstances; but we are in a Situation which requires us to run all Risques. No Danger is to be considered when put in Competition with the Magnitude of the Cause and the Absolute Necessity we are under of increasing our Stock. Enterprises which appear Chimerical, often prove successful from that very Circumstance, Common Sense & Prudence will Suggest Vigilance and care, when the Danger is Plain and obvious, but where little Danger is apprehended, the more the enemy is unprepared and consequently there is the fain'd Prospect of Success.[5]

George Washington and the American colonies were not the only ones with supply problems. The British colony of Bermuda, a small

3. Washington to Governor Jonathan Trumbull, August 4, 1775, GWP.
4. Washington to Governor Nicholas Cooke, August 4, 1775, GWP.
5. Washington to Governor Nicholas Cooke, August 4, 1775, GWP.

island in the Atlantic Ocean about 900 miles east of Charleston, South Carolina, was not concerned with war materiel but rather the food for its very survival. Bermuda, with a population of about 12,000, consisted of land only 14 miles long and 1 mile wide. The island's residents could only grow enough food to support themselves for about two months of the year. Historically, Bermuda's food supply depended upon trade with North America. This was a potential disaster for Bermuda.[6]

The governor of Bermuda, George James Bruere, was a representative of the King and strove to support the British government's positions. The Bermuda Assembly, including the powerful and influential Tucker family, had other ideas. Henry Tucker, the family patriarch, and the family openly condemned the British colonial policies, calling them "unconstitutional acts." In 1774, he denounced the British Parliament for "obstinacy" and wrote, "I think the collonies ought to hazzard every thing rather than to submit to slavery . . . for if the Parliament of great Britain have a right to dispose of the American's property as they please, call it by what name you will there can be no greater marks of Slavery." Very naturally, he was concerned for not only American property rights but also those of his own extended family.[7]

Bermuda, and the Tuckers, were in a difficult situation. The Continental Congress, in response to the Coercive Acts, enacted a trade embargo to go into effect in 1775 which would prohibit exports to British territory including Bermuda. If Bermuda could not obtain foodstuffs from North America it would be in desperate circumstances. However, if Bermuda was perceived to be supporting, joining, or even sympathetic to the American colonies it would face possible retaliation from the British. The tiny island was extremely vulnerable and could not be defended by the inhabitants nor the American colonies. The Royal Navy could control and threaten Bermuda's existence simply by placing a ship or two at its harbor to interrupt shipping.

Henry Tucker, however, took action. He instructed his son St. George Tucker, an attorney in Virginia, to write Thomas Jefferson and other delegates to the Continental Congress in Philadelphia. In a letter to Jefferson, St. George Tucker explained the dire need Bermuda

---

6. Phillip Hamilton, *The Making and Unmaking of a Revolutionary Family, The Tuckers of Virginia, 1752-1830* (Charlottesville, University of Virginia Press, 2003),10.

7. Hamilton, *Tuckers*, Letter Henry Tucker to his son St. George Tucker, July 31, 1774, 30-31.

had to continue its commerce with the American colonies. He also wrote that the Bermudians "consider the Americans as Brethren, and their Souls are animated with the same generous Ardor for Liberty that prevails on the Continent; they are most Zealous Friends to the Cause of America, and would readily join with it, in any Measures to secure those inestimable privileges now contending for; in short, they consider the Cause as their own, and with pleasure behold every step that has been taken in support of it."[8]

In addition, St. George Tucker also told Jefferson that Bermuda, being defenseless, could not declare their allegiance with the American colonies. However, he felt "authorised" by "some of the principle Gentlemen of the Island" to suggest that if the Continental Congress would allow commerce between the American colonies and Bermuda "no commodities shall be reshipped thence [from Bermuda] to any other place which the Congress may think proper to have no Commerce with." In addition, it would be agreed that Bermuda would only import from Great Britain "the absolute necessaries of life."[9]

Jefferson replied that a "relaxation of our terms . . . might be mutually beneficial to us." He then suggested that a visit from "some body with some kind of public authority as well to give information of facts, as to satisfy the Congress that the inhabitants of Bermuda will enter into such engagements" would be helpful.[10] Henry Tucker and other prominent Bermudians personally went to Philadelphia to plead their case. There, members of the Continental Congress informally suggested that if ships laden with munitions were to come from Bermuda they would be permitted to return with food supplies.

Henry Tucker, and his extended family, looked at the Royal powder magazine on Bermuda as a source of war materiel that could be handed over to the Americans in exchange for food. The magazine was at a remote location and virtually unguarded making it an easy target.[11]

On July 15, 1775, the Continental Congress passed a resolution stating that vessels importing munitions would be permitted to sail from the colonies carrying cargoes of foodstuffs. Discreetly, Bermuda was not specifically named.

8. William Bell Clark, editor, *Naval Documents of the American Revolution*, vol. 1, (Washington, DC, US Navy Department, 1964), Letter St. George Tucker to Thomas Jefferson, June 8, 1775, 635.
9. Clark, *Naval Documents*, vol. 1, Letter St. George Tucker to Thomas Jefferson, June 8, 1775, 635.
10. Thomas Jefferson to St. George Tucker, June 10, 1775, GWP.
11. Hamilton, *Tuckers*, 31.

Unbeknownst to George Washington, the wheels for an attempt to capture the powder had been set in motion. The details of the raid are lost as the Bermudians who assisted in the mission vanished into the night and kept their involvement to themselves. However, Governor Bruere described the raid on the powder magazine as follows:

I had less suspicion than before, that such a daring and Violent attempt would be made on the Powder Magazine, which in the dead of night of the 14th of August was broke into on Top, just to let a man down, and the Doors most Audaciously and daringly forced open, at the great risk of their being blown up; they could not force the Powder Room Door, without getting into the inside on Top. They Stole and Carried off about one Hundred Barrels of Gun powder, and as they left about ten or twelve Barrels, it may be Supposed that those Barrels left, would not bare remooving. It must have taken a Considerable number of People; and we may Suppose some Negroes, to assist as well as White Persons of consequence. . .

The next morning the 15th instant (of August), one sloop Called the *Lady Catharine*, belonging by Her Register to Virginia, George Ord Master, bound to Philadelphia, was seen under Sail, but the Custom House Boat could not over take Her. And likewise a Schooner Called the *Charles Town and Savannah Packet*, belonging to South Carolina, from South Carolina Cleared out at Bermuda the 11th of August with 2,000 Sawed Stones for Barbadoes John Turner Master. And was seen under Sail the same day, at such a Distance off, that the Custom House Boat could not over take either of the Vessels. It may be supposed that neither of the vessels came near the Shore, to take in the Powder, if they did carry it away, but it is rather to be imagined that it must have been Carried out by Several Boats, as both these Vessels, Sailed from a Harbour at the West End, twenty Miles off, of the Magazine.[12]

The Bermuda legislature, of which Henry Tucker as well as other family members and prominent citizens were a part, offered a reward to anyone who gave evidence to convict those who aided the Americans in stealing the powder. Bruere offered a personal reward, and a pardon, hoping that an informer would come forward. The situation was fascinating as it was an open secret that many islanders,

---

12. Clark, *Naval Documents*, vol. 1, Letter Governor Bruere to Lord Dartmouth, August 17, 1775, 1169; Clark, *Naval Documents*, vol. 2, Letter Governor Bruere to Lord Dartmouth, September 13, 1775, 91.

with the connivance of prominent citizens, aided in the powder raid by transporting over 100 barrels of powder to the shore and then ferrying them out to the Americans. Yet, to the frustration of Governor Bruere, he was unable to obtain sufficient evidence.

These clandestine maneuverings by the Bermudians and the Continental Congress were kept a very close secret as the British could easily have thwarted any attempt on the powder stored at Bermuda. Washington himself was not advised of the raid possibly because it had not occurred to anyone that their commander, at his headquarters in Cambridge, would be considering such a distant naval strike.

Nicholas Cooke, Governor of Rhode Island, wrote Washington on August 11, 1775, advising Washington he had learned that Bermudians had been in contact with delegates to the Continental Congress in Philadelphia asking that food be allowed to be exported to Bermuda. These men had also mentioned the powder at Bermuda might be easily taken. Cooke wondered if Washington still wanted Rhode Island to mount the operation against the Bermuda powder magazine.[13]

Washington, not knowing that the Continental Congress had sanctioned a raid on Bermuda, continued to pursue his own attempts to acquire the powder. On September 2 Nicholas Cooke wrote Washington with the welcome news that Rhode Island had resolved to send the armed sloop *Katy*, commanded by Captain Abraham Whipple, to Bermuda to seize the powder. Captain Whipple asked that Washington supply him with a letter for the people of Bermuda stating that if they assisted in obtaining powder Washington would recommend to the Continental Congress that Bermudians be permitted to obtain provisions. The letter was not to be disclosed unless Whipple could not acquire the powder without assistance of the local people.[14]

Washington supplied a letter "to the "Inhabitants of the Island of Bermuda" to Cooke but cautioned that he "shall depend upon Capt. Whipple's not making use of it, except in Case of real Necessity." Washington, a military commander, did not want to involve himself in international politics; therefore, he included the clause about "real necessity." However, Washington was determined to obtain the powder at whatever cost.[15]

13. Governor Cooke to George Washington, August 11, 1775, GWP.
14. Governor Cooke to George Washington, September 2, 1775, GWP.
15. George Washington to Inhabitants of Bermuda, September 6, 1775, GWP.

Captain Abraham Whipple sailed on Tuesday, September 12. He was ordered "if possible to take the powder into possession without any communication with the Inhabitants." Cooke advised Washington, "I have given it to him strictly in Charge not to make Use of your Address [letter] unless in Case of absolute Necessity."[16]

Meanwhile, Captain Ord brought the *Lady Catherine*, with the load of gunpowder, into Philadelphia. The Captain of H.M.S. *Rose*, James Wallace, wrote Vice Admiral Samuel Graves September 9th advising him of the arrival of a vessel "from Bermuda belonging to Philadelphia which had broke open in the Night and taken out of the Magazine of that Island 126 barrels of gunpowder."[17]

On September 9, 1775, the *Pennsylvania Evening Post* newspaper carried a brief article, "New York, September 7. Extract from a letter from Bermuda, dated August 21. 'Upwards of one hundred barrels of gun-powder have been taken out of our magazine; supposed by a sloop from Philadelphia, and a schooner from South Carolina. It was very easily accomplished, from the magazine being situated far distant from town, and no dwelling house near it.'" Other newspapers reprinted the article immediately.[18]

As the powder had already been seized efforts were made to recall Captain Whipple's expedition to Bermuda, but the ship sent after him was unable to find the *Katy* at sea. When Whipple reached Bermuda he put in at the west end of the island. His arrival caused something of a panic among the Bermudians as his was thought to be a British warship. Women and children scattered inland. After showing his instructions and his commission, but not Washington's letter, he was warmly greeted. Five members of the King's Council boarded the *Katy* where Whipple was assured that the islanders were friends of the American cause. The islanders who took part in the powder raid, while unknown specifically, were suspected by Governor Bruere; this suspicion "made them obnoxious to the enemy [the British], reducing them to a disagreeable situation" according to Governor Cooke. Captain Whipple returned to Rhode Island on October 20 and returned Washington's letter.[19]

---

16. Governor Cooke to George Washington, September 14, 1775, GWP.

17. Clark, *Naval Documents*, vol. 2, Captain Wallace to Vice Admiral Graves, September 9, 1775, 59. Force, *American Archives*, Series IV, vol. 3, Pa. Committee of Safety, September 20, 1775, report of powder received from Captain Ord., 864.

18. *Pennsylvania Evening Post*, September 9, 1775.

19. Governor Cooke to George Washington, October 25, 1775, GWP.

Although Captain Whipple came home empty handed George Washington's powder crisis was relieved when supplies came in from a variety of sources including the Pennsylvania Committee of Safety. The Committee sent Washington 4012 pounds of powder on September 4th which may have included the powder from Bermuda.[20]

Bermuda was on the brink of famine for the rest of the war. Some provisions came from the American colonies in exchange for items such as salt. The British also provided some supplies.

The *Charles Town and Savannah Packet*, commanded by Captain John Turner, despite Governor Bruere's suspicions, was not involved in the Bermuda powder raid. All the Bermuda powder appears to have been taken to Philadelphia by Captain George Ord in the *Lady Catherine*. The confusion arises because at about the same time a load of powder was captured by the South Carolinian, Admiral Clement Lempriere. However, that powder came from a British ship seized near St. Augustine. The capture was unrelated to the Bermuda events. Contemporary and modern accounts of the Bermuda raid accepted Governor Bruere's report naming the two ships he suspected.[21]

20. Force, *American Archives*, Series IV, vol. 3, Pa. Committee of Safety, September 20, 1775, report of powder received from Captain Ord., 864.

21. For the unrelated seizure of the British ship near St. Augustine see: Clark, *Naval Documents*, vol. 1, Arthur Middleton to William Henry Drayton, August 11, 1775, 2211; Henry Laurens to the Committee of Beaufort, August 12, 1775, 1130. Clark, *Naval Documents*, vol. 2, Captain James Wallace to Vice Admiral Graves, September 9, 1775, 58; Vice Admiral Graves to Captain James Wallace, September 17, 1775, 129.

Benjamin Franklin's Failed Diplomatic Mission

❄ GENE PROCKNOW ❄

Benjamin Franklin's Revolutionary War diplomatic successes have been well chronicled. He was instrumental in persuading King Louis XVI to enter into a military alliance with the fledgling United States and for negotiating the Treaty of Paris with the British ending the Revolutionary War. Less remembered is Franklin's first diplomatic mission after the onset of hostilities.

Capitalizing on the capture of Ft. Ticonderoga, the Patriots invaded Canada to drive out the British and unite the thirteen colonies with Canada. Initially the invasion was slow moving, but successful. The Canadian cities of St. Johns, Chambly, and Montreal fell to Patriot attackers and the Continental army swept to the gates of Quebec, the strategic key to remaining Canadian positions held by the British. However, a December 31, 1775, assault failed and an enfeebled Patriot army camped outside the city walls.

With the Continental army deteriorating from disease and a lack of provisions and anticipated British reinforcements, something had to be done to sustain the Patriot conquest of Canada. Maj. Gen. Philip Schuyler, commander of the Northern Department, reiterated a previous request that the Continental Congress send a delegation to win over the Canadians. Congress thought that Canada should send a delegation to Philadelphia similar to the other colonies.[1] Given the now dire situation, Congress reconsidered and authorized a diplomatic commission to travel to Montreal to persuade the Canadians to join the thirteen colonies in rebellion against British rule.

1. Justin H. Smith, *Our Struggle for the Fourteenth Colony—Canada and the American Revolution* (New York & London: Knickerbocker Press, 1907), 2:325.

THE COMMISSION

On February 15, 1776, Congress established a three person diplomatic commission consisting of Benjamin Franklin, Samuel Chase, and Charles Carroll. Franklin, a member of Congress, was the most experienced diplomat as he had represented colonial interests in Britain before the rebellion. Chase, a member of Congress from Maryland, was selected to demonstrate that Protestants and Catholics could live harmoniously within one political entity, and he was a good friend of northern commander General Schuyler. Charles Carroll, who was fluent in French, was selected because of his Catholic faith and his enormous personal wealth. Congress also requested that Carroll's cousin, the Reverend John Carroll, a practicing priest, accompany the commission to interact with the Canadian religious authorities.[2]

After over a month of deliberations, Congress formally charged the Commission with the objective of convincing the Canadian populous to join the thirteen colonies in separating from Britain. The commissioners were authorized to offer the following inducements.[3]

Free and undisturbed Exercise of their Religion
Possession and Enjoyment of their Estates
Rights to enact laws governing their colony
Representation in Congress
Establishment of a free press
Mutual defense

Fleury Mesplet, a French-speaking printer from Philadelphia, accompanied the commissioners to publish materials sympathetic to the Patriots. Mesplet carried a printing press, as the only press in Canada was located in British controlled Quebec. Congress believed that a publishing operation was critical to widespread dissemination of its proposals thereby engendering Canadian support for joining rebellion against British rule.[4]

Another important component of the commission's charge was expansive military powers. Military officers were subordinate to their command and the commissioners were authorized to sit and vote in councils of war. The commissioners had the authority to settle disputes between the Continental army and the Canadians (including

2. *Journals of the American Congress from 1774 to 1788*, February 15, 1776 (Washington: Way & Gideon, 1823), 265.
3. *Instructions and Commission from Congress to Franklin, Charles Carroll and Samuel Chase for the Canadian mission, March 20, 1776*, franklinpapers.org/franklin//framed Volumes.jsp, accessed November 16, 2014.
4. Smith, *Our Struggle for the Fourteenth Colony*, 334.

The Patriot Commissioners: Charles Carroll, Benjamin Franklin, and Samuel Chase. (*Maryland Department of Education, Library of Congress*)

several jailed Canadians) and to enact regulations concerning relations. Further, Congress furnished blank officer commissions to form up to four new regiments and to enlist willing volunteers among the Canadian populace.

Lastly, the commissioners sought to secure the allegiance of the Native American tribes who straddled the border between Canada and New York (including modern day Vermont). At the very least, they sought the tribes' neutrality as the New Yorkers and New Englanders recollected the fearful Indian attacks during the French and Indian War. The commission was also charged with encouraging good relations and trade with Indian Nations. Passports were authorized to facilitate trade and to keep the peace.

THE RECEPTION

The late winter journey from Philadelphia to Montreal required Benjamin Franklin and the commissioners to travel through wilderness country, to brave wintery elements, and to sleep in makeshift quarters. The 70-year-old Franklin was uncertain that he could complete the arduous journey and wrote to Josiah Quincy:

> I am here on my Way to Canada, detain'd by the present State of the Lakes, in which the unthaw'd Ice obstructs Navigation. I begin to apprehend that I have undertaken a Fatigue that at my Time of Life may prove too much for me, so I sit down to write to a few Friends by way of Farewell.[5]

5. Letter dated April 15, 1776, from Benjamin Franklin to Josiah Quincy, Sr., franklin-papers.org/franklin//framedVolumes.jsp, accessed December 12, 2014.

Franklin persevered and arrived in Montreal on April 29, 1776. Brig. Gen. Benedict Arnold and a salute from the cannon of the city's citadel welcomed Franklin and the other two commissioners. A grand party and feast was held to celebrate their arrival and to impress the local inhabitants of the importance of the Commissioners.[6]

However, the reception from the general population was considerably muted. When Maj. Gen. Richard Montgomery, leader of the Patriot forces in Canada first came to Montreal on his way to Quebec, the Canadians provided supplies and assistance. However, his defeat gave pause to the Canadians in giving additional support. Lacking hard currency, the Patriots could only offer relatively worthless Continental dollars for needed goods and services. This led Canadians to believe that Congress was bankrupt and they would not honor Continental dollars. In fact, Franklin had to find a fellow traveler to exchange Continental currency into silver to pay for a calash (a two wheeled, one horse vehicle) to take them into Montreal.[7]

On May 1, the commission wrote to Congress requesting twenty thousand pounds to prosecute the war effort. The money would be used to establish a bank to exchange Continental notes and to pay off existing debts. Further, Franklin indicated that without this money, it was impossible to propose a union of Canada with the thirteen colonies.[8]

The intended good will by Father John Carroll engaging with his Canadian ecclesiastical counterparts did not generate pro-Patriot support. Carroll briefly met with Father Peter R. Floquet, a Jesuit priest in Montreal. Father Floquet was open to speaking, possibly because he was concerned with Patriot backlash against Catholics in Maryland and Pennsylvania. To further incent Father Floquet, the Patriots restored his Montreal residence to him that had been requisitioned for military use. However, all other Catholic priests followed Bishop of Quebec Monseigneur Briand's orders forbidding any contact with Father Carroll and the Patriots.[9]

The Canadian clergy believed that they had positive assurances of religious freedom under the Quebec Act from the British government and only unsubstantiated promises from the Patriots. The clergy expe-

6. Brant Mayer, ed., *Journal of Charles Carroll of Carrollton* (Baltimore: Maryland Historical Society, 1876), 92-93.
7. *The Commissioners to Canada to John Hancock, May 1, 1776,* franklinpapers.org/franklin//framedVolumes.jsp, accessed November 16, 2014.
8. *The Commissioners to Canada to John Hancock, May 1, 1776,* franklinpapers.org/franklin//framedVolumes.jsp, accessed November 16, 2014.
9. Henry De Courcy, *The Catholic Church in the United States, 2nd Edition,* John Gilmary Shea, ed. (New York: Catholic Publishing House, 1856), 46-50.

rienced first hand intolerance from Brig. Gen. David Wooster, a Patriot officer serving in Canada, and became aware of Congress's harsh denouncements of the Roman Catholic faith. Further, some of the colonies prohibited Catholic priests from serving as missionaries among the Native Americans and harshly treated those that disobeyed the ban. These experiences led the Canadian Catholic Church to reject John Carroll's entreaties and to support the British.[10]

Compounding the funding and religious issues, the Canadians observed many disheartened Patriot soldiers abandoning the campaign and returning home at the end of their enlistments. Canadians increasingly perceived that the Patriots were not committed, so why should any Canadian enlist to fight the British?

Col. Moses Hazen in a letter to General Schuyler summed up the situation with respect to the local population, "we no longer look upon them as friends, but, on the contrary, waiting an opportunity to join our enemies . . . who would wish to see our throats cut, and perhaps would readily assist in doing it."[11]

The military situation was increasingly bleak. There were only 3000 men remaining in the northern army versus the planned 8000 complement. Smallpox further decimated the ranks.[12] The current Patriot positions were not defensible given the expected large number of British army and navy reinforcements. On May 6, Franklin and the other two commissioners recommended that the Continental army be withdrawn from Quebec and Montreal to defend the northern entrance of Lake Champlain.[13]

THE OUTCOME

Historian Justin Smith hypothesized that if Montgomery and Arnold were successful in capturing Quebec at the end of 1775, the Canadians would have sent representatives to the Continental Congress and joined the rebellion. He cites as evidence the initial support along the Patriot invasion paths down the St. Lawrence and Chaudière River

10. Smith, *Our Struggle for the Fourteenth Colony*, 334-35.

11. Letter From Colonel Hazen to General Schuyler, April 1, 1776, *American Archives: Documents of the American Revolution, 1774-1776*, lincoln.lib.niu.edu/cgi-bin/ amarch/getdoc.pl?/var/lib/philologic/databases/amarch/.14244, accessed November 21, 2014. For more information on Colonel Hazen and his support of the Patriot cause, see allthingsliberty.com/2014/11/top-5-foreign-continental-army-officers/.

12. *The Commissioners to Canada to John Hancock, May 1, 1776*, franklinpapers.org /franklin//framedVolumes.jsp, accessed November 16, 2014.

13. *The Commissioners to Canada to John Hancock, May 6, 1776*, franklinpapers.org /franklin//framedVolumes.jsp, accessed November 16, 2014.

valleys.[14] However strong, any early Canadian support evaporated by the time Franklin and the other commissioners arrived in Montreal. The Patriots had earned enemies among the population with broken promises and worthless currency.

Since the commission carried little hard currency and none was likely to arrive in time, Franklin quickly realized that it would be impossible to win over the Canadians to the Patriot cause. Franklin rightly discerned that with the Quebec Act that guaranteed French Canadian cultural, religious, and legal customs, there was no burning platform for rebellion against British rule.

The Canadian population now viewed the Continental army as an invading and occupying force. Further, the Americans were regarded with suspicion of not sharing the same respect as the British for the French Canadian way of life. There was the strong possibility that the populace would take up arms against the Patriots.

Given these poor prospects for success and his declining health, Franklin departed Montreal on May 11 to return to Philadelphia. Reverend Carroll accompanied him, as he could make no headway with the French Canadian religious authorities. The other two commissioners, Charles Carroll and Samuel Chase, remained in Montreal for another twenty days and departed only when the military situation deteriorated and the fall of Montreal to the British was imminent.

Franklin's outreach to the seven Indian tribes of Canada was also not successful. Initially, the Native Americans pledged neutrality, probably because there were few British forces outside of Quebec. However, the Great Council of the Onondagas reported that they received a hatchet (a symbol of alliance) from the British authorities but refused to give it up to the Patriots until a council of the entire Seven Nations could be conducted. The commissioners suspected that the tribes were delaying taking sides to see who was likely to prevail.[15]

Never again would the Patriots invade Canada nor seriously pursue a political combination. However, Franklin learned valuable lessons as part of this mission. He realized that proper funding to procure logistics and army supplies were critical to the Revolution's success. Without the means to pay for goods and services the Continental army would be treated as an occupier wherever it went.

On the positive side, Franklin procured a soft marten fur cap to protect him from the Canadian cold and wind. This cap would make

14. Smith, *Our Struggle for the Fourteenth Colony*, 446.
15. *The Commissioners to Canada to John Hancock, May 6, 1776*, franklinpapers .org/franklin//framedVolumes.jsp, accessed November 16, 2014.

him famous in Parisian society as a country sage and homespun American.[16]

In France, Franklin was strikingly more successful in winning the hearts and minds of both the French government and people. During his time in Paris, he secured vital funding and military support for the fledgling Patriot cause. Franklin's Canadian diplomatic mission provides another example that highly successful people generally "fail" early in their careers. These failures provide life lessons that lead to future successes. In Franklin's case, they contributed to brilliant and extraordinary diplomatic and political successes!

16. Walter Isaacson, *Benjamin Franklin—An American Life* (New York: Simon & Shuster, 2003), 306.

Governor Franklin Makes His Move

❀ THOMAS FLEMING ❀

New Jersey governor William Franklin is one of the forgotten major players in the American Revolution. By the fall of 1775, he was the only royal governor in the thirteen rebellious colonies who had not fled or been chased from his post by the mounting tension between the Americans and the mother country. But William's real prestige derived from his name. He was Benjamin Franklin's son.*

Dr. Franklin, as Benjamin was known, thanks to an honorary degree from the University of Edinburgh, had returned from eleven years in London earlier in the year. In the course of this controversy-filled decade, he had become the spokesman not only for Pennsylvania but for all the colonies. On shipboard he had written the longest letter of his life. It began with two deeply meaningful words: "Dear Son." The letter described Franklin's secret negotiations with the British government, which had convinced him that George III and the men around him were determined to subdue and humiliate the Americans. It closed with urgent advice that William should resign his royal office as soon as possible and join the resistance to Britain's arrogant pretensions to imperial power.

To Ben Franklin's dismay, William declined to take this advice. He told his father he felt "obligated" to the king and his government for keeping him in his office in spite of their disagreements with his father. Not even the bloody battle of Bunker Hill, which exploded six weeks after Ben arrived in Philadelphia, changed the governor's mind. Almost as dismaying was Ben's discovery that a hefty percentage of

*This article is adapted from the author's book *The Man Who Dared The Lightning: A New Look At Benjamin Franklin* (New York: Oxford University Press, 1971), recently released as an eBook.

the Continental Congress, which was meeting in the Pennsylvania State House, was equally reluctant to break with the king.

Soon after Bunker Hill, Ben Franklin wrote a declaration of independence and a rudimentary constitution which he called "Articles of Confederation and Perpetual Union." He was stunned to discover that the documents had horrified most of the members of Congress. Ben's political enemies in Philadelphia pointed to the fact that his son had not resigned as royal governor and circulated a rumor that Ben was a secret agent for George III.

Late in August, Ben journeyed from Philadelphia to Perth Amboy, New Jersey, the site of the royal governor's handsome house. Both men sensed their argument was coming to a climax. Neither was aware that their discussion was fatally influenced by the distant past. William was illegitimate. He had grown up in a household dominated by his viper-tongued stepmother, Deborah, while his father was absorbed by business and politics.

William's resentment of this unhappy childhood colored everything he heard from his father. At least as important was the influence of William's deeply religious English wife, Elizabeth, whom he had met in London when he journeyed there with his father in the 1760s. She had convinced the governor that it would be a grievous sin to revolt against their king.

The elder Franklin was bewildered by William's disagreement with his support of the revolution that was rumbling around them. Only twelve years ago, father and son had journeyed to Perth Amboy to install William as royal governor. Applause and approval had been showered on them from all sides. Now, a decade had turned the world upside down. The father stressed the steady escalation of the conflict and its continental nature. George Washington had come from distant Virginia to Massachusetts to take command of the "Grand American Army" besieging the British in Boston.

Ben told William the latest news from Europe—the British were hiring thousands of German troops to bolster their army. He argued that no matter how many foreign troops they hired—George III was reportedly also negotiating with the Russians—he could never conquer America. The most his army could do was set up some enclaves along the coast. The moment the king's soldiers ventured into the interior, they would be trapped and annihilated.

The heart of Benjamin's argument was the importance of William acting now. Timing was crucial. Congress would soon appoint generals to serve under Washington. William's service in the French and Indian War made him well qualified for one of these commissions. If he preferred a political post, there would soon be numerous tasks he was even more qualified to undertake. When it came to national reputation, he was one of the few men in the colonies who could match George Washington.

William shook his head and argued back. He told Ben most colonists were not in favor of independence. Only a small faction favored this drastic, treasonous step. Earlier in the year, the rebels in New Jersey had formed a Provincial Congress. When they levied taxes and drafted men into a militia, a negative reaction had swept the state.

The governor insisted that the pro-independence minority had forced the British government into acts of war, such as Bunker Hill. He flourished a letter from Lord Dartmouth, the American secretary in the British cabinet, urging him to press the New Jersey legislature to consider a recent conciliatory proposal from Prime Minister Lord North. Finally, William scoffed at the idea that America, a country that had trouble paying its royal governors' salaries, could win a war that would cost millions against the richest most powerful nation on earth.

Mournfully, the unhappy father rode back to Philadelphia. A few days later, William sent him copies of Lord Dartmouth's letter, and the minutes of recent sessions of the New Jersey Assembly, in which there had been no hint of revolutionary tendencies. The governor signed the letter, "Your ever dutiful and affectionate son."

On November 15, 1775, Governor Franklin made his move. He summoned his colony's assembly to meet in Burlington, New Jersey. He was betting on his long tenure in office, his famous name, and his frequent declarations that the rights of the people and the prerogatives of the Crown were equally dear to him. Other factors further increased his chances of success. New Jersey was largely rural. It had no big cities in which agitators could fester. Nor was there a newspaper to fan the flames of resentment.

On November 16, Governor Franklin told the Assembly that he was troubled by the "present unhappy situation of publick affairs." He declared that he wished to say nothing that would "endanger the harmony of the present session." He then proceeded to say a great deal that endangered the harmony of the whole American Revolution. He told the legislators that "His Majesty laments their neglecting the resolution of last February 20th." This was the offer from Britain's prime minister to exempt from further taxation any colony that voted to contribute its just share to the common defense of the empire.

The governor's father had described this so-called "Conciliatory Resolution" as the equivalent of a highwayman brandishing a pistol at a stagecoach window. But William Franklin's solemn voice and earnest manner gave no hint of this opinion. He went on to tell the assemblymen why he had chosen not to flee to one of the British men of war that were anchored in New York harbor. He did not wish the king to think New Jersey was in "actual rebellion" as other states obviously were. Everyone knew His Majesty was taking "all necessary steps" for putting down the rebellion with the same severity that had seen the defeat of recent uprisings in Scotland and Ireland. William professed to be deeply distressed at the thought that New Jersey might be exposed to such punishment. He begged the assem-

Lithograph of William Franklin from a Bas-relief. (*New York Public Library*)

blymen to persuade the people not to bring "such calamities" on their peaceful, prosperous province.

If they did not agree with him, the governor continued, if they wanted him to depart, all they had to do was tell him. He was well aware that "sentiments of independency" were being voiced by some people. Essays in newspapers in Philadelphia and New York ridiculed those who feared "this horrid measure." Then, with masterful persuasion, William told the assemblymen they would do their country "an essential service" if they declared their sentiments in "full and explicit terms" that would "discourage the attempt."

Not a word was spoken against the governor's exhortation. William made sure this tacit agreement would continue by announcing that the king had granted a request New Jersey had been making for a decade. They would be permitted to print 100,000 pounds in bills of credit, which would serve as badly needed paper money. The assembly responded by voting to form a committee that would petition George III "to use his interposition to prevent the threatened effusion of blood" and to express their great desire for the "restoration of peace and harmony on constitutional principles." Even more startling were resolutions sent to New Jersey's delegates in the Continental Congress, forbidding them to vote for "any propositions . . . that may separate the colony from the mother country."

It was a truly incredible performance, the incredibility magnified tenfold by its time and place, less than a half day's journey from the Continental Congress in Philadelphia. At that seat of rebellious government, delegates discussed enlarging George Washington's army and worried about the problems being encountered by the army they had sent into Canada earlier in the year to bring the "fourteenth colony" into their revolution. Also on the docket was advice to several colonies to form their own governments and take no more orders from royal officials. Engulfed in this ever swifter current toward independence, the congressmen could not believe their eyes or ears when they heard what Governor Franklin and his assembly were doing across the Delaware River in Burlington.

It did not take a Machiavelli or a Julius Caesar to discern that if New Jersey's petition got to George III and he bestowed still more proofs of his generosity from his ample exchequer, the chances were alarmingly good that other wavering colonies such as Maryland and New York (which had already ordered their delegates not to vote for independence) would have second thoughts about loyalty to the penniless Continental Congress.

At this point in 1775, the percentage of Americans who favored independence was still relatively small. This was especially true in New Jersey. In many counties, the voters who favored independence barely numbered a hundred. If the king had even one or two opportunities to display his generosity (based, of course, on a colony's "submission") the deep wellsprings of feeling for England which were still a living reality in almost every American's consciousness would have swiftly swept the independence men into an impotent minority.

Even more probable was the instantaneous jealousy that would have seized every colony if New Jersey, New York, and Maryland won special favors from the king. The Continental union might vanish in the smoke and flames of mutual recrimination, overnight. Almost singlehandedly, William Franklin was dueling his father and the rest of the Continental Congress for control of the continent.

The men meeting in Philadelphia were equally aware of the stakes. Although they had not yet agreed on where they were marching— toward independence or eventual reconciliation—they were in total agreement on maintaining a united front. The very day they heard the news of the New Jersey Assembly's petition, they resolved unanimously that in the "present state of affairs" it would be "very dangerous to the liberties and welfare of America if any colony should separately petition the king or either house of Parliament."

The Continental Congress appointed a three-man committee to communicate this decision to the New Jersey Assembly. The committeemen were John Dickinson of Pennsylvania, George Wythe of Virginia, and John Jay of New York. Dickinson had long been Benjamin Franklin's chief political foe in Pennsylvania. Now Benjamin had to watch his enemy undertake the task of rescuing the Revolution from his Loyalist son. It reduced Franklin's power in Congress to something very close to zero. A man who could not persuade his own son to join the cause was unlikely to be respected as a political leader.

The following day, December 6, 1775, Dickinson, Wythe, and Jay were in Burlington, where they asked for permission to address the assembly. Behind the scenes, Governor Franklin desperately lobbied influential members to refuse to listen to them. But this was asking too much of American legislators in late 1775. A superb orator, Dickinson soon convinced a majority that their petition was a surrender to Britain's divide and conquer tactics. Only if they persuaded Parliament that they were not "a rope of sand" would they ever win redress of their grievances.

John Jay followed Dickinson to the podium and made a shrewd suggestion. He pointed out that Congress had already presented an "Olive Branch Petition" to Parliament earlier in the year (John Dickinson had been its writer and sponsor). The British had ignored it with the pompous assertion that Congress had no legal standing. Wouldn't it be better to urge His Majesty and his friends to reconsider that perfectly reasonable plea for reconciliation, rather than submit one of their own? The assembly, already uncomfortable about their rebuke from the Continental Congress, seized on Jay's idea as a perfect out. They resolved that their petition be "referred" until the king responded to the olive branch plea.

Governor Franklin could only watch in frustration as his attempt to build a backfire against independence flickered out. He soon discovered that he had ignited another kind of blaze, crackling with suspicion and hatred, in New Jersey's independence men. Before the year 1776 ended, a still defiant William Franklin would be a prisoner in Connecticut. His father, abandoning all hope of becoming a leader in Congress, accepted the task of going to France to persuade England's inveterate enemy to become an ally of Revolutionary America. Ben Franklin's triumph in this seemingly impossible assignment would have a decisive impact on America's struggle for independence.

Russia and the American War for Independence

❀❧ NORMAN DESMARAIS ❧❀

The use of foreign troops in time of war was not an uncommon practice in the seventeenth and eighteenth centuries. Much as we have treaties, like NATO, for mutual support, eighteenth-century countries banded together, particularly along family lines, as royal families intermarried to secure and promote their economic and political interests.

When the troubles between England and her American colonies turned to armed conflict in 1775, the war was not popular in Britain. The country could no longer count on its usual sources for new recruits into the military as they did not support the war. Moreover, recruiting and training was a lengthy process, so, in conjunction with recruiting and training, Britain sought experienced soldiers. So Britain turned to foreign troops. She first turned to Russia for help.

Lord William Legge, 2nd Earl of Dartmouth, Secretary of State for the American Department, began making overtures to Catherine II, Empress of Russia even before King George III proclaimed the colonies in rebellion on August 23, 1775. (News of the king's proclamation didn't arrive in America until October 31, 1775.) Catherine had veteran troops available who had just fought a successful war against the Turks (1768 to 1774). She expressed her desire to have the continued good will of the King of England, but made no mention of supplying soldiers. The English envoy did not comprehend the significance of Catherine's shrewd remarks. When Britain made a formal request for a loan of 20,000 troops, the empress refused to send any help, due largely to pressure from Frederick the Great of Prussia. She expressed the hope that the American conflict might be settled by peaceful means.

Yet, the Earl of Dartmouth wrote to Major General William Howe on September 5, 1775, telling him that the Empress of Russia gave "the most ample assurances of letting us have any number of infantry that may be wanted." He requested 20,000 men and planned to send them to Quebec in the spring. He expected to have an equal number of British troops in North America to act with them.[1]

Reports on negotiations between Britain and Russia put the number of troops at between 13,000 and 100,000. They expected the number to be on the low side because the British people seemed rather averse to "hiring any more Troops, being already burdened with Taxes."[2]

France and Spain opposed Russia's entry into the war and planned to do their utmost to thwart Britain's effort. A schooner departed from Nantes, France on, October 11, 1775 and arrived at Providence, Rhode Island, about mid-November. The captain reported that the Empress of Russia had agreed to furnish Great Britain with a body of troops to serve in America and that "a great naval armament was preparing at Brest, said to be destined to intercept the Russian fleet in the Baltic."[3]

The news of possible Russian involvement created consternation in the colonies. When a privateer from Beverly, Massachusetts, captured five empty transports, part of a fleet of 200 vessels heading from New York to England, some people wondered whether she was going to bring over some Russians or provisions.[4]

However, Lord Dartmouth wrote to General Howe, on October 27, 1775, advising him that the prospect of troops from Russia was doubtful at best.[5]

1. C.O. 5, 92, folios 238—239d; entry in C.O. 243, 75-76; C.O. 5/ 92, fol. 238; C.O. 42, 34 fos. 165-1607d; entry in the C.O. 43, 8, 174-177, all in K. G. Davies, *Documents of the American Revolution 1770-1783* (Shannon: Irish University Press 1972, 1981), 10:74, 77. Extract of a Letter from Plymouth, Feb. 4, *New-York Gazette, and Weekly Mercury*. April 28, 1777. President Phillips Callback to the Earl of Dartmouth, January 5, 1776, C.O. 226/6, fol. 78. in Davies, *Documents*, 12:40.
2. Richard Harrison to Willing Morris & Co., Martinique, August 22, 1776, in *Naval Documents of the American Revolution*. (Washington, DC: Government Printing Office, 1962-2015), 6:277. Extract of a Letter from Captain Dennison, of the *Expedition* Transport, Halifax, September 2, 1776, *New-York Gazette, and Weekly Mercury*. January 13, 1777. *The Pennsylvania Ledger: or the Virginia, Maryland, Pennsylvania, & New-Jersey Weekly Advertiser*, November 9, 1776. *The Connecticut Gazette; and the Universal Intelligencer*, November 1, 1776. *Dunlap's Pennsylvania Packet or, the General Advertiser*, November 12, 1776. *The Virginia Gazette*, November 22, 1776, and November 29, 1776. *The Connecticut Courant, and Hartford Weekly Intelligencer*, October 28, 1776.
3. *Freeman's Journal, or New-Hampshire Gazette*, December 3, 1776. *Pennsylvania Journal*, January 29, 1777, and March 5, 1777. *Freeman's Journal*, February 11, 1777.
4. *Freeman's Journal*, December 10, 1776.
5. Dartmouth to Major General William Howe, C.O. 5, 92, fos. 275-277 D; entry in C.O. 5, 243, 91-93, all in Davies, *Documents*, 10:112.

General Howe replied to the Earl of Dartmouth, on November 26, 1775, proposing to strengthen Halifax, provide for the blockade of Boston, and take Rhode Island with 10 battalions the following spring. Each battalion would incorporate 100 hired Hanoverians or Hessians without officers and 100 volunteers of English militia. He also wanted to add 4000 Russians against an estimated 10,000 rebels in Rhode Island.[6]

George Sackville Germain, 1st Viscount Sackville, called Lord George Germain, had succeeded the Earl of Dartmouth by January 5, 1776. He wrote to General Howe approving his plan for the spring campaign. He estimated that Howe would need 6100 more men but thought that adding foreign troops to the British battalions would be liable to objections. He decided instead to raise the troops by recruiting. He acknowledged that the negotiations with Russia had failed but he was "in treaty with other states for different corps amounting in the whole to upward of 17,000 men, and I think those treaties are brought so near to an issue that they cannot fail." He expected to send 10,000 foreign troops to General Howe.[7]

General Howe wrote to Lord Germain, on November 30, 1776, proposing that the winter campaign shift to South Carolina and Georgia. He anticipated needing no less than 10 ships of the line and a reinforcement of 15,000 troops "which I should hope may be had from Russia or from Hanover and other German states, particularly some Hanoverian chasseurs." This would increase the army in the southern district to 35,000 effective men "to oppose 50,000 that the American Congress has voted for the service of next campaign."[8]

General Howe's request for 15,000 foreign troops "really alarmed" Lord Germain because he "could not see the least chance of my being able to supply you with the Hanoverians or even with the Russians in time." When Lord Germain realized that General Howe's army would consist of 35,000 men if he were reinforced with 4000 German troops (which he expected to procure) along with 800 additional Hessian chasseurs and about 1800 British recruits, he was satisfied that General Howe would have an army equal to his wishes. Lord

6. Howe to Dartmouth, November 26, 1775, C.O. 5, 92, fos. 318-327 d, in Davies, *Documents*, 10:138.

7. George Germain to Howe, January 5, 1776, C.O. 5, 93, fos. 1-9 d entry in C.O. 5, 243, in Davies, *Documents*, 10:175; 12:34. *The Parliamentary register; or, History of the proceedings and debates of the House of commons [and the House of lords . . . 1774-1780]* (London: J. Stockdale, 1802), 4:334.

8. November 30, 1776, Howe to Germain, November 30, 1776, C.O. 5/93 fol. 304, in Davies, *Documents*, 12:265.

Germain also thought that the enemy must be greatly weakened and depressed by Howe's successes and hoped that Howe would be able to recruit provincial troops, so he ordered cloth for 3000 additional uniforms and camp equipage for 8000 to be sent to General Howe.[9]

British relations with Russia seem to have improved by July 1777. General Howe thought the addition of 10,000 Russian troops "would ensure the success of the war."[10] British newspapers reported that Catherine the Great would send 30,000 troops to subdue the Americans and to maintain and recruit them for two years at her own expense if the British government would cede the island of Minorca to her. If Parliament acquiesced, the addition of Minorca to Russia's possessions in the Black Sea and her free navigation in the Archipelago would give Russia control of the entire Mediterranean and Levant (eastern Mediterranean extending from Greece to Cyrenaica) trade, making her the greatest maritime power in Europe.[11]

A letter from Stockholm dated July 30, 1777, erroneously stated that Britain, Russia, and the King of Prussia concluded a treaty which would add 36,000 Russians and 12,000 German troops to the army payroll. Britain would also raise 24 regiments of 500 men each in England and Ireland, bringing the army in America to at least 80,000 men.[12]

George III refused Russia's request for Minorca and the treaty was never ratified, so Russia never sent any troops to America. However, Catherine the Great proclaimed the League of Armed Neutrality on February 29, 1780. It was conceived by the Danes and subscribed to by Sweden and several other European nations to protect free trade between neutral countries and those at war. While it focused primarily on ships from the Netherlands, the league resisted all search efforts at sea. Russia even entered into a treaty to protect neutral shipping with Denmark and Sweden in wartime. England received the principles of the Treaty from her Russian ambassador on April 1, 1780, but would not recognize them as "rights" which would undermine her most effective military weapon, the blockade.

---

9. Germain to Howe, January 14, 1777, C.O. 5/94 fol. 1, in Davies, *Documents*, 14:32.
10. Howe to Germain, July 7, 1777, C.O. 5/94 fol. 260, in Davies, *Documents*, 14:129-131.
11. *Rivington's New-York Gazette: or the Connecticut, Hudson's River, New-Jersey, and Quebec Weekly Advertiser*, October 11, 1777.
12. *Pennsylvania Ledger: or the Weekly Advertiser*, November 19, 1777.

England disregarded Armed Neutrality, so Catherine created an armed fleet to enforce its principles and called on other nations to join. The fleet consisted of 84 Russian, Danish, and Swedish warships. Most of the European nations signed on, but, when Holland indicated her willingness to join, the British government declared war on the Dutch in December 1780 rather than have them enter into an alliance with the Russians.[13]

Catherine attempted to use the League of Armed Neutrality to mediate an end to the American War of Independence in December 1780 but negotiations broke down and the British surrender at Yorktown terminated the effort at a mediated peace.

13. *Encyclopedia of the American Revolution*, Harold E. Selesky, ed. (Detroit: Charles Scribner's Sons, 2007), 1:24-25. *The Encyclopedia of the American Revolutionary War: a political, social, and military history*, Gregory Fremont-Barnes, Richard Alan Ryerson, ed. (Santa Barbara, CA: ABC-CLIO, 2006), 2:694-696.

George Galphin and the War in the South, 1775–1780

❦ BRYAN RINDFLEISCH ❦

At the same time that George Washington and the Continental army besieged Thomas Gage and his forces at Boston in November 1775, Britain's Superintendent of Indian Affairs in the South, John Stuart, sent a letter to Gage. Within, Stuart warned Gage that his situation had grown considerably precarious in the South, as "the competition for the friendship of the Indian Nations in this district will be great." Yet if anyone was able to handle the complexities and nuances of England's alliances with Native Americans, it was Stuart, a former trader among the Cherokee who also cultivated personal ties with the Creek, Choctaw, and Chickasaw—the four major indigenous powers in the south. Why, then, did Stuart try and temper the expectations of his superiors, and as early as 1775? As Stuart's correspondence during the war reveals, he time and again took up the pen to complain that "the competition between me and the Rebel Agents for the Friendship of the Indians has been very great."

Who, or what, had Stuart so anxious about his chances to enlist indigenous leaders? As Stuart divulged, it was "The Person Employed by the disaffected of Carolina and Georgia to Counteract me . . . one George Galphin who has for many years past carried on an extensive trade to" the Native peoples in the South. Stuart feared Galphin's "weight and consequence, [which] has been greatly increased by his having been for several years past employed" by the empire "to conduct whatever business [it] had to transact in [the] nation[s]." In short, the revolutionaries had a Stuart of their own, and dare say, a man of greater means and connections in the Native South than Stuart himself.[1]

1. John Stuart to General Gage, November 15, 1775, *American Archives: Documents of*

It should come as no surprise, then, that Stuart attempted—rather unsuccessfully—to convince indigenous leaders not to listen to Galphin, for "Mr. Galphin is a Trader but he is not a Beloved Man; he tells you that he will supply you . . . But I will tell you the Truth; he cannot." According to Stuart, only when "the Rebels are reduced to Obedience and Reason" would Native peoples again "have plenty amongst you and be happy." When words failed, though, as they often did for Stuart in the first years of the war, he plotted with the governor of East Florida, Patrick Tonyn, to get rid of their Galphin problem. Tonyn cryptically instructed a group of Florida Loyalists under the command of Samuel Moore in early 1777[2] to proceed to Georgia and "do the Business without any of the Kings Warriors." What exactly was Moore's business? "to Kill [George] Galphin."[3]

the American Revolution, 1774-1776, ed. Peter Force, Series 5, Volume 3 (Washington, D.C.: Government Printing Office, 1837), 714-715 ("friendship"); John Stuart to William Knox, March 10, 1777, *William Knox Papers, 1757-1811,* Box 10: Indian Presents, Reminiscences, & Anecdotes, Folder 3, William L. Clements Library, University of Michigan, Ann Arbor, MI ("Rebel Agents"); John Stuart to the Earl of Dartmouth, October 25, 1775, *Early American Indian Documents: Treaties and Laws, 1607-1789, Volume XIV: South Carolina and North Carolina Treaties, 1756-1775,* ed. Alden T. Vaughan (Bethesda, MD: University Publications of America, 1989-), 380-381 ("Counteract me," "weight and consequence," "business").

2. Moore and his Florida Loyalists were infamously known among the revolutionaries in Georgia, having fled that colony at the outset of the war, afterwards organizing themselves into guerilla units that raided the Georgia frontier. As early as summer 1776, newspapers and correspondence between revolutionary leaders fixated on the attacks by "Messr. Moore . . . at the head of a body of plunderers, [who] have been *SENT* into the Province of Georgia. These freebooters, in the most cruel and wanton manner, destroyed the crops, broke up the plantations, drove off the cattle, and carried away the negroes belonging to several of the Georgia planters," leaving the province of Georgia "in the greatest distress." "Extract of a Letter to a Gentleman in London," August 20, 1776, *American Archives,* Series 5, 1:1076.

3. John Stuart to the Lower Creeks, December 4, 1775, *Early American Indian Documents: Treaties and Laws, 1607-1789, Volume XII: Georgia and Florida Treaties, 1764-1775,* ed. John T. Juricek (Bethesda, MD: University Publications of America, 1989-), 493-494 ("Beloved Man," "Truth," "Obedience"); Patrick Tonyn to John Perryman, January 24, 1777, *Board of Trade and Secretaries of State: America and West Indies, Original Correspondence, Board of Trade: East Florida, 1763-1777,* Colonial Office Records, CO 5/557, British National Archives, Kew: Great Britain, 321-322 ("do the Business"); Robert Scott Davis Jr., "George Galphin and the Creek Congress of 1777," in *Wes Taukchiray Papers—Galphin File,* MS #198u-200u, South Caroliniana Library, University of South Carolina, Columbia, SC, 8 ("Samuel Moore"); John Rutledge to Unknown, August 30, 1777, *John Rutledge Papers, 1739-1800,* MS mfm R. 281, Slide 3510, South Caroliniana Library, University of South Carolina, Columbia, SC ("to Kill Galphin").

Upon receiving intelligence that a "gang of the Florida Scout . . . are after Mr. Galphin," Gen. Lachlan McIntosh of the Continental army scrambled to "collect all [our] Regiment that can be got together . . . to intercept [that] party." However, McIntosh failed to reach Galphin in time, and Moore's "Party . . . way-laid the Road on the day when Mr. Galphin was to have set out with [their] Indian [allies]" from his Silver Bluff plantation. But, as luck would have it, Galphin "received Information of it" ahead of time, undoubtedly from his Creek supporters Nea Mico and Neaclucko of Cusseta. Galphin therefor remained behind while a unit of the Georgia militia, led by Capt. John Gerard, took Galphin's place in escorting their indigenous allies back to Creek country. Despite the armed escort, though, Moore and his men, mistaking Gerard for Galphin—"they being much alike"—still ambushed the militia and during the melee, shot Gerard dead. Although the militia, and the Creeks under their protection, returned fire and gave chase "till they [the Loyalists] took to a Swamp," Moore and his men ultimately escaped, all the while believing they had killed Galphin. As Stuart shortly thereafter gloated in his letters to London, "We have a flying report that Mr. Galphin is Dead!" But even when Stuart learned the truth that Galphin still lived, he tried to arrange Galphin's assassination again, sending the same man to finish the job. Only this time, Galphin was waiting. In the dead heat of July 1778, a motley crew of Georgia militia and Creek Indians—sent by Galphin—"discovered . . . Moore" and during their brief exchange of gunfire, "Moore . . . was killed, and 9 of his gang taken prisoner."[4]

So what can this strange series of events, and more so Stuart's fears and anxieties about his rival, tell us about the American Revolution? For starters, George Galphin was not only an important figure, but an essential component of the American war effort in the South.

---

4. Samuel Elbert to General Lachlan McIntosh, August 16, 1777, *The Papers of Lachlan McIntosh, 1774-1799*, Georgia Historical Society, Savannah, GA ("after Mr. Galphin," "Regiment"); John Rutledge to Unknown, August 30,1777, *John Rutledge Papers, 1739-1800* ("way-laid the road," "Information," John Gerard, "much alike"); "A Talk from Nea Mico and Neaclucko to George Galphin," October 13, 1777, *George Galphin Letters, 1777-1779*, in *The Papers of Henry Laurens*, Roll 17: Papers Concerning Indian Affairs, South Carolina Historical Society, Charleston, SC (Nea Mico and Neaclucko); July 8, 1778, *Gazette of the State of South Carolina*, South Caroliniana Library, University of South Carolina, Columbia, SC ("Swamp," "discovered," "prisoner"); John Stuart to William Knox, August 26, 1777, *Board of Trade and Secretaries of State: America and West Indies, Original Correspondence, Secretary of State: Indian Affairs, 1763-1784*, Colonial Office Records, CO 5/78, British National Archives, Kew: Great Britain, 220-221 ("Dead").

However, historians of the Revolutionary War have altogether neglected, or outright dismissed, this man and his efforts to counteract
British efforts to draw the Creek, Cherokee, Choctaw, and Chickasaw
nations into the conflict.[5] One could legitimately argue that Galphin
was the one man who stood in the way of the revolutionaries losing
the South between 1775 and 1778, before the British switched their
focus from the northern colonies to the south as part of their
"Southern Strategy." In fact, Galphin proved so important in undermining British influence in the Native South that British leaders determined the only way to gain the upper hand was to kill Galphin and
remove him from the equation altogether.

Now who was George Galphin? As colonial newspapers attest, he
was "a Native of Ireland—and a Gentleman, distinguished by the
peculiar Excellency of his Character—of unbounded Humanity and
Generosity—incapable of the least Degree of Baseness—and so much
esteemed throughout the whole Creek Nation" and other indigenous
societies in the South. Yet Galphin hailed from humble beginnings as
the eldest son of a poor linen-weaving family in County Armagh,
Ireland. In 1737, he left Ireland for South Carolina where he entered
the deerskin trade as a lowly Indian trader for the firm Archibald
McGillivray & Co. But over the course of three decades, Galphin rein-
vented himself as a reputable trader and merchant, and established a
reputation as one of the most trustworthy and dependable intermedi-
aries for Native and European peoples in the South, which only added
to the weight of his growing political and commercial importance. As
the naturalist William Bartram observed, Galphin "possessed the most
extensive trade, connexions, and influence, amongst the South and
South-West Indian tribes." In particular, Galphin owed much of his
importance to his Creek wife Metawney of Coweta, who ushered
Galphin into the Creek world and facilitated his relationships with her
clansmen like Escotchaby and Sempoyaffee, two of the primary headmen of the Lower Creeks during the mid to late eighteenth-century.[6]

5. It should be noted that the Cherokee were the exception to the rule here, as a portion of the Cherokee nation, known as the Chickamagua "secessionists," led by the
young warrior Dragging Canoe, seized the chaos of the revolution as an opportunity
to expel Euro-American settlers from Cherokee territories. The resulting, so-called
"Cherokee War of 1776" stood in stark contrast to the neutrality of the Creek, and to
a lesser degree, the Chickasaw and Choctaw. For further information, refer to Tyler
Boulware, *Deconstructing the Cherokee Nation: Town, Region, and Nation among
Eighteenth Century Cherokees* (Gainesville: University Press of Florida, 2011).
6. Galphin's family and friends testified after his death that he "had a considerable and
decided control and influence over the Indians . . . That this influence arose as well

These men in turn propelled Galphin into the major political and commercial circles of the Native South, elevating Galphin to a position as one of the premier cultural brokers between indigenous and European worlds, especially for the Creeks and the British empire. Such connections throughout the Native South also attracted a wealth of imperial and colonial authorities, as well as transatlantic merchants, who flocked to Galphin in search of political and commercial relationships with him. For when it came to Indian affairs or the deerskin trade in the South, nothing happened without Galphin knowing about it or having a hand in it. Galphin was, for all intents and purposes, a one-man force of nature, often called upon by colonial and imperial administrators, like James Habersham, to serve at the empire's behest. As Habersham confided to Galphin, "you have it more in your power than any person I know to induce the Creeks" or other indigenous peoples to a particular purpose.[7]

Of course, then, the revolutionaries wanted someone with Galphin's prestige and connections that rivaled, if not eclipsed, Stuart's own. It is no coincidence that Continental army generals, such as Benjamin Lincoln, and Continental Congress delegates, like Henry Laurens, approached Galphin as early as October 1775, as "We think it of great moment that you Should have a personal interview with [the] Indians" on their behalf. As many of these revolutionaries understood, the Native peoples of the South—and particularly the Creek nation—held Galphin in high regard. According to indigenous leaders like the Tallassee King, Galphin "was looked upon as an Indian." Also, contrary to Stuart's claims, many headmen perceived "Mr. Galphin [as a] Beloved Man," and as one who "had the Mouth of Charleston," a title by which Native leaders recognized—and even

from his extensive and honorable trade amongst them, his connexion with one of their women of Indian family distinction, and by whom he had children, as for his kindness and hospitality toward the Indians, always receiving them with good humor and furnishing them amply with such necessaries, as they stood in need of at his hospitable dwelling at Silver Bluff as at his trading houses in the Indian nation." "Bonds, Bills of Sale & Deeds of Gift," October 27, 1809, *Le Conte Genealogical Collection, 1900-1943*, MS #71, Book D, Box 6, Folder 9: Galphin, Hargrett Rare Book & Manuscript Library, University of Georgia, Athens, GA, 270-272.

7. February 14, 1774, *South Carolina Gazette, 1732-1775*, MS CscG, South Caroliniana Library, University of South Carolina, Columbia, SC ("Native of Ireland," "esteemed"); Thomas P. Slaughter, ed., *William Bartram: Travels & Other Writings* (New York: Library of America, 1996), 259-261 ("connexions"); James Habersham to George Galphin, October 8, 1771, *Habersham Family Papers, 1712-1842*, MS #1787, Folder 4, Georgia Historical Society, Savannah, GA ("more in your power").

designated—Galphin as their proxy to the Carolina and Georgia colonies. Further, the revolutionary leadership knew that Stuart hated Galphin with a passion, having written to his acquaintances in London that "I never suffered myself to be duped by him, for neither his knowledge nor intelligence were never necessary for me." In Stuart's mind, Galphin was a rival to his own power as the Superintendent of Indian Affairs, as Galphin was not "in any respect responsible to the Superintendent, [who] may with impunity oppose his measures and . . . render them abortive." In short, Galphin was a massive thorn in Stuart's side, and the revolution's leaders sought to exploit such a rivalry.[8]

However, Galphin was at best a reluctant revolutionary. Even though he promised the American rebels to do all "in my power . . . to keep the [Indians] peaceable," he admitted that "I am sorry an Independence is declared for I was still in hopes affairs would have been settled, but now it is all over." In fact, he dreaded "they were [all] in Hell . . . now as there is an Independence declared" as there would be "so many brave men killed & God knows when there will be an end to it."

Galphin's initial reticence to support the revolutionary movement stemmed from his fears of what the war might do to his family. To Galphin, family meant everything; he surrounded himself with, employed, protected, and bequeathed all his wealth to his kinsmen. The Galphin clan in North America included his Creek, Irish-French, and African children; his Scots-Irish sisters, nephews, nieces, aunts, and uncles; his Anglo and Scots-Irish cousins, nephews, and nieces; as

8. South Carolina Council of Safety to George Galphin, October 22, 1775, *The Papers of Henry Laurens, Volume X: December 12, 1774–January 6, 1776*, ed. Philip M. Hamer and David R. Chesnutt (Columbia: University of South Carolina Press, 1988), 491-492 ("great moment"); Tallassee King to the Governor & Council of Georgia, September 22, 1784, *Creek Indian Letters, Talks & Treaties, 1705-1837*, W.P.A. Georgia Writers' Project, MS #1500, Box 60, Hargrett Rare Book & Manuscript Library, University of Georgia, Athens, GA, 161-163 ("as an Indian"); "Letter from Timothy Barnard to the Cussetas," June 2, 1784, *Creek Indian Letters, Talks & Treaties, 1705-1837*, 140-142 ("Beloved Man"); Tallassee King's Son to the Governor & Council of Georgia, n.d. 1783, *Creek Indian Letters, Talks & Treaties, 1705-1837*, 117-120 ("Mouth of Charleston"); James Graham to John Graham, n.d. 1776, *Board of Trade and Secretaries of State: America and West Indies, Original Correspondence, Secretary of State: Miscellaneous, 1771-1778*, Colonial Office Records, CO 5/154-157, British National Archives, Kew: Great Britain, 367 ("duped by him"); John Stuart to the Earl of Hillsborough, June 12, 1772, *Documents of the American Revolution, Volume V: Transcripts, 1772*, ed. K.G. Davies (Shannon, Ireland: Irish University Press, 1972-), 114-117 ("abortive").

well as his Creek, French, and Irish wives and mistresses.[9] Needless to say, Galphin was a family man, and dutifully feared for the futures of his children and kinsmen. But when push came to shove, Galphin embraced the rebellion, as rumors spread that Stuart intended to incite the Native South against the revolutionaries. Fearing for the safety of his family, Galphin felt "'twas a Duty Incumbent on me . . . knowing my interest in the Creeks was so great, that it was not in the power of any Man [i.e., Stuart] to set them upon us if I opposed them." By siding with the rebels, Galphin gambled everything on a revolution he did not necessarily believe in, motivated by his concern for family and their futures now threatened by the empire. As Galphin reveals to us, then, one's loyalties during the war were just as much defined by one's personal circumstances as they were by imperial or republican ideologies and identities.[10]

To deal with the imminent threat that Stuart posed to the colonies, the South Carolina and Georgia Councils of Safety—later followed by the Continental Congress—quickly appointed Galphin their "Indian commissioner." But in assuming such a role, Galphin demanded the American "Indian Department" operate out of his home at Silver Bluff, staffed by the family and friends he surrounded himself with. Galphin

9. Galphin and Metawney had three Creek children—George Jr., John, and Judith—while Galphin's relationship with his French mistress, Rachel Dupree, produced two children, Thomas and Martha. In addition, Galphin was a large slave-owner and violently exploited the sex of his female slaves, including Nitehuckey by whom he had a daughter Rose, another slave named Rose by whom he fathered a daughter Barbara, along with the slave Sappho by whom he had two daughters, Rachael and Betsy. Even though born into slavery, Galphin's African children were taken from their mothers, put into the Galphin household, and freed by Galphin in his last will and testament (1776). As for Galphin's extended family, he surrounded himself with his sisters from Ireland, Martha Crossley and Margaret Holmes, who brought their entire families to Galphin's Silver Bluff planation in the 1760s. The Crossley and Holmes families included Martha's husband-in-law William and their five children, and Margaret's husband-in-law William and their several children, including David Holmes who went on to become Galphin's right-hand man in the deerskin trade. Finally, Galphin invited and provided for his various nieces, nephews, uncles, aunts, and cousins of the Pooler, Pettycrew, Young, Trotter, Rankin, Robson, Lennard, McMurphy, Dunbar, Barnard, and Foster families (all a mix of Anglo, Irish, and Scottish descent). *Last Will and Testament of George Galphin,* April 4, 1776, 000051 .L51008, South Carolina Department of Archives and History, Columbia, SC.
10. George Galphin to Timothy Barnard, August 18, 1776, CO 5/77, British National Archives, 559-563 ("power," "Independence," "Hell," "God"); George Galphin to Henry Laurens, February 7, 1776, *The Papers of Henry Laurens, Volume XI: January 6, 1776–November 1, 1771,* ed. Philip M. Hamer and David R. Chesnutt (Columbia: University of South Carolina Press, 1988), 93-97 ("Duty").

thereafter transformed his plantation into a base of revolutionary resistance. In particular, he mobilized his connections in the Native South to create one of the largest information-gathering infrastructures in that region. As Stuart lamented, "it is impossible to prevent the Rebels having Emissaries and every sort of Intelligence . . . as every Trader has his Packhorsemen, and hirelings, and there is one perhaps two, three Traders in every Town of the [Indian] Nations with their hirelings." He concluded, "there cannot be then by any wonder that Mr. Galphin finds Spies and Tools amongst them." To make matters even worse for Stuart, Galphin maintained old—and cultivated new— alliances with many of the indigenous leaders in the South, a number of whom refused to go to war for either side, which was more than enough for Galphin. Furthermore, leaders like Captain Aleck of Cusseta, the Tallassee King and his "Son," the Handsome Fellow of Okfuskee, and Wills Friend, acted as Galphin's "Informer[s]" and relayed information to his "Spies and Tools." Galphin then redirected such information to the Councils of Safety, Gen. Benjamin Lincoln in Charleston, and to the Provincial and Continental Congresses.[11]

Galphin also converted Silver Bluff into a base of operations for the Continental army, allocating plantation resources and manpower to support the war effort. In 1776 and again in 1778, Galphin conspired with Gen. Charles Lee to lead an "irruption into . . . East Florida" with Lee at the head of an army, while Galphin would calm "the minds of the Creeks," a plan which Lee considered "of the highest consideration." In preparation for the expeditions, Galphin modified his "trading boats" to be troop carriers "fitted up in the manner of Spanish Launches with a piece of cannon in the prod," with intent "to go for [St.] Augustine" to seize that British fortification. Spanish observers in Havana marveled at "Maestre Galfen" who readied weapons, provisions, and soldiers for transport to East Florida. Despite Galphin's logistical maneuverings, the expeditions never materialized because plans for the invasion were discovered by British spies. Yet the Continental army also used Silver Bluff as a supply depot and a staging ground against Loyalist guerillas, leading to the construction of a "train of Artillery," an army hospital, and a permanent garrison on the plantation. As word of his "unwearied exertions" spread, most of those

---

11. Henry Laurens to George Galphin, October 4, 1775, *The Papers of Henry Laurens, Volume X*, 447-449 ("Indian Commissioner"); John Stuart to Patrick Tonyn, July 28, 1777, CO 5/557, British National Archives, 687-689 ("Emissaries," "Tools"); John Pigg to George Galphin, June 13, 1778, *George Galphin Letters, 1777-1779* ("Informer").

in support of the revolution knew Galphin's name, including George Washington.[12]

Of even greater importance, Silver Bluff emerged as the center for negotiations with the Native peoples of the South. For instance, in fall 1776, Galphin opened his doors to Creek leaders from the towns of Cusseta, Yuchi, Okfuskee, Tallassee, Hitcheta, Coolamies, and others, where he cautioned them not to listen to "the Kings people" and to remain "steadfast friends," offering a wealth of "goods for you here." In speaking to those Native headmen, Galphin reaffirmed his fictive familial ties to them, counseling "My Friend[s], I hope you nor none of your people will concern" yourself with the war. Native leaders responded in kind, that they "look upon Messr. Galphin . . . not only as Elder Brother but as Father and Mother," and that "Whatever Talks Galphin . . . shall send . . . [we] will stand to [it]." And in keeping with the familial theme, Galphin framed the Revolutionary War in terms that he and his indigenous allies understood best, that it was a "Family Affair between England & this Country," or a "dispute between a Father & his Children."[13]

12. "Opinion of the Georgia Council of Safety," August 19, 1776, *American Archives,* Series 5, Volume 1, 1052 ("irruption"); Charles Lee to the President of South Carolina, August 1, 1776, *Charles Lee Letterbook, July 2–August 27, 1776,* MS P3584, South Caroliniana Library, University of South Carolina, Columbia, SC, 50 ("minds"); Thomas Brown to John Stuart, September 29, 1776, CO 5/78, Reel 7, 544-549 ("trading boats," leaked information); Juan Joseph Eligio de la Puente to Diego Joseph Navarro, April 1, 1778, *Transcriptions of Records from Portada del Archivo General de Indias,* Texas Tech University in Seville, Spain, Edward E. Ayer Manuscript Collection, MS #1236, Newberry Library, Chicago, IL ("Maestre Galfen"); Benjamin Lincoln to Brigadier General Moultrie, April 22, 1779, *Benjamin Lincoln Papers, 1635-1974* [microfilm], Reel 3, University of Texas at Arlington, Arlington TX, 281-282 ("Artillery"); Benjamin Lincoln to George Galphin, July 9, 1779, *Benjamin Lincoln Papers, 1635-1974,* Reel 3, 385 ("hospital"); "Return of the Georgia Brigade of Continental Troops Commanded by Colonel John White," June 25, 1779, *Benjamin Lincoln Papers, 1635-1974,* Reel 4, 17 (garrison); Major General Robert Howe to General Gorge Washington, November 3, 1777, in *The Papers of George Washington: The Revolutionary War Series, Vol. 3,* ed. Philander D. Chase (Charlottesville: University of Virginia Press, 1985), 103-104 ("exertions").
13. George Galphin to the Creek Indians, Fall 1776, CO 5/78, Reel 7, 551 ("King's People," "many Ships," "goods," "Family Affair," "My Friend"); "Talks from the Commissioners of Indian Affairs for the Southern Department at Salisbury," November 13, 1775, *Henry Laurens Papers, Kendall Collection,* in *William Gilmore Simms Papers,* MS P, South Caroliniana Library, University of South Carolina, Columbia, SC ("Father"); "Journal of a Conference between the American Commissioners and the Creeks at Augusta," May 16-19, 1776, *Early American Indian Documents, Volume XII,* 183-190 ("Elder Brother").

While Galphin advocated for—and largely secured—the neutrality of the Creek and other Native populations in the South during 1776 and early 1777, the assassination attempt on his life dramatically changed things. In Galphin's mind, Stuart and his "Cowardly Dogs" had crossed a line and there was no turning back, particularly after Stuart put out a "£500 Reward for me Dead or live." From here on out, Galphin labored zealously to banish British agents from their stronghold in Creek Country, setting in motion what became known as the "British Expulsions of 1777."[14] Rallying his Native allies in fall 1777, Galphin managed to evict all of Stuart's traders and spies in the nation. As headmen from the town of Cusseta recalled that event, their warriors forced the British to "run off in the Night to Pensacola, after they were gone the Cusseta Women went over to their houses and pulled them down." Some of those British agents, like William McIntosh, barely escaped with their lives, after "a fellow called Long Crop from the Cussetas with some others yesterday came over here with a View to take my Scalp, [but] he mist his aim." Shortly after, Galphin reveled in the fact that he and his allies "got all Stuarts Commissioners Drove out of the nation [and] the [Creek] plundered . . . upwards of 100 horse Loads of ammunition and other goods that was Carried up there to give the Indians to Come to war against us." It seemed, then, by the end of 1777, Galphin had seized the upper hand, while further heartened by news from the north that a British army surrendered at Saratoga.[15]

However, the war took a darker turn for Galphin and the south in 1778 when the empire implemented its "Southern Strategy." Largely a response to France and Spain's entrance into the war that transformed that conflict into a global war, Britain turned its attentions toward the south in hopes of enlisting the large number of African slaves, Loyalists, and Native peoples to fight against the revolutionaries,

14. For the particulars of the "British Expulsions of 1777," see Bryan Rindfleisch, "'Our Lands are Our Life and Breath': Coweta, Cusseta, and the Struggle for Creek Territory and Sovereignty during the American Revolution," *Ethnohistory* Volume 60, No. 4 (Fall 2013), 581-603.

15. George Galphin to Henry Laurens, June 25, 1778, *The Papers of Henry Laurens, Volume XIII: March 15–July 6, 1778*, ed. Philip M. Hamer, David R. Chesnutt, and C. James Taylor (Columbia: University of South Carolina Press, 1992), 513-515 ("Dogs," "Reward"); "A Talk from the Head Men of the Upper and Lower Creeks—Nea Micko and Neaclucko to George Galphin," October 13, 1777, *George Galphin Letters, 1777-1779* ("Night," "Cussitaw Women"); William McIntosh to Alexander Cameron, July 6, 1777, CO 5/78, Reel 7 ("Long Crop"); George Galphin to Henry Laurens, October 13, 1777, *The Papers of Henry Laurens, Volume XI*, 552-553 ("plundered").

thereby freeing the British army to protect other parts of the empire, particularly the West Indies. After a string of British victories at Savannah and Augusta in December 1778 and January 1779, Galphin found himself cut off from his American allies and forced to fend for himself. Shortly thereafter, a band of Loyalists raided Galphin's stores, depriving him of a great quantity of trade goods he used to ensure the neutrality or support of indigenous leaders. Moreover, Galphin recognized that not only he, but also his entire family was in danger. Therefore, when the British threatened to come "upon us Like a Clape of thunder," Galphin wrote to his allies that "georgia is taken by the kings troops & all Continental troops is taken out of it." After which, Galphin guided his family away from Silver Bluff, "travel[ing] all night" until they reached a safe haven, where Galphin then "left them . . . & Returned back" to face the impending arrival of the British army. As Galphin intimated to his family and friends, "I Shall Stand as Long as I Can."[16]

Yet the British were not Galphin's only problem. Cut off from the lifeline of trade that sustained his efforts to keep the Native South peaceable or at least neutral, Galphin was at the mercy of what little supplies the Georgia revolutionaries had on hand. It wasn't nearly enough. After 1778, Galphin endured a chronic shortage of goods that he could send to his indigenous allies, whereas Stuart enjoyed the full commercial might of the empire. To compound matters, those in the South Carolina Provincial Congress challenged Galphin's loyalty to the revolution. As Henry Laurens informed Galphin, there was "an attack upon your Character" by one Dr. David Gould and "Reverend [William] Tennant who had twice before intimated doubts of your attachment" to the cause. In particular, Gould and Tennant alleged that Galphin—unable to risk giving away supplies from his already depleted stores—angrily swore at them and stated, "Damn the Country [for] I have lost enough by it already." Such rumors about Galphin's hesitant loyalty persisted throughout the war. However, the greatest blow to Galphin came from his own family when two of his nephews—and intended successors—David Holmes and Timothy

---

16. George Galphin to Henry Laurens, December 29, 1778, *The Papers of Henry Laurens, Volume XV: December 9, 1778–September 1, 1782*, ed. Philip M. Hamer, David R. Chesnutt, and C. James Taylor (Columbia: University of South Carolina Press, 1999), 19-21 ("thunder," "kings troops"); George Galphin to Henry Laurens, March 28, 1779, *George Galphin Letters, 1777-1779* ("all night," "Returned back"); George Galphin to Henry Laurens, December 29, 1778, *The Papers of Henry Laurens, Volume XV*, 19-21 ("Long").

Barnard defected. Together, Holmes and Barnard redirected a significant portion of Galphin's resources to Stuart and the British, largely
in hopes of monopolizing "the Trade . . . to West Florida" then under
British control. To Galphin's horror, his nephews also joined Stuart as
"Commissioner[s] for exercising the Office of Superintendent of
Indian Affairs." This betrayal stung Galphin so badly that he filed a
codicil to his last will and testament by which he disinherited Holmes
and Barnard.[17]

To make matters even worse, the frontier inhabitants of Georgia—
even those who sided with the revolutionaries—undermined
Galphin's efforts to maintain peace between indigenous and Euro-
American peoples. As Galphin confided, "most of [those] people . . .
has wanted an Indian War Ever Since the Difference between
America & England, & [do] everything in their power to bring it on."
In one particular instance, backcountry residents invaded one of
Galphin's councils with Native leaders, where they threatened "three
or four Indians" and declared to Galphin "they will kill them wherever they meet him." On another occasion, Galphin alone faced the
wrath of these people, "Some of [whom] Said I had got the better of
them now in keeping the Indians peaceable, but it would not be Long
before they would Drive me and the Indians both to the Devil." Or
more explicitly, they "would Come & kill me & the Indians." Galphin
now found himself threatened on all sides; with the British army nearly upon him, without the supplies necessary to give indigenous allies
and neutrals, betrayed by members of his own family, and even suspected and threatened by those on the side of revolution.[18]

In early 1779, British forces under the command of Archibald
Campbell occupied Silver Bluff, renaming that place Fort
Dreadnought while putting Galphin under house arrest until he could

---

17. Henry Laurens to George Galphin, October 4, 1775, *The Papers of Henry Laurens,
Volume X*, 447-449 ("Character," "Tennent," "Damn"); James Durouzreaux to Galphin
Holmes & Co., December 15, 1775, *Henry Laurens Papers, Kendall Collection* ("West
Florida"); John Stuart to George Germain, 10 August 1778, CO 5/79, Reel 8, 27-29
("exercising"); April 6, 1776, *Last Will and Testament of George Galphin* ("disinheritance").
18. George Galphin to Henry Laurens, October 26, 1778, *The Papers of Henry Laurens,
Volume XIII*, 452-454 ("America & England"); George Galphin to William Jones,
October 26, 1776, *American Archives,* Series 5, Volume 3, 648-650 ("three or four");
George Galphin to William Jones October 26, 1776, *American Archives,* Series 5,
Volume 3, 648-650 ("wherever"); George Galphin to Henry Laurens, December 22,
1777, *The Papers of Henry Laurens, Volume XII: November 1, 1777–March 15, 1778*, ed.
Philip M. Hamer, David R. Chesnutt, and C. James Taylor (Columbia: University of
South Carolina Press, 1990), 175-177 ("Devil").

be put on trial for "high treason." But even though a prisoner of war, Galphin continued to undercut British Indian affairs in any way he could. For instance, he managed to sneak a year-long correspondence between himself and his revolutionary allies, at one point optimistically stating "we should still be able to drive the Enemy off or pen them up." In addition, Galphin continued an under-the-radar diplomacy with Native leaders, such as the Tallassee King, who ventured to Silver Bluff under the pretense of seeing their "friend." At one of these clandestine meetings, Galphin boasted that "We've been at war with the English for four years, and they couldn't beat us, what can they do now that the French and Spanish are on our side?" In return, the Tallassee King presented Galphin with a "white wing and Beads" to signify their continued support of the revolution. And when American propagandists learned of Galphin's intrigues, they used his example to inspire resistance against the English occupation of Georgia, citing "the unwearied endeavors of Mr. Galphin [to keep] the Indians" on their side. As British officials noted with anxiety, notwithstanding "the Submission of Mr. Galphin . . . a few days ago 18 of Galphin's party of Creek Indians returned in a Transport from visiting him . . . [and] have lately behaved very much Amiss." However, Galphin could not prolong the inevitable for long, particularly after the surrender of Charleston in May 1780, which for all intents and purposes secured British control over the South. As he awaited trial, all Galphin could do was watch as his wealth—intended to support his family—vanished before his eyes, confiscated under the Disqualifying Act of 1780. Galphin thereby lived out his final days being threatened with execution, cut off from his family and friends, and as witness to a British army seemingly on the verge of crushing the revolution. On December 1, 1780, George Galphin died a prisoner in his own home, never to see the dramatic reversal of American fortunes in 1781.[19]

19. January 30, 1779, *Journal of an Expedition against the Rebels of Georgia in North America under the Orders of Archibald Campbell, Esquire, Lieut. Colol. of His Majesty's 71st Regimt.* (Darien, GA: Ashantilly Press, 1981), 52-53 ("Campbell," "Galphin's capture"); "Memorial of Lachlan McGillivray on behalf of George Galphin," June 8, 1780, *Colonial Records of the State of Georgia, Volume XV: Journal of the Commons House of Assembly: October 30, 1769–June 16, 1782,* ed. Allen D. Candler (Atlanta: Franklin Publishing Co., 1907), 590-591 ("high treason"); George Galphin to Henry Laurens, March 18, 1779, *George Galphin Letters, 1777-1779* ("drive the enemy"); "A Talk delivered by George Galphin . . . to the Tallassee King and a Number of Warriours and Beloved Men," November 7, 1779, *George Galphin Letters, 1778-1780,* Edward E. Ayer Manuscript Collection, Vault Box Ayer MS 313, Newberry Library, Chicago, IL ("French and Spanish"); "A Talk delivered at Silver Bluff to George Galphin by the Tal-

While indigenous leaders like the Tallassee King and Fat King of Cusseta mourned the passing of their "old friend" and affirmed "Mr. Galphin's . . . good Talk . . . that we the red People and the white should live in Peace," they also promised to keep Galphin "in continual remembrance." But the same could not be said of the revolutionary movement and its leaders. For some inexplicable reason, Galphin has been exorcised from the collective memory of the American Revolution, a national forgetting that neglects not only the vital contributions of this man, but also the nature of the Revolutionary War in the south between 1775 and 1778. For most people today, the war from 1775 to 1778 unfolded solely to the North where Washington battled the Howe brothers and Henry Clinton, or Horatio Gates, Daniel Morgan, and Benedict Arnold surrounded and defeated the British at Saratoga. But what is lost in that narrative are the messy realities and dangerous possibilities in the South, in which powerful indigenous nations could have sided with the British and thereby tipped the balance of the war. But because of George Galphin and his labors from 1775 to 1778, that never happened, and the war in the North proceeded as it did because the revolutionaries did not have to contend with British strength in the South.[20]

So what did Galphin's family receive for his services rendered? Financial collapse, the loss of the family's patriarch and other kinsmen, and more surprisingly, a blackened reputation that persisted throughout the centuries. As early as 1800, the Georgia and federal legislatures both questioned whether or not Galphin "was a friend to the Revolution." Then, in 1809, family and friends were forced to testify that "Galphin . . . during the American war . . . [was] attached to the Common Cause" and, by "his utmost exertions," kept the Native peoples of the South "from taking part on either side of the political

lassee King," November 3, 1779, *George Galphin Letters, 1778-1780* ("white wing"); December 25, 1779, *Virginia Gazette, 1732-1780,* Issue 46, page 2, MS 900200 .P900049, South Carolina Department of Archives and History, Columbia, SC ("unwearied endeavors"); Alexander Cameron to the Commissioners of Indian Affairs, August 1780, CO 5/81, Reel 8, 592 ("Submission," "Amiss"); "British Disqualifying Act of 1780," July 1, 1780, *The Revolutionary Records of Georgia, Volume I: 1769-1782,* ed. Allen D. Candler (Atlanta: Franklin-Turner Co., 1908), 348-349.

20. "Talk delivered by the Tallassee King to the Governor & Council," September 20, 1784, *Georgia Creek Indian Letters, Talks & Treaties, 1705-1837,* 159-160 ("old friend," "remembrance"); "Talk from the Fat King of the Cussitaws," December 27, 1782, Telamon Cuyler Historical Manuscripts, 1754-1905, MS #1170, Series 1, Folder 25, Hargrett Rare Book & Manuscript Library, University of Georgia, Athens, GA ("good Talk").

question." In conclusion, it was determined that Galphin was "a decided Friend of the American Revolution." But then again in 1850, members of the House of Representatives declared "Galphin was not known to have been a Whig" and had by some unfathomable "act of ... toryism," betrayed the revolution. And such rumors and half-truths continued. It is about time, then, that the record should—and can—finally be set straight. While George Galphin was a reluctant revolutionary, he proved to be one of the Revolutionary War's most important figures in the South.[21]

21. "Bonds, Bills of Sale & Deeds of Gift," November 13, 1800, *Le Conte Genealogical Collection, 1900-1943*, Box 6, Folder 9: Galphin, 224-229 ("friend to the revolution"); "Bonds, Bills of Sale & Deeds of Gift," October 27, 1809, *Le Conte Genealogical Collection, 1900-1943*, Box 6, Folder 9: Galphin, 270-272 ("Common Cause," "exertions," "political question," "friend"); July 6, 1850, *Congressional Globe: Debates and Proceedings of the Thirty-First Congress*, First Session, The Library of Congress, Washington, D.C., 931 (memory.loc.gov/cgi-bin/ampage) ("Whig," "toryism").

"The Sale of the Hessians" and the Franklin Legend

HUGH T. HARRINGTON

Since 1874 a growing assumption, indeed an assumption expanding to the status of "fact," has arisen that a document known as "The Sale of the Hessians" was a piece of propaganda written by Benjamin Franklin. A quick online search using the search terms of "Sale of the Hessians" and "Franklin" will bring up many books, college courses, and websites confidently proclaiming that Franklin wrote the piece. However, some hedge their bets just a bit by qualifying the statement, adding that "The Sale of the Hessians" is "assumed" or "probably" written by Franklin. Seemingly, none state that the author of the propaganda hoax is unknown.

There are three fascinating aspects of the story of "The Sale of the Hessians." The first, and the least significant, is the propaganda document itself. The second is the ready acceptance that it was written by Benjamin Franklin. The third, and the most significant aspect of "The Sale of the Hessians," is that there is no evidence at all that it *was* written by Benjamin Franklin.

The document known as "The Sale of the Hessians" is a fake letter dated February 18, 1777, purported to have been written by a "Count de Schaumburg to the Baron Hohendorf, commanding the Hessian troops in America."[1] Both the Count and the Baron are fictitious. The letter was written as satire in order to make the German Count appear to be pleased with the Hessian deaths at Trenton (December 1776). The letter written in French states bluntly that the British pay for dead Hessians and therefore the more dead the better and in fact it is

---

1. The full text of the *Sale of the Hessians*, translated from French to English, may be found in John Bigelow, editor, *Life of Benjamin Franklin, Written by Himself,* (Philadelphia: J.B. Lippincott & Co., 1875), 2:395-399. books.google.com/ books?id =vv51SuTo9RcC&pg=PA395, accessed January 8, 2015.

preferable not to treat the seriously wounded and instead allow them to die. Frequently, modern authors claim the letter was designed to spur Hessian desertions.

Until 1874 there was no evidence that anyone attributed "The Sale of the Hessians" to Franklin. However in that year the Franklin biographer John Bigelow included "The Sale of the Hessians" in his book *The Life of Benjamin Franklin*. He commented, "Nor do I think I am doing Doctor Franklin any injustice in suspecting him of being its author. Since the death of Swift [Jonathan Swift, 1667–1745] who besides Franklin, was sufficiently a master of this kind of satire to have written it?"[2] Since then Franklin's alleged authorship has grown until it has become not only commonplace but seemingly required whenever "The Sale of the Hessians" is discussed in any format.

Yet, the sole evidence of Franklin's involvement in the "Sale of the Hessians" hoax boils down to Bigelow's "who besides Franklin" comment. That is hardly sufficient evidence to persuade anyone, which begs the question as to why Franklin's name is still connected with the hoax.

A 1983 article, "Franklin and 'The Sale of the Hessians': The Growth of a Myth" by Everett C. Wilkie, Jr. in *Proceedings of the American Philosophical Society*, thoroughly, and very convincingly, traces the entanglement of Franklin's name with "The Sale of the Hessians" hoax.[3] Wilkie maintains that there is no evidence prior to Bigelow that anyone connected Franklin with "The Sale of the Hessians," that there is no evidence that it was published prior to 1782 or that anyone in Europe "had any interest in it beyond the passing interest shown in such witty, ephemeral productions." Wilkie also asserts that Franklin could not write French well enough in 1777 to have written the piece.

Wilkie does leave one very slight possibility that Franklin was involved: Bigelow's argument based on internal evidence. However, Wilkie sums up his position by writing that "unless new more reliable evidence is forthcoming, there would appear to be little reason at all to attribute 'The Sale of the Hessians' to Benjamin Franklin."[4]

The little hole Wilkie left open, involving internal evidence, was effectively plugged by Jan Pilditch in 1988.[5] After comparing and con-

2. Ibid.
3. Everett C. Wilkie, Jr., "Franklin and 'The Sale of the Hessians': the Growth of a Myth,"*Proceedings of the American Philosophical Society,* 127: 202-212.
4. Ibid.
5. Jan Pilditch, "Franklin's Sale of the Hessians: American or European Satire?,"*Australasian Journal of American Studies,* 7: 13-22.

trasting various potential authors Pilditch concludes that, "far from Bigelow's assertion that 'who besides Franklin?', the internal evidence viewed alongside other American and European satires would seem to suggest, not Franklin and not American either."[6]

The editor of *The Papers of Benjamin Franklin*, William B. Willcox, agrees that there is no tangible connection between Franklin and "The Sale of the Hessians."[7]

One has to wonder just why Franklin's name is continually associated with "The Sale of the Hessians" by those who profess to be historians. Perhaps it's simply a good story and adds to the luster of Franklin. Or, perhaps it is just easier to repeat what others have repeated.

6. Ibid.
7. William B. Willcox, editor, *The Papers of Benjamin Franklin* (New Haven: Yale University Press, 1983), 23:480-484.

Enlisting Lasses:
Women Who Aspired to be Soldiers

❄ DON N. HAGIST ❄

Almost every student of the Revolutionary War has heard of Deborah Sampson, the Massachusetts woman who disguised herself as a man and served for over a year as a Continental soldier.[1] As fascinating as her case is, it was exceedingly unusual; although some historians have attempted to prove that many women served in the ranks either clandestinely or openly, there is scant evidence that more than three or four actually did so.[2] In general, one of the rites of enlistment was a physical examination, so the chances of a woman successfully joining an established military unit were slim.

On the American side it was perhaps easier because the military infrastructure was nascent, fragmented among the colonies and communities within them, and evolving as the war progressed. Women who attempted to enlist were nonetheless usually discovered. Lt. William Barton of the 1st New Jersey Regiment wrote a letter in November 1778 describing his own experience of meeting "a young lad" who wished to enlist. He gave money and lodging to the prospective recruit in the home where he was quartered. By the following afternoon a number of circumstances had raised his suspicion, so he called upon another officer to "officiate as Doctor in searching; he did, and soon made the Discovery by Pulling out the Teats of a Plump Young Girl, which caused great diversion." She was attempting to escape from her family because she'd been forbidden to marry a man

1. Alfred F. Young, *Masquerade: The Life and Times of Deborah Sampson, Continental Soldier* (New York: Alfred A. Knopf, 2004).
2. See Linda Grant de Pauw, "Women in Combat: The Revolutionary War Experience," *Armed Forces and Society* 7 #2 (Winter 1981), 209-226, and a rebuttal by Janice E. McKenney, "Commentary: 'Women in Combat' Comment," *Armed Forces and Society* 8 #4 (Summer 1982), 686-692.

she loved. The following morning the officer "ordered the Drums to beat her through the Town with the whores march; they did so which was Curious seeing her dressed in mens Clothes and the whores march Beating."[3]

On the British side, procedures for recruiting and training soldiers were far more standardized. During the entire eighteenth century, only three women are known to have successfully managed to become British soldiers, none during the American Revolution.[4] The notion of women clandestinely enlisting is a popular one, however, and in fact was equally popular during the era of the American Revolution. So popular, in fact, that the renowned playwright Richard Brinsley Sheridan used it as a plot device in his 1778 play *The Camp*. And newspapers reported several instances of women attempting to enlist, first during the flurry of recruiting that occurred when it became clear that the American war would be a long one, and again during the massive military buildup after France joined the war.

> Newcastle, December 30, 1775. Wednesday last, a good-looking girl, about twenty-seven years old, dressed in mens cloaths, applied to Serjeant Miller, the recruiting officer here for Frazer's Highland regiment, and desired to be enlisted in that body, which the serjeant agreed to, and gave her a shilling. Her sex, however, was soon after discovered. She said the cause of this act was from a quarrel with her father, whose cloaths she had absconded in: and notwithstanding her sex, she would have no objection to the army, as she thought the exercise not superior to her abilities. She was, however, discharged.[5]

> Yesterday a stout woman dressed in mens clothes enlisted in the Highland regiment, under the name of Peter Mitchel, and was sworn before a magistrate: a man came sometime after and claimed her as his wife—she said she was very willing to serve his Majesty, and was much abler than many of the recruits who had enlisted. She was discharged.[6]

---

3. Robert Fredilington, "A Diversion in Newark: A Letter from the New Jersey Continental Line, 1778," *New Jersey History* 105 #1-2 (Spring-Summer 1987). The spelling and grammar in the quotations has been modernized for readability.
4. Elizabeth Ewing, *Women in Uniform through the Centuries* (London: B. T. Batsford, Ltd., 1975).
5. *The Middlesex Journal, and Evening Advertiser* (London), January 4, 1776. Frazer's regiment was the 71st Regiment of Foot, raised in Scotland for service in America.
6. *Edinburgh Advertiser*, January 19, 1776.

"She Will be a Soldier" by Thomas Rowlandson, c. 1798. (*Anne S. K. Brown Military Collection, Brown University Library*)

Saturday last a young woman in Glasgow, of the name of Gardener, having got herself equipped in the Highland dress, was enlisted in General Fraser's Highland regiment. Unfortunately her sex was discovered, which has prevented her serving her King and country as a soldier.[7]

We hear from the north, that a few days ago, a servant maid, disguised in men's apparel, inlisted for a soldier with a recruiting party. After receiving the bounty money, she got leave to go home, under pretence of taking leave of her friends: With the bounty she paid off some debts, and then fled the country.[8]

We hear from Aberdeen, that about five weeks ago a young woman of the name of Black, enlisted herself for a soldier, and received pay ever since, till last week when a woman in a house which she sometimes frequented became amorous of the supposed

7. *Edinburgh Advertiser*, February 2, 1776.
8. *Edinburgh Advertiser*, March 22, 1776.

handsome young lad, and made such advances as brought on a discovery of the recruit's sex.[9]

The Beginning of last Week, a young Girl, about 17 Years of Age,
went from Barrow, near this Town, to Nottingham, and having
procured Man's Apparel, enlisted for a Soldier (being persuaded
thereto, as she says, by a Man where she lodged) and that Night
lay with the Serjeant but the next Day after being sworn, she was
taken to the examining Surgeon, to whom she confessed her Sex,
and was discharged. The Man who persuaded the thoughtless Girl
to this Frolick, was entrusted by her to exchange the Man's Cloaths
for her own at the Pawnbroker's, but instead of which he sold
them, and decamped with the Money, leaving the Girl in a
deplorable Situation, to lament her Credulity.[10]

Extract of a Letter from Plymouth Dock, June 25 . . . "on Sunday
last it was discovered that a Woman had enlisted and been for
some Time in the 13th Regiment in the Barracks at this Place. One
of the Shropshire Militia quartered at Plymouth, a Sweetheart of
her's at Wells, exposed her Sex. She was immediately discharged
and a Collection made to carry her home. It is surprising how very
soon she learnt her Exercise, having been but three Months in the
regiment, and yet expert."[11]

On Friday last, a young lady of a reputable family went and
enlisted herself at Tower-Hill in one of the regiments of guards
doing duty there; but upon going through the custom that is usually observed on such occasions, she was under a necessity of discovering her sex, being ordered and compelled to strip herself
naked, notwithstanding all her endeavours and entreaties to the
contrary. Upon being questioned by the serjeant with regard to the
occasion of so extraordinary an occurrence, she gave him the following relation: that her lover was an officer belonging to the regiment in which she had enlisted herself, but that he being for some
time gone to America, she had long wished for an opportunity to
go to him, and had pitched upon the above method as most con-
ducive to elude the vigilance of her friends, and expedite her
design. Upon its being remonstrated to her that it was very uncertain what time she might have gone to America, it depending in a
great measure on the progress she might make in learning her exer-

9. *Edinburgh Advertiser*, April 5, 1776.
10. *Derby Mercury*, January 17, 1777.
11. *St. James's Chronicle* (London), June 29, 1778.

cise, she practically cried that she had been long practicing before she came there, and was in every way qualified to do her duty as a soldier. She is a handsome young woman, is rather stout, and makes a very good appearance as a man.[12]

As intriguing and amusing as all these stories are, they lack the corroboration required to distinguish them from rumor. The accounts are so numerous, and so lacking in other substantiation, that we can only guess whether they're indicative of real determination among women to enlist or of a social preoccupation with the romantic notion of a woman soldier.

12. *Edinburgh Advertiser,* July 6, 1779.

Invading America: The Flatboats that Landed Thousands of British Troops on American Beaches

❀❂ HUGH T. HARRINGTON ❂❀

Amphibious operations, which involve landing troops and supplies from the sea to the land, are extremely difficult and require special techniques, close coordination between the navy and army, as well as specialized equipment. The British learned the required skills during the Seven Years' War. After a failed attack on the French port of Rochefort the British revised their amphibious command and control procedures, and designed purpose-built launches, known familiarly as flatboats, especially for landing on enemy beaches.[1]

Ideally, the troops would be taken as close to the shore as possible so they would have the shortest distance possible to wade ashore and be exposed to enemy fire. Standard longboats were unsuitable for landing operations due to their deep draft which could be up to five feet when loaded.[2] Also, the long and narrow design of a longboat made loading and unloading troops difficult as they would have to get past the oarsmen and the oars to exit over the sides.

In April 1758 the Lords Commissioners of the Admiralty approved the design for a shallow draft flatboat.[3] Two sizes were planned. One was thirty-six-feet long and ten-feet two-inches broad. It would carry about fifty men plus a naval officer, gunner, and twenty oarsmen. A

---

1. Robert Beatson, *Naval and Military Memoirs of Great Britain, from 1727-1783* (London: Longman, 1804), 2:167.
2. Hugh Boscawen, "The Origins of the Flat-Bottomed Landing Craft 1757-1758,"*Army Museum '84* (Journal of the National Army Museum, Royal Hospital Road, London, UK, 1985), 24.
3. Contemporary scale models, complete with Army and Navy figures, can be found at the National Maritime Museum, Greenwich, England.

smaller version was thirty-feet long, nine-feet nine-inches broad, and carried sixteen oarsmen. Both of these boats were only two-feet eleven-inches in depth with wide, rounded bows and transom sterns. Fully loaded they required only two-feet of water, which allowed them to get close to the beach.[4]

The British flatboats used in the American Revolution were, with minor variations, the same. Their capacity was about 10,000 to 12,000 pounds not including the oarsmen. Troops were packed in close together seated in two rows facing each other with their muskets standing upright between their knees. A sailor manned the tiller while twenty others sat outboard of the troops to man the oars. The flatboats could also be fitted with a mast, sails, and a small cannon, or swivel gun mounted in the bow.[5] The swivel gun added a slight bit of defensive firepower. However procedure dictated that the landing site would be heavily bombarded by warships prior to the landing. The flatboats were not meant to fight their way ashore.

Twin gangplanks were extended over the bow onto the beach allowing for fast and orderly entry and exit of the troops. The procedure was described by a witness:

> All these flat boats . . . were lying in one row along the shore, and as soon as the regiment had marched past, it formed up again close to the shore, and awaited the signal for entering the boats. Immediately on this being given each officer marched with his men to the boats, . . . then he and his drummer entered first and passed right through from the bows on shore to the stern, the whole division following him without breaking their ranks; so that in two minutes everybody was in the boat.[6]

On reaching the enemy shore the men would march out over the bow onto the beach and would be combat ready immediately. Just prior to hitting the beach the flatboat would drop a kedge anchor off the stern. When the troops had disembarked the anchor was pulled, oars backed, and the flatboat would head out to sea for another load.

One variation of the flatboat was constructed and used in Canada. Major General Phillips' brigade orders of June 3, 1776, state:

4.. Boscawen, *Origins*, 25.

5. National Maritime Museum, Greenwich, England.

6. Boscawen, *Origins*, 28. The quotation is from Count F. Kielmansegge, *Diary of a Journey to England in the Years 1761-1762* (London: 1902), 258-259. A division, in this context, is a company or half-company, about 50 men.

Lieut. [William] Twiss is to proceed to Three Rivers and give his directions for construction of Boats. The description of one of these Boats is, a Common flat Bottom called a King's Boat or Royal Boat calculated to carry from 30 to 40 men with stores and provisions, with this only difference, that the Bow of each Boat is to be made square resembling an English Punt for the conveniency of disembarking the Troops by the means of a kind of broad gang board with Loop-holes made in it for Musquetry, and which may serve as a Mantlet[7] when advancing towards an Enemy, and must be made strong accordingly.[8]

Documentation of such a gang board or ramp used elsewhere in the American Revolution has not been found. An image of flatboats with a similar "gang board" appears in a 1780 image "A View of Gravesend in Kent, with Troops passing the Thames to Tilbury Fort."[9] Such a gang board or ramp strong enough to provide protection from enemy fire would have been very heavy and may have caused stability problems for the flatboat. The infantry, being packed in tightly, would not have been able to use the gang board as a mantlet or fire through the loopholes.

Another modification to the flatboats allowed them to be used to carry artillery. Planks installed the length of the boat and gangplanks placed over the bows allowed the artillery to be wheeled on and off the flatboat.[10] The Robert Cleveley image of the landing at Kip's Bay clearly shows flatboats carrying artillery and others carrying infantry.[11]

The effectiveness of the flatboats was clearly demonstrated on the morning of August 22, 1776, in a spectacular display of organizational prowess and seamanship when the Royal Navy shifted the bulk of the British army from Staten Island to Gravesend Bay on Long Island. At 4 A.M. flatboats were at the beach at Staten Island to pick up the first wave of troops.

---

7. Mantlet, a portable defensive shield.
8. James Murray Hadden, *Hadden's Journal and Orderly Books* (Albany: Joel Munsell's Sons, 1884), 169.
9. "A view of Gravesend in Kent, with Troops passing the Thames to Tilbury Fort, 1780," British Museum, www.britishmuseum.org/research/collection_online/ collection_object_details/collection_image_gallery.aspx?assetId=904082&objectId=33124 10&partId=1.
10. Adrian B. Caruana, *Grasshoppers and Butterflies: The Light 3-Pounders of Pattison and Townshend* (Bloomfield, Ontario: Museum Restoration Service, 1980), 30.
11. Don N. Hagist, "A New Interpretation of a Robert Cleveley Watercolour," *Mariner's Mirror*, 94:3, 2008, 326-30.

The landing itself was covered by three frigates and two bomb-ketches which bombarded the beach prior to the landing. The landing however was unopposed. The Captain of H.M.S. *Eagle*, Henry Duncan, who was involved in the landing, records that:

> The flat boats were all assembled by four o'clock [a.m.] on the beach, under the particular command of Commodore Hotham . . . About eight the Phoenix fired a gun and hoisted a striped flag, blue and white, at the mizen top-mast head, as a signal for the troops to proceed to the shore. A little after eight all the ships with troops for the first landing were in motion; and the boats that had taken in about 1,000 troops from Staten Island began to move across towards Gravesend Bay, in Long Island. Half-past eight Commodore Hotham hoisted the red flag in his boat as a signal for the boats to push on shore. The boats immediately obeyed the signal, and in ten minutes or thereabout 4,000 men were on the beach, formed and moved forward. The wind blew down the harbour, but the flood tide had made up too strong for the ships to get down in their intended station; nevertheless, by twelve o'clock or very soon after, all the troops were on shore, to the number of 15,000, and by three o'clock we had an account of the army being got as far as Flat Bush, six or seven miles from where they landed.[12]

This landing involved seventy-five flatboats each carrying fifty infantrymen, plus eleven bateaux (long, shallow draft boat with pointed bow and stern). The first embarkation of 4,000 men consisted of the light infantry and the reserve. It is very significant that not only did these troops reach the beach quickly but that after their arrival they were immediately able to move out in an orderly fashion to secure the beach. The evening before the amphibious landing on Long Island the troops to be landed in the second and third waves were put on board transports. The second embarkation, from the transports, of 5,000 men was delivered to the beach by the flatboats so quickly after the first landing that they could have supported the light infantry should there have been opposition. While the flatboats made their way to the beach with this second wave of troops the now empty transports moved out and were replaced by transports containing more troops to be taken to the beach in their turn. Three hours after the first landing 15,000 troops were ashore along with their baggage, equipment,

---

12. Henry Duncan, "Journals of Henry Duncan," in John Knox Laughton, *Naval Miscellany* (London: Navy Records Society, 1902), 122-123.

and forty pieces of artillery.[13] Moving a combat force of this size so quickly had never before been seen on this continent.

Less than a month later, on September 15, the flatboats were again used with great success. Unlike the landing at Gravesend Bay the crossing of the East River from Long Island to Manhattan Island required an assault on a hostile shore.

During the night of the 14th the British anchored five warships with their broadsides facing the American position on shore, only three yards away.[14] The Americans had dug trenches in anticipation of a landing. However they were not prepared for the power of the Royal Navy's assault.

An American, Joseph Plumb Martin, was on the receiving end of the attack. He described seeing "their boats coming out of a creek or cover on Long Island side of the water, filled with British soldiers. When they came to the edge of the tide, they formed their boats in line. They continued to augment their forces from the island until they appeared like a large clover field in full bloom."[15] A British officer, Captain William Evelyn of the Light Infantry, recalled that "the water covered with boats full of armed men pressing eagerly toward the shore, was certainly one of the grandest and most sublime scenes ever exhibited."[16]

Francis, Lord Rawdon was in one of the eighty-four flatboats making up the landing force. As he "approached [we] saw the breastworks filled with men, and two or three large columns marching down in great parade to support them. The Hessians, who were not used to this water business and who conceived that it must be exceedingly uncomfortable to be shot at whilst they were quite defenceless and jammed so close together, began to sing hymns immediately. Our men expressed their feelings as strongly, though in a different manner, by damning themselves and the enemy indiscriminately with wonderful fervency."[17]

13. Beatson, *Naval and Military Memoirs of Great Britain from 1727-1783,* (London: Longman, 1804), 4:156-157.

14. Journals of HMS *Phoenix,* HMS *Roebuck,* HMS *Orpheus,* HMS *Rose,* HMS *Carysfort* in William James Morgan, ed. *Naval Documents of the American Revolution* (Washington: Department of the Navy, 1972), 6:838-840.

15. Joseph Plumb Martin, George F. Scheer, ed., *Private Yankee Doodle* (Boston: Little, Brown and Company, 1962), 33-34.

16. Henry P. Johnston, *Battle of Harlem Heights* (New York: The Macmillan Company, 1897), 34.

17. William P. Cumming and Hugh Rankin, *The Fate of a Nation, The American Revolution Through Contemporary Eyes* (London: Phaidon Press, 1975), 110-111.

British flatboat; detail from an ink and watercolor illustration of the British occupation of Newport, Rhode Island, 1776. (*National Maritime Museum*)

When the flatboats were within fifty yards of the ships the signal was given and the warships let loose their first volley upon the breastworks. To Martin "there came such a peal of thunder from the British shipping that I thought my head would go with the sound." Bartholomew James aboard HMS *Orpheus* wrote that "it is hardly possible to conceive what a tremendous fire was kept up by those five ships for fifty-nine minutes, in which time we fired away, in the *Orpheus* alone, five thousand three hundred and seventy six pounds of powder. The first broadside made a considerable breach in their works, and the enemy fled on all sides, confused and calling for quarter . . ." To Lord Rawdon it was "the most tremendous peal I ever heard. The breastworks were blown to pieces in a few minutes, and those who were to have defended it were happy to escape as quick as possible . . . We pressed to shore, landed, and formed without losing a single man . . ." HMS *Carysfort* "fired 20 broadsides in the Space of an hour, with Double headed round & Grape Shott."[18]

American captain Samuel Richards saw "a dense column of the enemy moving down to the waters edge and embarking on board flat boats. Knowing their object we prepared to receive them. As soon as they began their approach the ships opened a tremendous fire upon us. The column of boats on leaving the shore proceeded directly towards us; when arriving about half way across the sound [East

18. Journal of Bartholomew James and journal of HMS *Carysfort*, in Morgan, *Naval Documents*, 6:841, 849. Martin, *Private Yankee Doodle*, 34. Cumming, *Fate of a Nation*, 111.

River] they turned their course and proceeded to Kip's bay—about three quarters of a mile above us—where they landed; their landing there being unexpected they met with no opposition: the firing from the ships being continued—our slight embankment being hastily thrown up—was fast tumbling away by the enemy's shott. Our troops left their post in disorder. . ."[19]

The landing at Kip's Bay was entirely successful. The astonishing firepower of the warships combined with the efficient landing of numerous troops was far more than the Americans could withstand. This was shock and awe.

Such is the power of a well-orchestrated amphibious landing. Without flat-bottomed landing craft the Royal Navy and the British army would not have been capable of taking advantage of the enormous coastline of the United States. While the humble flatboats did not win the war for the British the boats did allow a strategy of mobility which was hoped would overcome the Americans whose movements were limited by the feet of the foot soldier.

19. Morgan, *Naval Documents*, 6:844-845.

British Fascination with Ethan Allen

GENE PROCKNOW

The American public's interest in Ethan Allen as a "larger than life" folk hero during and since the American Revolution is well documented.[1] After leading the capture of Ft. Ticonderoga in May 1775, Allen's notoriety as the leader of the Green Mountain Boys in the northern frontier, which subsequently became Vermont, spread throughout the thirteen colonies. Allen's seizure of Ft. Ticonderoga, regarded as the "Gibraltar of North America" and thought to be impregnable, instilled the widespread impression of him as a vaunted military commander. However, it would be Allen's only military victory.

Even in defeat Allen was portrayed as a hero. On September 25, 1775, British forces captured Allen while commanding a rash attempt to take Montreal far in advance of the main Patriot army. A widely popular American propagandist play entitled *The Fall of British Tyranny* chronicled a purported heroic last stand by Allen.[2] Adding to his courageous reputation Allen penned a narrative on his subsequent captivity, describing harsh internment conditions while persevering through immense physical discomfort.[3] His incarceration chronicle became the second most printed book in the United States during the

---

1. For a description of how biographers and historians created the reputation and legend of Ethan Allen see, John J. Duffy, and H. Nicholas Muller III, *Inventing Ethan Allen* (Hanover & London: University Press of New England, 2014).

2. For a complete assessment of the relationship between Ethan Allen's own captivity narrative and *The Fall of Tyranny* play see, Ennis Duling, "Ethan Allen and the Fall of British Tyranny: A question of What Came First", *Vermont History*, Vol. 75, No. 2, (Summer/Fall 2007), 134-140.

3. An advertisement in the July 28, 1779 edition of *The Pennsylvania Gazette* billed his captivity as " . . . the most remarkable Occurrences".

Revolution (Thomas Paine's *Common Sense* was the most printed).[4] Further, Allen's strident advocacy of Vermont's independence from New York and New Hampshire, including authoring numerous pamphlets and newspaper articles, generated additional publicity.

But what is lesser known is that the British populace was also fascinated with Ethan Allen. He was the first high profile prisoner garnered by British forces after the outbreak of hostilities and Allen was among the first and only prisoners shipped to England.[5] His presence immediately became a domestic British political issue and a rallying symbol for the opponents of King George's policies towards America. Given this fame, when it looked like Allen might lead Vermont back into allegiance with the Crown, he provided hope for a British turnaround and victory. Much of what the British people knew about Ethan Allen came from copious and widely disseminated newspaper articles.

BRITISH NEWSPAPER AND PERIODICAL REPORTING ON ETHAN ALLEN

The capture of Ft. Ticonderoga in the beginning stages of the Revolution is the dramatic episode which elevated Ethan Allen from a small time, backwoods agitator into a mythic internationally recognized character. However, initial British press reports highlight Col. James Easton's role in the assault.

> June 1775, *Scots Magazine*:
> The commanding officer came forth; Col. Easton clapped him upon the shoulder, told him he was prisoner; and demanded, in the name of America, an instant surrender of the fort, with all its contents, to the American forces.[6]

James Easton, a colonel in the Berkshire militia, brought news to the Massachusetts Provincial Congress, which was the initial source reported in the British press. Interesting there was no mention of Benedict Arnold, who claimed co-command of the fort's capture.[7]

Subsequent British press reports significantly elevate Ethan Allen's role in Ticonderoga's capture and his fighting reputation began to dra-

---

4. Willard Sterne Randall, *Ethan Allen: His Life and Times* (New York & London: W. W. Norton & Company, 2011), xiii.
5. Captured sailors around the British Isles were regularly imprisoned in England, but soldiers captured subsequent to the Ethan Allen group were incarcerated in British held North American territories.
6. Utilized digitized search capabilities of The British Newspaper Archive, www.britishnewspaperarchive.co.uk for quotes.
7. *The Scots Magazine*, June 1, 1775.

matically rise. Within two months, the British press placed Allen in the front ranks of American military leaders albeit laced with sarcasm aimed at the entire group.

August 3, 1775, *London Gazette*:
The Americans seem to out-number us in Generals, there appearing, from several of their accounts to be the following, viz. Gen. Putnam, Gen. Pomroy, Gen. Washington, Gen. Lee, Gen. Ward, and Gen. Doctor Warren, killed in the late engagement, besides other superior commanders, as Col. Ethan Allen at Ticonderoga, and Col. Henry, at Virginia, &c.

Following up on the success at Ticonderoga, Ethan Allen, without a formal military rank and commission led a group of Vermont and Canadian volunteers during the fall 1775 invasion of Canada. His volunteers advanced well in front of the main Patriot army in a reckless and foolhardy attempt to take Montreal. Allen and most of his men were captured in a brief, but bloody engagement with British forces a few miles from the city. Given Ethan Allen's stature as a leading Patriot leader and for being the "conqueror of the mighty Ticonderoga" his capture was widely reported. Further, after major British losses at Lexington, Concord, and Bunker Hill, this was the first clear-cut victory, which provided the British press with positive news to report.

November 8, 1775, *Kentish Gazette*:
. . . the rebels were defeated and fled, with the loss of about 15 or 16 killed, and between 30 and 40 made prisoners; among the latter was one Ethan Allen styling himself Colonel, and who commanded the party.

Derided as a "make believe" military officer fostering civil unrest, Allen's motives were seen as self-serving and economically driven. He was not portrayed as attempting to win political freedom, but capitalizing on domestic instability to loot goods and materials.

November 13, 1775, *Northampton Mercury*:
. . . taken Prisoners, with their Commander Allen, the Cause of all the Disturbances of this Province, and how it seems, had promised his Party the Plunder of Montreal.

December 1775, *Scots Magazine*:
Canadian Governor Guy Carleton believing that he was simply dealing with leaders of a civil insurrection, transported Ethan Allen and the other captured prisoners to England for trial and presumed

hanging. Allen was remanded to Sir Brook Watson, a British merchant for transport to Falmouth on the ship, Adamant. Allen
described Watson as a "man of malicious and cruel disposition."[8]

The arrival of the conqueror of the previously thought invincible
Ft. Ticonderoga was widely reported in the British press.

December 1775, *Scots Magazine*:
In the Adamant, Wilson, which arrived, December 23, at London,
from Quebec, were brought 40 prisoners taken from the provincials, among whom is the noted Ethan Allen. They were lodged in
Pendennis Castle.

The British government and public soon recognized that Governor
Carleton's initial move to punish Allen and his men as common criminals fomenting civil unrest was not a sustainable policy. As the
Americans captured British soldiers, it became readily apparent that
hanging Allen or other prisoners would result in American retaliatory
executions.

December 27, 1775, *Kentish Gazette*:
Many arguments have arose about what government mean to do
with the above prisoners; the great number of men in the hands of
the provincials, will surely prevent our proceeding with severity
towards them.

From the time of his capture, Allen was reportedly kept in chains
under harsh conditions. British press reports expressed concern that
British officers and men would receive the same treatment. In addition, they further questioned the wisdom of the British government's
American policies.

January 6, 1776, *Kentish Gazette*:
We hear that Ethan Allen, a provincial Colonel, was brought from
America to England hand-cuffed, and that the forty prisoners, who
were brought over with him, were never suffered to come upon the
deck for air during the voyage. Is not this cruelty exceedingly
impolitic? There is not a doubt that the Congress will return the
compliment on Noblemen's nephews, Colonels, Captains, and
other subaltern officers, taken at Fort St. John, as soon as they are
acquainted with the severity practiced on their countrymen. "The

8. For Allen's description of his treatment by Sir Brook Watson see, Stephen Care
Arch, ed., *A Narrative of Colonel Ethan Allen's Captivity* (Acton, MA: Copley
Publishing Group, 2000), 21.

destined cord" will not now be a dangerous experiment. But this is not the first blunder in this business, made on this side of the water.

Ethan Allen's imprisonment and treatment became a domestic political issue bandied in the press. British politicians opposed to the government's American policies hired Lord Ashburton, John Dunning, and John Alleyne as counsel to obtain a writ of habeas corpus.[9] The opposition politicians sought to establish under what authority were the American prisoners held and to provide access to the British civilian justice system.

January 26 1776, *Hibernian Journal Or Chronicle of Liberty*:
The SUPPORTERS of the BILL OF RIGHTS, the LONDON ASSOCIATION, and all TRUE PATRIOTS, are called upon to DEMAND an Extension of the Habeas Corpus to these Americans, and no longer permit the inexorable Tyranny of Ministers, to bid Defiance to Mercy and Justice.

Within a few weeks, Ethan Allen and his fellow prisoners are ordered to embark on the *Solebay* for return to America. The opposition continued to question the government's policies and sought answers to why they were sent back across the Atlantic.

January 11, 1776, *Bath Chronicle and Weekly Gazette*:
Col. Ethan Allen and the other prisoners in Pendennis castle, are ordered back to America in the first vessel to Boston. Government have expressed their dislike of the conduct of General Carleton in sending them over. When Mr. Watson was told of Allen and the others sent back as prisoners to Boston, he replied, It was punishment sufficient enough.

Throughout the year 1777, British newspapers reported specific American retaliation against senior British officers for Allen's reputed harsh treatment.

January 20, 1777, *Northampton Mercury*:
This severe treatment (of General Prescott) the Congress declared was intended as a Retaliation for the imprisonment of Ethan Allen.

Further, during 1777 there were attempts made by American generals Lee and Gates and the American Commissioners in Paris, to

9. Lord Ashburton, John Dunning represented Benjamin Franklin before the Privy Council in 1774 and was a leading opposition member of Parliament.

arrange for Ethan Allen's exchange and release. When a prisoner swap was finally consummated in May 1778, the reporting was rather matter of fact without recognizing a military rank for Allen.

June 13, 1778, *Newcastle Courant*:
Major General Lee is exchanged for Major General Prescott, and Lt. Col. Campbell of the 71st for Ethan Allen.

Ethan Allen did not appear in the British press during the years 1779 and 1780. However, in 1781, Ethan Allen prominently returned to the British news with the reported prospect of leading Vermont to rejoin the British Empire.

January 1781, *Scots Magazine*:
New York December 20. Nothing (according to accounts received from America towards the end of January) has more disconcerted or given to much vexation to the Congress, as the establishment, against their will or approbation, of a new State called Vermont, which is situated on the frontier parts of New Hampshire, Connecticut and New York, of extensive territory, fertile soil, and tolerably well peopled. A set of the leading people in this quarter of America, joined by many of the New Hampshire men, among whom the famous Ethan Allen is the principal mover, have drawn the lines of the state, established laws and regulations, expressly contrary to the will or wishes of Congress.

Mistakenly, several inaccurate reports of Ethan Allen and the people of Vermont rejoining the British forces were published.

February 1, 1781, *Stamford Mercury*:
The last accounts from America say, that our affairs wear a very favorable aspect in the neighborhood of Albany and Ticonderoga, where Col. Ethan Allen (the Arnold in that part of the country) has joined the King's troops, with a considerable body of men well armed and disciplined; and that the inhabitants, who have been hitherto some of the most violent in favour of rebellion, are coming over very fast to the royal cause . . .

February 22, 1781, *Bath Chronicle and Weekly Gazette*:
There is every reason to suppose that EA has quitted the rebel cause.

In fact, Allen's reputed return to allegiance to the Crown is given as a reason why the British had a clear chance at victory in early 1781.

March 12, 1781, *Aberdeen Journal*:
. . . that Ethan Allen has fortified himself near Ticonderoga, and defied the Rebels. Our troops at New York were in the highest spirits and amply supplied with beef, mutton, fish, fowl and liquors, while their enemies continued to be in the most wretched situation, without clothes, pay or provisions. In short, there now appears a real prospect of America being reduced to obedience in two or three months at largest.

Even after the American victory at Yorktown the British press continued to print stories on the negotiations between leaders of Vermont, including Ethan Allen, and the British governor in Canada, Frederick Haldimand.

October 25, 1783, *Ipswich Journal*:
Ethan Allen whose state is refused to be added to the thirteen, on his part as absolutely refuses his submission and asserts the independence of his district; the manner in which the population of Vermont increases, and the number of loyalists resorting thither, may prove matters of serious consideration on the continent of North America.

After the Treaty of Paris ending the Revolution, the British press continued to write about Allen. British papers covered Allen's participation in the Wyoming Valley jurisdictional dispute between Pennsylvania and Connecticut.[10] Later sarcastic reports of Allen's philosophical treatise "*Reason the only Oracle of Man*" were published.

February 3, 1787, *Northampton Mercury*:
Ethan Allan, who was in the Provincial service during the War, we hear, has dipped his Red Coat in Black of the deepest Tartarean Die, being now not only a Preacher, but the Author of a large Octavo Volume containing a new System of Deism of the most pernicious Tendency.

In death, however, the British newspapers paid more respect to Allen, including in his death notice a courtesy and a military title, honorifics omitted in the first derogatory reports of 1775.

May 12, 1789, *Leeds Intelligencer*:
On the 13th of February died in Vermont, North America, Ethan Allen, Esq. Brigadier General of the militia of that Sate, and well known during the disputes between this country and the US.

---

10. *Hampshire Chronicle*, October 2, 1786.

CONCLUSION

British newspapers prominently featured Ethan Allen with over 200 citations from 1775 to his death in 1789. His news coverage overshadowed the more famous in America Benedict Arnold, his co-commander at Ticonderoga and high profile turncoat who was named in less than 100 British newspaper articles during the same period.[11]

Ethan Allen touched a nerve, which greatly interested the British populace. He was one of the few Patriot captives brought to England and the most high profile. Further his willingness to stand up to governmental authority on both sides of the Atlantic contributed to his celebrity status. Many British readers, especially those in opposition to the war viewcd him as fighting for the common man and against governmental overreach.

11. Utilized digitized search capabilities of The British Newspaper Archive, www.britishnewspaperarchive.co.uk, for statistics on number of articles on Allen and Arnold.

The American Crisis Before Crossing the Delaware?

🎕 JETT CONNER 🎕

Did Thomas Paine's *The American Crisis* influence Washington's troops prior to crossing the Delaware River and fighting the Battle of Trenton?

Does saying so make it so? Perhaps, if said convincingly and repeatedly. But sometimes it's fair to ask: Who says so? And how do they know?

It is said that George Washington ordered the first number of Thomas Paine's *The American Crisis* series to be read to his ragged troops before boarding boats to cross the Delaware on the eve of the Battle of Trenton. Inspired by Paine's words, so the story goes, the suffering soldiers marched through that cold and stormy night and achieved a much-needed victory the next morning at Trenton.

The details of Washington's success at the first battle of Trenton are well known and documented, but what about Paine's role in the affair?

Paine published *The American Crisis, No. 1*, the first of thirteen numbered pieces in the series written during the course of the Revolutionary War, just a few days before the crossing, in December 1776.[1] Biographies, history books, and synopses found in many writings, at historical monuments, and on multiple websites, tell the story of Paine's famous words, "These are the times that try men's souls,"

---

1. The first *American Crisis* did not first appear in the *Pennsylvania Journal* as is often claimed, but instead was first published on December 19, 1776, as a pamphlet. The *Journal* suspended publication in early December, given the British threat to Philadelphia, and did not resume publication until late January 1777. The first half of *Crisis No. 1* did appear in the newspaper *Pennsylvania Packet* on December 27, 1776, with the second half published on January 4, 1777. For a review of the publication history of the pamphlet, see The Library of America, "Note on the Texts," Thomas Paine: Collected Writings, www.loa.org/volume.jsp?RequestID=95&section=notes, accessed January 17, 2015.

and the remarkable effect they had on Washington's regiments. But not everyone repeats the story.

Reading Paine's opening lines of *Crisis No. 1*,[2] it is not hard to imagine soldiers listening to Paine's provocative rebuke of "the summer soldier and the sunshine patriot," and exhortation that "the harder the conflict, the more glorious the triumph," then mustering the courage to row across the ice-clogged river and surprise the Hessian garrison at Trenton. It is a dramatic element entwined with the story of Washington's Crossing. But neither Washington nor Paine ever described the scene.

Though he acknowledged in his writings the positive effects the *Crisis* series had on morale and events—"His writings certainly have had a powerful effect on the public mind . . . "— nothing in Washington's published general orders or accounts of the battle in his letters to the Congress, or to military subordinates or friends or family members, links Paine or his words to the Battle of Trenton.[3]

For his part, Paine never mentioned that Washington ordered his first *American Crisis* to be read to the troops in any of his accounts recalling the writing and publishing of the piece, and he certainly was not there in person to do the reading himself or witness first-hand what happened. Paine had volunteered as aide-de-camp to General Nathanael Greene on Washington's retreat across New Jersey and the Delaware, reported on much that he had seen on that march, but he then took leave of Washington's troops to go to Philadelphia in early December 1776 to finish writing *Crisis No. 1* and get it published.

So, then, who told this tale about Paine's role on that Christmas night, 1776? And who continues to tell it today?

It seems that Paine's arch-enemy James Cheetham originated the story. In an early biographical sketch entitled *The Life of Thomas Paine*, published soon after Paine's death, Cheetham—acknowledging the uplifting effect that *Crisis No. 1* had on troop morale and Revolutionary events—wrote that prior to Washington's crossing of the Delaware, "The number was read in the camp to every corporal's guard."[4] But Cheetham, who was not an eyewitness to the event, pro-

---

2. Philip Foner, *The Complete Writings of Thomas Paine*, 2 vols. (New York: Citadel Press, 1969), 1:50.

3. Library of Congress, "George Washington to James Madison Jr., June 12, 1784,"*George Washington Papers*, lcweb2.loc.gov/cgi-bin/query/P?mgw:20:./temp/~ammem_QNRS, accessed January 16, 2015.

4. James Cheetham, *The Life of Thomas Paine* (New York: Southwick and Pelsue, 1809), 32; also online, archive.org/stream/lifethomaspaine00cheegoog#page/n48/mode/2up, accessed January 20, 2015.

vided no source for the assertion, and at least one researcher who has tried recently to confirm it could not.[5]

Nevertheless, over time the story continued to build and gain gravitas. The following serves as a representative sample.

Moncure Conway, writing in his four-volume collection of Paine's works in the nineteenth century, said of *Crisis No. 1*, "It was written during the retreat of Washington across the Delaware, and by order of the Commander was read to groups of his dispirited and suffering soldiers." Conway drew on Cheetham for the source.[6]

Phillip Foner, in his two-volume collection *The Complete Writings of Thomas Paine*, wrote of *Crisis No. 1*: "The soldiers who heard the words of Paine's great document—Washington ordered it read to his men—were inspired to face the floes, a blizzard and the swift current of the Delaware River on Christmas Eve and achieve the victory at Trenton which gave the Americans new courage." And he repeated the statement later: "Before the soldiers embarked to battle the floes, a blizzard, and the swift current of the river, they listened, at Washington's command, to a reading of Paine's new pamphlet." Foner mentioned Cheetham.[7]

Howard Fast: "Washington had the first *Crisis* paper in the morning [December 19] and read it through at luncheon on the same day. There is evidence that Washington was thrilled with what Paine had written, for he immediately ordered copies of the *Pennsylvania Journal* distributed up and down the river to every brigade, with instructions that it be read aloud at each corporal's guard." Fast offered no source or evidence.[8]

Eric Foner said that "In what he called a 'passion of patriotism,' Paine composed *The American Crisis*, which Washington ordered to be read to the troops on Christmas Eve shortly before the crossing of the Delaware." Foner cited Phillip Foner and David Freeman Hawke's biography *Paine* as sources, but Hawke did not mention Washington's orders to have *Crisis No. 1* read to the troops.[9]

---

5. William Dwyer, *The Day is Ours!* (New York: Viking Press, 1983), 399n.

6. Moncure Conway, *The Writings of Thomas Paine*, 4 vols. (New York: AMS Press, 1967), 1:169.

7. Foner, *The Complete Writings of Thomas Paine*, 1:xvi; 1:49. Curiously, Foner gets the date of the crossing wrong, twice, saying "Christmas Eve." It was Christmas night, 1776.

8. Howard Fast, *The Crossing* (Newark: New Jersey Historical Society, 1984).

9. Eric Foner, *Tom Paine and Revolutionary America* (New York: Oxford University Press, 1976), 139; David Freeman Hawke, *Paine* (New York, Harper & Row, 1974).

Scott Liell wrote that "At 2 A.M. on December 26, upon the banks [of] the Delaware River, Washington ordered that copies of Paine's new pamphlet be distributed throughout the ranks and that these words be read to his men as they were packed into the flat-bottomed Durham boats that would take them across the river to the Battle of Trenton." Liell cited Phillip Foner.[10]

Harvey Kaye stated: "Washington himself recognized the inspirational power of Paine's newest work and as part of the preparations for his now-famous Christmas Night attack on Britain's Hessian mercenaries occupying Trenton, he ordered his officers to read it to their troops." Kaye cited Richard Ketchum (see below) and David Hackett Fischer's *Washington's Crossing*, which relied on Cheetham.[11]

Craig Nelson described the publication of the first *Crisis* in his biography of Paine, and said: "One pamphlet made its way back to the very source of Paine's inspiration—the banks of the Delaware River. At dusk on December 23, 1776, General Washington ordered his officers to gather their men into small squads and read aloud what Paine had written." He gave no source for the story.[12]

On Washington's side of the story-telling, several works mention his orders to read *Crisis No. 1* to the troops. For example, Richard Ketchum asserted that the number "was read to Washington's troops on the west bank of the Delaware River, while they waited for the boats. . . ." But he offered no citation. And in *The Winter Soldiers* Ketchum continued: "All that Washington's men had to elevate their spirits were the words of Thomas Paine's *Crisis 1* which had been published a few days earlier in Philadelphia and which Washington ordered read to them while they stood quietly in the cold waiting to move down to McKonkey's Landing." Again, no evidence was provided.[13]

And Ron Chernow's *Washington, A Life* made this puzzling assertion about Paine's *Crisis*: "he published thirteen essays in a collection entitled *The Crisis*. . . . These essays appeared in pamphlet form on December 23 and Washington had them read aloud to small clusters of men up and down the Delaware." All of them? Chernow cited

10. Scott Liell, *46 Pages* (Philadelphia: Running Press, 2003), 143-144.

11. Harvey Kaye, *Thomas Paine and the Promise of America* (New York: Hill and Wang, 2005), 58.

12. Craig Nelson, *Thomas Paine: Enlightenment, Revolution and the Birth of Modern Nations* (New York: Penguin, 2007), 301.

13. Richard Ketchum, *The World of George Washington* (New York: American Heritage Publishers, 1974), 136; *The Winter Soldiers* (Garden City, NY, Doubleday, 1973), 295.

Nelson's biography of Paine as a source.[14] Several histories of the Revolution also mention *Crisis No. 1* and the role it played at the crossing.[15]

Not all biographical studies or historical accounts of the crossing mention Washington's orders to have *Crisis No. 1* read to the troops. Two early works, David Ramsay's *The Life of George Washington*[16] and Washington Irving's *The Life of Washington*,[17] did not mention Paine in association with the event. Neither did Joseph Ellis's *His Excellency, George Washington*.[18] David McCullough's *1776* did not repeat the story of Paine and Washington's orders, either.[19]

Absent Cheetham's account there might not be a story, if the brief survey of the literature above is any guide. Historical evidence to back up Cheetham's assertion is lacking. Historians who tell the story have leaned on Cheetham, or those before them who did so, as their only source, if they give a source at all. Maybe those choosing not to repeat the tale are uncomfortable because of this. But thinking there must be a basis somewhere for such a story, I tried to discover it.

My search of eyewitness accounts or of those who wrote about those with direct knowledge of the crossing yielded no evidence for Cheetham's assertion. For example, research on several soldiers who participated in and described the crossing turned up nothing about *Crisis No. 1*.[20] In addition, a search of published papers, autobiographies, and biographies of some of the most notable participants who either crossed the Delaware to fight at the first battle of Trenton, or who were in Washington's camp at some point just before the crossing, revealed nothing about Washington's orders and the first *Crisis*.

14. Ron Chernow, *Washington, A Life* (New York: Penguin, 2010), 271.

15. See, for example, William Stryker, *The Battles of Trenton and Princeton* (Boston and New York: Houghton Mifflin, 1898), 80-81; and Gordon Wood, *Revolutionary Characters* (New York: Penguin, 2006), 212.

16. David Ramsay, *The Life of George Washington* (London: Cadell and Davies, 1807), a very early biography of Washington that does not mention Paine in its account of Washington crossing the Delaware.

17. Washington Irving, *The Life of Washington*, 5 vols. (New York: G.P. Putnam's Sons, 1857).

18. Joseph Ellis, *His Excellency George Washington* (New York: Alfred A. Knopf, 2004).

19. David McCullough, *1776* (New York: Simon and Schuster, 2005).

20. Among writings of soldiers reviewed for this article are those of John Fitzgerald, Elisha Bostwick, John Trumbull, and John Greenwood, the latter who was 16 or 17 at the time of the crossing and who provides a most vivid and literate account. "Over the River," John Greenwood, *The Revolutionary Services of John Greenwood*, Isaac Greenwood, ed. (New York: De Vinne Press, 1922).

The latter include Nathanael Greene (Paine's commanding officer), Alexander Hamilton, James Monroe, Henry Knox and John Glover, all participants, and Joseph Reed and Benjamin Rush, who were in the camp prior to the crossing.[21] There is, as noted above, no written order in the Library of Congress' *George Washington Papers* pertaining to *Crisis No. 1*.

It is not unreasonable to assume that the first *Crisis* circulated and was read in Washington's regiments up and down the banks of the Delaware prior to the crossing. It certainly was published and in circulation prior to the event. Nelson stated that 18,000 copies of *Crisis No. 1* were printed in a first run, but offered no source. Other accounts stated that at least three editions of the pamphlet were published immediately after the first printing on December 19.

The Library of Congress has an original broadside of *The American Crisis No. 1* that appeared in Boston, in early January 1777.[22] And Cheetham did describe in *The Life of Thomas Paine* the positive effect the pamphlet had on nine New York Convention members ("they were rallied and reanimated") though he doesn't say exactly when it appeared in that city.[23] Still, it is reasonable to assume that Paine's pamphlet traveled fast and was likely read in Washington's camp.

But a reasonable assumption is not evidence. I am unable to find anything that supports Cheetham's assertion about Washington's orders and *Crisis No. 1*. Perhaps the story is true, but in this case saying so apparently makes it so. Chalk it up to tradition then, because after generations of historians telling it, the story by now is woven into the fabric of the history of the American Revolution. It's a good old story.

---

21. A sample list of sources includes Richard K Showman, *The Papers of Nathanael Greene* (Chapel Hill: University of North Carolina Press, 1976); Ron Chernow, *Alexander Hamilton* (New York: Penguin Press, 2004); Daniel Preston and Marlena DeLong, *The Papers of James Monroe*, 5 vols. (Westport, CT: Greenwood Press, 2003); North Callahan, *Henry Knox, General Washington's General* (New York: Rinehart and Co., 1958); George Athan Billias, *General John Glover and his Marblehead Mariners* (New York: Holt, 1960); William Reed, *Reprint of The Original Letters from Washington to Joseph Reed During the American Revolution*, archive.org/details/ reprintoforigina00wash, accessed January 19, 2015; David Freeman Hawke, *Benjamin Rush: Revolutionary Gadfly* (Indianapolis: Bobbs-Merrill, 1971), 139. Hawke quotes Rush on Paine's *Crisis*: "I believe his '*Crisis*' did as much mischief to the enemy and as much service to the friends of liberty as has been in the power of any one man to render this country with any other weapons short of the sword."
22. Library of Congress, memory.loc.gov/cgi-bin/query/r?ammem/AMALL: @field (NUMBER+@band(rbpe+03902300)), accessed January 21, 2015.
23. Cheetham, *The Life of Thomas Paine*, 32, archive.org/stream/lifethomaspaine00 cheegoog#page/n48/mode/2up, accessed January 20, 2015.

Incidents Near Fort Ticonderoga on June 17, 1777

✺ MICHAEL BARBIERI ✺

A soldier writes his wife:

Mount Independence, June 8, 1777

I heartily embrace the opportunity to write to you, hoping that these will find you and yours in good health as I am now. I have been vary hearty since I left home. I herd last week that you were all well. Mr. Church said Sarah had been sick but had got well again. I would have your write to me if you can. I want to hear how you make out. I have nothing in particular to write to you. June 10th I received your letter yesterday and was very glad to see it. I was down the lake as far as Cumberland Bay last week but we could not see anything. We keep out small scouts but never have seen any but once. There were a party came up to Split Rock but did not stay more than 3 days. By what we herd they will not trouble us this summer. The measles are amongst us. Carpenters has had them. Robert & several others expect to have them soon. The Tories are the greatest trouble we have. They have tried to spread the Small Pox but were found out. Rum is 10/- a Quart Sugar 2/6 per lb. Chees 2/6–tobacco 30 a lb. We have got our bounty. My Dear Wife after my regard to you, I don't know when I shall see you but would have you do as well as you can. Remember that god is as able to support you now as ever if you trust in him. I shall come home as soon as I can get a chance and so I remain you loving husband till Death.

Acquilla Cleaveland[1]

---

1. Acquilla Cleaveland, letter to wife Mercy, June 8-10, 1777; pension application of Mercy Cleaveland, page 25; *Revolutionary War Pension and Bounty-Land Warrant Application Files* (National Archives and Records Administration, M804, roll 574). Hereafter referred to as "Pension Files."

It is likely that by the time Mercy Cleaveland read this letter, her husband already lay in his grave. Four months earlier, he had enlisted as a private in Benjamin Whitcomb's Independent Corps of Rangers, a small group of men who functioned as scouts and spies for the Northern Department of the American army.[2] Cleaveland died on June 17, 1777, just one week after finishing his letter, during an Indian ambush of a party of Rangers returning from a scouting mission down the lake.[3] A minor occurrence in the overall history of the American Revolution, this small action has become lost in the myriad events of greater significance. However, judging from the number of letters, diaries, and journals that mention the ambush, it held considerably more significance for Acquilla Cleaveland's contemporaries. Like all combat, for those directly involved, it held mortal importance.

In early 1777, the American army on Lake Champlain struggled to gather the necessary strength to man its positions. Unlike the previous year when there had been well over ten-thousand men at Mount Independence and Fort Ticonderoga, late spring of 1777 found barely a quarter of that number defending the posts. Two conditions brought on the predicament. To the south, Washington had his own dire problems assembling sufficient numbers to counter the British threat to the areas around Philadelphia and New York. As a result, he had few troops to spare for the Northern Department. Acquilla Cleaveland pointed to the second condition when he wrote that rumors claimed the British did not plan to "trouble us here this summer." Many soldiers, civilians, and members of Congress felt the British would not mount an invasion out of Canada with the result that minimal effort went into strengthening the department.

Nevertheless, plans had to be made for defense. Lake Champlain ended twelve miles north of Ticonderoga at Crown Point and the southern extension of the lake, commonly called "the river," became very narrow. Only a quarter-mile of water separated Ticonderoga from a promontory called Mount Independence on the east shore. Since Ticonderoga had been built by the French to counter an attack from the south, the north-facing Mount offered better protection against an invasion coming up the lake from Canada. However, the Americans had "but 2200 effective, and these ill armed ill cloathed and unaccoutered," a number and condition considered inadequate for

2. The Northern Department of the army consisted of most of New York and Vermont.
3. Lakes Champlain and George flow north so anyone going from that area to Canada would go "down" the lake.

defending the extensive Ticonderoga complex.[4] Expanding the works on the east side of the lake meant taking men from the west side so, to compensate, the old "French Lines" just a few hundred yards out from the fortress became the main line of defense. Outside those lines, use of the old works that had been repaired and the newly built positions had to be kept to a minimum.

As well as devising a defensive strategy, the American commanders attempted to gain information about British plans by regularly sending scouting parties down the lake. Cleaveland had been on such a mission to Cumberland Bay the week before writing to his wife. Gen. Arthur St. Clair commented that "[t]these parties were generally selected from a corps of rangers, who had been accustomed to services of this kind."[5] St. Clair's comment referred primarily to two companies commanded by Capt. Benjamin Whitcomb and a smaller company of Vermont men under Capt. Thomas Lee that had been attached to Whitcomb's corps. The hazards of long distance scouting fell principally to these three companies—a total of less than one hundred men.

American scouting parties in the late spring of 1777 seldom traveled farther down the lake than Cumberland Bay near Plattsburgh, NY. The scouts should have gone beyond that point but intense Indian activity to the north severely restricted the success of such movement and drastically threatened the survival of the scouts. The Indians formed part of the British invasion army that the Americans did not expect to see that summer but which did exist. If the American scouts had been able to approach St. John's, another 45 miles down the lake, they would have seen the preparations taking place for the British army's southward movement but those activities remained undiscovered by the American scouts.

The army gathering in Canada represented part of an intricate plan devised by Gen. John Burgoyne who felt that since the heart of the rebellion beat strongest in New England, separating that area of the colonies from the rest would cause the rebellion to wither and die. To accomplish this dissection, he proposed that one force move up the Hudson River from New York City with Albany, New York, as the objective. A second force with the same objective would come from

---

4. Arthur St. Clair, letter to James Wilson, June 18, 1777; vol. 2, box 10, James Wilson papers (Collection 721, The Historical Society of Pennsylvania).
5. "Proceedings of a General Court-Martial, . . . for the Trial of Major General Arthur St. Clair, August 25, 1778," in *Collections of the New-York Historical Society for the Year 1880* (New York, 1881), 78. Hereafter cited as "Court-Martial of Gen. St. Clair."

the west via the Mohawk River. The plan would be completed by a third force, under his command moving south out of Canada, up Lakes Champlain and George to the headwaters of the Hudson River, and then follow that river down to Albany. The army gathering under Burgoyne included approximately 9,000 British and German regulars, French-Canadians, Loyalists, and Indians from several communities including St. Regis, Sault St. Louis, Lake of the Two Mountains, and St. Francis.[6]

The number of Indians with Burgoyne varied almost on a daily basis, but he expected to have 400-500 accompanying him. Most British officers regarded them with mixed feelings: "The Indians are cunning and Treacherous, more remarkable for rapid marches and sudden attacks than Courage."[7] The British did see some value in their methods and Burgoyne used them as a screen to sweep up anyone who might observe his army. He also used them in the same manner as Whitcomb's Rangers served the Americans—as long-range scouts. Lt. Thomas Anburey, an officer with Burgoyne, echoed St. Clair's comments about Whitcomb's Rangers when he said that the Indians "were of vast service in foraging and scouting parties, it being suited to their manner."[8] It was a party of Mohawks from Sault St. Louis, an Indian settlement also called Caughnawaga, west of Montreal, which brought about the actions on Tuesday, June 17, 1777.

On that day, with pleasant weather and little expectation of trouble from the British in Canada, the American camp at Ticonderoga had a relaxed attitude.[9] Around noon, the calm atmosphere changed dramatically when the long roll of the drums signaled a call to arms. The alarm had been occasioned by "two Men taken and two killed by a Party of Indians who had concealed themselves in the Bushes near our out Guards, and rushed suddenly upon some unarmed Men who had strolled out a fishing."[10] These men, from Hale's New Hampshire regiment, had gone out along the road between the French lines and

6. George G.F. Stanley, ed., *For Want of a Horse* (Sackville, New Brunswick, Canada: Tribune Press, 1961), 98n.

7. James Murray Hadden, *Hadden's Journal and Orderly Books*, Horatio Rogers, ed., (Albany, NY: J. Munsell's Sons, 1884), 15.

8. Thomas Anburey, *Travels Through the Interior Parts of America; in a Series of Letters by an Officer* (London: W. Lane, 1789), vol. I, 425 (Letter XXXIX).

9. Moses Greenleaf, "Breakfast on Chocolate:' The Diary of Moses Greenleaf, 1777," Donald Wickman, ed., *Bulletin of the Fort Ticonderoga Museum*, vol. XV, no. 6 (1997), 494.

10. St. Clair to Wilson.

A topographical drawing showing Fort Ticonderoga from the South Bay of Lake Champlain in 1759. (*Library of Congress*)

the mills on the La Chute River.[11] When they had walked only about one hundred rods (about a quarter of a mile) from the lines where a thousand men sat encamped, the Indians fell upon them.[12] Within moments, the Indians had completed their bloody work, dragged their prisoners into the woods, and begun their trek back to Canada.

The attack caught the American camp completely by surprise and assembling the pursuit party took some time. In addition to the lack of a party already under arms at the time of the attack, the Americans held the same opinions about fighting Indians in the woods as did the British, and the men felt a certain amount of reluctance to chase an unknown number of them through wooded terrain. By the time the pursuit finally left the camp, the Indians had an insurmountable head start and the Americans could not find them. According to Nathan Brown, the Americans learned a lesson from this incident: "I believe that the officers are all vare much Disapointed and will not tary after them again."[13]

The Indians knew that they had caused considerable confusion and that the Americans did, indeed, "tary after them." They certainly did not feel, as one American claimed, "pushed to that degree that they

11. Henry B. Livingston, Ticonderoga, to William Livingston, June 21, 1777, letter, *Livingston Papers*, Massachusetts Historical Society, Boston.

12. Nathan Hale, Ticonderoga, to Abigail Hale, Rindge, NH, letter, June 21, 1777, *Hale Family Papers, 1698-1918*, Manuscript Division, Library of Congress, Washington, D.C.

13. Nathan Brown, Mount Independence, to John Dudley, Raymond, NH, letter, June 23, 1777, *Dudley Papers*, File 1, document 3-b, New Hampshire Historical Society, Concord, NH.

flung away there packs and knives to facilitate there escape."[14]
Soldiers, and Indians, commonly took off their packs before engaging
the enemy in order to allow for easier movement, particularly in the
woods. The Indians may have taken theirs off before attacking the
fishermen but they certainly removed their packs a few miles north of
Ticonderoga on their return to Canada.

The attack on the men outside the American defenses did not end
the fighting for that day. Jabez Colton wrote a friend that "[s]oon after
this a Small Scout of our men returning home commanded by a
Leutenant, fell into an Ambuscade of these Indians."[15] The Indians had
successfully raided the front door of the American positions and now,
on their way back north, they discovered another party coming
towards them from the direction of Crown Point. Since close pursuit
from Ticonderoga did not materialize the Indians prepared for more
battle.

The Indians set up their ambush around one o'clock in the afternoon.[16] They chose a place called Taylor's Creek about halfway
between Ticonderoga and Crown Point where the approaching party
would be down in the bed of the waterway and paying more attention to crossing the creek than to their surroundings.[17] The Indians
numbered around thirty. Moving into the ambush was a group less
than half that size. Under the command of Lt. Nathan Taylor, at 22,
the youngest officer in Whitcomb's Rangers, the American party
included Acquilla Cleveland and a few other men from Whitcomb's
Rangers accompanied by some volunteers from other regiments—a
total of fourteen men. With the approaching party outnumbered,
unsuspecting, and distracted by crossing a stream, the Indians must
have felt confident of another success.

14. Ebenezer Stevens, Ticonderoga, to Samuel Philip Savage (President of the Board
or War), letter, June 24, 1777, Massachusetts Historical Society, Boston.
15. Jabez Colton, Mount Independence, to Reverend Dr. Stephen Williams,
Longmeadow, MA, letter, June 19, 1777, Fort Ticonderoga Collections [FTA M#-
1998].
16. Greenleaf, 494.
17. Surgeon's report, pension application of Nathan Taylor, "Pension Files," reel 2350,
image 565. Although a creek by that name does not show on contemporary maps,
there is a brook named Halfway Brook (shown as Grant's Creek on many current
maps) on William Brassier's 1762 map, *A survey of Lake Champlain, including Lake
George*. It is likely this is the area where the action occurred. In further support of this
is a contemporary comment that the lake was almost two miles wide at the point
where the ambush occurred. Inspection of the lake between the two forts shows that
although much of that stretch of the waterway is relatively narrow, it does widen considerably in the area where Halfway Brook enters the lake.

The party of Rangers certainly felt relieved to be within a few miles of Ticonderoga and their camp on Mount Independence. Earlier, they had passed by the American outpost at Crown Point and they would be home within one or two hours. They would have felt secure now that the most dangerous part of the mission had passed. With the Indians well hidden the two parties "were within ten steps of each other" when the Indians triggered the ambush.[18]

The Indians did not fire upon the scouting party without warning. Instead, "[t]he Indians Sprung up & ordered them To Surrender."[19] One Indian addressed the Rangers using the word "Sago."[20] Although the word had no direct English equivalent, "Sago" did not constitute a threat but rather carried the essence of a greeting one would extend to a friend.[21] Did this Indian think the Rangers were a Loyalist party? Did he suppose that the Rangers could be fooled into thinking the Indians sided with the American cause and thereby trick them into an easy capture? Was he actually sympathetic to the American cause and trying to warn them? The men of the scouting party did not care. All they knew was that a strange Indian had suddenly appeared very close to them in the wilderness and Taylor immediately ordered the men to fire.

The reaction surprised the Indians "so thay mad Very wild fires on owre men a pritey warm scurmidge Ensued for a few minets."[22] Outnumbered and nearly surrounded, Taylor and the rest of the party soon realized that they had to fight their way out. Following one of the classic military maneuvers with which to counter an ambush, Taylor and his men attacked a weak point in the Indians' position. They broke through the encirclement and, expecting hot pursuit by the Indians, fled toward Ticonderoga: "[O]ne of our men was a Bliged to swim through the Lack."[23] Although the Indians had the Rangers outnumbered and on the run, they did not pursue them back towards Ticonderoga. They knew that, by now, the Americans at Ticonderoga had a party after them and the noise of the musket fire had told that party just where to find them. Their confidence now shaken by the hard fighting of the Rangers, the Indians collected their casualties and continued down the lake leaving their packs to be found later by the Americans.

18. St. Clair to Wilson.
19. Hale to Hale.
20. Colton to Williams.
21. Author's conversation with George Larrabee, expert on northeastern Native Peoples.
22. Hale to Hale.
23. Brown to Dudley.

Reports of American casualties for the day varied. Lieutenant Taylor received a wound in the left shoulder. The ball entered near the top of his shoulder, ran across his shoulder blade and came out near his backbone.[24] He continued to serve in Whitcomb's Rangers for two-and-a-half more years until he finally had to resign his commission due to lingering effects of the wound. An unnamed soldier received a wound in the head.[25] Others certainly received wounds during the fight but, at this time, their names have not been discovered. Two men died in the ambush—one being Acquilla Cleaveland. Records indicate three men of Caleb Robison's Company in Hale's Regiment—Joseph Harris, Moses Copps, and Samuel Smith—all died that day. Whether they suffered their fate near the French lines at Ticonderoga or in the ambush has not been determined. Four other men—Israel Woodbury and Thomas Creighton of Hale's regiment, Edward Wells of Poor's regiment, and William Presson of Scammell's regiment—are all listed as missing at that time. Like those killed, it has not been determined if they became prisoners during the raid or the ambush.

The number of Indian dead and wounded remains more of a mystery. In the confusion of fighting in the woods, the combatants could not tell if their shots reached their targets but Taylor and his men knew that they had killed at least one Indian and suspected that they had inflicted other casualties. When a burial party went back the next day, they "found one Indian dead lying between two logs with his Powder horn and a Bullet Pouch. . . . Our men saw as they supposed signs of one or two more that were killed and draged into the lake."[26] Further, although the Indians succeeded in disguising how many casualties they had suffered by carrying off their dead, the Americans felt that "it is probable they must have met with some as they were within ten steps of each other."[27] Even with a smooth-bore musket, it is hard to miss a target at that range and the Americans often loaded with buck and ball which would increase the likelihood of their fire having an effect.[28]

If the Americans could believe the accounts given by the Indians to their British commanders, however, the Indians did not suffer many casualties in the action. The British officer in charge of the Indian

24. Surgeon's report, Nathan Taylor pension application.
25. Hale to Hale; Colton to Williams.
26. Ibid.
27. St. Clair to Wilson.
28. "Buck and ball" is nine or twelve smaller buck shot loaded on top of the normal full-size ball.

scouting parties, Lieutenant Scott, sent a report to Brigadier General Fraser telling him that one of the scouting parties "had met with a small party of the Enemy about 14 or 15 in Numbers, of whom his people killed 4, and took 4 prisoners; the Indians had one killed and one wounded; . . . They fell in with them some where near Ticonderoga."[29] The British accurately reported the size of the American party but the numbers of casualties and captured differed from American reports. Lieutenant Scott may have included in his report those killed and taken prisoner near the French lines or at some other time and place in the Indians' movements. Even with unclear casualty figures, the day's events appeared to have been a victory for the Indians.

In spite of the danger of the Indians still being in the area, Whitcomb and some of his men returned to the scene of the ambush the next day. They found and buried the two dead Americans, one of whom had been scalped by the Indians before they left the scene.[30] The Rangers returned to Mount Independence the next day after performing their melancholy duty.[31]

If there existed any sense of triumph for the Americans to take from these occurrences, it was that the Rangers had killed at least one Indian and wounded some others "so that our injuries are not altogether unavenged."[32] Benjamin Whitcomb made the best of the situation: "Thursday. This day pleasant wind variable Capt Whitcomb returns from Scout brings a Grand Scalp of the Coynawago's."[33] A touch of the excitement (and possible embellishment) the taking of this scalp brought to the American camp can be read in the lines, "and to our satisfaction the body of the Indian Chief with all his Ornaments on, of which they striped him, as well as his Scalp which were carried in triumph through our Camp."[34]

29. Stanley, 98.
30. No information has come to light as to how or when in the skirmish poor Cleaveland died or whether or not his body suffered from the scalping knife. Clues exist for some of the names of the other men taken and killed that day but who was involved where and what happened to whom has not yet been verified.
31. Colton to Williams.
32. St. Clair to Wilson.
33. Greenleaf, 495.
34. Stevens to Savage. No other sources claim the dead Indian to be a chief. If he had been a chief, it would seem that the British reports of the incident would have included that bit of information assuming, of course, that the other Indians told him that bit of knowledge. Another question is why did the Indians leave this body instead of taking it away with them as was their usual custom? It seems as though they would particularly have wanted to take the body of a chief with them. Did they simply not find

With the Indians getting so close to the American lines and a scouting party being ambushed such a short distance from home, many in the camps at Mount Independence and Fort Ticonderoga began to worry about the British plans. Did they, after all the rumors, intend to move up the lake? From that point on, St. Clair sent out more scouts than before and over a wider area: "I had all the ground between this and Crown-point, from the Lake some distance over the mountains, well examined yesterday with a heavy scout, but they discovered no enemy, nor appearance of any."[35] Although this particular scout had nothing to report, it went only as far north as Crown Point. On the 28th, a smaller party went farther north:

> My scout, on which I depended much for intelligence. is not yet returned, nor I fear ever will now. It consisted of three men only, the best of Whitcomb's people, and picked out by him for the purpose. The woods are so full of Indians that it is difficult for parties to get through.[36]

By the time of this scout, the army under Burgoyne had advanced several miles up the lake and had his Indians scouring the woods to prevent American scouting parties from discovering the move. Although the Americans apparently did not get captured or killed, they did not return in time to give St. Clair any information that could save the positions around Mount Independence and Ticonderoga.[37]

Four days after the action at Taylor's Creek, on June 21, Burgoyne made a speech to the Indians in which he complimented them and offered a reward for bringing in prisoners. At the same time he forbade their scalping any but the dead. Did the action of the 17th have

the body? According to Whitcomb's report, his burial party found the body near the dead Americans and they apparently found it with little trouble. The Indians took the time to scalp at least one of the dead Americans and they took the time to carry off their other casualties. Why not this one? If this Indian had been the one to stand up and say "Sago" to the Rangers, could it have been an intentional action by the rest of the Indians to leave this body and thereby condemn his soul to eternal disgrace?

35. Court-Martial of Gen. St. Clair, 21.

36. Ibid., 122.

37. Which individuals went on this scout is not known but the rolls for the companies under Whitcomb's command do not show any casualties around that time. Abel Rice, a sergeant in Whitcomb's Rangers, may have been one of those men. He returned to Ticonderoga from a scouting mission to find the British flag flying over the fort! Imagine the shock—instead of relaxing with his friends, he now had to travel through an unknown number of miles of enemy territory in search of an army the whereabouts of which he had no idea. He eventually found his way through the enemy lines without incident and rejoined the rest of the Rangers.

some influence on Burgoyne's speech? Offering the Indians a reward for prisoners minimized unnecessary killing such as that which had happened to the unlucky unarmed fishermen near the French lines. Burgoyne knew the coming campaign promised to be long and difficult and he felt it best to reinforce his expectations of the Indians before events such as those of the 17th became more frequent and the risk of unwanted and unnecessary actions became too high.

The events on June 17, 1777, proved to be the first in a series of actions which would cost the lives of many people, culminate in the battles at Saratoga, and alter the course of world history by helping secure the birth of the United States. Innumerable people over the interceding centuries have been aware of these results but what has been lost in the haze of history (but certainly remembered by Mercy Cleaveland—she still had her husband's letter over sixty years later) is that somewhere near a woodland creek between Ticonderoga and Crown Point are the graves of a few, including that of Mercy's husband, who died early in that struggle.

Forgotten Volunteers: The 1st Company, Governor's Foot Guard During the Saratoga Campaign

❦ MATTHEW REARDON ❦

It is considered the oldest, continuously serving military unit in the United States. The 1st Company, Governor's Foot Guard has as much a storied history as the state that it serves. It came into existence in 1771, when the Connecticut General Assembly approved a petition that had been submitted by a group of prominent Hartford citizens to form an independent militia company. Among them was Samuel Wyllys, the son of the secretary of state and future Continental army colonel. The petition created "a distinct military company by the name of the Governor's Guard . . . consisting of sixty-four in number, rank and file, to attend upon and guard the Governor and General Assembly annually on election days and at all other times as occasion shall require, equipped with proper arms and uniformly dressed."[1]

It would hold the name "Governor's Guard" until 1775 when a group of New Haven citizens, among them Benedict Arnold, petitioned the General Assembly to raise a second company in that city. It would be known as the First Company, Governor's Guard for only two years when in 1778, with the organization of the Governor's Horse Guards, they again modified their name to its current one, the First Company, Governor's Foot Guard.

It has been a long held tradition that the unit played a very minimal role during the Revolutionary War. Its official history, published in 1901, only mentions two occurrences where they believed that the company played a significant role during the conflict. The first being in the fall of 1780, where they provided a military escort to two French

1. Charles J. Hoadly, ed., *The Public Records of the Colony of Connecticut*, 15 vols. (Hartford, CT: Case, Lockwood, & Brainard Co., 1890), 13:544.

commanders, Gen. Comte de Rochambeau and Adm. de Ternay through the streets of Hartford where they were to meet with George Washington at the State House. They referred to it as "the most interesting and imposing event in their entire history."[2] The second event was the company's seemingly uneventful participation in the Saratoga Campaign.

During the unit's centennial commemoration an address was given by Col. Henry C. Deming in which he recounted the event:

> It was the darkest hour of the Revolutionary struggle. Burgoyne had broken through the gates of Canada, swept out from St. Clair from Ticonderoga, captured and dismantled all the fortresses from the foot of Lake George to the head waters of the Hudson, and was in triumphant progress to join Sir Henry Clinton and cut off New England from New York. . . . All the troops in the Eastern States were rallied to prevent the consummation of the fatal design. The Guard was not obliged to go. They were not liable to the draft. Their duty was limited to guarding the Governor and the General Assembly. Under no circumstance could they be forced to the front, unless the governor went in person. But . . . the Guard unanimously resolved to go and actually went, under Captain Jonathan Bull, and while an advanced guard of reinforcements hurrying to Saratoga, they were crossing the Rhinebeck Flats they were met by a messenger with the joyful intelligence that Burgoyne had surrendered, and wheeling about marched with alacrity, it is presumed, for the banks of the Connecticut.[3]

According to Deming, the company, as volunteers, had marched over ninety miles, only to be turned back, disappointed at not reaching the scene to participate in either of the battles of Saratoga. Only until recently, that was all that was known about their participation in the campaign.

The real story is that the Governor's Foot Guard played a much larger role in the Saratoga campaign than anyone had previously reported. In fact, they may have actually played a larger role in the war than previously believed. While researching another topic, I came across the pension application of John Roberts. According to his application, Roberts was born on September 15, 1759, and resided in

---

2. *History of the First Company Governor's Foot Guard, Hartford, Connecticut, 1771-1901* (Hartford, CT: Danforth Press, 1902), 11. The event is still commemorated every September by members of the company. Each "Rochambeau Day" current members reenact the march in Hartford.
3. Ibid., 10.

Hartford at the outbreak of the war. He never states his involvement in the Governor's Guard until 1777, but he mentions serving under officers that were part of the company. For his first term of service, Roberts, in May 1775, joined a company of volunteers in Hartford under Lt. William Knox, a member of the Governor's Guard, and marched to Fort Ticonderoga in New York. There they escorted British prisoners of war back to Hartford. Roberts remained as a prison guard until the following February, where he assisted the movement of military supplies to the Continental army then engaged in the siege of Boston.[4]

Roberts states that in June 1777 the First Company volunteered as a unit and was sent over sixty miles away to the Connecticut coastal town of Fairfield. There they served for three months, where they were "constantly employed in guarding the sound coast." Discharged on the first of September, they returned to Hartford.[5]

By the last week of September, a dispatch rider arrived in Hartford carrying requests for reinforcements from Maj. Gen. Israel Putnam, the commander of Continental forces along the Hudson River, then stationed at Peekskill, New York.[6] It was feared by Putnam that he was about to be attacked by a British force under the command of Sir Henry Clinton who was then moving up the Hudson River in order to cooperate with Gen. John Burgoyne.

It is here that we can join Deming's narrative of events. His assertions thus far were correct; the company, despite not being obliged to go, volunteered their services during the fall of 1777. However, it was not to reinforce Saratoga, but to aid Peekskill. Under the leadership of Capt. Jonathan Bull, Lt. William Bull, and Ens. James Tiley, they joined a drafted militia brigade under the command of Brig. Gen. Erastus Wolcott.[7] After marching over a hundred miles, they arrived in the Peekskill area on October 9, two days after the British captured Forts Montgomery and Clinton, just across the river.[8]

---

4. John Roberts Pension Application, National Archives and Record Services, Washington, D.C. In late 1776, Major Christopher French, who served in the British 22nd Regiment of Foot, was taken prisoner. He would be housed in the tavern belonging to William Knox and guarded/escorted by members of the Governor's Foot Guard.

5. Ibid.

6. Charles J. Hoadly, ed., *The Records of the State of Connecticut*, 4 vols. (Hartford, CT: Case, Lockwood, & Brainard Co., 1894-1942), 2:405.

7. Ibid.; John Roberts Pension Application.

8. Israel Putnam, *General Orders Issued by Major-General Israel Putnam When In Command of the Highlands, In the Summer and Fall of 1777*, Worthington C. Ford, ed. (Brooklyn, NY: Historical Printing Club, 1893), 82-83.

According to Roberts, when they arrived they did not serve with the other militia units. They were instead attached to the 3rd Connecticut Regiment, part of the Continental army.[9] This was probably because the regiment's colonel, Samuel Wyllys, was the prime organizer of the company and was its commander before the war. He apparently wanted his company to serve with him.

After the British established a base at Fort Clinton, they began launching naval raids up the river in attempt to help Burgoyne, who was then engaged near Saratoga. Since its capture, along with Fort Montgomery, Putnam had been moving his force northward along the east bank of the Hudson in order to observe British movements.

On October 16, a British force landed at Kingston, the wartime capital of New York, about sixty-five miles north of Peekskill. They marched inland, captured the city, and set it ablaze. Instead of marching to Kingston, Putnam, learning of Burgoyne's surrender at Saratoga, halted his force. That same day he issued a general order informing his men of the surrender and "Congratulates the troops and orders them to Halt and Remain . . . untill further orders and Cook Provisions & Refresh them Selves."[10]

The next day, George Clinton, the governor of New York, sent requests southward to Putnam for assistance. He feared the burning of Kingston was only the first of several intended British targets. He might have also been nervous that they might make an attempt to free Burgoyne's captured army. Putnam responded quickly by sending most of his force northward towards Rhinebeck, located just opposite of Kingston, the very same day.[11]

The 3rd Connecticut Regiment, with the Governor's Foot Guard, marched about six miles in the lead of the main force. While we cannot verify that the First Company was in the advance guard, like Deming asserted, we now know for sure that at least their regiment was in the lead.[12] They were also advancing, despite having heard of Burgoyne's surrender the previous day. This was in contradiction to Deming's statement because he stated that upon hearing the good news, they turned around and headed back to Connecticut. They did not turn around, but instead pressed ahead to Rhinebeck where they arrived on the 18th. There they were able to view the British force

9. Ibid., 83.
10. Ibid., 84.
11. George Clinton, *Public Papers of George Clinton, First Governor of New York, 1777–1795—1801–1804.* 2 vols. (New York: Wynkoop Hallenback Crawford Co., 1900), 2: 457-459, 460-461.
12. Ibid., 460.

that was still on shipping in the river.[13] Roberts noted this in his pension application that at this time they were "employed watching the movement of the Enemys ship board up the river."[14]

They would remain here for about a couple days, until the British commander, learning of the surrender at Saratoga and realizing that he was basically surrounded by thousands of American troops, withdrew first towards Fort Clinton and then eventually back to New York City.[15] The Governor's Foot Guard retired southward with the rest of the force back to Peekskill where they were discharged and sent home in early November, having served for about a month.[16] This would be the first and last documented time that they would serve outside the border of Connecticut during the war.

The service of the First Company, Governor's Foot Guard along the Hudson River during the latter parts of the Saratoga Campaign has been completely forgotten. It might be because they did not participate in the battles of Saratoga or because the members did not see the need to memorialize a month of service in a six year long war. Though the unit today does not claim to have served in a combat role, this month of service brought it very close. In thirty days, a unit that was organized to only serve the governor and General Assembly marched over three hundred miles. For about two weeks, they were under arms and part of an American army that was actively monitoring British movements up and down the Hudson River. Had the British continued raiding after Kingston, they probably would have seen combat. Even if this does not constitute the official guidelines to earn them a battle honor, their service during the fall of 1777 deserves to be so much more than just a footnote in the history of Connecticut and its contributions during the Revolutionary War.

---

13. Ibid. Putnam writes his letter from "Leroy Statsford," which is today Staatsburg. He claimed that Wyllys' Regiment was six miles ahead of his position, which is a close estimate to the distance between Staatsburg and Rhinebeck.

14. John Roberts Pension Application.

15. Brendan Morrissey, *Saratoga 1777, Turning Point of a Revolution* (Hailsham, UK: Osprey Publishing, Ltd., 2000), 86, 90.

16. John Roberts Pension Application. Roberts, beginning in 1780, went on to serve on the three privateers before the war ended. Serving on the *Active* in 1781, he might have participated with its captain in the defense of New London when it was attacked that September by the British. However, he makes no mention of participation.

Sir Henry Clinton Attempts to Save the Convention Army

✺ MICHAEL J. F. SHEEHAN ✺

In late October of 1777, America celebrated its first capture of a British army; General Horatio Gates had defeated General Sir John Burgoyne near the village of Saratoga in upstate New York. The prisoners, known as the Convention Army after the semi-treaty that effected their surrender, were moved to a camp outside of Boston. By the autumn of 1778, it had been decided that the Convention Army would be moved to camps in Virginia, relieving the burden on Massachusetts. In doing so, they would have to cross the Hudson River, and the place selected to do so was at the King's Ferry, between Verplanck and Stony Points.

As was customary in the Revolution, it was not the responsibility of the victorious army to supply those they captured. To that end, Washington ordered a boat from the British in New York to be permitted to pass "King's Ferry with Cloathing and other necessaries for the troops of the Convention," as they were due at the end of November.[1] The same day, Washington sent a letter to General Sir Henry Clinton, the British Commander-in-chief, to which he responded days later that he had "sent Major Bruen, Deputy Quarter Mr [Master] General of the Army to King's Ferry with the Money & Necessaries."[2] Not two and a half weeks later, on December 5, Washington received information from Col. Christian Febiger that "52

---

1. George Washington to James Clinton, November 14, 1778, Founders Online, National Archives founders.archives.gov/documents/Washington/03-18-02-0141. All letters from the National Archives or the Library of Congress accessed on November 1, 2014. Hereafter, the National Archives will be referred to as NA.

2. Sir Henry Clinton to George Washington, November 19, 1778, NA. founders. archives.gov/documents/Washington/03-18-02-0213. Major Bruer was from the 15th Regiment of Foot.

Vessels yesterday morning were . . . up the North River with flat bottom boats . . . we cannot tell what their object is . . . The enemy certainly must have some object . . . and I should suppose [it a] rescue of the Convention troops."[3]

A week earlier, Col. Beverly Robinson forwarded intelligence to General Clinton that the militia of Orange and Ulster counties and a portion of the Continental army were distracted by the recent attack at Cherry Valley and had been shifting towards Minisink, away from the Hudson. It was this letter on which Clinton later scribbled "occasioned my move to Verplanck's" for the purpose of rescuing "at least part of those troops [of the Convention]" which inspired him to move up the Hudson.[4] Capt. John Peebles of the 42nd Regiment of Foot said that by late on the 4th, they had advanced to "about 5 miles below Kings Ferry."[5] The troops aboard ship were under the overall command of Brig. Gen. Edward Matthew, "while Brigadier General Sir William Erskine marched by land as far as Tarrytown." In New York, the famous Jäger captain Johann Ewald recorded that Erskine had with him about two thousand men "advanc[ing] over the pass of Kings Bridge," and that the shipping had about four thousand. Clinton was to accompany the force on the Hudson.[6]

In a detailed letter to Washington, Major Richard Platt, adjutant to General Alexander McDougall, commander of the Highlands, described the British flotilla and movement of troops as actions unfolded on the 5th. After spotting the "eighteen Vessels anchored in Haverstraw Bay," McDougall ordered from West Point "Lt Col [Udny] Hay with 500 Pennsylvanians & Genl Nixon's Brigade" down

3. Robert Hanson Harrison to Nathanael Greene, December 5, 1778, cited as a note in GW to NG, December 4, 1778, NA. founders.archives.gov/documents /Washington/03-18-02-0389. The North River was an alternative term for the Hudson during the eighteenth century.

4. General Sir Henry Clinton, *The American Rebellion: Sir Henry Clinton's Narrative of His Campaigns, 1775-1782, with an Appendix of Original Documents.* William B. Willcox, ed. (New Haven, CT: Yale University Press, 1954), 114-15. Beverly Robinson had been living in the Hudson Valley since the early 1770s and so was useful to Sir Henry regarding the area. He commanded the Loyal American Regiment and his confiscated home was the headquarters for commanders of West Point.

5. John Peebles, *John Peebles' American War: The Diary of a Scottish Grenadier, 1776-1782.* Ira D. Gruber, ed. (Mechanicsburg, PA: Stackpole Books, 1998), 237. The point five miles below the ferry lies between Croton Point and the northern section of Hook Mountain, near the Hi Tor.

6. Clinton, *The American Rebellion*, 115. Johann Ewald, *Diary of the American War: A Hessian Journal,* Joseph P. Tustin, ed. (New Haven, CT: Yale University Press, 1979), 157.

A view of the Convention Army's encampment in Charlottesville, Virginia. (*Library of Congress*)

to and across King's Ferry.[7] During their march, the stores of flour and pork at King's Ferry had been sent to Haverstraw Village under the care of Col. Ann Hawkes Hay. Lt. Col. Udny Hay and General Nixon had arrived at Stony Point by 3 a.m. on the 5th and began crossing King's Ferry to the Verplanck side; this was slowed by there being only two boats (the rest having been previously sent up the river with stores). By daybreak, "3 companies of Col [Rufus] Putnam's Regt" were prevented from crossing by the advance of the British vessels. Instead, they marched south to take "post upon the Hill at Col [Ann Hawkes] Hay's . . . The enemy . . . debarked in 20 boats . . . and landed at Stony Point." Nixon's brigade "immediately moved towards them; but before [they] got within a Mile . . . [the British] set fire to two or three small huts." No sooner had they done so than they got into their boats and went back to the shipping "without destroying any Stores or taking any Cattle."[8]

Clinton recalled in his memoirs that he had encountered a "delay of four days in our passage up the river . . . [that] prevented the . . . attempt on [the American rear] . . . as I had come so far and the

7. Richard Platt to George Washington, December 6, 1778, NA. founders.archives. gov/documents/Washington/03-18-02-0415. Lt. Col. Udny Hay of Pennsylvania became Assistant Quarter Master of the region in the late war, and is not to be confused with Col. Ann Hawkes Hay of the 2nd Regiment Orange County Militia of New York.
8. Ibid.

weather fine for the time of year, I landed the flank companies and part of the battalion of Guards . . . at Stony Point."[9] Captain Ewald, who was not part of the expedition, recalled that they "arrived at Verplancks Point two days too late, wherupon they returned." Captain Peebles, who was part of the cruise up the Hudson but did not disembark from his vessel the *Royal Sceptre*, recalled that "a body of men landed from the Transports on the Jersey shore, & having marched a little way, a smoke arose that look'd very like the firing of small arms but believe it was only burning some houses tho' we saw about 200 of the rebels at a house a mile or two from thence the troops staid ashore about an hour & Reembark'd again." Peebles also agreed with Ewald and said that "Burgoynes people . . . cross'd the North River at Kings Ferry two days before we got there, so we came back again."[10]

Major Platt's letter reached Washington at Paramus, New Jersey, later on the sixth. Washington moved immediately to oppose the British in case they lingered in Haverstraw Bay. To Col. Thomas Clark of the North Carolina line, Washington wrote that Clark "Be pleased . . . to move the [North Carolina] Brigade . . . to a good piece of Ground seven or eight miles towards the Ferry . . . If the enemy should have landed any men, you will send out scouts to reconnoitre them . . . keep them from penetrating the Country." Washington also ordered the Pennsylvania and Virginia brigades of Generals Anthony Wayne and Peter Muhlenberg "to Suffrans," just in case Clark required backup.[11] Although Washington was quick to respond to Clinton's

9. Clinton, *The American Rebellion.* It is not quite clear what delay Clinton is referring to, as no other British memorialists of the event recall or record any delay, weather related or otherwise.

10. Ewald, *Diary of the American War,* 157; Peebles. *John Peebles' American War,* 237-38. The *Royal Sceptre,* which Peebles called a "Cork Victualer" must have been one of the transports. Since Peebles' unit was a Grenadier, or "flank," company it is not clear why he, nor anyone on his vessel did not join the other flank companies in landing. The mention of the "Jersey shore" refers to what is now the shore of Rockland County on the west side of the Hudson, as before the Revolution the area had been disputed between New York and New Jersey. The troops seen near a "house a mile or two from" Stony Point were the troops from Putnam's regiment, amassing on the hill above Hay's. That site is now the grounds of Helen Hayes Hospital, better known as the grounds of the "Treason House," in Haverstraw.

11. George Washington to Thomas Clark, December 6, 1778, NA. founders.archives. gov/documents/Washington/03-18-02-0412; Robert Hanson Harrison to Nathanael Greene, December 6, 1778. George Washington Papers at the Library of Congress, 1741-1799: Series 4. General Correspondence. 1697-1799. memory.loc.gov/mss/ mgw/mgw4/054/0900/0970.jpg. Clark, though a Colonel, commanded the brigade of North Carolinians.

movements, he was still puzzled as to the reason. In a letter to General McDougall, he confessed that he could not "account for this odd maneuvre of Sr Henry Clinton in any other way than by supposing that he was misinformed as to the quantity of Stores at the ferry, or that it was a demonstration above, to forage with more security below."[12]

As the next few days passed Washington sent his reports to various officers, members of Congress, and governors, it became clear that the British withdrawal was permanent; the Continental army and militia could now settle down into winter quarters and have a fairly peaceful Christmas while the Convention Army, still in the hands of the Americans, marched slowly to their new quarters in Virginia.

12. George Washington to Alexander McDougall, December 7, 1778, NA. founders. archives.gov/documents/Washington/03-18-02-0424.

Captain Gustavus Conyngham: Successful American Naval Captain or Accidental Pirate?

❈ LOUIS ARTHUR NORTON ❈

Shortly after the onset of the Revolutionary War, Americans started to harass British commercial shipping close-to-home. One ship captain who engaged in this type of naval warfare was Gustavus Conyngham. He was credited with the most ships apprehended, but received little gratitude, remuneration, or recognition in maritime history, and in performing his service, he may have been the Revolutionary War's inadvertent American pirate.

THE IMMIGRANT AND *CHARMING PEGGY*

Conyngham was born in County Donegal, Ireland, in 1747 and his family immigrated to America in 1763. Conyngham learned mariner's skills as an apprentice to a Captain Henderson.[1] He later became a captain in his own right and was invited to join Philadelphia's Society for the Relief of Poor, Aged & Infirmed Masters of Ships, known locally as the "Sea Captain's Club." In 1773, at the age of twenty-six, Captain Conyngham married Philadelphia's Anne Hockley. The intelligent, articulate Mrs. Conyngham would become a vital asset later in his life.

The Philadelphia shipping firm Conyngham and Nesbitt Company, partly owned by a cousin, gave Conyngham command of the brigantine *Charming Peggy*. The Maryland Council of Safety contracted Conyngham and Nesbitt Company to obtain desperately needed gunpowder and other military equipment. In September 1775 Conyngham sailed to France to obtain the supplies and hoped to smuggle them back to America.

---

1. Henderson's given name is not recorded.

In November he arrived at Dunkirk and tied up adjacent to a British transport under repair. The port's powder magazine was close by, but getting barrels of powder onboard in the shadow of a British ship presented a problem. In his attempt to move the precious cargo quietly at night, a crewman on the transport became suspicious. He alerted his captain who, in turn, told the local British consul about Conyngham's suspected deceit. The consul then contacted England's Ambassador to France, Lord David Murray Stormont.

Stormont, increasingly aware that the French public seemed supportive of the Americans, demanded that the French foreign minister do something about Conyngham who appeared to be on a clandestine mission to obtain arms for the rebels. French officials boarded *Charming Peggy*, but Conyngham learned of the raid's plan and jettisoned the powder. Without proof of contraband, the French could not hold *Charming Peggy*'s captain, so he sailed for Holland minus the needed cargo and continued to Texel Island. Dutch businessmen brought two vessels to Texel loaded with the desired cargo plus "flints, medicene, [and] cloathing."[2] Contrary winds detained Conyngham's departure and then misfortune struck. A *Charming Peggy* crewman told the local British consul about the vessel's quest. *Charming Peggy* was seized and Conyngham arrested. Ever alert, Conyngham and some of his crew disarmed the guards that had been placed onboard. In danger of recapture, the captain and crew made for the nearest port with the intention of selling *Charming Peggy* to the Dutch government. Because of local corruption, Conyngham was never paid for *Charming Peggy* and was thus forced to search elsewhere for another ship to obtain and deliver the contracted cargo.

SHIP-LESS

Benjamin Franklin, the American Minister to France, was about to implement General Washington's plan of asymmetrical warfare against British shipping to influence commerce, maritime insurance rates, and British morale while keeping more of His Majesty's vessels on patrol near the British Isles, away from North American waters. Conyngham, who made his way to Paris was recommended to Franklin as a potential Continental navy captain, one who might be effective in harassing nearby British shipping. Franklin filled out a blank Continental navy commission for Conyngham dated March 1,

2. Robert Wilden Nesser ed., *Letters And Papers Relating to the Cruises of Gustavus Conyngham, A Captain Of The Continental Navy 1777-1779* (Whitefish, Montana: Kessinger Publishing, 2006), 10.

1777. Signed by John Hancock, the president in Congress, no written expiration date or restrictive clause was contained in Franklin's blank commission.[3]

At the time, American commissioner Silas Deane was making lucrative commercial dealings with French businessmen and likely saw Conyngham perhaps as a privateer captain in whom he might invest. Privateering was an important Revolutionary War activity that authorized a vessel, but not its captain, to conduct privateer operations outside the borders of its home nation and profit from the sale of cargos and prizes taken. Ship owners applying for a letter of marque provided a detailed description of the vessel, its armament, and posted a bond to assure that vessel and enterprise would observe international laws and customs.[4] The vessel could attack the enemy within the time limits of the letter of marque. Failing to comply with the obligations meant the letter could be revoked, prize money refused, the bond forfeited, and legal damages could be sanctioned. First issued by state (colonial) legislatures on April 3, 1776, the Continental Congress also issued national letters of marque to capture British vessels and cargoes.[5] Whether these letters were issued as blank documents so that ship owners could apply them to vessels of their choosing is not documented. Blank congressional privateer commissions might have been obtained from Deane.[6] Privateering during this time was both potentially lucrative and dangerous. Britain declared America's revolutionary activities as illegal, thus privateers were considered pirates and, if caught, punished by hanging. No captured Revolutionary War privateer actually met death in this way.[7]

SURPRIZE

After commissioners of the United States learned that Conyngham was seeking a ship, he was given command of the lugger *Peacock*, an armed vessel he believed was purchased and fitted by order of these

---

3. Nesser, *Letters and Papers of Conyngham*, 1. Franklin and his commissioners recruited many outstanding European officers to be appointed generals including Gilbert du Motier, Marquise de Lafayette, Baron Friedrich Von Steuben, and Count Casmir Pulaski.

4. The bonds were $5000 for vessels under 100 tons and $10,000 for vessels exceeding 100 tons.

5. Library of Congress, *Naval Records of the American Revolution, 1775-1788*. Washington, DC: Government Printing Office, 1906, 10-11.

6. No documents written by or to Conyngham refer to his actions as privateering and serve as evidence that Conyngham did not think that he was acting as a privateer.

7. Donald Barr Chidsey, *The American Privateers: A History* (New York: Dodd, Mead, and Company, 1962), 54.

commissioners. Luggers and cutters, relatively swift and quite seaworthy crafts in turbulent waters, were good vessels for smuggling and interdicting shipping and readily available in Dunkirk. Conyngham renamed *Peacock* the *Surprize*, and recruited his crew largely from idle American sailors detained in French and Belgian ports, plus an assortment of foreign nationals. At the request of Compte de Maurepas, prime minister of France, no French sailors were included.[8] The French were serious about maintaining strict neutrality. Conyngham considered *Surprize* to be a Continental navy warship and his crew were to be "govern'd by the regulations made for Seamen in the Continental Service" and not owned privately.[9] Conyngham said in a narrative dated March 1779 that he "Went on a cruze under my former Commission U.S. Navy."[10] Adding to this perception, one of Conyngham's first lieutenants, Matthew Lawler, later wrote to Navy Board member Timothy Pickering stating that, to his knowledge, he served on a "continental Vessel."[11]

Instructions dated July 15, 1777, from another American commissioner stationed in France, William Carmichael, put a sharper focus on Conyngham's mission. In part they stated, ". . . you should not cruise against the Commerce of England, I beg and intreat you . . . that you do nothing which may involve your security or occasion Umbrage to the Ministry of France. Not withstanding which your stock is not abundant . . . or If attackd first by our Enemies, the circumstances of the case will extenuate in your favor of your conduct . . . . in essence you may defend yourself." But Carmichael went on to say that he was to proceed directly to America to deliver dispatches as soon as possible.[12] Conyngham ignored the order and set out to do more damage to British shipping.

Surprize sailed from Dunkirk into the narrow English Channel in May 1777 where he captured two vessels while at sea: a British mail packet *Prince of Orange* carrying mail to the Dutch seaport of Helvoetsluis and the brig *Joseph* carrying a cargo of wine. On May 9 he ordered his prize crews to make for land with the two prize vessels where they were to be repaired and sold. When *Surprize*, accompanied by the prize vessels approached Dunkirk's harbor, they encountered a pair of British navy ketches. The British vessels rammed him multiple times, in the hope of goading Conyngham into a fight. He

8. Nesser, *Letters and Papers of Conyngham,* 60.
9. Nesser, *Letters and Papers of Conyngham,* 216-219.
10. Nesser, *Letters and Papers of Conyngham,* 11.
11. Nesser, *Letters and Papers of Conyngham,* 223-224.
12. Nesser, *Letters and Papers of Conyngham,* 64-65.

did not fire a shot and decided to use the courts as a weapon and proceeded to the protection of the neutral harbor. Conyngham planned to sue the British government for payment of damages to his ships once they got safely to shore and keep his prizes as well. His seemingly logical plan failed miserably.

The 1713 Treaty of Utrecht between France and England explicitly closed the ports of either power to the enemies of each other. Thus outraged, the British ambassador vigorously protested to Compte Charles Gravier Vergennes in Paris objecting to the seizure of two of His Majesty's vessels in the English Channel. To emphasize the point, the British sent the 18-gun sloop *Ceres* to blockade Conyngham and his entourage. Thus the French had no choice. They arrested Conyngham and his crew and in doing so, seized *Surprize* and confiscated his Continental navy commission papers.[13]

Stories about Conyngham's [aka "Cunningham" in British broadsheets] seizure of the British vessels appeared in English newspapers. The British public had been told that they were easily winning the war against the rebelling colonies, but now this premise was being questioned. (In the press political cartoons of Conyngham as a pirate would heavily weigh on the American in the future.)

The British Admiralty sent two additional sloops of war to Dunkirk to join *Ceres* to aid in extraditing the Irish expatriate and his crew to England for trial. Fortunately Franklin had garnered sympathy for the American cause within the French court of Louis XVI. Conyngham, his crew, and the *Surprize* were released, but the Irish American was now a notorious criminal in the eyes of the British. A new Continental navy commission was delivered to Conyngham dated May 2, 1777, dutifully signed by Hancock. It validated Conyngham's service in the Continental navy and replaced his earlier commission document that had been seized and re-certified him as a captain in the Continental navy.

REVENGE

William Hodge, an American agent based at Dunkirk, sold *Surprize* to a French woman with Franklin's approval then purchased the cutter *Greyhound* built for speed. To make the purchase seem innocuous, Hodge drew papers that stated that *Greyhound* had then been resold to an Englishman named Richard Allen. Conyngham appeared uninvolved in Hodge's dealings.

---

13. The American naval captain's commission was taken to Versailles, not to be seen again for about a hundred and thirty years.

Everything seemed quite correct. Once Captain Allen sailed *Greyhound* well clear of Dunkirk's harbor, Allen "miraculously" became Gustavus Conyngham. Conyngham took command and renamed her *Revenge*, probably assuming his appointment as a Continental navy officer made the cutter *Revenge* a Continental navy ship. According to a March 1779 letter Conyngham stated, "I continued in Comd of her [*Revenge*]—Went on a cruze under my former Commision U.S. Navy."[14] Now at sea, *Revenge* armed with 14 cannon and 22 swivel guns and a crew of 106 (mostly veterans of *Surprize*) would create havoc with British shipping, capturing or destroying many of their sparsely armed smaller vessels.

When Conyngham took *Revenge* to sea on July 16 several British vessels chased and fired on him, but he escaped. The American captain later captured four British small merchant ships; among them was a mail packet with many letters onboard. Stories of the shipping captures caused great concern in London. During the years 1777–1778, the maritime insurance rates increased by twenty-eight percent, "higher than at any time in the last war with France and Spain."[15] "Not only did the British merchants ask for protection of warships for their merchantmen on distant voyages, but they even demanded escorts for linen ships from Ireland to England."[16] British cargoes were switched to French and other neutral nation vessels.

In a questionable decision, Conyngham landed his prizes at Dunkirk once again. An infuriated Stormont again protested to Vergennes. The French ministry ordered Conyngham's prizes returned to the British owners and imprisoned the American and his crew. William Hodge was incarcerated in the Bastille for deceiving the French government after outfitting a raider in the guise of a merchant-man.[17] Thus the English were temporarily placated having imprisoned the pirate Conyngham and Hodge the outlaw smuggler.

Hodge gained his freedom by the intervention of Franklin or Silas Deane, each of whom had political connections in the French Court. About this time, enmity between Arthur Lee and Deane started to surface overtly and Conyngham's ventures were given as one of the reasons for the animus. Deane as commissioner was asked to procure

14. Michael J. Crawford, ed., *Naval Documents of the American Revolution* (Washington, DC: Naval Historical Center, vol. 10, 1996), 901.
15. *Wharton's Diplomatic Correspondence of the American Revolution* (Washington, DC: Department of State, Vol. II,), 262 and 311.
16. Edgar Stanton Maclay, *A History of American Privateers* (New York: D. Appleton and Company, 1899), xii.
17. Nesser, *Letters and Papers of Conyngham*, 88.

arms for the Revolutionary War from European powers. Profiting from these dealings, although considered unlawful by today's standards, was normal business at the time. Deane, in particular, had dealings with playwright and staunch American supporter Pierre-Augustin Caron de Beaumarchais. Lee, apparently resentful of Deane's successes, initiated a campaign to denigrate Deane's character, accusing him of disloyalty, embezzlement, and charging for supplies that the French had given as gifts to America. These accusations were never verified, but they helped lead to Deane's ruin.

Conyngham and his crew eventually gained release from the French authorities and *Revenge* set sail, this time for the mouth of the Thames River. He scoured the shipping lanes off the English coast for quarry, capturing the schooner *Happy Return*, two brigs, *Maria* and *Patty*, and merchantman *Northampton*. Conyngham sailed west, rounded Scotland's Shetland Islands and sailed south near Ireland's west coast. The British were increasingly annoyed at Conyngham's piratical actions. Stormont now asked Vergennes to issue orders to arrest the "Dunkirk pirate" if he returned to France.

Meanwhile Conyngham was having difficulty finding British vessels that could be easily subdued, so *Revenge* headed south. Nearing the Spanish coast, Conyngham encountered a British warship. The ships exchanged several harmless shots, but *Revenge* had suffered some storm damage off the British Isles that affected her maneuverability. Feeling vulnerable, Conyngham decided to avoid the fight. Before long the British Admiralty learned that Conyngham had exchanged gunfire with a British warship off the Spanish coast. Assuming that he was seen taking refuge in Spain, they now sent a diplomatic protest to the Spanish government.

On September 1 the *Revenge* arrived at El Ferrol, on the northwestern coast of Spain. Conyngham had a new masthead crafted and other repairs performed, supervised by local American agents. In a document concerning payment he stated: "I pledge in case of need, my person, my belongings present and future, and generally and especially the armed sloop-of-war the *Revenge* which I command and the prizes and ransoms that I have already taken in virtue of a commission from the Congress. . . . .," further evidence that Conyngham believed that he was in command of a Continental navy ship and took personal responsibility for the vessel's well-being.[18]

Concerned about maintaining Spain's neutrality status, the El Ferrol governor ordered Conyngham to leave in early October 1777.

18. Nesser, *Letters and Papers of Conyngham*, 104.

Cruising off Cape Ortegal east of Bilbao, *Revenge* detained the French brig *Graciosa* en route from London to La Coruña with dry goods fully insured in England. The British merchants were shipping goods via a "neutral bottom" in order to avoid capture by the now notorious "Dunkirk pirate." Taking a nonaligned French vessel into a neutral Spanish port was a major diplomatic blunder. Once the prize crew sailed the French vessel to St. Sebastián, Conyngham's men were jailed and their prize brig *Graciosa* was quickly returned to her owners.

The report of this incident reached Paris further inflaming the enmity between Lee and Deane. The two American commissioners were in rare agreement, both being appalled by Conyngham's lack of judgment. Deane berated Conyngham in January 1778, writing, " Every such adventure gives our Enemies advantage against us by representing us as persons who regard not the Laws of Nations. . . .Your Idea that you are at Liberty to seize English Property on board of French or other neutral Vessels is wrong; it is contrary to the established Laws among the maritime Powers of Europe. . . ."[19] The captain apologized concerning this diplomatic misdeed and dropped all claims to the captured vessel and its cargo. Yet he pointedly questioned if British naval ships could confiscate goods from American vessels, then Continental navy vessels should be able to do the same. "Have we not a right to retaliate?"[20] Clearly Conyngham assumed he was acting under his Continental navy captain's commission and had the prerogative to engage the enemy. He also assumed that Lee was partly behind Deane's letter of reprimand of him.

Conyngham continued his hunt for British shipping. The first vessel he captured and burned was a small tender from the 28-gun British frigate *Enterprise*. The mother warship gave chase, but the swifter *Revenge* sailed out of range of the British warship's cannon. Five additional vessels surrendered to Conyngham through mid-March. These prizes were sent across the Atlantic to Newburyport, Massachusetts.

On February 6, 1778, the French signed the Treaty of Alliance that recognized the United States of America. Subsequently on March 17, 1778, the French government declared war on Great Britain, making French ports safe-havens for Conyngham, but he found himself still sailing off neutral territory. Communications concerning political events were slow to circulate, particularly among those at sea.

19. Nesser, *Letters and Papers of Conyngham*, 120.
20. Crawford, *Naval Documents*, 11: 956-957, Conyngham to Lee 1/13/1778.

Many Spanish merchants were increasingly sympathetic to the American rebellion, so Conyngham put into Cadiz, Spain, around the end of March 1778. The British blockaded Cadiz harbor with two frigates, but Conyngham managed to sail past them at night. He headed for the Canary Islands where he captured and burned several more ships, all the while evading other British frigates that were ordered to hunt him down.

Conyngham next boarded the Swedish brig *Henerica Sophia* that was carrying a cargo of dry goods; her destination was the Canary Islands port, Teneriffe. Previously Silas Deane had written Conyngham stating that only neutral vessels, "loaded with Warlike stores & bound to the Ports of our Enemy," could be detained.[21] Dry goods could not be classified as "Warlike stores" and Teneriffe was certainly not an enemy port. The taking of this vessel was equivalent to the recently bungled *Graciosa* affair. This ill-considered action caused letters of rebuke about the "American corsair named Cunningham" from Vegennes, Franklin, and other assorted foreign diplomats.[22]

The *Henerica Sophia* was the last ship that Conyngham captured in European waters. The daring American, however, was not done and now harassed shipping in the Caribbean. *Revenge* arrived in Martinique in late October. Conyngham went on to take five vessels in the Caribbean in November. At Martinique, Continental agent William Bingham cultivated a friendship with Conyngham. Bingham received a dispatch that Admiral Comte d'Estaing was bringing a French fleet and troops to Martinique, but he was notified that some British vessels were also in the area. On December 28 Bingham sent Conyngham to warn d'Estaing that a British squadron was likely to the windward of the French fleet and thus vulnerable in an attack. Duly forewarned, d' Estaing engaged and dispersed the British force. *Revenge*, a mere messenger, was a distant spectator and returned to the port of St. Pierre on January 2, 1779. This was an important Martinique seaport, a place to exchange smuggled arms into specie. About this time Bingham noted that there was a large store of military supplies on hand. He asked Conyngham to deliver fifty chests of weapons to Philadelphia for the use of the Continental army.

After being away from his family for three years, Conyngham was astounded by the firestorm of criticism and complaints he encoun-

---

21. Crawford, *Naval Documents*, 120.
22. Nesser, *Letters And Papers of Conyngham*, 138, 148, 149. Also Franklin's letter to Grand in *Wharton's Diplomatic Correspondence of the American Revolution*, Vol. II, 827-828.

tered when he arrived in America. The Marine Committee of Congress met in Philadelphia on January 4, 1779, recommending, "that Capt. Conyngham give an account of himself."[23] Some former crewmen who preceded him home claimed that they had not been paid their promised wages. He was also unaware that he had become embroiled in scandals surrounding Deane, Arthur Lee, and his brother Richard Henry Lee, now chair of Congress's Marine Committee, who set out to disgrace Deane. They alleged that both *Surprize* and *Revenge* were privateers and several partners along with Deane had profited handsomely from

Capt. Gustavus Conyngham, after a miniature by Louis Marie Sicari. (*USNHC*)

the prize money derived from Conyngham's cruises. Conyngham's initial cruises occurred when France was trying to maintain political neutrality, thus forcing him to disguise his prizes even though his actions were approved and encouraged by American commissioners. The resulting irregular marine warfare proved to be an effective strategy during the early stages of the Revolutionary War. Conyngham claimed his motive was to harass British shipping in their dangerous home waters. Any ensuing financial gains were secondary to his goal. Conyngham's arguments gained sympathy, if not complete success in all quarters.

Upon his return to the United States, Conyngham was no longer captain of what he assumed was the "Continental Navy Cutter *Revenge*." The merchant firm of Conyngham and Nesbitt purchased *Revenge*, a move completing a figurative maritime circle. The obvious choice for her captain was Gustavus Conyngham. The state of Pennsylvania, an unsuccessful bidder, chartered *Revenge* for a fortnight to protect Philadelphia's commerce on the Delaware River under a letter of marque and as a lawful privateer. By the end of April 1779, the letter of marque charter expired. When *Revenge* set out to the Capes of Delaware on a private cruise, it was without any governmental "paper cover."

PRISONER

While cruising in waters off New Jersey in May, Conyngham encountered the 20-gun HMS *Galatea*. *Revenge*, out-gunned and outmaneu-

23. Library of Congress, *Naval Records of the American Revolution*, 93.

vered, was forced to surrender. Sticking to maritime protocol, Galatea's captain, Thomas Jordan, RN, requested Conyngham's papers. Having none, Conyngham was placed in irons. Once *Galatea* docked in Tory New York, Conyngham was first taken to a wretched prison hulk anchored off Brooklyn, then jailed at the provost's prison where he was weighted down with fifty-five pounds of chains that were fastened to his ankles, his wrists, and an iron ring secured about his neck.

Starved and mistreated for some weeks, Conyngham was eventually brought before Commodore Sir George Collier. Collier ordered Conyngham extradited to Britain for trial and probably to be hanged. Jeered by a Loyalist crowd, Conyngham was first paraded through the streets on a cart to the dock and then rowed to the British packet *Sandwich* bound for London. Finally he was placed in the grimy foul-smelling hold for his voyage to England.[24] Before *Sandwich* sailed on June 12, 1779, the American was given the opportunity to write a letter to tell his wife Anne of his situation. Conyngham landed at Falmouth, and then he was sent to Pendennis Castle bound by heavy irons and confined in a small windowless cell sealed with an iron-bound bolted door.

Meanwhile Anne Conyngham used her husband's letter describing his inhumane treatment to appeal to Congress to obtain her husband's release. She contended that the British conduct violated international prisoner of war protocol. Early in the war Stormont had been asked that Americans held in British prisons be subject to an exchange of prisoners to which he condescendingly replied, "The King's ambassador receives no application from rebels, unless they implore his majesty's mercy."[25] Philadelphia's Society for the Relief of Poor, Aged & Infirmed Masters of Ships, learned of Conyngham's plight and angrily protested His Majesty's treatment of Conyngham before the Continental Congress.[26] In retaliation the Marine Committee ordered Lieutenant Christopher Hele, RN, formerly of HMS *Hotham* and confined in a Boston prison, placed in conditions similar to those of Conyngham.[27] This apparently brought the issue to the Admiralty's

24. Being hanged in public was a common punishment for pirates in England, although by the time of the reign of George III, it was less common. Perhaps Conyngham's Irish ethnicity precipitated his extraordinarily cruel treatment.

25. H. Hastings Weld, *Benjamin Franklin: His Autobiography; with a Narrative of His Public Services* (New York: Harper and Brothers, 1848), 497.

26. Library of Congress, *Naval Records of the American Revolution*, 110-111.

27. Library of Congress, *Naval Records of the American Revolution*, 114, and Nesser, *Letters And Papers of Conyngham*, 184, 192.

attention and led to Conyngham's imprisonment at Mill Prison (Old Mill) in Plymouth and he was now regarded as an exchangeable prisoner. At Old Mill, if one committed "the least fault as they termed it, [one would spend] 42 days in the dungeon on the half of the allowance of Beef & bread—of the worst quality. . . .dogs, cats rats even Grass eaten by the prisoners, thiss [sic] hard to be credited, but is a fact."[28]

While at "Old Mill," Conyngham tried several escapes. Once he nonchalantly walked out of the prison gate with a group of visitors, but was caught after he started to go his own way. In another attempt, he dressed in a dark suit, and while wearing wire-rimmed spectacles in the disguise of a visiting doctor, he pretended to be engrossed in a book and walked through the prison gates. Unfortunately a prison tradesman recognized Conyngham and he was recaptured. On one particular stormy day, when the guards were preoccupied with the weather, he slipped by the sentries again, but was soon captured. Finally on November 3, 1781, Conyngham succeeded in escaping with a group of about fifty other Americans who had dug a tunnel under the prison wall.[29]

Conyngham and a few fellow escapees eventually crossed the channel to Holland. John Paul Jones was at the Texel having recently docked there after his renowned *Bonhome Richard/Serapis* sea battle. Conyngham contacted Jones hoping to find passage home. When the two men met for the first time, Jones greeted Conyngham warmly. The two American "rogues" were briefly united onboard Jones's new command, the frigate *Alliance*. Both had successfully fought the British in their home waters and were now considered pirates in the English popular press. Jones wished to continue his raiding, so Conyngham left *Alliance* and sailed to Philadelphia on *Hannibal,* whose crew included ninety-five fellow escapees from British prisons.[30]

THE ITINERANT MARINER RETURNS

The Revolutionary War finally ended with the signing of the 1783 Treaty of Paris. Conyngham had been given two naval captain's commissions, signed by the president of Congress and one personally presented by the esteemed Benjamin Franklin, but Congress now ruled these commissions were considered temporary. Conyngham's cap-

28. Nesser, *Letters and Papers of Conyngham,* 11.
29. Nesser, *Letters and Papers of Conyngham,* 190.
30. Nesser, *Letters and Papers of Conyngham,* 12.

tain's rank in the Continental navy was denied and they refused to pay him for his naval service.[31] A persistent Conyngham went on to spend seven years attempting to persuade Congress to give him what he considered his federal back pay. Even Treasury Secretary Alexander Hamilton tried and failed to advance Coyngham's claim through Congress.[32]

Gustavus Conyngham served the cause of American independence with distinction and endured many hardships as an English prisoner. Because he had been issued a Continental navy commission, he assumed his actions were within the rules of maritime warfare. According to official records, neither *Surprize* nor *Revenge* is listed as Continental navy or privateer vessels. In summary, Conyngham had fought under an "expired" naval commission and neither of his vessels were Continental navy or letters of marque. Therefore his actions were, according to maritime law, technically those of a buccaneer. Legally Conyngham could have been tried and, if convicted, ingloriously hanged—albeit as an unwitting pirate.

Gustavus Conyngham died in Philadelphia on November 27, 1819, at seventy-two. Conyngham took thirty-one prizes, more than any other American naval officer in the Revolutionary War."[33] It should be noted that none of these vessels were British men-of-war therefore his actions were like those of a privateer. He also, perhaps unwittingly, became a pawn in the feud between Deane and Lee. Captain Conyngham was daring, imaginative, resolute, and resilient, but also naïve. His Revolutionary War captures, whether legal asymmetric warfare acts or guileless piracy, impacted British morale at home, tempered their commercial maritime activity, and contributed to the realization of America's independence.

31. Library of Congress, *Naval Records of the American Revolution*, 197.
32. Nesser, *Letters and Papers of Conyngham*, 213.
33. E. Gordon Bowen-Hassell, Dennis M. Conrad, and Mark L. Hayes, *Sea Raiders of the American Revolution: The Continental Navy in European Waters* (Washington, DC: Naval Historical Center, Department of the Navy, 2003), 41.

Great Intelligence Successes and Failures

✺ MICHAEL SCHELLHAMMER ✺

Good Revolutionary War commanders understood the value of intelligence on their adversaries. The great eighteenth century military theorist Marshal de Saxe, who was on every good general's reading list, wrote that to win in battle "nothing more is required than to keep good intelligence, to acquire a knowledge of the country, and to assume the courage to execute."[1] The Marshal made it sound simple. Both sides in the Revolution worked strenuously to gather intelligence through many methods including spies, reconnaissance, and civilian informants and guides. Sometimes the commanders successfully managed their assets to gain good intelligence, other times they failed. What follows are examples of when American leaders used their intelligence systems to gain the right information at the right time and capitalized on it for success, and other instances when the intelligence systems failed.

First, the successes.

LEXINGTON AND CONCORD

As a professional British army officer, Lt. Gen. Thomas Gage, commander of Crown forces in Massachusetts in early 1775, understood the value of intelligence and ran an effective network of operatives who monitored the increasingly defiant colonists. In late March his network revealed that the colonists cached weapons and gunpowder at the town of Concord. Gage planned to snuff out the growing opposition to Crown authority by raiding Concord to seize the arms.

Unfortunately for Gage, British preparations for the raid in early April signaled his plans. In Boston, silversmith Paul Revere headed a

---

1. Maurice, Comte de Saxe, *Reveries, or Memoirs, Concerning the Art of War* (Edinburgh: Sands, Donaldson, Murray and Cochran, 1759), 96.

group of workers, sometime referred to as the "Mechanics" that observed British activities and reported to the leaders of the Patriot "Sons of Liberty" such as Dr. Joseph Warren. Whig leaders also organized a network of dispatch riders in Boston and in country towns to spread warnings of any impending British strike.

Gage scheduled his raiding force to depart Boston on the night of April 18. That night, citizens encountered Crown patrols in the country and quickly sent warnings to the town of Lexington where John Hancock and Samuel Adams lodged, in case the redcoats planned to seize the two Whig leaders (although Hancock and Adams were actually not Gage's targets). Revere also sent Warren reports from his informants about soldiers preparing for a march. Gage's troops marshaling on Boston Common, visible to even casual observers, confirmed an imminent raid. Late that night Warren launched Revere and express rider William Dawes to Lexington to warn Adams and Hancock about the British movement.

It is not news, of course, that Revere and Dawes made their famous rides and delivered warnings to Adams and Hancock at around midnight. The bigger picture is that the Whig intelligence system operated exactly as it was designed; the Sons of Liberty informants reported British preparations to Patriot leaders; the leaders understood the information and reacted quickly, and multiple express riders, including Revere and Dawes, carried timely warnings to the forces that took action.

Thanks to the Patriot intelligence system, Capt. John Parker's Lexington Militia Company was one the units that mobilized in the early hours of April 19. Gage's troops reached Lexington soon after dawn and encountered Parker's men on Lexington Green, and the first shots of the rebellion followed.[2]

TRENTON

In December 1776 the American cause was in what General Washington called, with some understatement, a "melancholy situation." "With a handful of men," he wrote, "we have been pushed thro'

2. David Hackett Fischer, *Paul Revere's Ride* (New York: Oxford University Press, 1994), 78-85, 93-112, 138-148. See also Ray Raphael, "Paul Revere's Other Riders," *Journal of the American Revolution*, January 13, 2014, allthingsliberty.com/ 2014/01/ paul-reveres-riders/; Derek W. Beck, "Dissecting the Timeline of Paul Revere's Ride, April 9, 2014, allthingsliberty.com/2014/04/dissecting-the-timeline-of-paul-reveres-ride/; and J.L. Bell, "Did Paul Revere's Ride Really Matter?" April 21, 2014, allthingsliberty.com/2014/04/did-paul-reveres-ride-really-matter/.

the Jerseys, without being able to make the smallest opposition."[3] His army camped in eastern Pennsylvania and across the Delaware River Gen. William Howe's redcoats and Hessians held New Jersey with 17 dispersed garrisons.

Washington believed that Howe planned to take Philadelphia, and he looked for ways and places to knock his opponent on the defensive. "Find out some person who can be engaged to cross the river as a spy," he told his generals, "obtain some knowledge of the enemy's situation . . . get some person in to Trenton."[4] That was only one order among many in which Washington pushed commanders for intelligence. "Every piece of intelligence worthy notice you obtain, forward it to me by express," he told Brig. Gen. Philemon Dickson of the New Jersey militia, and "spare no pains, nor cost, to gain information of the enemy's movements, and designs" he directed Brig. Gen. James Ewing.[5] In response, Continental and militia units constantly skirmished with the isolated enemy outposts, and reported what information they learned in the process. By late December Washington was gaining a thorough picture of British and Hessian vulnerabilities in New Jersey.

On December 22, Col. Joseph Reed, Washington's adjutant, sent his general a detailed report with the latest intelligence from New Jersey and recommended an attack on Trenton.[6] Washington convened a council of war. The sum of available intelligence indicated that Trenton was unfortified, its garrison of two Hessian regiments was exhausted from almost constant fighting with the American militia, and their nearest support was six miles away. Washington approved the plan for an attack to take place on December 25–26.[7]

It is part of the American fabric that Washington's army crossed the Delaware on Christmas night and defeated the Hessian garrison at Trenton, achieving a victory that electrified the Patriot cause. Intelligence information, expertly gathered, understood, and applied, was a key factor in Washington's decision to fight this iconic battle.

3. Washington to Horatio Gates, December 14, 1776, *Writings of George Washington*, Vol. 6, accessed December 30, 2014, etext.virginia.edu.

4. Washington to the General Officers, December 14, 1776, *Writings of George Washington*, Vol. 6.

5. Washington to Brig. Gen. Philemon Dickson, December 12, 1776, and Washington to Brig. Gen. James Ewing, December 12, 1776, *Writings of George Washington*, Vol. 6, accessed December 30, 2014, etext.virginia.edu.

6. Joseph Reed to Washington, December 22, 1776, The George Washington Papers at the Library of Congress, accessed December 30, 2104, memory.loc.gov.

7. David Hackett Fischer, *Washington's Crossing* (New York: Oxford University Press, 2004), 191–205.

Capitalizing on the success at Trenton, at the end of December 1776 Washington assembled an army of about 5,000 Continentals, Pennsylvania and New Jersey militia, and even a detachment of Continental Marines in western New Jersey to secure a foothold in the contested state.

PRINCETON

On December 30 a patrol of the Philadelphia Light Horse learned from their British prisoners that Crown forces under Gen. Charles Cornwallis were concentrated ten miles away at Princeton, planning to attack the Americans at Trenton. The next day Pennsylvania's Col. John Cadwalader confirmed the information when he sent Washington a dispatch from a local intelligence operative, "a very intelligent young gentleman," who entered the British camp at Princeton and saw thousands of troops.[8] Heeding the warnings, Washington sent troops towards Princeton to delay the British advance.

Just as the intelligence indicated, Cornwallis moved to attack Trenton on January 2, 1777. Washington's delaying forces successfully slowed the advance and the forces clashed at the Second Battle of Trenton. Night halted the British attack and the Americans took defensive positions outside Trenton on the Assunpink Creek.

That night, Washington called a council of war and the senior officers reviewed their intelligence. From patrolling, Brig. Gen. Arthur St. Clair understood the approaches to the British camp at Princeton. Adjutant Joseph Reed, who attended school in Princeton, also knew the area. The council learned more about the terrain from locals. Information from Col. Cadwalader's spy also showed that the British camp was vulnerable to attack from the east. Such comprehensive knowledge of the enemy position contributed to the council's unanimous approval to attack Princeton.

Early in the morning the Americans slipped away from Assunpink creek and marched on Princeton. The Battle of Princeton on January 3 was hard-fought, and ended in a striking American victory that helped put Howe's forces in New Jersey on the defensive.[9]

BEMIS HEIGHTS

In June 1777, Gen. John Burgoyne pushed into the American northern frontier from Canada with 7,250 British, Hessian, and Loyalist troops.

---

8. Cadwalader to Washington, December 31, 1776, The George Washington Papers at the Library of Congress, accessed December 30, 2014, memory.loc.gov.
9. Fischer, *Washington's Crossing*, 277-289, 314-315.

The Americans contested his advance south. Three months later Burgoyne's expedition was on the west bank of the Hudson River reduced to about 6,000 men and short on provisions. In early October the Americans held a strong defensive line anchored to the west bank of the Hudson on a plateau known as Bemis Heights. The thick forests stymied Burgoyne's scouting efforts. To locate an open American flank, Burgoyne decided to launch a reconnaissance in force with 2,000 men. If the line was found weak, Burgoyne would continue pushing south.

The American commander, Maj. Gen. Horatio Gates, received a steady stream of intelligence on the British army from scouts and enemy deserters. Gates also understood the terrain. It was his engineer, Polish volunteer Col. Thaddeus Kosciuszko, who designed the Bemis Heights fortifications that blocked Burgoyne's path. On October 5 Gates correctly predicted to Washington "from the best intelligence [Burgoyne] has not more than three weeks provisions in store . . . so that, in a fortnight at farthest, he must decide whether he will rashly risk, at infinite disadvantage, to force my camp, or retreat to his den."[10]

Two days later on October 7, a British deserter informed the Americans about Burgoyne's preparations for an advance.[11] That same morning American pickets spotted British troops advancing and foraging for provisions. Gates sent his aide, Capt. James Wilkinson, to confirm the activity. Wilkinson reported to his general, "they are foraging, and endeavoring to reconnoiter your left; and I think Sir, they offer you battle. . . . I would indulge them."[12] Another reconnaissance by Maj. Gen. Benedict Arnold and Benjamin Lincoln confirmed that a large formation of British and Hessians was headed for the American lines.

Now aware that the advance was Burgoyne's expected "rash risk," Gates launched a counterattack with Col. Daniel Morgan's Virginia riflemen and two brigades. Vicious fighting over three hours beat back the British assault. The battle of Bemis Heights was Burgoyne's unsuccessful and final grasp for victory.

10. Gates to Washington, October 5 1777, George Washington Papers at the Library of Congress, accessed January 19, 2015, memory.loc.gov/ammem/ gwhtml/gwhome .html.
11. Lieutenant William Digby, journal entry for October 7, 1777, in *The British Invasion from the North, the Campaigns of Generals Carleton and Burgoyne from Canada, 1776-1777* (Albany: Munsell's Sons, 1887), 287.
12. General James Wilkinson, *Memoirs of My Own Times,* Volume I (Philadelphia: Abraham Small, 1816), accessed January 19, 2015, www.archive.org), 267-268.

Gates continued to receive valuable information from scouts and deserters until October 17, when Burgoyne, with his army's power exhausted, finally capitulated. It was the first surrender of an entire British army to the Americans and a significant turning point in the Revolution.

NEW YORK'S COMMITTEE FOR DETECTING AND DEFEATING CONSPIRACIES

In mid-September 1776, the Continental army was in danger of losing Manhattan to Crown forces and the Revolution was on shaky ground. In this tenuous atmosphere, convinced that they faced "the barbarous machinations of their domestic, as well as external enemies," New York's rebel government, the Provincial Convention, established a committee charged with "detecting and defeating all conspiracies . . . against the liberty of America."[13]

The committee began operating on September 28 and formed a secret service "to gain information respecting the most disaffected persons" to the American cause.[14] New York attorney and Continental Congress delegate John Jay headed the effort with the assistance of committee member Nathaniel Sackett. Their operatives, that eventually numbered about a dozen, penetrated Loyalist groups and delivered valuable counterintelligence information to the committee. When Gen. Washington began professionalizing the Continental Army intelligence networks in the summer of 1778, he called on Sackett to learn agent operations and tradecraft. Sackett's lessons contributed greatly to the successful methods used by the famous Culper spy ring in New York City.

Before its disbandment in January 1778, the committee reviewed over 500 cases of citizens accused of opposing the rebellion. The overall justness of such an organization and its process is certainly open to debate. Nevertheless, the Committee was one of America's first organized counterintelligence efforts and it laid the foundation for more effective intelligence activities. John Jay went on to become the first chief justice of the United States. Today he is considered to be one of the founders of American counterintelligence.[15]

13. *Minutes of the Committee and of the First Commission for Detecting and Defeating Conspiracies in the state of New York, December 11, 1776–September 23, 1778* (New York: New York Historical Society, accessed January 19, 2015, via www.archive.org), xiii.
14. *Minutes of the Committee and of the First Commission for Detecting and Defeating Conspiracies,* 2.
15. For thorough discussions on the Committee, see Alexander Rose, *Washington's Spies: The Story of America's First Spy Ring* (New York: Random House, 2007), 42, 48-51, and Kenneth Daigler, *Spies, Patriots, and Traitors: American Intelligence in the Revolutionary War* (Washington: Georgetown University Press, 2014), 111-125.

And the Failures . . . .

Battles are complicated events where conflicting or unclear information can confuse even good generals. Here are some examples of when American intelligence systems failed, usually with terribly tragic results.

THE QUEBEC EXPEDITION

In late 1775 the Continental Congress planned to neutralize threats from Canada by seizing Montreal. Gen. George Washington, commanding the Continental army at Boston, decided to support the effort by sending a force north from Boston through the Maine wilderness to seize Quebec. It seemed like a good idea at the time. Washington expected light resistance at Quebec and an easy passage through the highlands of Maine by way of the Kennebec and Dead rivers. "I made all possible inquiry as to the distance, the safety of the route and the danger of the season," he wrote, "but found nothing in either to deter me from proceeding."[16] He chose the rising star Col. Benedict Arnold to command the expedition.

Washington was way off. He gained much of his knowledge about the northern frontier from a 1761 map by a British army engineer and underestimated the ruggedness of the terrain.[17] Arnold's expedition departed in September and endured an exceptionally harsh passage through the Maine highlands that destroyed their supplies, bled off their numbers, and exhausted the soldiers. Arnold wrote to Washington during the trek, "I have been much deceived in every account of our route, which is longer and has been attended with a thousand difficulties I never apprehended."[18] Slowed by the difficult northward trudge, the expedition did not arrive outside Quebec until December 13. Then they faced British reinforcements that arrived only days before them. Arnold wrote Washington, "had I been ten days sooner Quebec must inevitably have fallen into our hands, as there was not a man there to oppose us."[19] Their second adversary, the brutal Canadian winter, also arrived.

16. Washington to the President of Congress, September 21, 1775, *Writings of George Washington, Vol. 3*, accessed January 5, 2015, etext.virginia.edu/washington/fitz-patrick/.
17. Robert McConnell Hatch, *Thrust for Canada: The American Attempt on Quebec in 1775-1776* (Boston: Houghton Mifflin, 1979), 62.
18. Arnold to Washington, October 27, 1775, George Washington Papers at the Library of Congress, accessed January 5, 2015, memory.loc.gov/cgi-bin/ampage?collId=mgw4&fileName=gwpage034.db&recNum=605.
19. Arnold to Washington, November 20, 1775, George Washington Papers at the Library of Congress, accessed January 5, 2015, memory.loc.gov/cgi-bin/ ampage?collId=mgw4&fileName=gwpage034.db&recNum=890.

A week later the other half of the American invasion force, Brig. Gen. Richard Montgomery's troops from Montreal, joined Arnold. The combined force attacked Quebec in a snowstorm in the early morning hours of December 31. The assault failed at the cost of 200 American lives. Montgomery was among the dead and Arnold severely wounded.

Had the Americans applied their intelligence more effectively, they could have avoided, or at least better handled, this dramatic but disaster-prone expedition.

BROOKLYN

In August 1776, 15,000 British troops under Gen. William Howe landed on Long Island, threatening New York City. In between them and Manhattan stood a fortified American defensive line south of Brooklyn.

Incorporating a rugged ridge known as the Gowanus Heights, the American line was a solid defense. But at that early stage of the war the Continentals lacked both a spy network on Long Island and an effective cavalry force. The result was that neither Gen. Washington nor Maj. Gen. Israel Putnam, the commander of the defenses, fully understood the battlefield or British intentions and movements. The Americans heavily defended and fortified three natural passes that formed avenues through the Heights; the Martense Lane Pass, Flatbush Pass, and Bedford Pass. But the Jamaica Pass, at the east end of the line, went unfortified. Only two battalions of riflemen under Col. Samuel Miles had orders to watch the area and report any enemy movement. The commander of the left of the American line, Maj. Gen. John Sullivan, also posted a patrol of five mounted officers to observe the Jamaica Road which ran through the pass. Sullivan later wrote that he was "very uneasy" about the road, "through which I had often foretold the enemy would come, but could not persuade others to be of my opinion."[20]

Sullivan's concern was valid. Howe's British troops thoroughly scouted the area and gained information from local Loyalists. His subordinate, Gen. Henry Clinton, also knew the area from time he spent there in his youth. "I took some pains to reconnoiter" Clinton wrote, which led him to realize that the Jamaica Pass offered an avenue to

---

20. Sullivan, letter dated October 25, 1777, in *The Bulletin of the Historical Society of Pennsylvania, Vol. I, 1845-1847* (Philadelphia: Merrihew & Thompson, 1848), "Papers Relating to the Battle of Brandywine," 52. Sullivan's letter could have been self-serving—he wrote it a year after the battle as part of his defense of his actions at the battle of Brandywine.

maneuver behind the Continental defenses.[21] Clinton suggested to Howe a British attack through the pass to turn the American flank.

Howe detested Clinton, but grudgingly agreed with the plan. On the night of August 26, Clinton marched east to Jamaica Pass with about 10,000 troops, two-thirds of the British force. They moved, unnoticed, within two miles of a brigade of New York militia under Brig. Gen. Nathaniel Woodhull. At Jamaica Pass, Gen. Sullivan and Col. Miles perceived signs of the enemy advance but whether they properly warned their senior commanders is unclear.[22] That night Clinton's troops captured Sullivan's mounted patrol and learned that Jamaica Pass was essentially unguarded.

The next morning, British and Hessian troops pinned down the Americans at the Martense Lane and Flatbush Passes. At about the same time Clinton and Howe personally led their main force through Jamaica Pass to overwhelm the American left flank. Putnam's defensive line crumbled and the troops retreated to Brooklyn.

Washington took personal command of the Long Island defenses but with his forces outnumbered and outflanked the situation was hopeless. On August 29 Washington evacuated his forces to Manhattan, which relinquished Long Island to the Crown for the rest of the war.

BRANDYWINE

In July 1777, Gen. Howe's army departed New Jersey by sea in a naval convoy of over 200 ships. Washington had little intelligence on its destination, and for weeks he thought that Howe was headed for the Hudson River, Philadelphia, or South Carolina. Howe's landing at the north end of the Chesapeake Bay at the end of August pointed to Philadelphia as Howe's target.

Washington chose to defend Philadelphia on the banks of Brandywine Creek, southwest of the city. The American defense adequately covered five fords across the creek, and Washington was wary of an enemy crossing on his open right flank. There, he posted Maj. Gen. John Sullivan and cavalry under Col. Theodorick Bland to cover three more fords and the vulnerable flank. But the American reconnaissance was, again, incomplete. Two miles to the west, beyond

21. Sir Henry Clinton, *The American Rebellion: Sir Henry Clinton's Narrative of His Campaigns, 1775–1782, with an Appendix of Original Documents*, William B. Willcox, ed., (New Haven: Yale University Press, 1954), 41.

22. See Barnet Schecter, *The Battle for New York: The City at the Heart of the American Revolution* (New York: Walker & Company, 2002), 133-135.

where Sullivan and Bland watched, two more fords crossed the Brandywine. Just as at Long Island, Howe found the fords thanks to thorough scouting and a local Loyalist. Much like Jamaica Pass, Howe knew that the open crossing offered an avenue to turn the American right flank.

The battle of Brandywine nearly repeated the battle of Brooklyn. On September 11 Howe launched a diversionary attack on the American front. At the same time Howe and Gen. Charles Cornwallis led a larger force to the northwest, crossed the Brandywine at the unguarded fords, and crashed onto the American right flank. Washington received so many confusing reports of the action that he later told Congress, "the intelligence received of the enemy's advancing up the Brandywine, and crossing at a ford about six miles above us, was uncertain and contradictory."[23] The Americans repositioned their line and fought stubbornly, but could not halt the British attack.

Washington withdrew his army east to the town of Chester and two weeks later Howe's army marched into Philadelphia.

CAMDEN

Gen. Horatio Gates, the famed victor of Saratoga, took command of the Continental army's Southern Department at a camp at Hollinsworth's Farm on the Deep River in North Carolina on July 25, 1780, already armed with intelligence. The bulk of the British and Loyalist army under Lord Charles Cornwallis was at Charleston, South Carolina. According to Gen. Thomas Sumter of the South Carolina militia, Lord Francis Rawdon held an exposed post at the town of Camden, South Carolina, with only 700 Loyalist troops. Gates decided to march to Camden and sweep away Rawdon's outpost, and his army departed on July 27.

Gates was making a series of intelligence mistakes. To begin with, he failed to understand his area of operation. His senior commanders suggested somewhat circuitous routes to Camden where the army could sustain itself, but Gates chose a route that was direct but heavy in Loyalist sentiment and barren of forage. This forced the Americans to consume meager rations of green corn, peaches, and thin soup that some officers thickened with wig powder. Gate's second error was that he moved with a cavalry force that was too small to adequately

---

23. Washington to the President of Congress, at midnight, Chester, September 11, 1777, *Writings of George Washington*, Vol. 9, accessed February 11, 2015, etext.virginia.edu/washington/fitzpatrick/. Adjutant General Pickering actually wrote this dispatch at Washington's direction.

scout ahead and keep track of enemy dispositions. "Fatal mistake!" observed the veteran cavalryman Lt. Col. Henry Lee.[24] The Americans closed on Camden on August 15 unaware that Cornwallis's army was not in Charleston, but actually concentrated at Camden.

It was on August 9 that Cornwallis, who "was regularly acquainted by Lord Rawdon with every material incident or movement" the Americans made, as he later wrote, learned that Gates was headed toward Camden.[25] Marching from Charleston, Cornwallis's army arrived at Camden two days before Gates. Continental and Loyalist cavalry patrols clashed the night of August 15, revealing the presence of Cornwallis's force. Gates's adjutant, Col. Otho Holland Williams, recalled that when Gates learned that he faced Cornwallis's entire army, "the general's astonishment could not be concealed." Gates called a council of war and asked his senior commanders, "Gentlemen, what is best to be done?"[26]

The council agreed that they had no choice but to fight Cornwallis the next day, and with that, Gates's subordinate commanders began sharing the intelligence mistakes. With roughly 3,000 soldiers the Americans outnumbered the British by about 800 men. Gates formed his line of battle in the early morning of August 16, but made the mistake of posting his most inexperienced soldiers, the North Carolina and Virginia militia, on the left of his line where they would oppose the most senior and experienced British brigade. As a former king's officer Gates should have known that by tradition, British commanders routinely assigned their most senior units to the right side of their battle lines. He also should have realized the advantage that gave the British against the militia he expected to fight them. The reasons for Gates's decision, and the extent that the subordinate American commanders accepted or disagreed with the assignment, is open to debate. Either way, the decision rebalanced the odds in Cornwallis's favor.

24. Henry Lee, *The Revolutionary Memoirs of General Henry Lee, Edited with a Biography of the Author by Robert E. Lee* (1812, reprint, New York: DaCapo Press, 1998), 172. Lee was not assigned to the Southern Department in August 1780, but I consider his professional observation valid.
25. Charles, Earl Cornwallis to Lord George Germain, August 21, 1780, State Records of North Carolina XV: 269-273, accessed February 11, 2015, www.battleofcamden.org /cornwallis2germain_txt.htm.
26. Otho Holland Williams, *A Narrative of the Campaign of 1780* (A. E. Miller, Charleston, South Carolina, 1822), accessed February 15, 2015, "Documentary History of the Battle of Camden, 16 August 1780," battleofcamden.org/.

Gates opened the battle by advancing the militia on the left of his line but Cornwallis immediately counterattacked against the move. The advance of the veteran British regulars set the American militia to flight. The American line crumbled and the cavalry of Lt. Col. Banastre Tarleton's British Legion swept in and completed the rout. American losses were probably 250 killed and 800 wounded, many of whom were captured, compared to 68 killed and 256 wounded in Cornwallis's army. The loss at Camden was an absolute disaster and a major blow to the American cause in the South.[27]

27. For a thorough assessment of how Gates and the entire Southern Department performed at this battle, see "Unlucky or Inept? Gates at Camden," by Wayne Lynch, allthingsliberty.com/2014/05/unlucky-or-inept-gates-at-camden/.

George Washington's Agent Z: The Curious Case of Lieutenant Lewis J. Costigin

KEN DAIGLER

One of the things that makes human intelligence operations so interesting is that you never know how, and for that matter whether, an operation will work out as planned.

Lt. Lewis J. Costigin's mission as a spy for George Washington did eventually work out. But, not the first time he tried in early 1777. In his second attempt in late 1778, he was able to report intelligence of value.[1] However, the circumstances under which he accomplished this were highly unusual, to say the least. The most surprising aspect of his successful mission was that he did it in British occupied New York City, dressed in his Continental army officer's uniform, openly walking around the city observing British activities and forces.

Costigin was a merchant in New Brunswick, New Jersey, prior to the war. In November 1776 he was a first lieutenant in the New Jersey Line of the Continental army. According to his pension statement:

> after the Battle of Trenton Col. Lourey the Company general informed him that information was received that Lord Cornwallis was approaching with his army from Brunswick to attack the army at Trenton and informed him that he was directed by Gen. Washington to select a suitable person to proceed to Brunswick to ascertain the strength of the British forces that guarded Gen. Lee and their baggage. And as he was a native of that place and had

---

1. In Colonial times the word "intelligence" had a broader meaning than is currently in use. It was used to refer to any information of interest or value, and in various documents the words information and intelligence were both used to refer to details on the enemy obtained by both public and nonpublic means.

been in the Mercantile business there and his family remaining in Brunswick that he was thought qualified for this undertaking upon which he volunteered his service and by the direction of Col. Lourey waited on Gen. Washington for his instructions after reviewing his orders he proceeded to Brunswick and procured all the information in his power . . . he was taken by a party of light horse . . . and was sent to New York a Prisoner of War where he remained as such for three years . . . and after such period of three years exchanged for a Captain of the British Army.[2]

That Costigin was captured in January 1777 is supported in his expense report for costs related to his intelligence activities in New York City which was forwarded to General Washington by Costigin's superior.[3] Apparently when captured he was in enough of a uniform of an American officer to be treated as a prisoner of war and not a spy. In any event, once a prisoner in New York City, he was placed on parole, which allowed him freedom of movement but involved three specific pledges he had to make against his honor as an officer:

He could not involve himself in any military activities.

He could not communicate with his military colleagues, nor publically criticize any British activities.

When summoned, he must present himself to British prisoner authorities.[4]

Costigin appeared to be forgotten, or ignored by the Continental army until August 21, 1778, when Washington sent a letter to Col. John Beatty, the Commissary General for Prisoners:

Lewis Johnson Costagan a Lieut. In the 1st Jersey Regt. Was taken prisoner early in 1777. I would wish that the speediest means may be used for the obtaining his Exchange, at the same time you will observe such caution in conducting the affair as not to alarm the enemy or induce them to detain him. You will not seem over anxious, and yet take such measures as cannot fail to procure his liberty.

As soon as he comes out you will be pleased to direct him to repair immediately to the Head Quarters of the army.[5]

2. Pension Statement of August 25, 1820, at www.fold3.com/image/#12766045. Pension: S. 43,337.

3. Letter from Matthias Ogden to George Washington, April 4, 1782, at founders. archives.gov/documents/Washington/99-01-02-08080.

4. Charles Henry Metzger, *The Prisoners in the American Revolution* (Chicago: Loyola University Press, 1971), 193.

5. David R. Hoth, ed., *The Papers of George Washington, Revolutionary War Series, vol. 16, 1 July–14 September 1778* (Charlottesville: University of Virginia Press, 2006), 343.

No official explanation has been found to explain this sudden interest in Costigin. However, in this same month Washington began planning the development of the Culper spy ring in New York City.[6] He was well aware that creation and operational development of that collection network would take time. However, he also needed current intelligence on enemy plans and activities in the city now that the British command had returned there. Perhaps Washington had in mind the use of Costigin, who had previously been selected as a spy and was known to Washington, as one measure to fill the intelligence gap until the Culper Ring could become operational.

In September, Costigin traveled from New York City to New Brunswick to await his formal exchange. Washington was informed of this in a letter from William Livingston, the governor of New Jersey, who wrote on September 21, 1778, that, "About a week ago arrived in Brunswick from New York one Crowel formerly a New Jersey man with a flag for his Boat from Admiral Gambier, for the sole purpose of his carrying to Brunswick Lewis Costigen & his family . . . "[7]

In his expense report to Washington relating costs of his intelligence collection activities in New York City, Costigin explained that at that time he was " . . . prevailed upon by the Solicitations of Major General Lord Sterling & Colonel Ogden To Stay in the City of New York after his Exchange for the space of Four Months, in order to procure & send out information respecting the movements of the Enemy."[8]

Interestingly, Costigin makes no reference to his involvement in intelligence activities in New York City in his pension application, even some forty years after the events. Also, he gives his time as a prisoner of war to be three years, when in actuality it was about two years. This may be due to his understanding that secrets are to remain so. It might also be that since the pension was based upon his military service, his intelligence role was not a factor to consider. A third possibility is that since pension applications required witnesses or written documentation, he may not have had such supporting evidence for his intelligence activities.

6. For information on the Culper Ring, see Michael Schellhammer, "Abraham Woodhull: The Spy Named Samuel Culper," *Journal of the American Revolution*, May 19, 2014, allthingsliberty.com/2014/05/abraham-woodhull-the-spy-named-samuel-culper/.
7. rotunda.upress.virginia.edu/founders/GEWN-03-17-02-0069 (accessed May 26, 2015).
8. Ogden to Washington, April 4, 1782.

It seems that after so many months wandering about New York City in his Continental army uniform Costigin had become an accepted part of the landscape. Upon his return from New Brunswick he apparently simply continued to walk about observing and talking with various people as before. While this may seem highly improbable in a logical sense, bureaucratic procedures in any large organization often create such errors. This would not be the last time it happened to the British army.[9]

However, having been legally exchanged Costigin was removed from the pledges that accompanied his parole. Thus, he could assist Washington by reporting on events in the city. Still, to protect his identity and his current non-parole status, Costigin needed to find a covert manner to get his reports to American lines, and he used the mark Z as his signature on these reports to hide his true identity. The only clue as to how he managed to smuggle his reports out of the city is in his expense report, wherein he notes a total expenditure of sixty-five pounds which included " . . . sending the intelligence procured to the American lines."[10]

Costigin's first, of a total of three, reports is dated December 7, 1778. It includes information on a variety of subjects, and refers to three other letters of which no record seems to exist. The report states:

After Observing the Troops in Motion on the ev'ning of the second I immediately dispatched a person with what I could gather—since which I forwarded three letters carrying ev'ry matter I could Possibly learn, which were near the Facts.

Last ev'ning Genl Clinton return'd to town, and the Troops disembarking, passing to Long Island and their different Cantonments thro' the Night.

Every Species of Provissions Especially Fresh are in great plenty, except Bread, and from the best authority I can assure you none have been issued for several days past. They are hourly expecting a fleet with flour from Home which is said to have sail'd some time ago.

9. The disinformation operation by Private Charles Morgan, of the New Jersey Light Battalion, prior to the Battle of Yorktown was also apparently assisted by British Army bureaucratic structure. Posing as a deserter, he convinced Cornwallis of false information regarding American capabilities. However, when he returned to American lines a few days later, it appears Cornwallis was not informed and continued to believe Morgan's information. See Kenneth A. Daigler, *Spies, Patriots, and Traitors: American Intelligence in the Revolutionary War* (Washington: Georgetown University Press, 2014), 225-27.
10. Ogden to Washington, April 4, 1782.

The Bedford of Seventy-four Gun is Order'd home, she having lost all her Masts cannot get them here, and goes under Juries, she belongd to Byron's fleet.

For fear of fire, Orders are Issued that all ships and Vessels remaining here to lay in New Town Creek, this winter where arm'd Vessels are to protect them.

In One of my last I Mention'd things coming [from] Shrewbury. Since I find that Most amazing Quantities come from that Quarter, within this Year not less than One Thousand Sheep, five Hundred Hogs, and Eight Hundred Quartr or up-wards's of good beef, a large Parcel of Cheese–besides Poultry–which give [good] support to the City.

Yesterday Arriv'd seven Prizes, Two [French] Vessels bound to America: Two with Tobaco from Virginia, the Others small West Indiamen.

It is reported that Genl Vaughen is shortly to go home.[11]

This report, while general in nature, does appear to be accurate in its details, and indicates that Costigin did enjoy freedom to walk about the city and collect local gossip. There are no documents suggesting that he received any response to this report, nor that he was given any specific reporting requirements for this or his future reporting.

His second report, sent some days later, does contain more useful intelligence, and would seem to indicate that he had developed some access to individuals with knowledge of British troop movements. It is dated December 13, 1778, and states:

Since my last, nothing having turn'd up untill this day. A fleet of Jamacia Men about thirty sail are geting into the North river and are to sail in a few days under convoy of a frigate–the Emerald Tomorrow the Amazon of 32 Guns sails for England, a number of Passenge among whom, Colo. Wm Bayard, Colo. Campbell of the 22nd Regt the Major of 16th Dragoon's name unknown, and a Parson stringer from Phila.

11. Edward G. Lengel, ed., *The Papers of George Washington, Revolutionary War Series, vol. 18, 1 November 1778–14 January 1779* (Charlottesville: University of Virginia Press, 2008), 376-77. Note: No previous reports from Costigin regarding supplies from Shrewsbury have been found.

Overleaf: a 1776 map of New York City. (*Boston Public Library*)

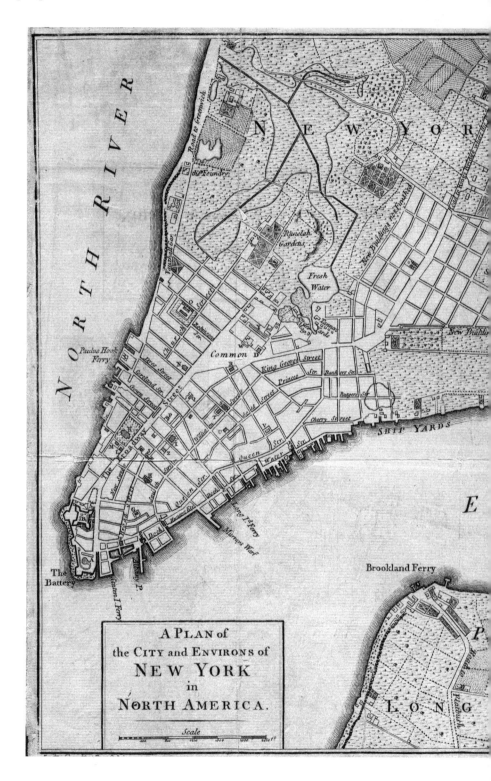

A PLAN of
the CITY and ENVIRONS of
NEW YORK
in
NORTH AMERICA.

Scale

As yet no Acct of the three fleets sail'd under Command of Major Genl Grant. Genl Cambell and Lieut. Colo. Campbell of the 71st now appointed a Brigr by the Commander in Chief: it is believ'd by all that Grant is gone to the West India: Genl Campbell being appoint'd Governor of Pensacola it cannot be a secret his destination: Colo. Campbell seem'd of more importance; I have paid ev'ry Attention to his line, and find he has from 3000 to 3500 Men, call'd here a pretty Command, and from the best Judges and men entituled to know ev'ry thing transacted. I am of Opinion they are intended for Georgia: from which they have high expectations not only from the weakness of the place, but likewise friendship of the Citizens of that Province–I this day saw Go'vernor Tryon in the City [he] having been very ill with the Gout is retu [returned] but cannot learn who is left in Command [of] the bridge. I this day also learned that the Light Infantry from Jamacia, with the 17th Dragoon's, and Cathcarts Legion, from Jerico, are Order'd to South and East Hampton's and as they [take] no Provisions with them, it is believ'd they will sweep all that Country.

Bread with the Army is exceedingly [short] but Large Quantities of Rice have been taken which serve as a Substitue–the Opinion of an evacuation still prevails among numbers of the inhabitants–but I must say I cannot as yet see any Probability of it.[12]

Costigin's final intelligence report is brief, and dated December 19, 1778:

Mr. James Willing, with Two Officers said to be deserters from the British service, at Pensacola have been lately taken in a small sloop from that Quartr bound as suppos'd to Philadelphia. The three on being brought to this place found means to make their escape from the prize, and got into the City.

Mr. Willing who is some way connected with Lawr. Kirtwright immediately repair'd to his house, but unhappily found no shelter there, he being a person of Consequence was given up and is now in confinement he being no Seaman, and taken unarm'd it is generally said he will be held up for Connelly–the other Gentlemen are not yet discover'd.

The Jamacia fleet have not yet sail'd and I find there will be in the whole 40 or 50 sail–a number of them Arm'd.[13]

12. Lengel, *The Papers of George Washington*, 399-400.
13. Lengel, *The Papers of George Washington*, 465.

From other correspondence, and Colonel Ogden's role as indicated in Costigin's pension paper and his operational expense report, it can be surmised that his reporting channel went directly to Ogden, and then to Ogden's Commanding Officer Lord Stirling (William Alexander), and from Stirling to Washington. It appears Stirling may have provided Washington with a consolidated intelligence report on New York City activities, but accompanied by the reports from each source.

Washington's only recorded reaction to Costigin's reporting was almost lost to history. On December 30, 1778, Stirling sent Washington a communication which included information from Costigin, but it is not clear which December report it was from.[14] On January 2, 1779, Washington responded to Stirling, "I am favd with yours of the 30th Ulto. I thank you for the intelligence it contains."[15]

However, also preserved is the draft of the correspondence, which reads: "I am favd with yours of the 30th Ulto with the information from Z inclosed. I thank you for that and what you have collected from other quarters."[16]

Another indicator that Washington appreciated Costigin's reporting comes from the fact that he was aware when Costigin's reports ceased to appear. In a March 15, 1779 letter from his Headquarters at Middle Brook, Washington wrote to Brigadier General William Maxwell, "We have heard nothing of a long time from Z. Has he dropped the correspondence? Or what is become of him. If we are to depend no further upon him, you should endeavor to open some other channel for intelligence—The Season advances when the enemy will begin to stir, and we should if possible be acquainted with their motions."[17]

Maxwell responded, on March 17, identifying who Z was and noting that he was no longer active as a reporting source: "We have several people in New York that would give us intelligence but we have none that will attempt to go for it; those that have gone formerly have been presented at the last Court, and Bills found against them; they

14. rotunda.upress.virginia.edu/founders/GEWN-03-18-02-0600 (accessed May 26, 2015).

15. rotunda.upress.virginia.edu/founders/GEWN-03-18-02-0625 (accessed May 26, 2015).

16. rotunda.upress.virginia.edu/founders/GEWN-03-18-02-0625 (accessed May 26, 2015).

17. rotunda.upress.virginia.edu/founders/GEWN-03-19-02-0483 (accessed May 26, 2015).

denyed the charges but are bound to the next Court so that we cannot get them to move The person, under the Carracter of Z is out
some time ago. I think he lives at Brunswick Viz. Costican."[18]

With this correspondence, Costigin's role in American intelligence
ends with the exception of his subsequent request for reimbursement
submitted through Colonel Ogden on April 4, 1782, and the brief
description of his intelligence role in his pension statement of August
25, 1820.

18. rotunda.upress.virginia.edu/founders/GEWN-03-19-02-0510 (accessed May 26, 2015).

Ann Bates:
British Spy Extraordinaire

❦ CHRISTIAN M. MCBURNEY ❦

With the recent popularity of spies in the Revolutionary War, led by AMC's *TURN* cable television series and the bestselling book *George Washington's Secret Six: the Spy Ring that Saved the American Revolution*, the impact that spies had on the outcome of campaigns and other aspects of the war has sometimes been exaggerated. Two examples are discussed in my book, *Spies in Revolutionary Rhode Island*. One of them concerns Ann Bates, the subject of this article.

One of the few known female spies on either side in the Revolutionary War, Ann Bates spied for the British during the Rhode Island Campaign of July and August 1778, the first time the French and American forces jointly cooperated to attack a British outpost. The joint expedition failed to capture the British garrison defending Newport, but the American army fought well at the Battle of Rhode Island on August 28, 1778.[1] Bates provided her British handlers with valuable intelligence, despite never setting foot in Rhode Island. However, she did not, as some historians claim, play a crucial role in the British triumph.

Born around 1748, Bates worked as a schoolteacher in Philadelphia. Because her husband was a soldier and gun repairman in the British army, she learned about weaponry and the importance of military information, such as the enemy's cannon, soldier, and supply totals. At some point during the British occupation of Philadelphia, Ann Bates met with John Craig (sometimes Craiggie or Cregge), a civilian active in British general Sir Henry Clinton's espi-

---

1. See Christian McBurney, *The Rhode Island Campaign: The First French and American Operation in the Revolutionary War* (Yardley, PA: Westholme, 2011), *passim*.

onage network. Craig judged her, accurately, as it turned out, to be intelligent and resourceful—just the right type to thrive as a spy. Bates performed a few secret tasks for Craig.

The Bates family's world changed dramatically when Clinton, the new commander in chief of British forces in North America, decided to evacuate Philadelphia in response to news of the alliance between France and America and the anticipated imminent arrival of a French fleet in Chesapeake Bay. After her husband joined Clinton's army, which marched out of Philadelphia on June 18, 1778, bound for New York City, Ann followed. When, on about June 26, she arrived in the city serving as British headquarters, she asked to see Craig. Instead, she was taken to meet with one of Clinton's spy handlers, Major Duncan Drummond. Drummond and Craig together persuaded Bates to spy for the British army. Drummond subsequently wrote: "a woman whom Craig has trusted often came to town last night. She is well acquainted with many of the R.A. [Royal Artillery] . . . It is proposed to send her out under the idea of selling little matters" in Washington's camp and there "she will converse with Chambers and will return whenever she may have learnt anything that deserves to be known."[2] Craig later received a nice finder's fee from the British secret service for bringing Bates to Duncan's attention.[3]

After a mere single day of training, on June 29, Ann departed New York City on her first mission. Using the cover name "Mrs. Barnes," Bates disguised herself as a peddler. She was given five guineas for expenses to buy items for a peddler's pack—thread, needles, combs, knives, and some medicines. On July 2, she arrived at Washington's camp at White Plains, New York. As "Mrs. Barnes," she freely traveled amongst the American soldiers and camp followers. Bates had been instructed by Drummond to find a disloyal soldier, named Chambers, and to glean any useful intelligence from him. However, she could not find him. Bates then resourcefully changed her mission to find out what useful intelligence she could. She listened in on conversations, located gun emplacements and counted artillery pieces. After finally selling most all of her merchandise, she made her way back to Drummond in New York City.

2. Undated note, probably by Major Duncan Drummond on June 28, 1778, Henry Clinton Papers 234:27, William L. Clements Library. This note has the same hand-writing as in the British Intelligence Memorandum Book noted in the note below.
3. Undated entry (near end of book), British Intelligence Memorandum Book, MMC-2248, Manuscript Reading Room, Library of Congress.

Bates began to spy on Washington's army at a time when it was sending Continental regiments eastward to augment the American army in Rhode Island. On July 29, 1778, Major Drummond dispatched Bates back to White Plains. Still disguised as Mrs. Barnes, the peddler, she evaded or passed through multiple military checkpoints and finally arrived at Washington's camp. She was again unable to locate Chambers, her contact. (She learned later that he had been killed in a battle in the Mohawk Valley.) Bates therefore spent the next three or four days wandering about the American camp, counting "119 pieces of cannon" and estimating the number of soldiers at 23,000. She spotted ten wagons rolling into camp "with wounded" in them. She also described the locations of the American brigades. She even boldly entered the residence temporarily being used as Washington's headquarters and spotted the commanding general, but did not learn any useful information there.[4] She was informed, however, that no American troops had yet been dispatched to Rhode Island. "During her stay amongst them," wrote Drummond after Bates's return to New York City on August 6, "she could neither learn nor see any detachment that had been sent to Rhode Island."[5]

Just two days later, Bates was sent back to White Plains for a third time, arriving on August 12. At Washington's headquarters she overheard an officer whom she thought was a general inform one of Washington's aides-de-camp (perhaps Alexander Hamilton) that 600 boats were being prepared for an invasion of Long Island by 5,000 troops (this attempt was never made). She also learned that about 3,000 Continentals and 2,000 militiamen had left camp for Rhode Island. Bates observed that with the departure of another detachment of 3,800 "picked men" to Dobbs Ferry, the American camp "was not

4. The information on Ann Bates, unless otherwise stated, is from British Intelligence Memorandum Book, July 21-November 10, 1778, MMC-2248, Library of Congress, and Petition of Ann Bates, March 17, 1785, British Treasury Papers, In-Letters, T1/611, British National Archives. Bakeless also relied on these sources, and Misencik relied primarily on Bakeless. See John Bakeless, *Turncoats, Traitors and Heroes* (New York: Da Capo Press, 1975), 252-58 and Paul Misencik, *The Original American Spies: Seven Covert Agents of the Revolutionary War* (Jefferson, NC: McFarland, 2014), 78-86. To the author's knowledge, as Bates's petition and the supporting documents are not held by any library or archives in the United States, the author has donated a copy to The David Library of the American Revolution, Washington Crossing, Pennsylvania. While the identity of the author of the intelligence book is not certain, it probably was penned by Major Drummond.

5. Journal, August 6, 1778, British Intelligence Memorandum Book, MMC-2248, Library of Congress.

near so numerous as when she was first there, nor their parades half so full." She estimated the strength of Washington's army had fallen to 16,000 or 17,000 troops. She counted fifty-one pieces of artillery on Saturday and saw nine more cannon arrive in camp the next day.[6]

Bates took pride in her role, writing in a petition for a pension in 1785 that "my timely information was the blessed means of saving the Rhode Island garrison with all the troops and stores who must otherwise have fallen a prey to their enemies." Duncan Drummond was asked to review Bates's petition, and he observed that "she asserts nothing but what is strictly true" and that "her information . . . was by far superior to every other intelligence."[7] Paul R. Misencik, who recently devoted a chapter in his book on spies to a detailed history of Ann Bates's espionage activities, called her Britain's "most effective" spy, in large part based on her supposed decisive role in the Rhode Island Campaign.[8]

Bates's role in the Rhode Island Campaign has been exaggerated. Mostly importantly, the timing is off. Early in the morning of July 22, 1778, Continental brigades commanded by James Varnum of Rhode Island and John Glover of Massachusetts, totaling 2,500 soldiers, set out on their 160-mile trek to Rhode Island. Later that morning, Washington appointed Major General Marquis de Lafayette to command the detachment, forcing the young French nobleman to gallop off to catch it.[9] Lafayette's Continentals reached Tiverton, Rhode Island, the staging area for the invasion of Aquidneck Island, on August 8. Accordingly, when Bates reported to Drummond on August 6 that no American troops had yet left for Rhode Island, she was incorrect. On August 19, after her next trip to the White Plains camp, Bates told Drummond of the movements of the two Continental brigades. She added that 2,000 militiamen accompanied this detachment, but this too was untrue.

When Bates returned to Clinton's headquarters on August 19 and belatedly warned of American troop movements to Rhode Island, it is said that this information led Clinton to reinforce the Newport garrison, which helped to defeat the combined French and American forces outside Newport.[10] However, this could not be accurate, as

6. Ibid., August 19, 1778.
7. Ann Bates's claim for compensation, March 17, 1785, British Treasury Papers, In-Letters, T1/611, British National Archives.
8. Misencik, *Seven Covert Agents*, 86.
9. McBurney, *Rhode Island Campaign*, 78.
10. Bakeless, *Turncoats, Traitors and Heroes*, 257; Misencik, *Seven Covert Agents*, 85.

Clinton never sent any reinforcements to Newport in August because the French fleet had arrived outside Narragansett Bay on July 29. Back on July 9, concerned that Newport would be exposed to an attack by the French fleet when it arrived, Clinton had prudently sent some 1,850 troops under Major General Richard Prescott, by boat through Long Island Sound to reinforce the Newport garrison.[11] However, this was weeks prior to Lafayette's Continentals departing White Plains for Rhode Island on July 22.

Still, Ann Bates was a remarkable woman and a valuable spy. Her ability to handle the physically grueling trips between her posts without resting long and getting past the many Continental army checkpoints was impressive. Bates's efforts proved that women could be valuable spies. They were often able to overhear secret information because they were considered unable to understand the complexity of military affairs. Disguised as a mere peddler, she was able to penetrate even Washington's headquarters. Bates was paid for each of the three trips she made to Washington's camp—twenty dollars, thirty-one dollars, and thirty dollars.[12]

The British spy Ann Bates continued to perform clandestine missions between 1778 and 1780. In September 1778, when she was on another mission infiltrating Washington's army, a deserter from the British Twenty-Seventh Regiment recognized her, but she was able to elude capture.[13] This event, however, led Ann to cease penetrating Washington's headquarters. Later, Ann was sent to escort from Philadelphia to New York City a female secret agent who had helped to turn Benedict Arnold. A series of safe houses provided shelter for the female spies until they came to the New Jersey shore of the Hudson River. To avoid both a storm and detection by Patriot scouts, the women had to stay hidden in a Loyalist's cellar for three days. Bates also provided her superiors with a report on Philadelphia shipping and the amount of flour to be found in its "rebel" mills.

When her husband was sent to Charleston following the British capture of the city in May 1780, Ann Bates travelled with the troops

---

11. McBurney, *Rhode Island Campaign,* 76.
12. Undated entry (near end of book), British Intelligence Memorandum Book, MMC-2248, Library of Congress.
13. Journal, undated (about September 30, 1778), British Intelligence Memorandum Book, MMC-2248, Library of Congress. See also Petition of Ann Bates, March 17, 1785, British Treasury Papers, In-Letters, T1/611, British National Archives ("an English deserter who knew me gave information who I was so that I was obliged to make a precipitate retreat for fear of being taken up as a spy").

to South Carolina but did not engage in any further espionage activities. The couple sailed to England in 1781. Later deserted by her husband and in dire financial straits, she successfully petitioned the British government for a small pension on the basis of her wartime spying.[14]

14. Bakeless, *Turncoats, Traitors and Heroes*, 258–62; Misencik, *Seven Covert Agents*, 86–91.

Hannah Caldwell's Death: Accident or Murder?

❄️ JOHN L. SMITH, JR. ❄️

There's nothing like the murder of a young, innocent woman to get patriotic fervor in an uproar. The death of Jane McCrea in 1777, supposedly at the hands of Indians commissioned by British Lt. Gen. John Burgoyne, outraged Patriots and led to a huge surge of recruiting in New York. The story then went down in American folklore. Aside from being the inspiration for the character of Cora Munro in the early classic *The Last of the Mohicans*, the legendary 1804 painting *The Death of Jane McCrea* still makes its way into videos and textbooks on the American Revolution.

But just three years later, another tragic death happened to an innocent New Jersey woman. Not quite getting the huge play Jane McCrea's death did, the death of Hannah Caldwell nevertheless sparked widespread anger with Patriots. And although not a famous painting hanging in a museum, Hannah's death is still to this day depicted on the seal of Union County, New Jersey. The (inaccurate) image shows a woman standing in her home's doorway being shot point-blank by a British redcoat soldier. Poor Hannah may have died, but the legend of *how* she died is very hard to kill. As recently as 2005, a popular-selling book said,

> Poorly trained or callous soldiers sometimes entered homes firing their weapons randomly at residents. One of their victims was Hannah Ogden Caldwell, the wife of a patriot clergyman, who was killed by a soldier entering the bedroom where she and her nine children had gathered. His shot tore open her chest and punctured her lung.[1]

1. Carol Berkin, *Revolutionary Mothers: Women in the Struggle for America's Independence* (New York: Alfred A. Knopf, 2005), 37.

Pretty heavy stuff, but a little short on facts—no matter which story you believe. Only one fact is for sure—Hannah Caldwell, inside of her own home that day in 1780, was killed by a musket bullet . . . or two.[2] However, past those details, how accurate is the story of her terrible murder? Well, maybe not much. Here are both sides of the story and you can be the judge.

THE BATTLE AND THE CALDWELLS

By the summer of 1780, the Revolutionary War had already shifted its focus to the southern half of the rebel states. But Hessian Gen. Baron Wilhelm von Knyphausen, commander of the British garrison in New York City, still wanted a crack at Gen. George Washington's army near Morristown, New Jersey. Before dawn on June 7, 1780, he moved his 6,000 troops from Staten Island across Newark Bay to Elizabethtown Point, New Jersey. But General Knyphausen ran right into New Jersey militia and a brigade of the New Jersey Continental line. The ensuing battle slowly pushed back the Americans, as both sides fought through the small village of Connecticut Farms (now Union Township, New Jersey). The Battle of Connecticut Farms is known in American history as being one of the last Revolutionary War battles in the northern front. It's also known for what happened to Hannah Caldwell there.

When the war broke out, Rev. Mr. James Caldwell had been pastor of the First Presbyterian Church in Elizabethtown. But strongly believing in the American cause, Caldwell joined the Patriot army and became chaplain of the New Jersey line. When his church and home were burned by Loyalists in January 1780, he moved his wife and nine children four miles inland to Connecticut Farms and then left for duty at Jockey Hollow, near Morristown.

Rev. Mr. Caldwell was away from home that morning of June 7, 1780, when the advancing British and Hessian troops moved through Connecticut Farms, chasing American troops, setting fires, and shooting back at Patriots firing from their open doorways and windows. Rev. Mr. Caldwell's wife, Hannah Caldwell, was in the parsonage home with their two youngest children, a four-year-old toddler and their sick nine-month old, Maria. The other seven children had been moved out of the area already. Seeing the battling militia and enemy troops approach down the road, Hannah rounded up some of the

2. Different accounts of Hannah's death speak of one or two musket balls hitting her in her chest. In support of the "redcoat soldier firing through the window" theory, it was supposed that two balls were "double loaded" into the musket barrel.

Caldwell's valuables like silverware and lockets. Many valuables were lowered down the well; others she stashed inside her pockets, then she returned inside the house. Also in the house with Hannah and her two children were a nurse, Constance Benward (sometimes called "Katy") and a housekeeper that the couple had taken in named Abigail Lennington.

THE CASE FOR MURDER[3]

Hearing the battle coming closer and closer, Hannah and the others went "to a back room, which was considered secure, with stone walls on three sides and one window on the north side."[4] Hannah reportedly sat on the bed with little Maria, telling the two other women present, "Don't worry, baby will be our protection. They will respect a mother."[5] Hannah handed the baby to Katy. Abigail went to look out of the single window in the house. She testified that she saw a "short thick man wearing a red coat"[6] come to the window, look in, and point his musket to the window. Abigail heard a crash and a boom accompanied by shards of broken glass being blasted into her face. Then, looking over toward the bed—she saw Mrs. Caldwell lying with her back on the bed. Hannah appeared to be dead with a bleeding bullet wound in her chest.

In a deposition, Katy states that the soldiers then entered the house looking for anything of value. They found Hannah's body and cut open her dress, discovering more valuables inside the pockets of the dead woman. They pulled the body to the floor and took the sheets and covers from the bed. Hannah's body was removed from the house by local friends just before the British troops burned the house. "The

---

3. *Union County Historical Society Proceedings*, Vol. 2 (1923-24), 10-15. The case for Hannah's deliberate murder was made by her husband, Rev. Mr. James Caldwell just three months after her death. In September 1780, he published the well-read pamphlet *Certain Facts Relating to the Death of Hannah Caldwell, Wife of Rev. James Caldwell*. It contained depositions (supposedly given to a magistrate) testifying to Hannah's murder. The statements were from witnesses Abigail Lennington and Catherine Benward, along with neighbor Mrs. Patience Wade (to whose house Hannah's body was carried) and wife to Deacon Caleb Wade. The pamphlet is at the Union County [NJ] Historical Society.

4. Joan N. Burstyn, ed., and The Women's Project of New Jersey, Inc., *Past and Promise: Lives of New Jersey Women* (Metuchen, NJ: Scarecrow Press, 1990), 13-14; detail of the inside of the house also confirmed in Thomas J. Fleming, *The Forgotten Victory—The Battle for New Jersey 1780* (New York: Reader's Digest Press, 1973), 161.

5. *Certain Facts Relating to the Death of Hannah Caldwell, Wife of Rev. James Caldwell.*

6. In a different reference to the supposed testimony (footnote 3), the soldier was described as "a shot [short] squatty soldier in a red coat."

soldiers burned nine other homes, as well as the schoolhouse, barns, and shops, before leaving the village."[7]

Depositions concerning Hannah Caldwell's death were gathered and published in newspapers as well as in a pamphlet just three months later. In the pamphlet, an angry and distraught Rev. Mr. Caldwell summed up her death as the work of the Royal Army carrying out the implied orders of General Knyphausen: "This was a violation of every tender feeling; without provocation, deliberately committed in open day; nor was it ever frowned on by the commander."[8] Public patriotic outrage mirrored Rev. Mr. Caldwell's claim:

> Some attempts were made by the Royalist party to escape the odium of the frightful outrage by pretending that Mrs. Caldwell had been killed by a chance shot. The actual evidence, however, sets beyond question the fact that one of the enemy was the murderer and there is much reason to believe that the deed was deliberately ordered by those high in authority.[9]

So shortly after the event, the Patriot story spin began in high speed . . . each version with its own variation of the heinous, outrageous murder. A noteworthy adaptation came from none other than famed Founding Era historian Mercy Otis Warren:

> This lady was sitting in her own house, with her little domestic circle around her, and her infant in her arms; unapprehensive of danger, shrouded by the consciousness of her own innocence and virtue; when a British barbarian pointed his musquet into the window of her room, and instantly shot her through the lungs. A hole was dug, the body thrown in, and the house of this excellent lady set on fire, and consumed with all the property it contained.[10]

Another celebrity of the time mentioned "Poor Parson Caldwell . . . ," none other than Maj. John André, who had just included a non-sentimental word about the traitorous Rev. Mr. Caldwell in an epic-

7. Burstyn, *Past and Promise*, 13.
8. Ellen Mackay Hutchinson Cortissoz, Arthur Stedman, ed., *A Library of American Literature: Vol. 3—Literature of the Revolutionary Period* (New York: Charles L. Webster & Company, 1888), 123; "The Death of Parson Caldwell's Wife."
9. Mary Simmerson Cunningham Logan, *The Part Taken by Women in American History* (Wilmington, DE: Perry-Nalle Publishing Company, 1912), 173.
10. Lester H. Cohen, ed., *History of the Rise, Progress and Termination of the American Revolution, interspersed with Biographical, Political and Moral Observation*, Vol. 1, by Mercy Otis Warren (Indianapolis, IN: Liberty Classics, 1988), 327-328.

ballad about a battle at Bull's Ferry, New Jersey in July 1780.[11] The third and final part of his poem *The Cow Chace, a Poem in Three Cantos* was in fact running in *The Royal Gazette* the day after André was captured as a spy in cahoots with Benedict Arnold.[12] Who says history doesn't take strange turns? In the book version of André's poem mentioning Rev. Mr. Caldwell, end notes actually give a passing nod of sentimentality toward Mrs. Caldwell herself:

> . . . whose Wife was barbarously shot by a newly enlisted Soldier of Knyphausen's command in the preceding Summer, on no other Provocation, as was alleged, than that she vituperated [insulted] him from her Window as he passed.[13]

An even worse spin, totally inaccurate, and sickeningly melodramatic was this account of Rev. Mr. Caldwell: "Returning to his home one day, he found his wife shot on his step-stone, and her babe creeping around in its mother's gore. He took the child in his hands, held it aloft toward heaven, baptized it in its mother's blood, and swore eternal hostility to a foe that would not spare women or children."[14]

The newspapers wasted no time in giving alarming accounts of the innocent mother's murder. The June 14 and 21, 1780, issues of *The New-Jersey Gazette* printed details:

> . . . a Soldier came to the House, and putting his Gun to the Window of the Room where this worthy Woman was sitting . . . shot her through the Lungs dead on the Spot."[15] After more lurid

---

11. Maj. John Andre, *The Cow Chace, a Poem in Three Cantos* (London, 1781; reprinted Albany, NY: J. Munsell, 1866), 43. The endnotes of the printed London book version of Andre's poem actually document much of the "evidence" for the innocence of the British in Mrs. Caldwell's death. Andre's poem ran initially in three issues of *The Royal Gazette* (New York) in 1780. The poem was then printed in book form by John Fielding of London in 1781, the year following the deaths of John Andre and Hannah Caldwell. The 1866 edition, from where the references in this article are culled, is a direct copy of the 1781 London edition. The preface of the 1866 version reads, "The present Edition is printed from the first, as it appeared at Intervals in the Columns of Rivington's Royal Gazette [no italics], of New York City. The original Notes as printed in that Paper, are here preserved as Foot Notes, while all the additional Notes are given at the End, with the Authorities from whence derived."
12. Andre, *The Cow Chace*, 51; "This Canto was first printed in Rivington's *Royal Gazette*, No. 416, September 24, 1780."
13. Andre, *The Cow Chace*, 52.
14. Matthew Hale Smith, *Bulls and Bears of New York: With the Crisis of 1873 and the Cause* (Hartford, CT: J. B. Burr & Company, 1875), 535.
15. *The New-Jersey Journal*, June 21, 1780; and Andre, *The Cow Chace*, 54.

details, the newspaper editorialized that at least she was killed instantly before her house was set on fire, so that's some consolation. "One of the barbarians advancing round the house, took the advantage of a small space, through which the room was accessible, and fired two balls into that amiable lady, so well directed that they ended her life "in a moment."[16]

The article in the second newspaper closed the final paragraph proclaiming, "This Melancholy Affair, with their cruel Burnings, has raised the Resentment of the whole Country to the highest Pitch."[17]

THE CASE FOR A TRAGIC ACCIDENT

Almost immediately after Hannah Caldwell was killed and her house burned, the hurricane of American public fury began against the enemy. The British felt the other side of the story needed to be told quickly! In a letter dated June 20, 1780, an anonymous British soldier requested that the British army's version of what happened be published in *The Royal Gazette* to correct the "many Falsehoods"[18] of the rebels' story about Mrs. Caldwell's death:

> Whilst the troops were advancing to Connecticut Farms, the rebels fired out of the houses, agreeable to their usual practice, from which circumstance, Mrs. Caldwell had the misfortune to be shot by a random ball. What heightened the singularity of this unhappy Lady's fate, is, that upon Enquiry it appears, beyond a Doubt, that the shot was fired by the rebels themselves, as it entered the side of the House from their direction, and lodged in the Wall nearest the Troops then advancing.[19]

If a murder trial of Hannah Caldwell had actually happened, a plausible witness for the defense would have been Ebenezer Foster,[20] a Loyalist who returned to New Jersey that day under the protection of General Knyphausen's soldiers (although the prosecution would've labeled Foster as a looter). Foster had been a justice of the peace in

---

16. *The New-Jersey Journal,* June 14, 1780; The New Jersey State Library Digital Collections, 312: www.njstatelib.org/slic_files/imported/NJ_Information/ Digital_ Collections/NJInTheAmericanRevolution1763-1783/9.9.pdf (accessed June 10, 2015).

17. *The New-Jersey Journal,* June 21, 1780; and Andre, *The Cow Chace,* 54.

18. *The Royal Gazette,* No. 389, June 21, 1780; also Andre, *The Cow Chace,* 58.

19. *The Royal Gazette,* No. 389, June 21, 1780; also Andre, *The Cow Chace,* 59-60.

20. Ebenezer Foster was described by James Rivington, the *Royal Gazette* publisher, as a "Gentleman of great Integrity, and a very loyal Subject." Andre, *The Cow Chace,* 58.

nearby Woodbridge, New Jersey, and his eyewitness account of the Hannah Caldwell incident, printed in the August 5, 1780, issue of *The Royal Gazette*, paints a compelling testimony,

> I soon saw a Group of Soldiers in and about said House, and on my nearer Approach, heard some of them mention (rather piteously), a Woman's being shot in the house, as soon as the Crowd dispersed, I entered the House and not without Difficulty, found her laying on her Back on a Bed that stood in a small, dark, back Bed room, (for I don't recollect that it had any Window) tho' it had two Doors that opened into other Apartments. She was to Appearance death, and had a Cloth carelessly thrown over her Face, which I did not remove but left her, expecting the Troops would soon march, when her Friends might take Care of her . . . I followed, and did not return in less than three Hours, when some Person who was near Mr. Caldwell's House, told me the Woman was stripped, and thrown off the Bed, but that a British officer's coming in, had prevented the soldiers from carrying off her Cloaths. On entering the House I found her laying on her Face on the Floor beside the Bed, and most of what Cloaths had been pulled off by her Side. I concluded that she had been taken off the Bed that the Bedding might be taken from under her . . .[21]

Foster goes on to describe his crime scene investigation and from that examination, drew an inevitable Loyalist conclusion:

> We then examined every Circumstance in our Power, in order if possible, to discover the Cause of the Lady's Death, who by this Time we had heard was Mrs. Caldwell. We found that on Account of a Pantry that was building on the back Side of the House, a small Spot of Covering had been pulled off opposite to the Bed whereon the Lady sat, the only Ball we could discover that had touched the House was the one that killed her. It appeared to have come from a northern Direction (in the Course of the Rebel fire) and passed between the Joints of the plastered Wall, it seemed to have passed so far above the Bed as to have hit her above the Girdle and its passing through her left Breast, I account for by supposing her to have been in a stooping Posture . . .[22]

21. *The Royal Gazette*, No. 402, August 5, 1780; also Andre, *The Cow Chace*, 56; and William Scudder Stryker and William Nelson, ed's., *Documents Relating to the Revolutionary History of the State of New Jersey*, Vol. IV—Archives of the State of New Jersey (1914), 564-566.
22. *The Royal Gazette*, No. 402, August 5, 1780; also Andre, *The Cow Chace*, 57; and *Documents Relating to the Revolutionary History of the State of New Jersey*, 564-566.

Foster's account couldn't be contradicted because the evidence (the Caldwell house) had been burned to ashes. The fire started by the British destroyed any evidence indicating the musket ball's point of entry—whether through the window or the side wall. But Foster insisted that the shot that killed Hannah came from a northerly direction and therefore irrefutably showed that Mrs. Caldwell had been killed by friendly American fire.

However, a prominent American countered that the Foster theory was really just a lame excuse to cover up murder. Who said that? A source from on-high: the first chief justice of the United States Supreme Court, John Marshall. Writing some years later, Marshall recounted the incident of "Mrs. Caldwell, the wife of the clergyman . . ." and severely scolded the British for their pathetic cover-up story:

> Ashamed of an act so universally execrated, it contended by the British, that this lady was a victim of a random shot, and even that the fatal ball had proceeded from the militia; in proof of which last assertion, they insisted that the ball had entered on that side which looked towards the retreating Americans. But it was notorious that the militia made no stand at the farms, and a pathetic representation of the fact, made to the public by the afflicted husband, received universal credence and excited universal indignation.[23]

Discounting the British claim that the American Mrs. Caldwell was killed by American friendly fire, Chief Justice Marshall said the American militia, in the northern direction from the Caldwell house, was running from the British and Hessian troops. But was the Battle of Connecticut Farms near the Caldwell house that simplistic?

Tim Abbott is a Litchfield Hills, New Jersey, resident with an interest in the Revolutionary War and Knyphausen's 1780 raid in particular. In reading Foster's slightly slanted conclusion, Abbott has written,

> And what of the claim that the shot came from the American lines to the north? That is an odd direction. Maxwell's men [Continental Army Brig. Gen. William Maxwell] were initially arrayed along a ravine running roughly southwest to northeast and facing a royalist advance from the southeast. The patriots then withdrew to the northwest along a road toward Springfield as their left flank was turned by another royalist column that advanced from the east or

---

23. John Marshall, *The Life of George Washington: Commander in Chief of the American Forces* (London: T. Gillet, 1805), 276.

northeast of their position. Shots 'from the north' could therefore have come from either side.[24]

So Abbott is saying that the positions of the two armies around the Caldwell house were fluid and were always shifting places back and forth as the battle happened. Bullets were flying north and south from both sides as soldiers moved. Assuming that the outright window murder of Hannah Caldwell didn't happen, and that she was tragically killed by a random ball entering a wall and striking her during the battle . . . then the musket ball in reality could've been fired from either a Patriot gun or a Royal gun.

After reading Rev. Mr. Caldwell's own 1780 pamphlet laying out the testimony of the two witnesses and a neighbor in his case for murder, historian Thomas Fleming expressed the opinion, "A reading 200 years after the event, without the hatreds engendered by a civil war, makes it clear that it was a military accident."[25] Maybe . . .

WERE THE CALDWELLS TARGETED IN A NEW JERSEY HIT?

After Rev. Mr. Caldwell's wife was killed and their house burned, there were whispered conspiracy theories abounding that the Caldwells had been targeted for assassination by Loyalists because of allegiance to the American rebellion. The *New-Jersey Gazette* of June 21, 1780, fanned those now-spoken claims,

> In the Neighborhood lived the Rev. James Caldwell, whose Zeal and Activity in the Cause of his Country had rendered him an Object worthy of the Enemy's keenest Resentment. His Vigilance and Attention had always evaded every Attempt to injure him, and therefore it was now determined to wound him in an unguarded Part . . . He had been warned of their utmost Hatred of him.[26]

Murder contract or not, in 1781 (a little over a year past the killing of his wife), Rev. Mr. James Caldwell was shot and killed by a sentry, who was arrested, put on trial, and hung for murder. The prosecution could never produce any evidence showing that the sentry had been hired by the British or Loyalists to kill Caldwell.

---

24. Walking the Berkshires, "We are Avenging the Cause of Virgin Innocence," greensleeves.typepad.com/berkshires/knyphausens_raid_1780/ (accessed June 10, 2015).

25. Thomas J. Fleming, *New Jersey—A History* (New York: W.W. Norton & Company, Inc., 1984), 77.

26. *The New-Jersey Gazette*, June 21, 1780; and Andre, *The Cow Chace*, 53.

Was Hannah Caldwell murdered or just the unlucky victim of an army musket ball? Was James Caldwell murdered or just an accidental casualty of an untrained sentry? Unless some unknown, absolute document surfaces somewhere, the controversy will rage on.

THE COUNTY SEAL CONTROVERSY ALSO RAGES ON

The New Jersey village of Connecticut Farms, where Hannah Caldwell died, became Union Township in 1808. As the area grew in the nineteenth century, Union Township was absorbed into the new Union County in 1857. Every good county needs a seal, an emblem symbolizing an aspect of the county. Not wanting the usual depictions of wheat stalks or fish, Union County of course decided to show Hannah Caldwell being murdered.

So, since 1857, the logo of Union County, New Jersey, shows Hannah standing *outside* of her house (since showing her *inside* the house would be hard to illustrate) and a redcoat soldier shooting her like it's the opening of deer season.

Over the years, some people have objected to the seal on the grounds that it's the only municipal seal that shows a "homicide" or that it's historically inaccurate. True and true. But instead, a 2011 battle erupted between Union County and a political activist who used the county seal in her public TV broadcasts. The county said she couldn't use the trademarked seal. The whole thing became a First Amendments rights case, which was just settled last year in federal court. The court ruled that as an insignia of a U.S. municipality, the graphic belonged to "the people."[27]

No mention was ever made in the court ruling that the seal still shows poor Hannah Caldwell being shot to death on purpose. What's still with that? Justice really *is* blind sometimes.

---

27. Nj.com, "Union County unable to prohibit critic from using its seal, federal judge rules" www.nj.com/union/index.ssf/2014/06/union_county_must_allow_critic_to_use_it_logo_federal_judge_rules.html (accessed June 13, 2015).

Lafayette's Second Voyage to America: Lafayette and *L'Hermione*

❦ KIM BURDICK ❧

In 1775, Gilbert du Motier de Lafayette was an eighteen-year-old French soldier assigned to military maneuvers at Metz. At Metz, he attended an official dinner where the Duke of Gloucester, younger brother of England's King George III, was expounding upon the American Revolution.[1] Amazed by what he heard, Lafayette later wrote, "My heart was enlisted, and I thought only of joining my colors to those of the revolutionaries."[2]

When Louis XVI forbade this young French soldier to go to America, Lafayette deliberately disobeyed orders, leaving France with Baron DeKalb and a dozen friends and colleagues. They set sail from Spain in Lafayette's ship *la Victoire* on April 20, 1777, reportedly heading for Santa Domingo.[3] Landing in South Carolina, they made their way 650 miles to Philadelphia, where, on July 31, Lafayette was commissioned "Major General without pay."[4] Lafayette's first sight of the American troops came on August 8 when George Washington reviewed the Continental army.

A month later, at the Battle of Brandywine (September 11, 1777), a bullet filled Lafayette's boot with blood. Now twenty years old, he spent the winter with Washington's army at Valley Forge and in late May was the hero of an action in nearby Barren Hill, Pennsylvania. Other adventures followed at Monmouth and Rhode Island in 1778.

1. At thirteen, Lafayette became a sous-lieutenant in the King's Musketeers. By seventeen he was a captain in the Noailles Dragoons and later captain in that corps.
2. Quoted in James Gaines, *Liberty and Glory: Washington, Lafayette and their Revolutions* (New York: W.W. Norton and Company, 2007), 37.
3. Letter to Adrienne Lafayette from aboard *la Victoire,* June 1777. Christine Valadon, translator, Cleveland State University Special Collections. Reel 23, Folder 202.
4. Andreas Latzko, *Lafayette: A Life* (New York: Literary Guild, 1936), 52.

With no new military orders, coupled with unhappy news from France about the death of his tiny daughter, and the inability to recoup his investments due to *la Victoire* foundering off the eastern seaboard in the summer of 1777,[5] Lafayette became restless. He requested a leave of absence to briefly return to France.

Monsieur Gerard, the French minister at Philadelphia, wrote ahead to the government in Paris, "You know how little inclined I am to flattery, but I cannot resist saying that the prudent, courageous, and amiable conduct of the Marquis de Lafayette has made him the idol of the Congress, the army, and the people of America."[6]

Upon his arrival, Lafayette's wife, Adrienne de Noailles de Lafayette, wrote, "Monsieur de Lafayette has returned, as modest and charming as when you last saw him, his sensibility undiminished . . . [He] is now in the king's disfavor and is forbidden to appear in any public place. We hope this will not last long . . . nor will he be able to leave for some time after the restriction ends since he must take advantage of the king's good will when it is offered to him."[7] Lafayette formally apologized to the king for having left France without permission,[8] and soon began lobbying him for ships and supplies for America. By March 1779, Ben Franklin reported from Paris that Lafayette had become an excellent advocate for the American cause at the French court. The following year, the success of Lafayette's efforts would be apparent.

On February 21, 1780, Lafayette wrote from Versailles "It seems to be settled that on March 4, I shall find a fast-sailing frigate at Rochefort ready to take me directly to Boston. It will carry neither arms nor clothing but only a few packages of presents for my division. I shall provide a list of what should be carried over with me."[9]

---

5. Laura Auricchio, *The Marquis: Lafayette Reconsidered* (New York: Alfred A. Knopf, 2014), 78.

6. Rupert Sargent Holland, *Lafayette for Young Americans* (Philadelphia: George W. Jacobs & Co., 1923; reprinted Ulan Press, 2012).

7. Stanley J. Idzerda, ed., *Lafayette in the Age of the American Revolution: Selected Letters and Papers, 1776-1790* (Ithaca: Cornell University Press, 1979), 2:230. Idzerda notes: "A nineteenth century note in the hand of Lafayette's secretary has a marginal note: 'Upon Lafayette's first return it was thought that, in order to maintain the king's dignity, which Lafayette had greatly offended by his disobedience, he must be exiled for several days and forbidden to see anyone but his family.'"

8. Lafayette to Louis XVI. Paris, February 19, 1779, in Idzerda, *Lafayette in the Age of the American Revolution,* 232.

9. Ibid., 355.

About the same time, thirty-four year-old Louis de La Touche was called upon to report to the mouth of the Charente River no later than February 20 to await the specific orders regarding a mission from the navy minister. The aristocratic La Touche was the son of a naval officer, and a nephew of Charles de La Touche Tréville, squadron chief. The frigate at Rochefort was *l'Hermione*, one of the king's best ships. The ship's crew included a number of officers, a surgeon, and a priest. About half the three hundred and thirteen working on board were sailors whose responsibilities were to maneuver the ship and man the cannons, but La Touche did not yet know what this mission would be.

March 5, 1780, was an important day for America. On that day, Louis XVI issued the orders: "Monsieur le Marquis de Lafayette will hasten to join General Washington whom he will secretly inform that the King will send at the beginning of spring, help consisting of six ships and approximately 5,000 infantrymen."[10] A list of the ships and supplies the French contemplated sending can be found in the correspondence between Chevalier de Fleurieu and French minister of the navy, Gabriel de Sartine (1729–1801), dated March 5 and 6, 1780.[11]

Lafayette was now authorized to communicate to Washington that the French troops "shall be simply auxiliaries, and with this title they shall come under the orders of General Washington. The French General shall receive the orders of the American commander in chief in all things except what pertains to the internal management of his own troops . . . In case operations by land should not require the concert of the squadron, it will be free to cruise at such a distance from the coasts as the Commandant shall think best for doing the most harm to the enemy."[12]

The secrecy of the mission was communicated to the commander of the navy at Rochefort who received word that the details of the mission were not to be shared. De Sartine informed ship's captain La Touche that Lafayette was to have decent lodging on board *l'Hermione* and, according to strict orders from the king, was to present the list of his four officers and eight servants to La Touche. No additional pas-

10. Glenda Cash, trans., *Le journal de bord de l'Hermione (Journal of the Hermione)*, www.poplarforest.org/Democracy-Lafayette/logepisodes.htm.

11. Idzerda, *Lafayette in the Age of the American Revolution*, 368.

12. Stephen Bonsall, *When the French Were Here* (Garden City & New York: Doubleday, Doran and Company, 1945), 15.

sengers were to be permitted on board. The password would be "Saint Louis and Philadelphie."[13]

In the midst of the excitement, on March 9, 1780, Rochambeau's appointment to the American mission was announced. John Adams, from his diplomatic post in Paris, reported that Lafayette, unhappy at having been passed over for Rochambeau, made a silent statement of protest, bidding adieu to his monarch "in the Uniform of an American Major General." Adams noted that when Lafayette appeared before Louis XVI in American attire, his uniform "attracted the Eyes of the whole court." Adams was sure that the sword Lafayette was carrying that day was the one commissioned for him by Congress. It "is indeed a Beauty," Adams conceded, "which Lafayette shews with great Pleasure."[14]

Lafayette left immediately for Rochefort where *l'Hermione* was waiting for him in the river at Port des Barques. Final preparations took place on March 11. The four officers designated by Lafayette boarded, then a careful search of the decks was made to assure no unauthorized passengers had come on the ship. *L'Hermione* finally set sail for America on the night of March 14 or 15.[15]

Lafayette's autobiography states, "This expedition was kept very secret; Lafayette had preceded it on board the French frigate the Hermione; he arrived at Boston before the Americans and English had the least knowledge of that auxiliary reinforcement."[16]

Lafayette was now twenty-two years old, a husband and father of two surviving children. Captain Latouche[17] wrote de Sartine: "I will have for M. le Marquis de La Fayette all the consideration and attention not only prescribed in your orders, but those that my heart dictates for a man whose actions have inspired in me a great desire to make his acquaintance. . . . I will offer him the choice of my room or the one next to mine which previously served as Council Room."[18]

On March 20, stormy seas and wind resulted in damage that forced *l'Hermione* back toward Ile d'Aix. A small boat was launched to retrieve a replacement part. La Touche took the opportunity to send

13. *L'Hermione* was commissioned in May 1779 under the command of Louis-René Levassor Latouche-Tréville, later to become the Comte de Latouche. A Rochefort-born aristocrat, he later became a noted admiral during the French Revolutionary and Napoleonic wars, 1801. Cash, trans.,*Le journal de bord de l'Hermione.*
14. Auricchio, *The Marquis,* 86.
15. Cash, trans., *Le journal de bord de l'Hermione.*
16. Lafayette, *Memoirs, Correspondence and Manuscripts,* 251.
17. Lieutenant de vaisseaux was Louis-René Levassor, Comte de Latouche-Tréville.
18. Cash, trans., *Le journal de bord de l'Hermione.*

word of Lafayette's good health and well-being on board *l'Hermione*. The repair was made, but now *l'Hermione* was further delayed by lack of wind. Finally, once at sea, *l'Hermione* had an exchange of cannon fire with a British ship. On April 10, a sailor died from a fever similar to typhoid. A few days later, a repair had to be made in the uppermost section of a mast and a malfunction in a compass caused frustration. Finally, the American coast came into view on Thursday, April 27, and by 2:00 in the afternoon *l'Hermione* found shelter in the small port of Marblehead, sixteen miles from Boston. La Touche noted that "Brigadier General Glover came on board to see Monsieur the Marquis de La Fayette."[19]

Lafayette wasted little time in sending a communique to George Washington, alluding to Louis XVI's still-secret news:

> Here I am, My dear General, and in the Mist of the joy I feel in finding Myself again one of your loving Soldiers I take But the time of telling you that I Came from france on Board of a fregatt Which the king Gave me for my passage–I have affairs of the utmost importance that I should at first Communicate to You alone . . . and do Assure You A Great public Good May derive from it.[20]

At 2:30 in the afternoon of April 28, 1780, *l'Hermione,* with French flag flying high, arrived in the port of Boston and saluted the American flag that was displayed at the fort on Castle Island with thirteen cannon shots. Word that the ship had been sighted spread through the city, and the wharves were lined with people. As Lafayette left the ship, he was saluted by La Touche and his crew.

La Touche wrote to de Sartine that day of the eventful crossing and the enthusiasm raised in Boston by the return of the young major general. "Mr. the Marquis de La Fayette enjoyed good health throughout the crossing . . . He received the most distinguished honors of the people with bonfires and shouts of joy, respect no less shown by the officials of the State, their pleasure at seeing him again. On the docks the crowd demonstrated with cries of joy and musket fire. La Fayette went ashore at 1:00 stirring the level of celebratory noise even more."[21]

The arrival of Lafayette at Boston "produced the liveliest sensation, which was entirely owing to his own popularity, for no one yet knew what he had obtained for the United States. Every person ran to the

19. Ibid.
20. Lafayette (at Boston harbor) to Washington, April 27, 1780, Lafayette Papers, 2:364-68.
21. Cash, trans., *Le journal de bord de l'Hermione.*

shore; he was received with the loudest acclamations, and carried in triumph to the house of Governor Hancock, from whence he set out for head-quarters."[22]

The excitement was confirmed by Abigail Adams in a May 1 letter to her husband: "Last week arrived at Boston the Marquis de la Fayette to the universal joy of all who know the Merit and Worth of that Nobleman. He was received with the ringing of Bells, firing of cannon, bon fires, etc."[23]

Lafayette left Boston on May 2 to travel to Washington's headquarters at Morristown, New Jersey. Festivities like those that had greeted him in Boston erupted in every town Lafayette passed through on the two hundred and fifty mile journey. "It's to the roar of cannon that I arrive or depart; the principal residents mount their horses to accompany me," Lafayette wrote his wife Adrienne. "In short, my love, my reception here is greater than anything that I could describe to you."[24]

From the harsh winter at Morristown, New Jersey, to the dwindling number of troops, to Benedict Arnold's censure for misdeeds while governing Philadelphia, things seemed to be going from bad to worse. The position of the army had, in fact, become desperate. There was no money, so the men had not been paid in months. There was no food. Clothing and shoes were almost nonexistent, and many men went about barefoot and in rags. Ammunition was in even shorter supply than weapons.[25] 1780 had not started well, but Lafayette's arrival indicated that perhaps things would soon improve.

On May 16, 1780, the Continental Congress "Resolved, That Congress consider the return of the Marquis LAFAYETTE to America, to resume his command in the army, as a fresh proof of the distinguished zeal and deserving attachment which have justly recommended him to the public confidence and applause; and that they receive with pleasure, a tender of further services of so gallant and meritorious an officer."[26]

---

22. Marie Joseph Paul Yves Roch Gilbert de Motier Lafayette. *Memoirs, Correspondence and Manuscripts of General Lafayette. Vol 1.* (New York and London: Published by His Family, 1837; reprinted Forgotten Books: Classic Reprint Series, 2012), 251.

23. Abigail Adams to John Adams, 1 May 1780. Massachusetts Historical Society, www.masshist.org/digitaladams/archive/doc?id=L17800501aa&bc=%2Fdigitaladams%2Farchive%2Fbrowse%2Fletters_1779_1789.php, accessed March 14, 2015.

24. Auricchio, *The Marquis*, 86.

25. Olivier Bernier, *Lafayette: Hero of Two Worlds* (New York: E.P. Dutton, 1983), 93.

26. *Journals of the Continental Congress* (Washington, DC: Library of Congress, nd), 17:432.

In June, Lafayette received a letter from Boston patriot Samuel Adams who wrote:

> I had for several months past been flattering myself with the prospect of aid. It strongly impressed my mind from one circumstance which took place when you was at Philadelphia the last year. But far from certainty, I could only express to some confidential friends here, a distant hope, though as I conceived, not without some good effect: at least it seemed to enliven our spirits and animate us for so great a crisis. I was in the Council Chamber when I received your letter, and took the liberty to read some parts of it to the members present. I will communicate other parts of it to some leading members of the House of Representatives as prudence may dictate, particularly what you mention of the officers' want of clothing.
>
> I thank you my dear sir for the friendly remembrance you had of the hint I gave you when you was here. Be pleased to pay my most respectful compliments to the Commander in Chief, his family, &c. and be assured of the warm affection of your obliged friend and very humble servant, Samuel Adams[27]

On April 30, La Touche reported by letter to French navy minister de Sartine that there had been some minor damage to *l'Hermione* but also proudly reported that the copper sheathing of the frigate was in perfect condition. *L'Hermione* put to sea again on June 2, 1780.

Although *l'Hermione* is most significant to American history for bringing Lafayette across the Atlantic with the crucial news that French reinforcements of troops, frigates, supplies, and money were coming to our assistance, she was involved in the American Revolution until after Yorktown.[28] On June 7, 1780, soon after depositing Lafayette in Boston, *l'Hermione* battled the 32-gun British frigate HMS *Iris* just south of Long Island.[29] The two ships exchanged a fierce cannonade for an hour and a half, during which La Touche was hit in the arm by a musket ball and *l'Hermione's* rigging was damaged. A year later, *l'Hermione* was one of three supporting frigates in the fleet of Admiral Destouches in a clash between the British fleet and

---

27. Samuel Lorenzo Knapp, *Memoires of Lafayette* (Boston: Knapp, 1824), 47, memory.loc.gov/ammem/index.html, accessed April 2, 2015.

28. Roger Marsh and Fiona Clark Echlin, "*L'Hermione*—building the Frigate of Liberty," *Ships in Scale*, March/April 2014, www.galleryhistoricalfigures.com/LafayetteHermione.pdf.

29. Naval War College Blog. Newport, Rhode Island, navalwarcollegemuseum.blog spot.com/2013_04_01_archive.html#uds-search-results.

seven French ships of the line.[30] On May 4, 1781, *l'Hermione* was in Philadelphia where the Continental Congress honored her service in the previous year's actions up and down the coast. Shortly thereafter, she was engaged in the naval battle of Louisbourg on July 21. On September 28, 1781, as the allied American and French armies began establishing their siege lines around Yorktown, and ships of the French fleet began blocking the entrance to the Chesapeake Bay, *l'Hermione* arrived with powder and supplies. At the end of the battle, along with the frigate *Diligente*, and forty-four gun ship *Romulus*, *l'Hermione* wintered in near Yorktown, sailing home to France in February 1782.[31]

A NEW *L'HERMIONE*

The story of Lafayette and *l'Hermione* has captured the attention of French and American citizens. A recreation of *l'Hermione* was conceived by members of the Centre International de la Mer in 1992, at almost the same time Americans began to seriously study French aid and historic locations along the Yorktown campaign route. Construction of *l'Hermione-Lafayette* began in 2007, and the Washington-Rochambeau Revolutionary Route (W3R) was approved by Congress. Now these international olive branches will meet, with a beautifully recreated French tall ship, *Hermione-Lafayette*, due to set sail in the spring of 2015, from the mouth of the river Charente in Port-des Barques where Lafayette boarded in March 10, 1780.

The tall ship's voyage will be a 3,819 mile transatlantic crossing using eighteenth century technology. *L'Hermione–Lafayette*'s route will not be in historical sequence as hurricane season will be taken into account. *L'Hermione–Lafayette* will land at Yorktown, Virginia, where the original had engaged in the blockade that led to the British defeat and will spend the months of June and July 2015, stopping at twelve historic ports along the Yorktown Campaign route. Related festivities, harkening back to Lafayette's 1780 voyage to America, will bring both the story and the W3R National Historic Trail alive.

Note: Since this article was first published, *L'Hermione–Lafayette* completed its historic voyage and is now back in France.

30. Albert Durfée McJoynt, "French Naval Leaders and the French Navy in the American War for Independence," www.xenophongroup.com/mcjoynt/ marine.htm, accessed March 28, 2015.
31. Jacques de Trentinian, "De Grasse's Naval Army (March 1781—April 1782)," xenophongroup.com/mcjoynt/degrasse_fleet2.htm, accessed March 28, 2015. See also: www.nps.gov/waro/learn/news/upload/February-2015-Highlights-Final.pdf, accessed March 28, 2015.

Fortifying Philadelphia: A Chain of Redoubts and Floating Bridges

豁 BOB RUPPERT 豁

On August 25, 1777, Gen. William Howe with 17,000 men landed at Head of Elk, Maryland; he was 57 miles south of the city of Philadelphia. Over the next month, he battled the Continental army at Brandywine Creek and the South Valley Hills before marching into Philadelphia on September 26.

Because he planned to spend the winter in the city, he needed to be guaranteed the delivery of supplies before the Delaware River froze. Before this could occur his army had to accomplish several things as quickly as possible: take control of Chester and Billingsport, the two towns on the Delaware between Head of Elk and Philadelphia; subdue the American forces in Fort Mifflin and Fort Mercer, the two forts guarding the approach to Philadelphia; and remove the *Chevaux de Frise* that the colonists had secured to the Delaware riverbed. Amazingly, all of this was accomplished between October 1 and December 1, 1777.

To protect the city from an attack by Washington and the Continental army, General Howe ordered his chief engineer, Capt. John Montresor, to build a chain of 10 redoubts across a 2 1/2 mile stretch of land to the north and 2 floating bridges across the Schuylkill River to the west. Because many of the soldiers were involved in the taking of Fort Mifflin and Fort Mercer, inhabitants from the city had to be hired to help build the redoubts and floating bridges. The story of this construction project has been left to us in the diaries and journals of those who were there.

September 27–29: "This afternoon began to reconnoiter the heights near this city, for forming the defense of it, by Field Works, running from the Schuylkill to the Delaware Rivers. This I [Captain John Montresor] was given to understand was our present grand object . . .

I attended him [General Howe] and settled for the payment of the Inhabitants that could be procured to work. Allowance 8 shillings a day to four and eight pence per day . . . We found in the city about 50 Boats of all sorts and procured a Durham boat from Frankford creek that will hold 100 men";[1] "Early this morning I begun on fixing the Situation for forming a chain of redoubts for the defense of the city. This afternoon I attended Lord Cornwallis in viewing the Position I had fixed on for the works . . . North of the city."[2] "Engineers begun to mark out the defences . . . several new boats discovered."[3]

October 1–3: "Several Scows, Flat Boats and others found and brought to Town that were hid in the marshes."[4] "At 10 this morning signed the order for Provisions for 340 Inhabitants to work on the redoubts . . . At 11 this morning orders from the General by Captain Mulcaster for me to attend principally to the 2 outer faces of all the Redoubts first & to begin immediately on the Schuylkill and works from it."[5] "[E]ach redoubt was to be occupied by a captain, two lieutenants, and fifty men, who were relieved each day."[6]

To hurry construction of the bridge, huts were built nearby to house the workers who would otherwise have had to proceed each morning from their homes or regimental encampments.

October 17–20: "This day principally employed . . . in transporting the materials for the Bridge . . . at Grey's ferry."[7] "The detachment from Wilmington and . . . Chester arrived on the opposite side at 2 o'clock p. m. . . . With the detachment arrived the Engineer."[8] "The Commander-in-Chief with the army marched from Germantown to the heights North of Philadelphia . . . and encamped in the rear of the 10 redoubts."[9] "The ten newly erected but not completed redoubts which lie scattered from the Delaware to the Schuylkill are in front of our camp."[10] Similar accounts are related by Capt. Johann Ewald, Lt.

1. G. D. Scull, "Journal of Captain John Montresor, July 1, 1777 to July 1, 1778, Chief Engineer of the British Army," *Pennsylvania Magazine of History and Biography*, 6 (1882), 42-43, hereinafter cited as Montresor.
2. Ibid., 43.
3. Ibid.
4. Ibid., 44
5. Ibid.
6. Bruce E. Burgoyne transl. and edit., *Johann Conrad Dohla, A Hessian Diary of the American Revolution* (Norman: University of Oklahoma Press, 1990), 68-69.
7. Montresor, 50.
8. Ibid.
9. Ibid., 51.
10. Ernest Kipping, transl., and Samuel Stelle, annot., *The Diary of General William Howe's aide de camp Captain Friedrich von Muenchhausen* (Monmouth Beach, NJ: Philip Freneau Press, 1974), 40, hereinafter cited as Muenchhausen.

Gen. Archibald Robertson, Lt. Col. John Simcoe, and Maj. John André.[11] "At just past 10 this morning, the Engineers finished the Floating Bridge across Schuylkill upwards of 400 feet."[12]

The pontoon bridges were made with flat-bottomed boats, to which were attached joists and floor planks. The bridges served multiple purposes: they facilitated the movement of supplies, the movement of information, and the movement of troops.

October 21–24: "Began on the Tete de Pont [a defensive work at the end of the bridge on the enemy's side] on the west side of the Schuylkill . . ."[13] "At 3 o'clock p.m. the works for the tete de pont at Gray's Ferry ordered to be stopt and the Detacht. . . . bridge to be taken up and carried to Middle Ferry."[14] "This night made work for 30 men on each side of Middle Ferry house to cover the workmen making the Floating Bridge."[15] "finished 3 Lodgments for 40 men each as a Tete de pont opposite on West Side of Schuylkill. Began this morning to lay the Bridge and Middle Ferry and I completed it this afternoon."[16]

October 28–30: "At 2 p. m. the floating Bridge at Middle Ferry was carried down the Schuylkill by the N. E. Stormy High tide and rapid stream and Ebb together."[17]

"The same Tide which troubled us produced greater Derangement in the projects of the Enemy. Their Bridge over the Schuylkill was broke by it, and 12 of their Boats six of them large ones, . . . drifted to us."[18] "This night the Rebels set fire to several of our boats that formed our Bridge at Middle Ferry."[19]

11. Johann Ewald, *Diary of the American War*, Joseph Tustin, ed., (New Haven, CT: Yale University Press, 1979), 96; Harry Miller, ed., *Archibald Robertson, Lieutenant-General Royal Engineers, His Diaries and Sketches in America, 1762-1780* (New York: New York Public Library, 1930), 153; John Graves Simcoe, *A Journal of the Operations of the Queen's Rangers* (New York: Bartlett & Welford, 1844; reprinted New York: New York Times & Arno Press, 1968), 17; John Andre, *Major Andre's Journal, Operations of the British Army, June 1777 to November 1778* (Tarrytown, NY: William Abbatt, 1930; reprinted New York: New York Times & Arno Press, 1968), 59.
12. Montresor, 51.
13. Ibid., 52.
14. Ibid.
15. Ibid., 53.
16. Ibid.
17. Ibid. 54.
18. "Journal of Major Francois Louis Teissedre de Fleury, dated 27-30 October 1777," in George Washington Papers, Series 4 (Library of Congress).
19. Montresor, 54.

Overleaf: Detail from "A Survey of the City of Philadelphia, 16 November 1777," by John Montresor, showing the numbered redoubts. (*Library of Congress*)

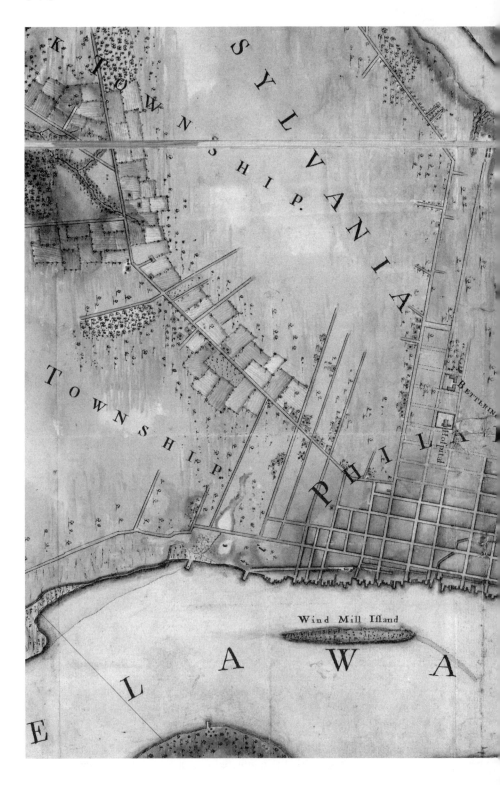

November 5–19: "Began on another floating bridge across the Schuylkill at Middle Ferry. . . . "[20] "Brought up 20 anchors for the Bridge."[21] "Bridge across Schuylkill . . . passable for Horse and foot."[22] "Bridge across Middle Ferry . . . finished."[23] "The 1st grenadiers, 1st light infantry and 33rd . . . crossed the Schuylkill at the bridge and marched under the command of Lord Cornwallis to Chester."[24] " . . . our well fortified camp, the right flank of which is anchored on the Delaware and the left on the Schuylkill. In front we have 10 well placed redoubts."[25] "They have thrown up very strong lines across—from River to river . . . ten . . . very strong redoubts, ditched, friezed, picketed and abbatised; every one which cross fire and flank their lines."[26]

The redoubts were "at a distance of four hundred Yards from each other,"[27] connected by a dense abatis.

December 1–10: "Return of the Number and Nature of Ordnance in the severall Redoubts."[28] Column 1 identifies the redoubt, columns 2 thru 7 identify the cannonball size, the material the cannon was made of, and the number of cannon, and column 8 identifies howitzers:

Redt.	18 Prs. Iron	12 Prs. Med	12 Prs. Iron	8 Prs. Iron	6 Prs. Brass	4 Prs. Brass	How 5 1/2 Iron
#1	2					2	2
#2			2				
#3					2		
#4				2			
#5			2				
#6					2		
#7		2					1
#8					2		
#9		2					
#10	2						

20. Ibid., 56.
21. Ibid.
22. Ibid., 57.
23. Ibid.
24. Andre, *Major Andre's Journal*, 64.
25. Muenchhausen, 44.
26. "Letter from Richard Platt to General John Lamb, in British Defences of Philadelphia," John F. Watson, *Annals of Philadelphia* (Phildelphia: Stoddart & Co., 1881), 610.
27. "To George Washington from Major John Clark, Jr., 17 November 1777," *The Papers of George Washington*, Revolutionary War Series, Frank E. Grizzard, Jr. and David R. Hoth, ed. (Charlottesville: University of Virginia Press, 2002), 12:285-86.
28. "Return of the Number and Nature of Ordnance in the severall Redoubts," Collection: Montresor Family Archives on microfilm (1993), Harold Finigan.

"In each of the ten redoubts, guard houses are being built. They are fully supplied with artillery and ammunition."[29] "A pontoon bridge was laid across the Schuylkill at Grey's Ferry."[30]

December 22: "Sir Wm. Howe moved out from Philadelphia with 7000 men across the Schuylkill over the 2 floating bridges and so to Darby leaving Lt. General Kniphuysen [with 6000 men] in command at Philadelphia."[31]

Darby was three miles west of the Schuylkill River. "A scanty supply of forage and fresh food . . . induced General Howe to cross the Schuylkill on the 22nd with a larger part of the army and encamp on the left of the main road this side of Derby in a line four and a half miles long . . . "[32] His force included three jäger companies with half of them mounted, two battalions of light infantry, British and Hessian grenadiers, four troops of light dragoons, the Anspach Brigade, and 200 wagons. Washington prepared a plan for a Christmas day attack, but when Howe pulled his forces back to the Schuylkill the plan was no longer viable.

December 28–30: "At About 8 in the morning the army marched toward Philadelphia. The Light infantry took post above the bridge at Grey's until it was taken up."[33] "The several brigades daily move into the eleven redoubts along the line from their quarters. The redoubts are numbered beginning on the Delaware, the 1st, 2nd, and 3rd are occupied by the English Guards and the Queen's Rangers, the 4th by the 1st English Brigade, the 5th by the 2nd, the 6th by the 4th, the 7th by the 3rd, the 8th, by the 5th and the 2nd Battalion of Anspachers, the 9th by Stirm's brigade, the 10th by Woellwarth's, and the 11th by the Hessian grenadiers."[34]

The redoubts when completed ran from the mouth of Conoquonoque Creek near Willow Street on the Delaware River to the "Upper Ferry" on the Schuylkill River. They were numbered according to their placement along the chain; their locations, identified by current street names, were as follows:

29. Bernard A. Uhlendorf & Edna Vosper, eds., "Letters of Major Baurmeister," *Pennsylvania Magazine of History and Biography*, 60 (1936), 44.

30. Andre, *Major Andre's Journal*, 71.

31. Ibid., 195.

32. Bernard A. Uhlendorf, trans, annot., *Confidential Letters and Journals 1776-1784 of Adjutant General Major Baurmeister of the Hessian Forces* (New Brunswick, NJ: Rutgers University Press, 1957), 148; "To George Washington from Major John Clark, Jr., 23 December 1777," *The Papers of George Washington*, 12:680-81.

33. Andre, *Major Andre's Journal*, 73.

34. Uhlendorf & Vosper, eds., "Letters of Major Baurmeister," 49-50.

#1 was located near Green and Oak streets on the Delaware River;

#2 was located west of North Second and Noble streets;

#3 was located between North Fifth and Sixth streets and Noble and Buttonwood streets;

#4 was located on North Eighth Street between Noble and Buttonwood streets;

#5 was located on North Tenth Street between Buttonwood and Pleasant streets;

#6 was located on Buttonwood Street between North 13th Street and North Road;

#7 was located on North Schuylkill Eighth Street between Pennsylvania Ave. and Hamilton Street;

#8 was located on North Schuylkill Fifth Street and Pennsylvania Ave;

#9 was located on North Schuylkill Second Street near Callowhill Street;

#10 was located on the Schuylkill River at the "Upper Ferry," near present-day West River Drive and Spring Garden Street.[35]

Two additional redoubts were constructed about one-eighth of a mile in advance of this chain of ten to watch the Wissahickon and Germantown roads. Also a dam was constructed across the Cohocksink Creek causing the nearby meadows to be covered with water. This formed a water barrier immediately to the west of Redoubt #1.

March 19: "Began to repair the Parapets at the Redoubts."[36]

April 20–24: "Engineers marked out two advanced works in the Lines."[37]; "Begun on our advanced works in Front of the lines consisting of 400 men for the working party. Two semi-circular Redoubts, one for 100 men to the left one for 50 in the right."[38] "Two redoubts are to be constructed about 600 paces in front of our lines on well selected, commanding heights toward Germantown."[39]

May 12–14: "Some of the redoubts were dismantled without my knowledge, rather unmilitary."[40]

June 3–18: "Redoubts dismantled of their Field train (artillery) and some iron . . . 12 Pounders and some old ones, sent all without my

35. www.northamericannforts.com/East/pa.html—molndal.
36. Montresor, 197.
37. Ibid., 201.
38. Ibid.
39. Muenchhausen, 51.
40. Montresor, 286.

knowledge."[41] "This morning early the Kings Troops evacuated the city of Philadelphia and the several redoubts and works that form its defences and retired by land to Gloucester Point 4 miles below it on the Pennsylvania Shore."[42]

Montresor's extensive fortifications north of Philadelphia were never attacked during the British stay. When the British departed in June of 1778, they dismantled or abandoned the works that had taken so much effort to construct. The Historical Society of Pennsylvania has on display the entire "Plan of the English Lines Near Philadelphia 1777." It was drawn by Lewis Nicola one month after the British army evacuated the city. The plan, in great detail, outlines all twelve redoubts, the abatis, stockades, and a cremaillered work. Today no trace of them remains.

41. Ibid., 288.
42. Ibid., 292.

The Loyalist Refugee Experience in Canada

＊ ALEXANDER CAIN ＊

In the aftermath of General Burgoyne's defeat at Saratoga, many Loyalists in the New York and Hampshire Grant regions chose to flee to the safety of Canada rather than face the prospects of poor treatment, forfeiture of property, and imprisonment at the hands of local rebels. When Loyalists left their communities and traveled north to Canada, they usually followed one of two routes. Loyalists from New York typically followed an overland route through Native American territory to Lake Ontario. Because much of the travel was along forest trails, Indian guides were essential.[1] Unfortunately for many refugees, the route included passage through territory held by the Oneidas, allies of the Americans. Likewise, refugees had to avoid Continental and militia detachments that actively patrolled the region. Once clear of enemy territory, refugees crossed Lake Ontario at Oswego or followed the southern shore of the lake to the Niagara River.[2] The trip along the Niagara was often difficult, especially in time of spring floods.

Those refugees from the Hampshire Grants usually followed a combined land and water route along Lake Champlain and the Richelieu River to Montreal.[3] The roads followed were often muddy and in poor condition. Refugees could only use pack horses, ponies, or hand and horse carts for their belongings and provisions. Securing water transportation was critical to the flight north.[4] While travelling

1. Janice Potter MacKinnon, *While the Women only Wept* (Montreal: McGill-Queen's University Press, 1993), 89.
2. Ibid., 87.
3. Ibid., 88.
4. Those Loyalists who failed to secure boats often found themselves trapped in the Hampshire Grants.

on water, refugees were often forced to seek shelter on insect-infested or low-lying islands in the middle of Lake Champlain. Because of the difficulties of this combined land-water passage, Loyalists were forced to travel in groups whose members could share the burden of carrying boats and provisions.

Some Loyalists might be lucky enough to make the trip in thirteen days, but most took much longer. An expedition of women and children that had to move slowly, was not lucky enough to make good connections with boats, and experienced bad weather could take from two to three months to reach the Quebec Province.[5] The delay in travel combined with the rugged country took its toll on the clothing of Loyalist women and children.[6] Likewise, it was not uncommon for refugees to exhaust their supplies and be forced to survive on nuts, roots, and leaves.[7]

The experience of Loyalist Mary Munro highlights the hardships Loyalist women encountered during the Revolutionary War. Mary Munro had been forced to flee from her home in Shaftsbury to Canada following the defeat of Burgoyne. As they traveled towards Lake George to join others en route to Canada, they lightened their load by discarding food and "most of their wearing Apparel . . . After much difficulty, [they] arrived at Lake George and . . . lay in the woods Six days almost perished with Cold and Hunger . . . until three other families arrived . . . [afterwards they] prevailed on the commanding officer at Fort Edward to give them a boat and a flag, they set off across Lake George."[8] Unfortunately for Mary, they were "discovered by a party of Indians from Canada—which pursued them . . . as a result of the excessive hardships they underwent," Mary and her

5. Ibid., 89.
6. Henry Watson Powell to Governor Frederick Haldimand, July 10, 1779, Haldimand Papers, Add Mss 21,793, British Library (hereinafter HP). One traveler wrote, "the wet Weather, the Badness of the Roads, and the various Difficulties of so long a Journey, at this late season of the Year which seemed at once to encounter me, were sufficient to discourage one who had scarce ever been from Home before. But the Prospect before me of pursuing my original Plan of Life, and enjoying Peace with all its attendant Blessings made me look upon the Fatigues of the Way as Trifles. When travelling through the Wet and Dirt, I would say to myself by way of comfort this will make a fair Day and good Roads the more agreeable. And indeed we should not know the Value of good Things did we not sometimes experience their contrary Evils." Richard Cartwright Jr. "A Journey to Canada, c. 1777," www.62ndregiment.org /A_Journey_to_Canada_by_Cartwright.pdf.
7. MacKinnon, *While the Women only Wept*, 89-90.
8. Memorial of Captain John Munro, August 17, 1784, AO 13/56, National Archives of Great Britain. MacKinnon, *While the Women only Wept*, 92.

children were "very sickly the whole Winter" after arriving in Canada. The toll the journey took on Mary was sadly announced by her husband when he declared "the children recovered but Mrs. Munro never will."[9]

The British government controlling Canada was ill prepared for the arrival of thousands of men, women, and children who Governor Frederick Haldimand fittingly described as "loyalists in great distress."[10] As a result, the Crown adopted a policy similar to governmental treatment of the poor in England. Incoming Loyalists were questioned to determine what trade or profession they possessed and then were dispatched to specific locations to seek employment. Destitute Loyalists, including the sick, infirm, children, women with infants, and cripples, were assigned to refugee camps and placed on public assistance. However, "public assistance" in the eighteenth century differed greatly from modern practices. Under eighteenth century British policies, those on public assistance received only bare necessities at minimal costs. More importantly, those on assistance were expected to work in exchange for aid. At many refugee camps, women and children were expected to make "blanket coats, leggings at cheaper rates than the Canadians."[11] To keep expenses low, Loyalist women and children were mustered once a month so they could be inspected to determine whether or not they still qualified for public assistance.[12]

Unfortunately, the efforts of the British government to provide asylum for the Loyalists were often in vain and as the years progressed, existing difficulties were compounded with an ever greater influx of refugees. Housing was the greatest problem. On September 14, 1778, Haldimand's secretary, Conrad Gugy, complained about the lack of pine wood to construct necessary housing for the refugees.[13] By December and the onset of the Canadian winter, Loyalist housing was not complete.[14] On January 7, 1779, Haldimand demanded to know

9. Memorial of Captain John Munro, AO 13/56.
10. Haldimand to Lord George Germain, October 14, 1778, HP 21,718. Estimates place the number of non-military Loyalists in Canada following the defeat of Burgoyne at over one thousand men, women, and children. By 1780, the number of Loyalist refugees in Canada had grown to five thousand. By 1784, the number would increase to seven thousand.
11. Regulations as to the Lodgings and Allowances for Loyalists, March 6, 1782, HP 21,825.
12. Ibid.
13. Conrad Gugy to Haldimand, September 14, 1778, HP 21,824. Construction of the first set of barracks was not completed until November 8, 1778. Gugy to Haldimand, November 8, 1778, HP 21,824.
14. Gugy to Haldimand, December 20, 1778, HP 21,824.

why officials assigned to Machiche had not yet built a saw mill necessary for the construction of housing and military barracks.[15] British
authorities even experienced difficulties establishing a schoolhouse for
refugee children.[16]

Living quarters for Loyalist refugees were cramped at best. In
December 1778 one hundred and ninety six refugees at Machiche
were distributed among twelve buildings. The following year, over
four hundred refugees were placed in a mere twenty-one buildings.
Records suggest that these structures were only eighteen by forty feet
in size.[17]

Throughout the fall months of 1778, British officials likewise struggled to supply the Loyalists with rations, candles and blankets.[18] By
1783, over three thousand Loyalists were in need of basic clothing,
including over three thousand pairs of stockings and shoes and sixteen
thousand yards of linen and wool.[19] The following year, British officials warned that several refugees had died "owing as they think for
the want of provisions and clothing."[20]

Food supplies and cooking equipment were exceedingly difficult to
procure as more Loyalists arrived in Canada. Fresh meat was continuously scarce[21] and full rations often withheld.[22] Conrad Gugy complained to Haldimand that the children at Machiche were severely
malnourished and many mothers were depriving themselves of their
own food in an effort to keep their children alive.[23] To complicate

15. Haldimand to Gugy, January 7, 1779, HP 21,824.
16. Gugy to Haldimand, March 6, 1779, HP 21,824; Gugy to Haldimand, March 14,
1779, HP 21,824.
17. List of Loyalists and Their Families lodged at Machicheat This Date, December 2,
1778, HP 21,825; Gugy to Haldimand, November 16, 1778, HP 21,824.
18. Gugy to Haldimand, October 30, 1778, HP 21,824; Gugy to Haldimand,
November 8, 1778, HP 21,824; Gugy to Haldimand, November 16, 1778, HP 21,824.
19. Estimate of Clothing Required to Clothe the Above Numbered of Refugees,
Agreeable to the Proportions Heretofore Granted, 1783, HP 21826. That same year
loyalists at Sorel were supplied with "360 yards of linen cloth, 149 yards of wollen
cloth, 73 blankets, 110 pairs of stockings, 106 pairs of shoes and 10 pairs of short leggings and mitts." Haldimand to (?), December 1783, HP 21,826.r. It should be noted
there were over 600 Loyalists in and around Sorel at the time of this issuance.
20. Stephen Delancey to Robert Matthews, April 26 and May 4, 1784, HP 21,825.
21. Gugy made no less than two requests in November 1778 for provisions of fresh
beef for the Loyalists at Machiche. Gugy to Haldimand, November 8, 1778, and
November 16, 1778, HP 21,824.
22. Matthews to Abraham Cuyler, November 18, 1782, HP 21,824.
23. Major John Ross to Sir John Johnson, September 11, 1780, HP 21,824. Daniel
McAlpin would also complain about the state of Loyalist children and families under
his care. "All are in a state of distress . . . and are in urgent need of help." Daniel
McAlpin to Haldimand, July 1, 1779, HP 21,819.

matters, in 1778, the refugees at Machiche were only issued twenty-four kettles and eight frying pans.[24] To alleviate this problem, Loyalists were encouraged to grow or secure their own food. To assist in this venture, Mr. Gugy established a pasture for fifty cows and a garden for growing vegetables at Machiche.[25] Unfortunately, the efforts to establish self-sufficiency among the Loyalists failed miserably. By 1780, over two hundred and sixty-two men, three hundred and eight women, and seven hundred and ninety eight children at various refugee camps outside of Montreal alone were receiving public assistance in the form of food supplies from the government.[26]

The treatment of African-American Loyalists during the American Revolution, including those in Canada, was especially problematic. British authorities encouraged slaves to profess their loyalty to the Crown in exchange for freedom. However, once escaped slaves reached British lines, African-Americans found that the promises were not always fulfilled. Some were taken prisoner and either claimed as property by their captors or sold for profit. Likewise, British officials consistently maintained that former slaves of Loyalists had to be returned to their masters. Only a few were allowed to serve as soldiers. Many Loyalist officers protested the treatment of African-American Loyalists. One officer, Daniel Claus, asserted that African-American soldiers were often of great help to scouting and raiding parties. He then noted sadly that sixteen blacks he had brought in as recruits "for their loyalty . . . now are rendered Slaves in Montreal."[27]

From the refugee perspective, most were horrified at their living conditions and lack of provisions. As one group of Loyalists opined, "we shall not be able to overcome the Seveir and approaching hard winter . . . [in] a Strange and Disolate place where [we] can get nothing to Work to earne a Penney for the Support of Each Other . . . much more the Bigger part of us Without one shilling in our pockets and not a Shew on our feet."[28] Another Loyalist complained that his refugee camp was a "drowned bog without water."[29] Many refugees

24. Gugy to Haldimand, November 16, 1778, HP 21,824.
25. Haldimand to Germain, October 15, 1778, HP 21,819.
26. MacKinnon, *While the Women only Wept*, 107-110.
27. Daniel Claus to Haldimand, December 9, 1779, HP 21,774, MacKinnon, *While the Women only Wept*, 102.
28. Petition by His Majesty's Faithful Subjects Emigrated Under the Conduct of Captain Michael Grass from New York to This Place, Sorel, September 29, 1783, HP 21,825.
29. Gugy to Haldimand, October 2, 1778, HP 21,819; Petition to Mr. Gugy, November 12, 1778, HP 21,819.

accused Gershom French, a Loyalist in charge of supplies at Machiche, of abusing Loyalists and diverting basic materials to himself.[30]

To contain the impact of refugees on the Quebec Province, British authorities restricted Loyalists and refused to let them travel outside of their respective camps. As a result, refugees quickly discovered that they could not supplement their meager supplies with trips to neighboring towns and villages. Services, including laundry, were subject to price fixing under the threat of being removed from public assistance.[31] Likewise, requests to sell goods, including alcohol, to complement their meager living conditions were summarily denied.[32]

An even greater concern amongst refugees was the presence of camp fever which was quickly spreading through the refugee sites. Other deadly diseases present at the camps included malaria, small pox, and pneumonia.[33] Loyalists chaffed at the government's downplay of the camp conditions and the assertion that their complaints were "frivolous."[34] According to a letter from Gugy to Stephen DeLancy, inspector of the Loyalist camps, he was "well aware of the uniform discontent of the Loyalists at Machiche . . . the discontent . . . is excited by a few ill-disposed persons. . . . the sickness they complain of has been common throughout the province, and should have lessened rather than increased the consumption of provisions."[35]

As years passed and Loyalists continued to be confined inside refugee camps, families and individuals collapsed under the psychological burden. Long-term absences of Loyalist men on military missions only exacerbated the situation. There was one recorded incident of infanticide at Carleton Island where a mother killed her newborn.[36] Marriages crumbled, alcoholism rose, suicides increased, and emotional breakdowns became commonplace.[37] In short, death and tragedy surrounded the Loyalists in Canada.

30. Complaint by John Peters, January 20, 1780, HP 21,827.
31. "The loyalist women receiving rations are to wash for the non-commissioned officers and men of the volunteers at four coppers a shirt and in proportion for other things." Haldimand to Lieutenant French, July 14, 1780. HP 21,821.
32. Claus to Haldimand, November 19, 1778, HP 21,774.
33. Ross to Haldimand, November 25, 1782, HP B125, 85. MacKinnon, *While the Women only Wept*, 118.
34. Gugy to Haldimand, October 2, 1778, HP 21,824.
35. Gugy to DeLancy, April 29, 1780, HP 21,723.
36. Ibid.
37. W. Stewart Wallace, *The United Empire Loyalists: A Chronicle of the Great Migration, Volume 13* (EBook, 2004), www.gutenberg.org/files/11977/11977.txt. See also Tuttle to Matthews, July 11, 1781, HP 21,819; MacLean to Matthews, November 24, 1779,

From the British perspective, Haldimand became exasperated with the refugees in his colony and described them as "a number of useless Consumers of Provisions."[38] He summarized the distaste British authorities had for the grievances from unappreciative Loyalists when he told a prominent refugee "His Excellency is anxious to do every-thing in his power for the Loyalists, but if what he can do does not come up to the expectation of him and those he represents, His Excellency gives the fullest permission to them to seek redress in such manner as they shall think best."[39] In short, Haldimand utilized Loyalist dependency to maintain government control over the refugees. The Loyalists were forced to choose between accepting their camp conditions or fend for themselves.

HP 21,789; St. Leger to Haldimand, November 16, 1782, HP 21,789; Claus to Haldimand, June 14, 1784, HP 21,774. There are period accounts of several "insane loyalists" being sent from refugee camps to hospitals in Quebec.
38. Haldimand to Johnson, May 23, 1780, HP 21,819; Haldimand to Powell, March 15, 1780, HP 21,734.
39. www.canadiangenealogy.net/chronicles/loyalists_quebec.htm.

How was the Revolutionary War Paid For?

JOHN L. SMITH, JR.

It's one thing to make speeches about declaring independence, or to assemble militias and discuss battle tactics against the enemy.

It's quite another thing to pay for it all.

So how do you pay for a war that no one expected to last eight years?

Great Britain possessed world wide colonies, tremendous wealth, the ability to tax its subjects, and excellent credit ratings in the well-established world credit market. But how did the fledgling American confederation of thirteen states and a weak Congress go about funding their own rebellion?

History books and many teachers will imply that the French money and supplies before and after the Battle of Saratoga made all of the difference in America winning the war. While the French assistance certainly helped, it actually did a disservice to the Americans who basically paid for their own rebellion . . . the merchants, suppliers, planters and growers, average families, and of course the soldiers of the Continental army. Let's look at the total picture of how the War for Independence was paid for—100 percent of which was paid for by Americans themselves through taxes, bonds, IOUs, and by paying off all foreign loans.

Glossary of terms to know for this article:

SPECIE—any precious metal used as currency, like gold or silver.

FIAT CURRENCY—any currency that's valuable only because the issuing government says it is.

FACE VALUE—the value of a currency that's printed on the money itself.

Estimated Funding Sources
War for Independence[1] (in millions of pounds sterling)

	Sterling (£)	Percentages
Fiat Currency		
States' Money	64	39
Congress Money	46	28
Total Fiat Currency	110	67
Borrowed Funds		
States' Indebtedness	23	14
Congress Debt Certificates	16	10
Congress Foreign Loans	10	6
Congress Domestic Bonds	6	3
Total Debts	54	33
Total Cost of War (rounded up)	165	100

From 1775 to 1783, America used a variety of methods to pay for the war; some of which would seem very familiar to us even today. Here they are in order of percent contributed to the war effort:

1. *The Thirteen States Printed Their Own Money (39%)*: We know that the thirteen colonies/states acted as individual sovereign countries in their time. That included the right to tax its citizens and to print money. So to pay for the food and supplies of its own militias, the states printed lots of money. But because taxes were such a hot button, for obvious reasons, the decision to tax residents to give value to the new currency was put off to sometime in the future (most states started in 1777). Some states also confiscated and sold Loyalist properties. But taxes also served as a mechanism to take currency out of circulation, therefore preventing inflation and keeping prices stable. That technique worked for a while until, as discussed below, the value of the federal Continental dollar started a tailspin and the confidence of all printed money started to drop.

2. *Congress Printed Its Own Money (28%)*: Since Congress didn't have the power to tax and there was no organized national bank, printing money was the primary source of funding Congress used dur-

1. The table has been produced based upon "Ferguson's estimate of the total cost of the war": Edwin J. Perkins, *American Public Finance and Financial Services, 1700-1815* (Columbus: Ohio State University Press, 1994), 103, Table 5.4. Economic historians will recognize the invaluable research and work of two individuals in particular that this article draws from: Merrill Jensen, and especially his graduate student E. James Ferguson, who in the 1950s and 1960s, developed, tested, and published much of the statistical work that is still used today in the study of the Founding Era finances. Edwin J. Perkins is another good authority.

ing the Revolutionary War starting in 1775. And it printed *a lot* of money—the printing presses worked non-stop from 1775 to 1781! Lacking precious metals to mint coins, Congress printed paper notes that represented the equivalent value in specie. All types of weird denominations of a dollar were created, like "One Third of a Dollar" and so on. The two biggest problems with the so-called Continental dollars were that 1) there were so many printed and out there in circulation and 2) that they weren't backed by specie (which is like gold or silver) even though the dollar's face value said "This Bill entitles the Bearer to receive ONE Spanish milled DOLLAR or the value thereof in Gold or Silver . . . " But that wasn't true at all. The dollars were actually backed by nothing and as the war dragged on, people figured that out, which is why the term "Not worth a Continental"[2] came into being. The never-shy Mercy Otis Warren called the dollars, "immense heaps of paper trash."[3] The printed currency also carried such snazzy sayings as "Mind Your Business," "Death to Counterfeiters," and "A Lesson to arbitrary Kings, and wicked Ministers." Each piece of currency was personally signed and numbered by an official to make them look more valuable and to discourage counterfeiters. But after a while, counterfeiting became a very serious problem with Continental dollars and, as a sabotage tactic, the British became pretty good at it. In fact, some eagle-eyed citizens got to the point where they could spot counterfeit dollars because they looked *too* good.

It turns out that as the war waged on, the confidence in the Continental dollar started dropping like a rock because they were so numerous and backed by nothing. After all, it is thought that in 1775 there was only $12 million in specie in the whole thirteen colonies and none of it was in Congress's hands. Since Congress printed $12 million in Continental dollars just getting the presses going and the ink flowing, you could see why a currency crisis was in the works. In all, during the Revolutionary War, Congress printed almost $242 million[4] in face value Continental currency. The true specie amount was about $46 million, as shown in the above chart.

2. *Proceedings of the Twenty-First Continental Congress of the Daughters of the American Revolution*, 21 (1912), 799.

3. Mercy Otis Warren, *History of the Rise, Progress and Termination of the American Revolution interspersed with Biographical, Political and Moral Observations*, II; Lester H. Cohen, ed. (Indianapolis: Liberty Classics, 1988), 287.

4. To be exact—Congress issued $241,552,780 in face value Continental currency during the Revolutionary War. Eric P. Newman, *The Early Paper Money of America. 3rd edition* (Iola, WI: Krause Publications, 1990), 16. E. James Ferguson puts this face value total at $227.8 million which includes the 1780-81 new emissions, saying "The actual

3. *The Thirteen States Issued Their Own Debt Certificates (14%)*: Most of these were like state-issued war bonds. Also called "bills of credit," they were "interest bearing certificates" with the buyer putting up their land as collateral. The patriotic buyer would then (or so they were told) get their principal back plus interest—assuming America won the war! As support for the common defense, states would also issue these as "requisition certificates" to vendors or suppliers to pay for food and supplies if the Continental Army happened to be camped in their state.

4. *Congress Issued Its Own Debt Certificates (10%)*: These certificates were also called (in politically correct verbiage of its time) "involuntary credit extensions" because they paid no interest and their value, tied to the Continental dollar, dropped like lead daily. These were mostly given out by the Continental Army quartermaster corps to citizens when buying or confiscating materials. In the last two years of the war, the Continental army soldiers were also paid in these, so you can see why there was much grumbling—and mutiny. Some discharged soldiers sold their certificates to investors for literally pennies on the dollar.

5. *Congress Received Loans from Europe (6%)*: Before Saratoga, France had been smuggling small amounts of gunpowder and supplies to us through a dummy corporation. Although there was some bickering about whether these were loans or gifts, America tried to repay France in tobacco and IOUs. After the victory at Saratoga, from 1778 thru 1783, Ben Franklin and Silas Deane negotiated with France to give America six huge loans which just about broke the French Treasury. Following Yorktown, the world credit rating for England fell while the rating for America shot straight up. So in Amsterdam, John Adams easily raised $2.8 million for America at a favorable 5% interest rate (signifying low risk), and another $2.2 million from Dutch investors and the Spanish Crown. Some of the loans were used to keep the Continental Army intact in 1782–1783, but a lot of the money was spent in Europe to buy military supplies or to just make interest payments to keep America's credit door open. With the signing of the peace treaty, even British investors wanted in on loaning America money!

Occasionally it's brought up that the United States completely defaulted on its loans from France. That's not entirely true. In 1785 the

sum in circulation may never be known." E. J. Ferguson, *The Power of the Purse: A History of American Public Finance 1776-1790* (Chapel Hill: University of North Carolina Press, 1961), 43. Counterfeited currency was also in circulation.

cash-strapped Congress halted interest payments to France and defaulted on scheduled payments due in 1787 because the states were forwarding so little money. But with the establishment of the Constitution and the order that it brought to American finances, Secretary of the Treasury Alexander Hamilton was able to take action. "In 1795, the United States was finally able to settle its debts with the French Government with the help of James Swan, an American banker who privately assumed French debts at a slightly higher interest rate. Swan then resold these debts at a profit on domestic U.S. markets. The United States no longer owed money to foreign governments."[5]

6. *Congress Sold Bonds to Wealthy, Patriotic Americans (3%)*: Similar to World War II savings bonds, these war bonds paid about 6% interest—again, *assuming America won the war.* Although some bonds were sold in Massachusetts, Connecticut, and Pennsylvania (the possible site of the new government if America won the war), these bonds weren't a huge success. For one, private loans paid more interest and if defaulted upon, could at least be recovered in an English court even if America lost. And two—well, a lot of the wealthiest Americans were Loyalists. The bonds were a bet that America would win the war. But if America lost, it was thought that just holding the bonds could indicate to the victorious British Crown that you supported the traitors. Not a good thing.

DOWNWARD DOLLAR PLUNGE AND NEAR BANKRUPTCY

In tag team timing, from 1777–1780 Congress first took the lead in financing the war. By 1780, the states had their financial plans working well enough that they took the lead from 1780–1783 while Congress completely reorganized its financial house. It needed to! In July 1777, a Continental dollar had already dropped two-thirds of its value. It stabilized a little with the French alliance, but then again started a downward spiral. By 1780, Congress revalued its dollar as officially only one-third of its 1775 value. But the new and improved dollar still plummeted to the point where, by 1781, it took 167 dollars to equal the previous one dollar.[6] So what did Congress do? They

5. U.S. Department of State—Office of the Historian; Milestones: 1784–1800, "*U.S. Debt and Foreign Loans, 1775–1795*," history.state.gov/milestones/1784-1800/loans; (accessed January 12, 2014).

6. Jack P. Greene and J.R. Pole, eds., *The Blackwell Encyclopedia of the American Revolution* (Cambridge: Blackwell Publishers, 1994), 364, Table 1. Taken from E. J. Ferguson, *The Power of the Purse: A History of American Public Finance 1776-1790* (Chapel Hill: University of North Carolina Press, 1961), 32.

couldn't tax, so they printed even more dollars to be able to buy an ever-shrinking amount of goods and services. Prices were skyrocketing with severe depreciation and hyperinflation happening everywhere. States were still demanding that taxes be paid. It was a crisis, which threatened the existence of the new republic.

By 1781 and in desperation, Congress put strong-willed financier and congressman Robert Morris into the new office of Superintendent of Finance. Some of the first emergency actions Morris took were to devalue the dollar, and then he squeezed about $2 million in specie from the states. But in a very controversial move, he suspended pay to the Continental army enlisted soldiers and officers. Instead, he decreed that the army be paid in debt certificates or land grants until the peace treaty was signed. In 1782, the new consolidated national debt was so enormous that Morris suggested Congress only pay the interest on the debt, saying (this may sound familiar in today's world) " . . . leave posterity to pay the principle."[7]

Morris is a much checkered personality in American history and because of his bad personal land speculations leaving him owing $3 million, he ironically spent 1798–1801 in debtor's prison. But it should never be forgotten that more than once Morris used his own fortune or credit to keep the country afloat during its worst hours. "My personal Credit, which thank Heaven I have preserved through all the tempests of the War, has been substituted for that which the Country has lost . . . I am now striving to transfer that Credit to the Public."[8]

ECONOMIC AFTERMATH OF THE REVOLUTIONARY WAR

America's Revolutionary War was very expensive. Not only did it sap economic resources in the country, the depreciated currency acted (as wise Ben Franklin put it), "among the inhabitants of the States . . . as a gradual tax upon them."[9] And this was to a people who had been used to a life of light taxation before hostilities broke out. In the "be careful what you wish for" department, two economic historians speculated, " . . . that Britain was probably a 'victor' in defeat, for, after

7. C.P. Nettles, *The Emergence of a National Economy 1775-1815* (New York: Holt, Rinehart and Winston, 1962), 33. In Jack P. Greene and J.R. Pole, eds., *The Blackwell Encyclopedia of the American Revolution*, 370. Morris spells "principal" as "principle."
8. Robert Morris to Benjamin Harrison, 15 January 1782, in *The Papers of Robert Morris, 1781-1784*, E. J. Ferguson, ed. In Charles Rappleye, *Robert Morris: Financier of the American Revolution* (New York: Simon & Shuster, 2010), 259.
9. Jared Sparks, ed., *The Works of Benjamin Franklin . . . with Notes of a Life of the Author*, II, (Boston: 1836-1840), 424. From John J. McCusker & Russell R. Menard, *The Economy of British America 1607-1789* (Chapel Hill: University of North Carolina Press, 1991), 373.

independence, U.S. taxes rose precipitously. From 1792–1811, U.S. per capita tax rates were over ten times higher than the imperial taxes levied by the British from 1765 to 1775."[10] But we know it wasn't about taxes alone. It was about liberty and rights. "The colonists paid a high price for their freedom."[11]

The predictable recession broke out following the Revolutionary War, with data showing the "period of contraction" (a.k.a. recession) running consecutively from 1782–1789.[12] Indeed, for a point of reference we all can relate to, financial history professors McCusker & Menard point out that during the Great Depression (between 1929–1933), per capita GNP fell by 48 percent. It's estimated that those same economic markers (between 1775–1790) fell by 46 percent.[13]

The British war cost added a new national debt of £250 million onto their huge debt left from the French and Indian War of £135 million. The new debt carried an annual interest payment of £9.5 million alone. The loss of the war brought down the Lord North government within the halls of Parliament.

The Spanish war costs were pretty marginal reflecting their cursory involvement in the whole thing. It totaled to about 700 million *reales*, which Spain covered by taxing their colonies and issuing royal bonds.

The French war cost equaled over 1.3 billion livres in loans and supplies to America, plus the huge extra expenses to equip and send the French army and navy to America, and to attack British outposts around the world. Added to the 3.3 billion livres France owed from the French and Indian War, the resulting economic chaos eventually led to the French Revolution, which brought down the heads (literally) of the monarchy and nobility.

The American war costs, as shown in the above table, totaled approximately £165 million in 1783 values. It's always tricky to convert 200-year-old currencies gathered using imprecise war records—but that amount could roughly add up to about $21.6 billion in 2010 dollars.[14]

10. Lance Davis and Robert Huttenback, quoted in Edwin J. Perkins, *The Economy of Colonial America, Second Edition* (New York: Columbia University Press, 1988), 208.
11. McCusker & Menard, *The Economy of British America 1607-1789*, 374.
12. McCusker & Menard, *The Economy of British America 1607-1789*, 63, Table 3.4.
13. McCusker & Menard, *The Economy of British America 1607-1789*, 373-374.
14. This computation converting from 1783 sterling pounds (£) to 2010 dollars ($) was done converting "real value" over time. The generally-accepted Web site used was MeasuringWorth.com: www.measuringworth.com/ (accessed January 12, 2014). Edwin J. Perkins in *The Economy of Colonial America* (Appendix) computed $14.9 billion in 1985 real value dollars.

In America, the chaos of funding the American Revolution glaringly showed the weaknesses in the Articles of Confederation and a weak central government. George Washington had known all too well the many times in war he had begged for any money or supplies from a helpless Congress or indifferent states.

The establishment of the Constitution in 1787 brought fiscal stability to America, which was near collapse just after it had earned and paid for its liberty. It brought order to the national finances. It created a common market, common currency, it regulated trade and commerce, consolidated and funded the national debt, established a national bank, and gave Congress the authority to tax.

Okay, so maybe "gave Congress the authority to tax" wasn't such a good idea.

Thanks to the office of the Historian of the U.S. Department of State and its Special Assistance group for supplying valuable source material regarding the American payment of foreign loans during the post-war period.

Faking It: British Counterfeiting During the American Revolution

STUART HATFIELD

The American Revolution was very much a case of David versus Goliath. A relatively small group of colonists decided that they wanted to break free of the home government, which in this case just happened to be one of the most powerful nations on the globe. Almost overnight the thirteen separate colonies had to form a central government to unify the people, a military to defend the people, and a central economy to pay for it all. It was a daunting task that had to be accomplished while undergoing an invasion by the British army, which would continue to make mincemeat out of whatever forces the Americans could throw at it. The British army, however, had just as many uphill battles to fight. Lack of men and supplies, a chain of command that stretched almost three thousand miles, and a population in the colonies that could range from hostile to very supportive to outright ambivalent. For the British army, meeting the Americans on the field of battle would lead to many victories, but never any that would bring an end to the war. Something besides the force of arms would be needed to bring the colonies to their senses.

To this end a campaign was devised to undermine the nascent American economy in an attempt to achieve a twofer. If the economy was in shambles the Americans would not be able to purchase the men and material needed to continue the war. At the same time, by undermining the economy they would also be undermining the American Congress, which was acting as the central government. Perhaps if people lost faith in the Congress, they would realize that the war could not be won, and they would all return to the fold. While it is hard to say whether anyone in the British government sat down and actually put together a comprehensive plan, it is obvious that several different measures were undertaken. These included attempts to limit American trade with foreign nations using the all-powerful British Navy to interdict as much overseas commerce as possible as well as searching vessels from "neutral" countries for war materials in route to America. This move in particular was frowned upon by many European nations.

While these activities were effective to a point, the most effective strategy that was tried, and one that very nearly succeeded, was the massive undertaking of counterfeiting Congressional paper currency to the point of making it almost worthless, thus crashing the American economy. No economy, no more war. In looking at this strategy three questions must be asked: How were the fake notes produced and circulated? Was it effective in undermining the economy? Finally, was this a sanctioned strategy by the British, one that they knowingly pursued? Looking at the counterfeiting strategy through these questions presents an intriguing, and often overlooked aspect of the American Revolution.

HOW WAS IT DONE?

For the majority of the war the city of New York was under control of the British. It was here that the majority of the counterfeiting was done. For the most part it was not difficult as many of the advanced security measures that are used today to dissuade such actions were not in use. Even though bank notes had individual handwritten serial numbers and signatures, these were no deterrent as they were easily forged. In addition, most of the Continental currency that was printed by legitimate services was done on the cheap, with little eye to quality. This made the process of counterfeiting it much easier. Often the fake currency could be easily spotted because it was of higher quality than the legitimate bills. The paper was usually a higher quality and the engraving was of a much higher quality on the professionally done counterfeits.

One thing that set the legitimate currency apart was the special paper used, common paper infused with blue fibers and flakes of mica that set it apart from normal paper (a similar method is used today, which makes it much harder to simply photocopy a hundred dollar bill and spend it at the local grocery store). While the paper itself was special it was far from rare. In fact at one point British ships were intercepted on their way to New York that were found to be carrying not only the ink for counterfeiting but massive amounts of the paper. The American frigate *Deane*, on August 9, 1779, captured the *Glencairn* out of Glasgow. The report of Commodore Samuel Nicholson of the

Deane to the Continental Congress, as published in the *Virginia Gazette* of October 2, 1779, stated:

> On board the *Glencairn*, a person says he had in charge a box, which was to be delivered to some person in New York, but upon our coming up with them and the ship striking, threw it overboard; upon which we went immediately after it, and with difficulty got it before it sunk, when upon examination we found it contained materials for counterfeiting our currency, consisting of types, paper with silk and isinglass in it &c. We have however determined to secure the person, as we believe him to be the sole intender of the villainy: The box we have on board and shall bring it with us to Boston.

As for how the bills were put into circulation, there were several methods. One involved finding men who had deserted the Patriot cause and fled to British lines, lining their pockets with the fake cash, and convincing them to cross back over and spend what they could. Of course they would have to be careful as to not arouse suspicion, but with this method hundreds of fake Continental dollars could be put in circulation at a time. The practice was risky. A soldier named David Gambell of the 8th Pennsylvania Regiment, for example, had deserted and upon being captured was found with counterfeit money in his possession. He was court-martialed and sentenced to death by order of General Washington.[1]

Another method of dissemination was less subtle. Often in the New York newspapers were advertisements looking for people travelling into the colonies who would be willing to "wallpaper" with Continental bills. In the April 14, 1777, edition of the *New York Gazette* an ad appeared that specifically requested people to take into the other colonies "any number of counterfeit notes." The advertisement came to the attention of General Washington who on April 18 sent a copy to Congress, writing that the scheme "shows that no artifices are left untried by the enemy to injure us."[2]

It was not just civilians of questionable loyalty that were tasked with spreading the fake currency. British soldiers who became prisoners of war were on occasion charged with using counterfeit Continental money to purchase supplies, most notably after the cap-

1. John Whiting, *Revolutionary Orders of General Washington* (New York: Wiley and Putnam, 1844), 118.
2. John Fitzpatrick, ed., *Writings of George Washington* (Washington, DC: U.S. Government Printing Office, 1904-37), 7:433-35.

ture of General Burgoyne's army in 1777. According to the surrender
terms the British were to be allowed to return to Europe. Congress,
however, refused to allow their return, claiming several instances of
British violations of the surrender terms. Among congressional complaints was the "spending habits" of the British prisoners when pur-
chasing supplies from the locals. When General Howe was informed
of the issues he denied the use of counterfeit currency in a letter to
General Washington, calling the accusation that the men were knowingly spreading fake currency "too illiberal to deserve a serious
answer."[3]

WAS IT EFFECTIVE IN UNDERMINING THE ECONOMY?

Without a doubt the massive amount of counterfeiting in all forms
had a major effect on the young nation's economy. As the war progressed the value of the dollar fell dramatically for several reasons.
One was the lack of any sort of backing to bolster its value. Paper
money is basically a promise that it is worth what it says it is. Without
massive gold and silver reserves backing it up the dollar was subject to
fluctuation that was based on the strength of the promise, and in this
case the strength of the people making the promise, that is, Congress.
As such it was very much tied to the fortunes of the army. When the
army had success the value of the dollar rose, while failure caused it
to plummet; with a few exceptions the army had little success. This
led to the devaluation of the currency which made it hard to purchase
supplies and necessities that the army needed to win the victories that
could cause the currency to be worth something again. Yes, the circle
was a vicious one.

With the specter of fake currency compounding the problem of the
already low value, it meant that large numbers of people in the
colonies were simply not willing to sell supplies to Congress or the
army for paper money. This often led to the army having to "requisition" supplies leaving the people with at best useless stacks of paper
money and at worst written receipts that could be turned in for reimbursement, someday. On the other hand, the British army could usually go to the same people and offer specie (gold or silver), quickly
becoming the preferred people to sell to. Even in a rebellion principles
sometimes took a back seat to feeding a family.

How effective was the influx of counterfeit money in undermining
Congress? Good enough that even John Adams had to remind his

3. The Writings of George Washington, edited by Jared Sparks, Boston, 1834, vol. v,
535 (Appendix).

wife Abigail to be very wary of taking any paper money. In a letter home during the war Adams admonished his wife:

> How could it happen that you should have five counterfeit New Hampshire money? Can't you recollect who you had it of? Let me entreat you not to take a shilling of any but continental money or Massachusetts, and be very careful of that. There is a counterfeit continental bill abroad sent out of New York, but it will deceive none but fools, for it is copper plate, easily detected . . . [4]

The biggest and most visible sign of how the counterfeiting was affecting the economy and the country at large was Congress passing a law that made counterfeiting a capital crime. Under English Law the act was already considered treason and punishable by death and while most colonies had some sort of law on the books regarding counterfeiting, they mainly dealt with British money specifically. That left Congress having to create laws which sometimes mirrored existing ones, but took the new national status into account. Once that law was passed anyone caught and convicted of making or passing the fake Continental currency would be sentenced to death. A number of high profile cases caught the imagination of the public and were followed by even General Washington himself. To this end in 1780 Congress even took the extraordinary step of offering a bounty on counterfeiters, "two thousand dollars in the present Continental currency to any person or persons who take and prosecute to conviction." This reward was worth about ten dollars specie at the time.[5] Often the spread of the fake money was compared to the spreading of a plague, and the eradication of the plague was taken very seriously.

Still, even when at one point the amount of counterfeit currency in circulation may have exceeded the amount of legitimate currency, the economy hung on by its eye teeth and never fully collapsed. Congress continued to shore up the system by instituting price and wage controls as well as securing loans from European powers. The Treaty of Alliance with France in 1778 went a long way to bolstering the confidence the people had in the Congress and the army, which helped prevent a war-ending panic. Speaking of the army, while far from ever sweeping the British from the field as the war progressed, they began showing a tenacity and competence that also helped to instill the desperately needed confidence.

4. John Adams to Abigail Adams, May 25-27, 1777. *Adams Family Papers: An Electronic Archive*. Massachusetts Historical Society, www.masshist.org/digitaladams/.
5. *Journals of the Continental Congress, 1774-1789. Edited from the original records in the Library of Congress* (Washington, DC: U.S. Government Printing Office, 1904-37), 17:530.

As the value dropped, Congress had no choice but to print more money, driving the value down even further. By 1781, the exchange rate was $225 paper currency to $1 specie. This was at a time when the average Continental army private made $5 a month in Continental scrip, if he was paid at all.

Joseph Plumb Martin, a soldier from Connecticut, relayed in his memoirs that to earn a little extra (having not been paid in many months) he assisted in a roundup of runaway slaves that had fled to the service of the British after the siege at Yorktown in 1781 had ended:

> . . . the fortune I acquired was small, only one dollar; I received what was then called its equivalent, in paper money, if money it might be called, it amounted to twelve hundred (nominal) dollars, all of which I afterwards paid for one single quart of rum; to such a miserable state had all paper stuff, called -money- depreciated.[6]

It was not just the soldiers that felt they were getting short shrift from the poor value of the dollar. In 1781 the people had had enough and in the May 12 edition of the Rivington's *Royal Gazette* the following story took over the front page.

> The Congress is finally bankrupt! Last Saturday a large body of the inhabitants with paper dollars in their hats by way of cockades, paraded the streets of Philadelphia, carrying colors flying, with a dog tarred, and instead of the usual appendage and ornament of feathers, his back was covered with the Congress' paper dollars. This Bankrupt. example of disaffection, immediately under the eyes of the rulers of the revolted provinces, in solemn session at the State House assembled, was directly followed by the jailer, who refused accepting the bills in purchase of a glass of rum, and afterwards by the traders of the city, who shut up their shops, declining to sell any more goods but for gold or silver. It was declared also by the popular voice that if the opposition to Great Britain was not in future carried on by solid money instead of paper bills, all further resistance to the mother country were vain, and must be given up.[7]

This was a telling account of the effect of the poor value of the scrip and the effect that it had on the people. Though it is true that Rivington's newspaper was published with a Loyalist leaning, there is much to be seen from the perspective of one's enemy. This sentiment

6. Joseph Plumb Martin, *A Narrative of a Revolutionary War Soldier* (New York: Signet, 2001), 208.

7. Frank Moore, *Diary of the American Revolution. From Newspapers and Original Documents* (New York: Scribner & Sons, 1859), 2:425-26.

however was felt all across the fledgling nation. Had Congress been able to stop the rampant inflation and build confidence in its own brand, the economy and the war effort would have been stronger. Having the marketplaces filled with illegitimate currency went a long way to effecting dissatisfaction.

WAS THIS A SANCTIONED STRATEGY BY THE BRITISH?

Almost certainly it was. At least, many of the preeminent men of the revolution believed so. In a 1777 letter home John Adams stated the opinion of most the members of Congress: "Their principal dependence is not upon their arms, I believe, so much as upon the failure of our revenue. To think they have taken such measures, by circulating counterfeit bills, to depreciate the currency, that it cannot hold its credit longer than this campaign. But they are mistaken."[8] In just the following year Thomas Paine, in a 1778 letter to president of the Congress Henry Laurens, suggested appealing to General Howe in New York to become involved in cases of suspected forgery:

> I write this, hoping the information will point out the necessity of the Congress supporting their emissions by claiming every offender in this line, where the present deficiency of the law, or the partial interpretation of it, operates to the injustice and injury of the whole continent. I beg leave to trouble you with another hint. Congress, I learn, has something to propose through the commissioners on the cartel respecting the admission and stability of the continental currency. As forgery is a sin against all men alike, and reprobated by all civil nations, query, would it not be right to require of General Howe the persons of Smithers and others in Philadelphia suspected of this crime? And if he or any other commander continues to conceal or protect them in such practices, that, in such case, the Congress will consider the crime as the act of the commander-in-chief ? Howe affects not to know the Congress; he ought to be made to know them; and the apprehension of personal consequences may have some effect upon his conduct.[9]

8. Charles Francis Adams, *Letters of John Adams, Addressed to His Wife. Edited by His Grandson, Charles Francis Adams* (New York: Hurd and Houghton, 1876), 1:263.

9. Frank Moore, *Materials for History Presented from Original Manuscripts* (New York: Kenger Club, 1861), 108. "Smithers" is most likely James Smither, a well-known engraver in Philadelphia who was commissioned to create the engraving plates for Congress. It was later thought that he was involved in counterfeiting and when charged with high treason in 1778 he fled to New York. After the war he returned to Philadelphia and resumed his trade.

Was this a sanctioned strategy by the British? While most of the evidence is circumstantial, certainly the practice was not discouraged by the authorities in New York or London. The question was answered in part later in the war when an American privateer intercepted a British vessel that was carrying a letter written by General Henry Clinton, the commander-in-chief of the British forces in America, to Lord George Germaine, British secretary of state. The letter was dated January 30, 1780; it read:

> I should be wanting to my civil commission, in closing this letter, without a few reflections on the present state of the money of America. Every day teaches me the futility of calculations founded on its failure. No experiments suggested by your Lordship; no assistance that could be drawn from the power of gold, or the arts of counterfeiting, have been left unattempted. But the currency like the widow's cruize of oil, has not failed the Congress . . . I shall, nevertheless, my Lord, continue while I have the honor to command in America, assiduous in the application of those means entrusted to my care; if they cannot work its destruction, yet they embarrass Government.

The letter was eventually allowed to be printed in the *Pennsylvania Journal* on April 8, 1780. The letter was republished in England later that year.[10] More than anything else this letter from Clinton shows that he was not only aware of and encouraging the counterfeiting strategy, but also seems to have been a little disappointed that the goal of crashing the American economy had so far failed.

CONCLUSION

Benjamin Franklin, when he wrote his memoirs, looked back on the time of the flood of fake currency:

> Paper money was in those times our universal currency. But it being the instrument with which we combated our enemies they resolved to deprive us of its use by depreciating it; and the most effectual means they could contrive was to counterfeit it. The artists they employed performed so well that immense quantities of these counterfeits which issued from the British government in New York were circulated among the inhabitants of all the states, before the fraud was detected. This operated considerably in depreciating the whole mass, first, by the vast additional quantity, and

10. John Almon, *The Remembrancer or Impartial Repository of Public Events* (London, 1780), 10:40.

next by the uncertainty in distinguishing the true from the false; and the depreciation was a loss to all and the ruin of many. It is true our enemies gained a vast deal of our property by the operation but it did not go into the hands of our particular creditors, so their demands still subsisted, and we were still abused for not paying our debts![11]

While it can be said that the British commanders, both Howe and Clinton, were certainly aware of the massive counterfeiting offensive, it seems that the actual execution of the plan was carried out on a "street" level. Using various methods of disseminating that counterfeit currency, some subtle, some very bold, they were able to put massive amounts of it into circulation. Once in circulation it had the effect of destabilizing what was already an unstable currency, leaving the American economy teetering and the people's faith in Congress shaken. In most every way the planned economic offensive very nearly achieved its purpose of bringing an end to the rebellion.

It was only through the vigilance of Congress and the will of the American people that this outcome did not happen. It nonetheless had a lasting effect on the economy, the devaluation of Continental currency leading to the massive personal debts that plagued many veterans and merchants in post-war years. Eventually this culminated in what became known as Shay's Rebellion, and the need for a strong central government gave birth to the Constitution. Interestingly, even into the modern era the idea of counterfeiting a nation's money as a form of economic warfare has survived and has been put into practice numerous times.[12] While Britain may have been the first to use this method, they certainly were not the last.

11. Benjamin Franklin, *Memoirs of the Life and writings of Benjamin Franklin* (London: H. Colbrun, 1812), 3:106.
12. For example, during WWII Germany tried to flood the world market with counterfeit Bank of England notes; Lawrence Malkin, *Krueger's Men: The Secret Nazi Counterfeit Plot and the Prisoners of Block 19* (Boston: Little, Brown and Co., 2006). Dick K. Nanto (12 June 2009). More recently, North Korea has conducted counterfeiting operations against the US dollar. North Korean Counterfeiting of U.S. Currency, Congressional Research Service, RL33324, accessed September 20, 2015. Both of these operations ultimately failed, but illustrate that once a good weapon for war is found, it generally tends to stick around.

Ten Disabled British Pensioners

DON N. HAGIST

Wars were fought by soldiers, but it is the campaigns and commanders that are remembered and studied. This is a shame because the soldiers had a remarkable range of fascinating experiences, often more
exciting than those of the policymakers they served. And yet, the farther back in history one goes, the fewer personal stories of soldiers
survive. The names of most British soldiers who served in America
can be found on regimental muster rolls, but those administrative documents give only a few career details. Only a few personal narratives
by British soldiers who served in the American Revolution are known
to exist.[1] There is, however, a vast trove of records that contains some
precious details about what many of these men experienced.

British soldiers could get pensions if they served well and survived
their ordeals; in fact, it was just about the only profession that offered
a pension during the eighteenth century. A board of examiners
recorded the name, age, place of birth, trade, and length of service of
each pension applicant.[2] In addition to these demographic details,
they recorded the infirmity that prevented the man from earning his
own living, thereby making him a worthy candidate for government
support. Reading through these lists, we find a broad array of maladies
induced by military service: rheumatic, lost the use of his hand, drop-

---

1. Only eleven lengthy narratives of British soldiers are known to exist. Two are avail-
able in stand-alone books: Don N. Hagist, *A British Soldier's Story: Roger Lamb's
Narrative of the American Revolution* (Baraboo, WI: Ballindalloch Press, 2004), and
Joseph Lee Boyle, *From Redcoat to Rebel: the Thomas Sullivan Journal* (Bowie, MD:
Heritage Books, 1997). The remaining nine are published in Don N. Hagist, *British
Soldiers, American War: Voices of the American Revolution* (Yardley, PA: Westholme
Publishing, 2012).
2. Out Pension Admission Books, WO 116, British National Archives.

sical, asthmatic, sore legs, lost his sight, fits, and a host of other ailments including the catchall "worn out." Fewer than half of the men who served in America eventually applied for pensions (often long after the war due to lengthy military service),[3] but these pension board ledgers are often the only source of personal data that we have.

The discharge papers of some pensioners also survive.[4] A discharge is a document given to the soldier to prove that he had been legally released from his military obligation; most are printed forms with individual details handwritten into blank spaces. In addition to the personal data recorded in the admission ledgers, the discharges often include one or two sentences describing the soldier's infirmities, sometimes including dates and locations where wounds or injuries were received. From these records we learn, for example, that John Hawkins of the 22nd Regiment, discharged in 1796 after serving for 24 years, was "Paralytic and was wounded in the neck 25th May 1778 at Bristol in New England, in the right thigh at Bedford, and lost the use of his right side in the West Indies,"[5] and that Isaac Miller, a 24-year veteran of the 35th Regiment, suffered from "a wound he received in the left Leg, at the attack of the American Intrenchments at Bunker Hill the 17th of June 1775, in consequence of which & the rheumatism he contracted in America from the Climate."[6]

There are hundreds of similar statements among the discharges; the collection contains over 250 volumes, each containing documents for about 500 soldiers; I've read though the first fourteen volumes so far, tedious but rewarding work with microfilm at the British National Archives. As fascinating and enlightening as these statements of battle wounds are, affording personal insight on many of the war's great clashes, the discharges also reveal the many other hazards of military life. Among the hundreds of men who were simply "worn out" or contracted chronic illnesses are dozens of accidents and mishaps that speak to the variety of experiences that soldiers had.

---

3. Men who died in the service or deserted clearly did not apply for pensions. Discontinuities in service and other factors make it impossible to determine a precise number or portion of soldiers who served in America and later received pensions. Extensive study of the 22nd Regiment of Foot has shown that about half of the men who could eventually apply for pensions actually did so; the actual number may be higher.

4. Soldiers' discharges, WO 121, British National Archives. WO 97 and WO 119 also contain discharges. All of these pertain to men who were granted pensions; the discharges were apparently held by the pension office.

5. Discharge of John Hawkins, WO 121/26/357.

6. Discharge of Isaac Miller, WO 121/6/44.

From my notes on several hundred pensioners, below are ten of the more interesting and revealing descriptions of disabilities incurred as a result of service in the American Revolution:

1. JOHN HAWKINS, a writing clerk from Shankill near Lurgan in County Armagh, Ireland, joined the army in 1775 when he was 24 years old. He enlisted in the 37th Regiment of Foot. Although he was not discharged until 1788, his discharge reveals that he had been wounded during his second year of service; he was granted a pension because of "being wounded in the head in the action at Brandywine the 11 of September 1777 and Melancholy." His melancholy did not stop him from serving another ten years in a garrison battalion in Great Britain.[7]

2. SAMUEL NEWLY (sometimes written Newby) had been with the 10th Regiment of Foot since 1758, and in North America since 1767, when war broke out in Boston in 1775. He spent thirty years in the army, taking his discharge in 1788 when he was 51 years old. He came through this long service without injury but, a musician by profession, he was "worn out on account of his long service and Constant Practice on Musical Wind Instruments." He nonetheless reinlisted in the 54th Regiment and served another five years.[8]

3. ROBERT CHAPMAN enlisted with a recruiting party of the 54th Regiment of Foot in 1777 when his regiment was already at war in America. A 20-year-old bricklayer from Fakenham, Norfolkshire, he spent the next 15 years in the army. When the war ended, the 54th Regiment was sent to Canada for several years. It was here that Chapman acquired "a lame Foot occasioned by being Frost bit in the Province of New Brunswick when on duty as an Escort to a Courier going to Canada."[9]

4. WILLIAM McCREALLY, a blacksmith from Disset Martin in Londonderry, Ireland, joined the 3rd Regiment of Foot in 1773 when he was only 15 years old, a unusually young enlistment age. During his fifteen years in the army he suffered not only from the enemy but from the forces of nature. After "having received a Ball in his leg, at the Eutaws in America" in September 1781, he went with his regiment to the West Indies. There he had "both his arms broke in a Hurricane in Jamaica."[10]

5. CHARLES SMITH was a ten-year veteran in the 44th Regiment of Foot when he was "wounded at the Battle of Brandy Wine in his left

7. Discharges of John Hawkins, WO 121/1/6, WO 121/145/604.
8. Discharges of Samuel Newly (Newby), WO 121/5/34, WO 121/142/357.
9. Discharge of Robert Chapman, WO 121/14/442.
10. Discharge of William McCreally, WO 121/5/117.

"British Army Veterans Meet" by E. Fitzgerald. (*Anne S. K. Brown Military Collection, Brown University Library*)

arm" in September 1777. The weaver from Payton, Lancashire, who had enlisted in 1767 when he was 30 years old, continued to serve until 1790. This was in spite of an ordeal he survived when his regiment was sent to Canada part way through the war; he had "his right arm broken & the use of two fingers of his left hand destroyed when shipwrecked on his passage from New York to Quebec."[11]

6. JOHN HOPWOOD was a butcher, a useful trade in an age when armies had to slaughter cattle in order to provide fresh meat for soldiers. A native of Hutton, Yorkshire, he'd enlisted in 1771 when he was 28 years old and served until 1792, spending his entire career in the 54th Regiment. His disabilities were partly due to the harsh life of a soldier and partly from practicing his trade, "being rheumatic and having lost the use of the two first fingers of his right hand, occasioned by an accident when killing cattle for the use of the army in 1778."[12]

7. SAMUEL SHEPHERD, from St. James, London, proved that the army's butchers didn't always have enough to work with. When he was discharged in 1788 after having served 15 years in the 31st Regiment of Foot, much of the time in Canada, the 36 year old had "an inveterate scurvey from living upon salt provisions for eleven years in America."[13]

---

11. Discharge of Charles Smith, WO 121/8/51.
12. Discharge of John Hopwood, WO 121/14/459.
13. Discharge of Samuel Shepherd, WO 121/5/152.

8. HENRY BROWN served in three different regiments during his twenty years as a soldier. When he was discharged in 1790, the stocking maker from Dufftile, Derbyshire, was just 39 years old. Besides having been hurt "in America where he received a wound in the left knee" as a soldier in the 70th Regiment of Foot, he'd had an ignominious encounter with what was usually considered one of the soldier's best friends; he was "bruised in the side & privates by a fall of a cask of rum on board the Charlestown frigate since which he cannot retain his water."[14]

9. ARCHIBALD MACENDOW—a name that was spelled various ways—was born in 1754 in Ardnamarchan, Argyllshire, Scotland. When a new regiment, the 71st Regiment of Foot, was raised in Scotland for the war in America in 1775 he answered the call for recruits. MacEndow served for the entire war and took his discharge when it was over, but did not apply for a pension until 1792. The pension examining board recorded that he "was disabled at the siege of York Town in Virginia by the kick of a horse in the forehead and afterwards taken prisoner and when released he returned to his familiy in the highlands where he has lived since, subject to convulsion fits, which and real poverty, prevents his coming to solicit the pension sooner."[15]

10. JOHN WALLACE enlisted in the 76th Regiment of Foot as soon as the regiment was created in 1777, part of an expansion of the army in response to a widening war. The native of Kelso in Roxburghshire, Scotland, was 26 years old when he left his trade as a baker to become a soldier. On July 6, 1781, he was part of a rear guard of about twenty men that was attacked by a large American force at the Battle of Green Spring, Virginia; they fought desperately for some two hours, and Wallace was one of only a few who escaped unscathed. But at Yorktown the following month he was not so lucky; thunderstorms rolled through the area and he "lost his left eye by lightening on duty in America." After the war "He went home to his friends in the Highlands of Sutherland, who in his absense had disposed of his little property, a house & garden. He then came to work at his Trade as a baker till his other eye in consequence of the suffering of the first was so dim he could not see sufficient to get his living."[16]

14. Discharge of Henry Brown, WO 121/8/258.
15. Discharge of Archibald MacEndow, WO 121/14/368.
16. Discharge of John Wallace, WO 121/3/341.

Indian Patriots from Eastern Massachusetts: Six Perspectives

✵ DANIEL J. TORTORA ✵

Joseph Paugenit, Jr., Jonas Obscow, Anthony Jeremiah, Simon Peney, Obadiah Wicket, and Alexander Quapish. These are not household names to the average history enthusiast. But they are among the two hundred Indians from eastern Massachusetts who fought in the Revolutionary War. Few people are aware of the contributions that these and another thousand or more Native soldiers—Catawba, Lumbee, Mohegan, Oneida, Penobscot, Stockbridge, and others— made to the American cause during the Revolutionary War.[1] Similarly, few people are aware of the circumstances that led eastern Indians to wartime military service.

For the 1,700 remaining Indians in eastern Massachusetts, much had changed in the 150 years since the Pilgrims arrived. Life was characterized by poverty and land loss. Many Indians lived on small reservations or in isolated enclaves, subjected to the whims of inept colony-appointed agents called "guardians." Disease, despair, and alcohol abuse led to low life expectancies. Women peddled baskets and worked as housekeepers or herbalists. Men carved out a niche as warriors in colonial militias. Others were wanderers—traveling farmhands and laborers. Still others labored as whalers on long journeys from southern New England ports. Intermarriage was common. Some now

---

1. National Society Daughters of the American Revolution, *Minority Military Service, Massachusetts: 1775–1783* (Washington, D.C.: National Society Daughters of the American Revolution, 1989), 5.

lived in small cabins. Many had adopted Christianity. But traditions remained strong and kinship networks were still intact.[2]

In 1775, Massachusetts Indians had numerous reasons for enlisting. Many wished to carry on a family tradition of military service. Most Massachusetts Indians fought for the American cause out of economic necessity. Others had no choice; as servants they were forced to fight in the military by their masters. Just as their reasons for enlisting varied, their wartime experiences were equally unique. Some eastern Massachusetts Indians proved to be brave and bold soldiers, while others fell short of this distinction.

TRIBAL AFFILIATION OR COMMUNITY	PERCENTAGE OF TOTAL	APPROXIMATE NUMBER
Natick[3]	4.5	9
Ponkapoag	4	8
Aquinnah Wampanoag	5	11
Mashpee Wampanoag	22.5	46
Unknown/Other	30	60
Nipmuc	2.5	5
Herring Pond Wampanoag	2.5	5
Other Wampanoag	29	59
TOTAL	100	203

The following profiles reveal the representative experiences of six Indian Patriots during the Revolutionary War.

THE WARRIOR TRADITION: JOSEPH PAUGENIT, JR.

Many Indians fought to fulfill family tradition, or because that's what Indians did. Indians from the Christian communities of Natick and Ponkapoag (present-day Canton) in particular, had a long tradition of military service to Massachusetts. In 1756, Joseph Paugenit and his wife Zipporah, two Natick Indians, requested disability assistance from the Massachusetts legislature. Joseph sustained serious wounds while serving in a provincial regiment during the French and Indian War. Because he could no longer work, he and Zipporah sank into poverty. Yet five days after the first shots were fired at the Battles of

2. Jean M. O'Brien, "'Divorced' from the Land: Resistance and Survival of Indian Women in Eighteenth-Century New England," in *After King Philip's War: Presence and Persistence in Indian New England*, ed. Colin G. Calloway (Hanover, N.H. and London: University Press of New England, 1997), 145.

3. Researchers disagree on the precise number of Natick Indians who served in the Revolutionary War, classifying some veterans as Indian and others as African American.

Lexington and Concord in 1775, Joseph's son, also named Joseph, joined the American cause.[4] Despite the dangers and risks, Joseph Paugenit, Jr. was carrying on his family's warrior tradition. The young Paugenit signed up for three years of service.

Paugenit, whose name derived from an Indian word for "codfish," was one of sixteen Indians who fought at the Battle of Bunker Hill in 1775. Four others came from Massachusetts. Paugenit would later fight at Harlem Heights in 1776 and at one or both of the Battles of Saratoga in 1777. He died in a military hospital in Albany in 1777, either due to fatal injuries or smallpox. He was only 23 years old.[5]

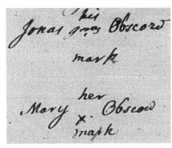

A detail from the petition of Jonas and Mary Obscow, Natick Indians, May 27, 1772. (*Massachusetts Archives Collection, 33:559*)

THE DEBTOR: JONAS OBSCOW

Many Massachusetts Indians saw combat because they were poor and had no other options. On May 27, 1772, Jonas and Mary Obscow petitioned the Massachusetts Council. Sickness had afflicted the family for several years. "Several of their children have died," the petition stated, and they "have become justly indebted to physicians and others." The two Natick Indians, perhaps under duress from their colony-appointed agents, sought to sell what many Indians held most dear—a tract of land. The Massachusetts Council granted the Obscows' petition and thirty-seven more acres fell out of Indian hands. This was a familiar tale for Massachusetts Indians at the time.[6]

4. Robert D. Hall, Jr., "Praying Indians in the American Revolution," lecture transcript, February 8, 2004, needhamhistory.org/features/articles/indians-american-revolution/; Eric Grundset, ed., *Forgotten Patriots: African American and American Indian Patriots in the Revolutionary War* (Washington, D.C.: National Society Daughters of the American Revolution, 2008), 130.
5. Jean M. O'Brien, *Dispossession by Degrees: Indian Land and Identity in Natick, Massachusetts, 1650–1790* (Cambridge, UK: Cambridge University Press, 1997), 95; George Quintal, Jr., *Patriots of Color: 'A Peculiar Beauty and Merit': African Americans and Native Americans at Battle Road & Bunker Hill* (Boston: Division of Cultural Resources, Boston National Historical Park, 2004), 43–44, 169.
6. Petition of Jonas and Mary Obscow, May 27, 1772, Massachusetts Archives Collection, 33:559–60.

Eastern Massachusetts Indians like Obscow were quick to join the military to escape poverty and woe. Obscow left his wife and seven-year-old child and joined a militia company in May 1775. He saw action in Cambridge. Like so many eastern Massachusetts Indians, the lure of enlistment bounties and clothing soon drew him to the Continental Army. Indian enlistees in the Continental army could choose between a "bounty coat" or its cash equivalent. Obscow opted for the coat on November 21, 1775. Indians were seldom treated as equals in civilian white society. But military service offered impoverished minorities equal enlistment bounties, equal pay, and camaraderie. Obscow's exact fate remains unclear; he apparently saw action in Rhode Island in 1778, but he never returned home.[7]

THE SEAFARING INDIAN: ANTHONY JEREMIAH

One of the several niches that eastern Massachusetts Indians had carved out for themselves in the eighteenth century was working as sailors on merchant vessels or as whalers. It is no surprise that some Indians saw service on the seas; they already possessed the requisite nautical experience. Anthony Jeremiah, a Nantucket Indian, was one of these men.

Jeremiah fought bravely in the Continental navy. Affectionately known aboard as "Red Jerry," or "Red Cherry," he served as a gunner under Captain John Paul Jones on the *Alfred*, the *Ranger*, and the *Bonhomme Richard*. In September 1779, Jeremiah survived the battle off the English coast between the *Bonhomme Richard* and the *Serapis*. Then, with tomahawk in hand, Jeremiah joined the boarding party that overtook the *Serapis* and compelled its surrender.[8] It was a shining moment for both Jeremiah and the American cause.

After the Revolutionary War, Indians in eastern Massachusetts would continue to travel in search of work. Some went back to sea as sailors on merchant ships or as whalers. This work again meant extended absences from reservation lands which were becoming

7. Massachusetts, Secretary of the Commonwealth, *Massachusetts Soldiers and Sailors of the Revolutionary War*, 17 vols. (Boston: Wright and Potter Printing Co., State Printers, 1896–1908) [hereafter cited as *MSS*], 11:619; Receipt for Wages, Camp at Cambridge, June 7, 1775, American Revolutionary War Manuscripts Collection, Boston Public Library; Petition of Mary Obsco[w], June 6, 1783, Massachusetts Archives Collection, 134:508.
8. "Red Cherry, A Naval Hero," *Daughters of the American Revolution Magazine* 54 (February 1920): 96. DAR researchers found no manuscript references to Jeremiah, though he does appear on a muster roll. Forgotten Patriots Research Files, Washington, D.C., Files to be Processed, Box 22.

This engraving (ca. 1779–1790) by Balthasar Friedric Leizelt depicts the battle between the *Bonhomme Richard* and the *Serapis*, in which Anthony Jeremiah fought. (*Library of Congress*)

fewer and smaller. Men like Jeremiah found a home on the high seas until the collapse of the whaling industry in the mid-nineteenth century.

THE LOUSY SOLDIER: SIMON PENEY, AND THE DESERTER: ABEL SUPPAWSON

A few Indians, like portions of the non-Indian population, proved to be poor soldiers. On March 20, 1781, Simon Peney, a Mashpee Indian, was sentenced to receive 80 lashes "on charge of stealing cider." The sentence was soon dropped. But on May 13 that same year, Peney was sentenced to receive 50 lashes "on charge of repeated absence from roll-call without leave." Peney was listed as deceased in August, and then, inexplicably, was sick one month later.[9]

A search of ads in war-era newspapers reveals that, like non-Indians, Indians also deserted their units and returned home. Enoch Cloas of Nantucket apparently eluded capture.

But Abel Suppawson of Cape Cod was less lucky. In 1778, Suppawson, a veteran of the Battle of Bennington and the Battles of Saratoga, deserted his company in the 14th Massachusetts Regiment. Yet, consistent with the equal treatment Indians received in the army,

9. *MSS*, 12:116.

Deserter ad from the
New-England
Chronicle, July 11,
1776. Enoch Cloas is
probably the same
Enoch Closs, a
Delaware Indian who
ran away from the
Indian Charity School
in 1765.

DESERTED *from Captain*
Treſſcott's Company, in the 6th Regiment of Foot,
in the Continental Service, an Indian Man, named
Enoch Cloas, about 6 Feet high; had on a blue out-
Side Jacket, round-bound Hat. He belongs to
Nantucket, and it is thought he has gone that Way.
Whoever ſhall take up ſaid Cloas, and return him
to ſaid Regiment, now in Boſton, ſhall receive Five
Dollars Reward, and all neceſſary Charges, paid
by   LEMUEL TRESSCOTT, Capt.
Boſton, June 19th, 1776.

officers afforded Indian offenders with leniency. Suppawson was
spared a harsh punishment, and was returned to action. Nonetheless
he died later that year.[10] Soldiers from all racial groups included some
unreliable soldiers. Indians were no exception.

THE PENSIONERS: ISAAC WICKHAMS AND OBADIAH WICKET

Only two of the Massachusetts Indians that served in the
Revolutionary War received federal pensions. Transience, low life
expectancy, and the difficulty of gathering supporting testimony of
whites—decades after the war had ended—contributed to this under-
whelming number. Mashpee Wampanoag Isaac Wickhams served
from 1780 to 1783. He fought in one of the light infantry companies
under Lafayette and witnessed Cornwallis's surrender at Yorktown.
When he applied for a pension in 1818, Wickhams was suffering from
"chronic lameness" and was eking out a humble subsistence in an "old
house 10 by 14 feet one story." He purchased a cow with his first pension payment. In later years, Wickhams testified on behalf of other
pension applicants and their widows. In time, he became the oldest
living Mashpee veteran.[11]

10. Ibid., 15:261; Massachusetts, et. al, eds., *The Acts and Resolves, Public and Private, of
the State of Massachusetts, 1777–1778* (Boston: Wright & Potter, 1918), 473–74 (June 23,
1778); "The Number of the Indians belonging to Potenomacut," December 1, 1765,
Massachusetts Historical Society manuscript. Transcript posted on wolfwalker2003.
home.comcast.net/~wolfwalker2003/potenomacut1765.pdf.
11. Isaac Wickham, S34534; Job Tobias, B.L. Wt. 1927-100, pp. 11–12; and Josiah
Crocker, W14358, Revolutionary War Pension and Bounty-Land Application Files, p.
23, National Archives and Records Administration, Washington, D.C., microfilm publication M804, record group 15. Viewed on Fold3; United States. Census Office, *A
Census of Pensioners for Revolutionary or Military Service* (Washington, D.C.: Blair and
Rives, 1841), 27.

That same year, 1818, Wickhams was also conned into signing a fraudulent petition contrary to the best interests of Indians on the Mashpee Plantation.[12] So much for veterans' benefits!

The other Massachusetts Indian pensioner was the Herring Pond Wampanoag Obadiah Wicket (also spelled Wickett), a household servant turned soldier. He claimed to have witnessed the execution of British spy Major John André in 1780. Thus far the evidence is inconclusive, but genealogists and local historians believe Wicket relocated to present-day Greene or Leeds, Maine (not far from present-day Auburn and Lewiston), and died there in 1819. In 1933, a town historian ordered and installed a veterans' tombstone to mark Wicket's reported final resting place.[13]

THE (FINALLY) HONORED INDIAN: ALEXANDER QUAPISH

The Natick Indian Alexander Quapish was born around 1741. A year after his wife died, and after being mustered for the Lexington Alarm, Quapish enlisted in the Continental Army in May 1775. He served under the command of Captain Daniel Whiting in Colonel Jonathan Brewer's regiment. He fell sick and was nursed by a teenaged soldier and his family in the "Needham Leg," the predominantly Indian enclave that is now part of Natick. Quapish died on March 23, 1776. His exact cause of death is unknown.[14]

After 227 years, Quapish and sixteen other Indian veterans finally got their due. In a ceremony led by Robert D. Hall, Jr., a Needham historian and a researcher for the Massachusetts Department of Veterans' Services, volunteers placed markers and flags throughout a cemetery containing the Indians' remains. In 2006, descendants of the Natick Indian veterans held another ceremony and unveiled monuments listing Natick veterans of color. In 2010, Boston National Historical Park posted a student-narrated video on Alexander Quapish. And a few years later, the Indian's terminal convalescence was referenced in artist Ted Clauson's *Needham Cares* sculpture, located outside the high school in that town.[15]

12. William Apess, *On Our Own Ground: The Complete Writings of William Apess, a Pequot*, ed. Barry O'Connell (Amherst: University of Massachusetts Press, 1992), 232.
13. Obadiah Wicket, S34535, Revolutionary War Pension and Bounty-Land Application Files, National Archives and Records Administration, Washington, D.C., microfilm publication M804, record group 15. Viewed on Fold 3; Albert S. Bryant to Ferd Stevens, February 2, 1939, private collection; interview with Leeds historian Marilyn Burgess.
14. Quintal, *Patriots of Color*, 186.
15. Hall, "Praying Indians"; Quintal, *Patriots of Color*, 186; Peter Schworm, "Honoring Sacrifices of 'Praying Indians,'" *Boston Globe*, May 30, 2006; "Patriots of Color Alexan-

While the individual stories of these Indians can be exciting, the collective reality is sobering. The eastern Massachusetts Indians who fought and died for the American cause were poor and desperate common soldiers. Following a long tradition of service to Massachusetts, they sought a better life and a share in the freedom and liberties that the United States claimed to be fighting for. Indian soldiers did not receive the acknowledgement they deserved while they were alive. After the war, widows struggled to pick up the pieces. Poverty, land loss, transiency, and general mistreatment remained the norm. But the experiences of these six Native Patriots, now better understood and better commemorated, offer a glimpse into the struggles and contributions of the first Americans. And they reveal one of many moments in American history in which Indians fought alongside non-Indians to forge a better future together.

der Quapish," June 25, 2010, www.youtube.com/watch?v=NifJfB0-r20; "Ted Clauson: Needham Cares" International Sculpture Center Directory, www.sculpture.org/portfolio/sculpture_info.php?sculpture_id=1014784.

A Melancholy Accident:
The Disastrous Explosion
at Charleston

JOSHUA SHEPHERD

For Sir Henry Clinton, the capitulation of Charleston, South Carolina, constituted not only the most stunning British victory of the war, but something of a personal vindication as well. In truth, the May 12, 1780, surrender of the vital southern port was a staggering blow to the Patriot war effort. Clinton enthusiastically claimed to have captured about 6,600 men, and without question, the Continentals of America's Southern Army had been captured nearly en masse.[1] Additionally, the British were left in possession of a ponderous amount of rebel ordnance, ammunition, and supplies. But in the wake of the overwhelming victory, such a vast haul of rebel materiel would ironically lead to one of the worst disasters of the war.

On May 14, Maj. Peter Traille, Clinton's chief of artillery, conducted an initial inventory of the captured stores. In addition to over three hundred pieces of artillery, the British were in possession of at least 5,416 muskets and well over thirty thousand rounds of fixed small arms ammunition. In the immediate aftermath of the capitulation, however, a thorough listing of captured arms was impossible. "Large Quantities of Musket Cartridges, Arms, and other small Articles" were not included in the return, reported Traille. "The scattered Condition

1. Sylvanus Urban, ed., *The Gentleman's Magazine and Historical Chronicle*, volume 50 (London: J. Nichols, 1780), 339. Letter, Sir Henry Clinton to Lord George Germain, June, 4, 1780. Clinton reported that he had taken 5,617 troops, plus an estimated 1,000 sailors. For a closer examination of the numbers, see Edward McCrady, *The History of South Carolina in the Revolution, 1775-1780* (New York: Macmillan Company, 1901), 507-510.

of the different Stores not admitting of collecting them in so short a Time, a more exact Account will be given as soon as possible."[2]

The following morning, British artillery officers, who were tasked with securing American munitions, were overwhelmed with even more captured rebel arms. The American militia, many of whom sat out the official surrender on May 12, were ordered to parade and give up their arms. American Maj. Gen. William Moultrie was somewhat amused that a fear of British retribution swelled the ranks of the militia to "three times the number of men we ever had on duty." The citizen soldiers surrendered a motley assortment of weapons, which were loaded onto wagons and taken into the center of Charleston. However, there seems to have been a woeful disregard for basic safety protocols. American officers claimed to have warned the British that some of the muskets were loaded, however at least one weapon reportedly discharged from rough handling.[3]

In Charleston, the weapons were delivered to a storehouse which the Americans had used as an improvised arsenal. As a means of implementing Britain's "southern strategy," such a disparate collection of militia arms was earmarked for the eventual use of Carolina Loyalists.[4] The building held, in addition to arms, an American stockpile of roughly 4,000 lbs of fixed ammunition. Heading up the British work party at the arsenal was Capt. Robert Collins of the Royal Artillery; by most accounts, he was a competent professional and regarded as "a valuable officer."[5]

Despite the intended use of the captured arms, Capt. Johann Ewald, a company commander in the Hessian Jaeger Corps, entered town that afternoon in the hope of acquiring a few of the muskets; either by purchase, or, he hoped, gratis through "the good offices" of

2. Franklin B. Hough, *The Siege of Charleston, by the British Fleet and Army Under the Command of Admiral Arbuthnot and Sir Henry Clinton* (Albany, New York: J. Munsell, 1867), 117-118. Major Peter Traille, Return of Ordnance and Ammunition in Charleston, May 14, 1780.

3. William Moultrie, *Memoirs of the American Revolution, so far as it Related to the States of North and South-Carolina, and Georgia* (New York: David Longworth, 1802), vol. 2, 108-109. See also William Gilmore Simms, *South Carolina in the Revolutionary War* (Charleston: Walker and James, 1853), 155. Both Moultrie and an unidentified American subaltern reported accidental discharges prior to the explosion.

4. Banastre Tarleton, *A History of the Campaigns of 1780 and 1781, in the Southern Provinces of North America* (London: T. Cadell, 1787), 24. Tarleton indicated that the arms were "for the use of the friends to the British government in the province of South Carolina."

5. Roger Lamb, *An Original and Authentic Journal of Occurrences During the Late American War, From its Commencement to the Year 1783* (Dublin: Wilkinson & Courtney, 1809), 296.

Captain Collins. Accompanied by one of his lieutenants, Johann Wintzingerode, Ewald headed for the magazine where the arms were being secured. The pair was less than a hundred yards from the building when Ewald bumped into a servant who informed him that an old friend, Capt. Georg Wilhelm Biesenrodt, was sick in a nearby home.[6]

"Since I did not know how long the siege corps would remain together," Ewald explained, he immediately decided to visit Biesendrodt and return to the storehouse later that afternoon. While his lieutenant waited in a nearby coffeehouse, Ewald accompanied the servant to Biesenrodt's quarters, which was in the neighborhood. Ewald had just stepped through the door of the house when the unexpected happened.[7]

"Such an extraordinary blast occurred," wrote Ewald, "that the house shook."[8] It was, in fact, a thunderous explosion that rocked the entire city. General Moultrie, who just then was near the corner of Broad and Meeting streets in the city center, recalled that the "houses of the town received a great shock, and the window sashes rattled as if they would tumble out of the frames."[9] The shock waves terrified city residents, and Ewald recalled that "dreadful cries arose from all sides" of the town. When he ran into the street, the Hessian captain was dumbfounded. The storehouse which he had nearly entered not ten minutes earlier had clearly experienced a catastrophic accident; the sky above the building was filled with "a thick cloud of vapor."[10]

The structure itself had been demolished by the explosion, which filled the sky with a deadly form of shrapnel.[11] "The muskets flew up into the air," wrote Jaeger Capt. Johann Hinrichs, and "ramrods and bayonets were blown onto the roofs of houses."[12] Immediately rushing

6. Johann Ewald, *Diary of the American War: A Hessian Journal*, trans. and ed. Joseph P. Tustin (New Haven: Yale University Press, 1979), 239.

7. Ewald, *Diary of the American War*, 239.

8. Ewald, *Diary of the American War*, 239.

9. Moultrie, *Memoirs of the American Revolution*, 109-110.

10. Ewald, *Diary of the American War*, 239.

11. The exact location of the explosion is uncertain. Edward McCrady, *History of South Carolina in the Revolution, 1775-1780* (New York: The Macmillan Company, 1901) places the explosion on Magazine Street between Archdale and Mazyck (now Logan) streets, page 505. Moultrie, in *Memoirs*, wrote that one of the bodies struck the steeple of "the New Independent Church" which stood "a great distance from the explosion," page 109. The present day Unitarian Church, 4 Archdale Street, is now on that site which is at the eastern end of Magazine Street.

12. Bernhard A. Uhlendorf, ed., *The Siege of Charleston, with an Account of the Province of South Carolina: Diaries and Letters of Hessian Officers from the Von Jungkenn Papers in the William L. Clements Library* (Ann Arbor: University of Michigan Press, 1938), 197-199.

to the building, Ewald was witness to deep horrors that he would never forget. The streets were littered with about sixty people "burnt beyond recognition, half dead and writhing like worms, lying scattered around the holocaust." Amid the confusion, he lamented, "no one could help them." The American militia, who were still milling about after surrendering their weapons, raced to the scene of the disaster and, joined by British troops and local slaves, frantically set to work fighting fires which had spread through the neighborhood. Ewald, generally an accurate and impartial witness, recorded that the danger was not quite passed. "Many of those who hurried to the scene," he claimed, "were killed or wounded by the gunshots which came from the loaded muskets in the cellars."[13] There was, however, little time to waste. The fires spread rapidly and eventually engulfed structures near the city's primary powder magazine.[14] "At last," reported Moultrie, "some timid person called out, that 'the magazine was on fire.'"[15]

Pandemonium ensued. Under the deluded fear that the main magazine was about to explode, workers fled in a contagious panic. Both British and Americans raced pell-mell through the streets in a virtual stampede. Were it not for the horrific nature of the disaster, the chaotic scene presented a comic spectacle. "I have heard some of them say," remembered Moultrie, "that although they were so confoundedly frightened at the time, they could not help from laughing, to see the confusion and tumbling over each other."[16]

When particulars of the disaster reached Moultrie near St. Michael's Church, the general concluded that it was no laughing matter. Familiarized with the disposition of American arms and munitions, Moultrie immediately advised bystanders to get as far away from the city's magazine as possible. The building was filled with a reported 10,000 pounds of powder and if ignited, he feared, "many of the houses in town would be thrown down." Heading for safety at the shoreline of Charleston's South Bay, Moultrie met with a British officer who was clearly agitated. When informed that the magazine contained such a ponderous amount of powder, the redcoat blanched and blurted out "Sir, if it takes fire, it will blow your town to hell!" Moultrie agreed; "it would give a hell of a blast," he responded.[17]

---

13. Ewald, *Diary of the American War,* 239.

14. The Powder Magazine, which dates from about 1713, survived the threat of fire and is currently preserved as a museum. See www.powdermag.org. Located at 79 Cumberland Street.

15. Moultrie, *Memoirs of the American Revolution,* 110.

16. Moultrie, *Memoirs of the American Revolution,* 110.

17. Moultrie, *Memoirs of the American Revolution,* 110-111.

Incendie by Pierre Quentin Chedel. (*Anne S. K. Brown Military Collection, Brown University Library*)

In the wake of the disaster, Crown troops were understandably suspicious that the defeated Americans were guilty of sabotage. Nearing the relative safety of the shoreline, Moultrie was accosted by a furious Hessian officer. "You, General Moultrie," shouted the German, "you rebels have done this on purpose, as they did at New York." Taken into custody, Moultrie was confined in a nearby home with a number of other Americans, but succeeded in slipping out a note of protest to British Maj. Gen. Alexander Leslie. Leslie immediately dispatched a staff officer, who ordered off the Hessian guards and then offered Moultrie an apology for the incident.[18] Nevertheless, recorded an anonymous American subaltern, the British remained considerably alarmed. "Patrols in the streets till the fire was extinguished," he wrote, "Their whole garrison under arms."[19]

When work finally proceeded on fighting the blaze, a good bit of the neighborhood had been destroyed. Capt. John Peebles of the 42nd Foot recorded that "a Barrack, the gaol, & house of Correction, in which were a good many people," was burnt, but by evening the

18. Moultrie, *Memoirs of the American Revolution*, 111.
19. Simms, *South Carolina in the Revolutionary War*, 156.

flames were put out by the efforts of townspeople, militia, and slaves.[20] The smoldering ashes revealed a grisly sight. The tremendous power of the blast had left unspeakable devastation. Moultrie later claimed that the body of one unfortunate victim had struck the steeple of Charleston's Independent Church, where marks of the incident were visible for days.[21] "We saw a number of mutilated bodies hanging on the farthest houses and lying in the streets," wrote Johann Ewald, who witnessed charred arms and legs scattered in every direction. "Never in my life, as long as I have been a soldier," concluded Ewald, "have I witnessed a more deplorable sight." For a hardened veteran who had seen extensive action since the New York Campaign, it was no mean observation.[22]

Precise figures for the number of victims to the disaster would remain elusive. Among the dead were Captain Collins, artillery Lieut. John Gordon, a lieutenant of the 42nd, 17 English and two Hessian artillerymen, and a Hessian grenadier. Perhaps the most unfortunate victims were the hapless civilians who lived near the scene of the explosion, not to mention "the lunatics and negroes," wrote the unidentified subaltern, "that were chained in gaol for trifling misdemeanors." Rumors abounded in the aftermath of the incident, and estimates of those killed by the blast ranged upwards of 300.[23] Perhaps the most reasonable estimate was that of Maj. William Croghan of the 1st Virginia, who informed a friend that "near a hundred lives" had been lost.[24]

Regardless of the exact figures, the incident was a tragic, and likely needless, loss of life. The precise cause of the disaster, however, will never be known for certain; everyone in a position to know exactly what occurred was killed by the explosion. The anonymous American subaltern who recorded the event in his journal wrote that although some of the British persisted in suspecting rebel duplicity in the catastrophe, "the more sensible" were certain that the explosion was occasioned by the rough handling of loaded muskets.[25] Such a conclusion

20. John Peebles, *John Peebles' American War: The Diary of a Scottish Grenadier, 1776-1782.* Edited by Ira D. Gruber. (Stroud, Gloucestershire: Sutton, 1997), 374.
21. Moultrie, *Memoirs of the American Revolution*, 109.
22. Ewald, *Diary of the American War*, 239.
23. Peebles, *John Peebles' American War*, 374. Simms, *South Carolina in the Revolutionary War*, 155. Ewald, *Diary of the American War*, 239.
24. Robert W. Gibbes, ed., *Documentary History of the American Revolution: Consisting of Letters and Papers Relating to the Contest for Liberty, Chiefly in South Carolina . . . 1776-1782* (New York: D. Appleton & Co., 1857), vol. 2, 133. Letter, Major William Croghan to Michael Gratz, May 18, 1780.
25. Simms, *South Carolina in the Revolutionary War*, 155.

came to be the general consensus. Johann Ewald, a fairly dispassionate observer, likewise thought that "as one might assume," a musket discharged accidentally while being stored in the arsenal, igniting a powder keg. "The entire disaster had occurred," he thought, "through carelessness."[26] To Captain Peebles, who lost a fellow officer from the 42nd Foot, the entire affair was "a melancholy accident," as well as a pointless disaster. "Very Strange Management," he observed, "to Store up loaded Arms in a Magazine, of Powder."[27]

For his part, Ewald viewed his narrow escape from the catastrophe with the grim resignation of a professional soldier. "From this incident," he wrote, "I realized once more that if one still lives, it is destined that he shall live. One should do as much good as possible, trust firmly in the Hand of God, and go his way untroubled."[28]

26. Ewald, *Diary of the American War*, 239.
27. Peebles, *John Peebles' American War*, 374.
28. Ewald, *Diary of the American War*, 240.

Murder Along the Creek: Taking a Closer Look at the Sugarloaf Massacre

THOMAS VERENNA

On September 11, 1780, a detachment of forty-one Northampton County, Pennsylvania, militiamen was surprised by a force consisting of thirty Seneca warriors and Tories. When the fighting was over, fifteen American patriots lay dead on the ground.[1]

As the summer of 1780 began to wane, a detachment of forty-one of the veteran Van Etten's Company was assigned to an imposing twenty-five-year-old Captain named Daniel Klader. Klader would lead these men into hostile and physically demanding terrain on a mission that culminated in tragedy.[2]

These two quotes, taken from Rogan H. Moore's book (which many historians consider to be the modern day authoritative source on the Sugarloaf Massacre), demonstrate what can happen when myth and folklore transition into historical memory. Some facts aren't in dispute, of course. In early September 1780, a detachment of volunteer militia *did* venture into the northwestern frontiers of Northampton County as part of an ongoing frontier war with the natives and Tories. On September 11 they *were* attacked and defeated along the Little Nescopeck. There is even a monument at the site with a bronze plaque, listing fifteen names of those soldiers who supposedly died at the site, placed there in 1933 by the local chapters of the Sons and Daughters of the American Revolution. A little further back is a headstone inscribed with the name "Daniel Klader, Captain, Van Etten's Co., Northampton Co. Militia, Died 1780."

---

1. Rogan H. Moore, *The Bloodstained Field: A History of the Sugarloaf Massacre, September 11, 1780* (Bowie, MD: Heritage Books, 2000), 7.
2. Moore, *The Bloodstained Field*, 29.

However the event itself has raised many questions because of the limited scope of the resources about the events. *What* exactly was this detachment doing in this part of the wilderness? *Who* was leading it? *Why* had they been so soundly defeated? Did *fifteen* men really die during the battle? Well, the answers aren't as readily apparent as Moore suggests. In fact, Moore gets a great deal wrong. To be fair, it isn't necessarily Moore's fault. Moore's narrative about the Sugarloaf Massacre has dominated the retelling precisely because he is using a narrative that goes back generations. The resources he used are themselves terribly unreliable. From printed articles full of wild local lore from the end of the nineteenth century to books on the region's history written by historical societies of the 1920's, it is hard to find a careful examination of this massacre anywhere. Let's remedy that.

After the Wyoming and Cherry Valley Massacres, Washington commanded General Sullivan to launch a brutal scorched-earth campaign against the Indians.[3] It was the hope of Washington, Sullivan, and the backcountry inhabitants of Pennsylvania's frontier that this campaign would drive the Indians out of reach of the homesteads and plantations; their close proximity had made it easy to launch attacks and raids on the civilian populations for generations (it didn't help that settlers continued to encroach upon American Indian land granted under treaty).

For the most part, the Sullivan campaign only fueled the Indian and Loyalist resolve to continue their raids. These attacks were continuous throughout the years of 1778[4] and 1779. Repeated requests for help were largely ignored by President Joseph Reed in Philadelphia[5] and when Sullivan was asked for aid, he saw his campaign as the

---

3. "The expedition you are appointed to command is to be directed against the hostile tribes of the six nations of Indians, with their associates and adherents. The immediate objects are the total destruction and devastation of their settlements and the capture of as many prisoners of every age and sex as possible. It will be essential to ruin their crops now in the ground and prevent their planting more." George Washington to Maj. Gen. John Sullivan, May 31, 1779; accessed June 9, 2015: founders.archives.gov/documents/Washington/03-20-02-0661.

4. *Pennsylvania Archives* (Harrisburg: State Printer, 1907) Ser. 1, Vol. 7, 572. In July 1778, Northampton County lieutenant John Wetzel wrote, "Col Strouds, informing me that he hourly expected an atack from the Indians, (their being a Large Bodey of them the numbers not yet known) at the Minesinks." Colonel Stroud was the militia commander for the northern militia district that encompassed the region most directly at risk of enemy raids.

5. *Pennsylvania Archives* Ser. 1, Vol. 7, 579: "The unexpected Incursion has given us great Concern, but as we hope there will be sufficient Vigor & Spirit in the Inhabitants to repel those Wretches, who cannot be sufficiently numerous or terrible to require more Resistance than the People can give."

greater importance and refused.[6] Even after attacks on defensive stations like Fort Freeland, in Northumberland County, in which a militia garrison was attacked and defeated, no help was granted.[7]

Following Sullivan's campaign, things quieted down primarily due to the coming winter season. But with spring, things began to heat up once more. On April 27, 1780, Lt. Col. Nicholas Kern, a veteran of the current war who had barely escaped capture at the Battle of Long Island in 1776,[8] hurriedly scribbled a note to Samuel Rea, county lieutenant. In his note, he relayed information about a new incursion. Apparently he wrote so fast that he did not have time to think about spelling (he was in the danger zone):[9]

> Excuse haste, we have this meiunet returned from a scout, where we found mr. Benjamin Gilberts house And gice mill & saw mill totally consumed with phire, and likewise Benjaman Peirts house, and the people Carryed of prisoners fifteen in Number by the enemy . . . We have had some scouting partyes But as Vallenteers

6. *Pennsylvania Archives* Ser. 1, Vol. 7, 594. Sullivan wrote to Hunter: "Your letter Dated the 28th Ins't I rece'd this Day, with the Disagreeable inteligence of the loss of Fort Freeland, your situation in Consequence must be unhappy, I feel for you, and could wish to assist you, but the good of the service will not admit of it, The Object of this Expedition is of such a nature, and its Consequences so Extensive that to turn the course of this Army would be unwise, unsafe & impolitic." Not everyone in Sullivan's command agreed with this decision, however. Col. Adam Hubley, also at Wyoming with Sullivan, wrote to Reed indicating that he felt that diverting some assistance to the settlements in Northampton and Northumberland would actually benefit the expedition as it would stop the war party from harassing Sullivan's army as it moved north. Leaving them unchecked, Hubley argued, would put them in a position to cut Sullivan off from the south and leave them vulnerable. See his letter in *Pennsylvania Archives* Ser. 1, Vol. 7, 596-597.

7. *Pennsylvania Archives* Ser. 1, Vol. 7, 589-591; Col. Samuel Hunter, commanding Fort Augusta, wrote to General Sullivan for assistance on July 28, 1779: "Yesterday Morning, Early, there was a party of Indians & Regular Troops Atacted Fort Freeland; the Firing was heard at Boon's place, when a party of Thirty men turned out from that under the Command of Cap't Boon, but, before he Arrived at Fort Freeland the Garrison had Surrendered, and the British Troops and Savages was paraded Round the Prisoners, & the Fort & Houses adjacent set on fire. Cap't Boon and his party fired briskly on ye Enemy, but was soon Surrounded by a large party of Indians; there was thirteen Killd of our People and Cap't Boon himself among the Slain. . . . The Town of Northumberland was the Frontier last night, and I am afraid Sunbury will be this night . . . . There was about three Hundred of ye Enimy, & the one third of them was white men, as the Prisoners informs us, that made their Escape."

8. See my article 'The Spartans of Long Island,' *Journal of the American Revolution* (November 12, 2014); accessed June 9, 2015: allthingsliberty.com/2014/11/ the-spartans-of-long-island/.

9. *Pennsylvania Archives* Ser. 1, Vol. 8, 213.

will not stay above two or three Dayes from home at once, it is of no use to the inhabitants as security.

On May 1, Rea forwarded on this news to Reed, telling him that he planned to call up an additional company of militia to secure the frontiers. Things in Northampton County were falling apart. Rea stressed that though the time had come to elect new officers for the militia, the commissions had come in late from the state, so he had not yet had time to arrange elections. Without officers, the militia could not be called. It didn't help that the officers were *themselves* discipline problems.[10] Reed's response underscores the reputation that the drafted militia from Northampton County had gained:

> We observe you have called the Militia which we approve provided they will seriously employ themselves in their proper Duty but we must express our Disapprobation of their rendezvousing in Large Bodies in Taverns & spending their time in Amusements.[11]

In the same letter, Reed reassured Rea that the measures taken by the Supreme Executive Council would help ease the burden of the county by reinstating the scalp bounty, as indicated above, but also by an additional measure:

> We have concluded to raise a Company immediately upon the Terms proposed in the enclosed Papers, & that no Time may be lost, we desire you . . . to appoint the Officers agreeable to the Plan inclosed, & set them immediately to recruiting Men.

The plan to which Reed refers was an ordinance passed in the Council on May 10, 1780, called "An Act for the Greater Ease of the Militia and the More Speedy and Effectual Defence of this State." This ordinance called for the establishment of a single company of volunteers, to be distinguished from the drafted militia, that would serve not less than seven months, from the middle of June to the middle of January, and would be outfitted, then ordered out to deal with the threats to the north. Rea apparently met his quota in time to organize the company according to the ordinance, as the muster roles indicate that the company formed on June 15, 1780.[12]

---

10. *Pennsylvania Archives* Ser. 1, Vol. 8, 221.
11. *Pennsylvania Archives* Ser. 1, Vol. 8, 222. In the militia's defense, they were accustomed to receiving a double rum ration during the Philadelphia Campaign (in lieu of actual money, which apparently the state just didn't have) and, as one might imagine, it was hard to break the habit.
12. *The Statutes at Large of Pennsylvania from 1682 to 1801*, Vol. 10 (Philadelphia: Clarence M. Busch, 1904), 191.

On July 4, Rea was making progress:

I have filled up the Commissions for the following officers, Viz., Capt. Johannes Van Etten, Lieutenant John Fish, and Ensign Thomas Syllaman. According to orders I have collected the Volunteirs at the County Town, and find that there is but fifty, but they are dayly Comeing in. I have ordered them up to the frontier of this County.[13]

Johannes Van Etten had organized a defense against the raid a few weeks previous, mentioned above. But just who was Johannes Van Etten? According to a document in one of the John Van Etten pension files, "There are several of the name in the service, and we are having difficulty in identifying ours from the others."[14] This is problematic for most people engaged in ancestry research, but for someone trying to pinpoint which officer was where and who did what task, it means tedious work. Moore apparently made the mistake that many do— conflating multiple individuals with the same name as if they were all one person.[15] Moore writes, for example, that "Captain Van Etten, the son of Jacob Van Etten . . . served with distinction during the French and Indian War." Yeah, no, that isn't correct.

While Johannes Van Etten was no slouch when it came to fighting on the frontier, he was not a captain during the French and Indian War; that was his *brother* John.[16] In fact, Johannes Van Etten was a member of his brother's ranging company, commissioned in Northampton County by Benjamin Franklin, during that war.[17]

---

13. *Pennsylvania Archives* Ser. 1, Vol. 8, 386. In all, the company would muster with eighty-three privates and fifteen officers and NCOs. James Scooby, a sergeant upon enlisting, was advanced to 2nd Ensign on September 1. Thomas Syllaman would apparently either decline his commission as Ensign or was replaced, as Henry Bush would show up as 1st Ensign on the returns. In addition, John Moyer was made 2nd Lieutenant.

14. So stated by Commissioner of the Bureau of Pensions in 1923, Mabel Knight; the John Van Etten Mabel was looking for was Johannes Van Etten's son, John.

15. Moore, *The Bloodstained Field*, 25-26.

16. In a letter addressed to Governor Morris, John Van Etten distinguishes himself and his brother Johannes in actions against the Indians. See the *Pennsylvania Archives* Ser. 1, Vol. 2, 720-721.

17. Franklin established a set of unique instructions for John Van Etten's company, including the keeping of a daily journal. His instructions, along with the organization of the company, partial muster roll, and daily rations, is at; "The Organization of John Van Etten's Company, January 12, 1756," accessed June 11, 2015: founders.archives. gov/documents/Franklin/01-06-02-0142. Van Etten's daily journal, or at least a few months of it, can be found in the *Pennsylvania Archives* Ser. 1, Vol. 3, 222-235.

Around the time that the Revolutionary War broke out in 1775, John moved away with his family; to where and at what time of the year, it is unclear (but he no longer shows up in Northampton County on tax records after that period).[18] By late 1777, after the Militia Law was passed, Johannes finally shows up on returns as an elected captain of a militia company in the northern militia district (or the 6th Battalion District in 1777).[19] Whether he saw service during the Philadelphia Campaign is unclear, though again we have an instance of rumor and folklore.[20]

Regardless, he had proven his determination in the defense of the frontiers. He had even turned his home into a garrison for the purpose of providing a safe haven for the region. Thus Van Etten was elected as the captain of volunteers for the county of Northampton. But what would be the purpose of the volunteers? Where were they going and what would be their task?

Disaffection ran high in Northampton County, but after Sullivan's campaign, those most agitated with constantly being disarmed and taxed removed themselves to the farthest parts of the county, in the area known as Fishing Creek and Catawissa.[21]

---

18. John lived in Forks Township, just a few miles from the town of Easton. Johannes, however, had a plantation in the northern part of the county.

19. There are some early returns in 1775 that show a John Van Etten as a captain of Associators, but it is unclear if it is John, the brother (before he moved), or Johannes, or even Johannes' son John who was old enough by that time and who would also be elected captain in the militia later in the war.

20. According to an early secondary source, "The troops of Northampton county were present at the disastrous battle of Germantown, and Captain Van Etten's company suffered severe losses." William J. Heller, ed., *History of Northampton County [Pennsylvania] and the Grand Valley of the Lehigh*, Vol. 1 (New York: American Historical Society, 1920), 136. No records exist that Van Etten fought at Germantown. Even if he had been on active duty at the time of the battle, the position of the militia on the flank of the army saw little (if any) action. The notion that they suffered heavy casualties is a fiction. It is likely that this early historian saw Van Etten's name on the Northampton County officers' rolls in 1777 without realizing the distinction between inactive duty rolls and permanent billet rolls indicating active service. Read more about the muster roll distinctions in my article "Explaining Pennsylvania's Militia," in Todd Andrlik, *et al.*, eds., *Journal of the American Revolution: Annual Volume 2015* (Yardley: Westholme, 2015), 212-213 (especially n.20).

21. According to the deposition of Thomas Hewitt of Cumberland County, written August 29, 1780, "They have lived peaceably at home in the most Dangerous times . . . . Every Incursion the Enemy has made into this County and all the Disaffected families in this fly there for protection, whilst the well-affected are oblidged to Evacuate the County, or shut themselves up in Garrison." From the *Pennsylvania Archives*, Ser. 1, Vol. 8, 528; *cf.* the deposition of Henry O'Niell, *Pennsylvania Archives*

When Lt Col. John Butler began recruiting for the crown in 1778, he found more than enough to fill his ranks from these regions. Those who did not elect to fight were more than happy to shelter Indians loyal to the Crown and pass along Patriot militia movements and intelligence as they came to hand. As early as April, hunters were complaining of the discharging of guns in the wilderness near Fishing Creek.[22] Shortly after, Tories and Indians were raiding the countryside using the northern regions of Northampton and Northumberland, using Catawissa and Black Creek as a base of operations as they had during the French and Indian War.

Reed firmly believed that routing these inhabitants and depopulating the region, either by force or through harassment, was the key to lasting security for the well-affected frontier communities.[23] It was the hope that the Seven Months Men, as they were called, would discourage the raids.

According to the pension file of Henry Bush, an ensign in the company, Van Etten's men first marched from Easton to Stroudsburg (named after Colonel Stroud), likely staying at Fort Penn or Fort Hamilton as a garrison for about two weeks. From there they

Ser. 1, Vol. 8, 527-528. See also my article "Disarming the Disaffected," *Journal of the American Revolution: Annual Volume 2015*, 107-120.

22. *Pennsylvania Archives* Ser. 1, Vol. 8, 156: "I will not trouble you with the distress of this County, They will no Doubt be painted to Council in lively Colours, and indeed the Picture cannot be over charged, nor should I at this Time write to you, But for a strong Belief and Persuasion, that a Body of Indians are lodged, about the head of Fishing and Muncy Creeks . . . . This is what we wish; Many of our Hunters who went late last Fall into that Country (which is a fine one for hunting) were so alarmed with constant Reports of Guns which they could not believe to be whitemens that they returned suddenly Back. We are not strong enough to spare men to examine this Country and Dislodge them. . . . This is a strange divided Quarter–Whig Tory, Yankey, Pennamite Dutch Irish and English Influence are strangely blended."

23. *Pennsylvania Archives* Ser. 1, Vol. 8, 167. As Reed explained on April 7, 1780, to Samuel Hunter:

"It is our earnest Desire that you would encourage the young Men of the Country to go in small Parties & harass the Enemy. In former Indian Wars it was frequently done & with great Advantage. . . . Last French War Secret Expeditions were set on foot by the Inhabitants which were more effectual than any Sort of defensive Operations. We most earnestly recommend it to you to revive that same Spirit & any Plan concerted with Secrecy & Prudence shall have our Concurrence & Support." Unfortunately, Reed's strategy was wrong. He failed to take into account how Loyalist opposition to the new American government would play out on the frontier. During the French and Indian War, for the most part, the majority of the backcountry supported operations into the wilderness. This was not the case in 1780. Tories were everywhere on the frontiers and they filled the ranks of Loyalist irregular units.

marched to Fort Allen.[24] At this point the company broke into detachments to garrison different defensive forts and block houses. In one of the most erudite and comprehensive (and accurately recollected) pension depositions I've come across, Henry Davis, another member of the company and survivor of the massacre, dictated:

> The Declarant further states that on the fifteenth day of June AD 1780 he entered the United States service as a volunteer in the (5th) fifth company of the third Battalion of Northampton County Pennsylvania Militia under Captain Vannata (or Vannaten) and that he served in said company until the fifteenth day of the next January 1781 making seven months and that he got no discharge when he left the service. & that John Fish was first and John Myers was second Lieutenant in the company, Nicholas Carns [Kerns–ed.] ye Major (as he thinks) and John Sigfreit was Colonel [it was the other way around–ed.] part of the time and Brown a part. That he was in one battle with the Indians commonly called the Seven Months Battle–in the Nescopeck Valley in Pennsylvania that he resided in Northampton County when he entered the service this time, marched along the frontiers of the North East part of Pennsylvania–lay part of the time at Gnaddenhutten and part at a place called the Minnysinques [the Minisink–ed.] and part of the time at Captain Vannata's fort at his own house in Pennsylvania.

In early September, Van Etten's men went on the offensive. Moore incorrectly suggests that Colonel Hunter placed an individual named Daniel Klader in charge of this offensive detachment, apparently magically giving him a commission as captain.[25] But according to Samuel

---

24. Pension file deposition states: "And this declarant further states that in the spring of the next year, according to the best of his recollection, he volunteered as an Ensign . . . in a Company of Militia commanded by Captain John Vanetten a low Dutchman . . . He entered at Easton, Penn., & marched to Stroudsburgh—at this place the Company remained about two weeks & then marched about 8 miles distant from Stroudsburgh to a place called Fort Allen, at which place they remained three or four months, then marched to Brink's Fort (?) about ten miles & remained there the remainder of the seven months."

25. Moore writes, "Colonel Stephen Hunter . . . ordered Captain Daniel Klader to take command of a detachment of Van Etten's Volunteer Militia. Klader was directed to select the best of Van Etten's Company for a dangerous mission that would take them into hostile country. . . ." *The Bloodstained Field*, 35. It should be noted that Colonel Hunter's name was Samuel, not Stephen. Moore probably got his information from the very-dated work of Henry C. Bradsby, *History of Luzerne County, Pennsylvania: With Biographical Selections, Vol. 1* (Luzerne: S.B. Nelson, 1893), 200, to which is found the claim, "Col. Hunter had determined to make a demonstration against this Tory

Rea, the detachment marched out from Gnaddenhutten on September 8 seemingly at *Rea's* orders, not Hunter's (which makes sense because a colonel from Northumberland had absolutely zero authority over the county lieutenants or the militia of Northampton), to begin their trek into the Sugarloaf Valley:

> Having had Sundry alarms & small parties of the Enemy having made incursions into the remote parts of it who plundered & burnt several Houses we thought it our indispensible Duty to send out a part of men as a Scout which consisted of forty one men part Militia & part of the Volunteers . . . to make such Discoveries as they could, and examine into the Reasons why a Number of Families on the Enemies Boarders remain on their Farms without Molestation or apprehension and give us information of the same, who accordingly marched from Canaudenhutten (a small old Moravian Town Situated behind the Blue Mountains on the west Branch of the Delaware) on the Eighth Inst.[26]

Of the battle, there exists only one contemporary eyewitness account. In the pension deposition of Peter Krum, a private in the company, it states that:

> A part of the company was sent to Black Creek to which he belonged. The Captain and Lieutenant went along, when they reached Black Creek they were attacked by the Indians and they were defeated. There were of their company . . . seven killed and three prisoners taken. The lieutenant was one of the prisoners . . . the Indians attacked them while eating dinner, the balance retreated about as he supposes twenty miles . . . He remained there on the

settlement, and arranged with Capt. Klader, of Northampton County, to join him in the enterprise, but the enemy had heard of the contemplated movement and proceeded to thwart it . . . . It is now pretty well known that this party knew that Capt. Klader intended to join Col. Hunter in the expedition up the river." This is good fiction, but not good history. So good, in fact, that it was picked up by F.C. Johnson in *The Historical Record, Vol. 6* (Wilkes-Barre: Press of the Wilke-Barre Record, 1897), 132. As happens with most fictional narratives, the story was embellished more and more; this time it included all sorts of details about how the men of the militia detachment spent their time before being ambushed—including the belief that "their guns were scattered here and there, some stacked, some leaning against stumps or logs, others lying flat on the ground" and "Some [men] were on the ground . . . one man was leaning against a tree with his shoes off cleaning them out, others had gone for grapes . . . of which party one had climbed a tree and was picking and eating the grapes from the vine." Yes, it is quite a descriptive narrative. A shame there is no evidence to support any of it.

26. *Pennsylvania Archives* Ser. 1, Vol. 8, 560-561.

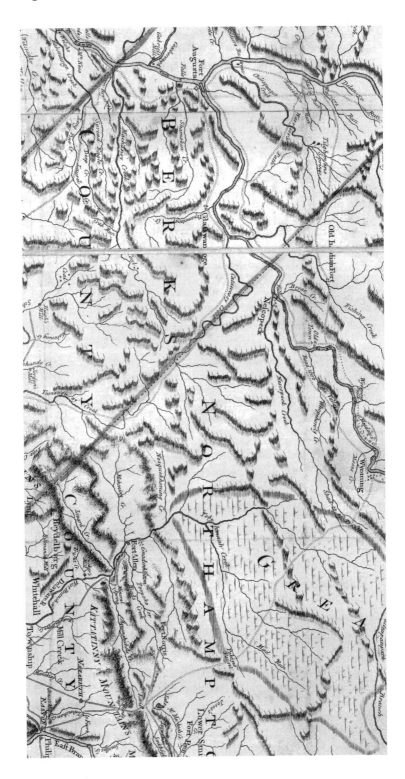

frontier until his term of service was expired without any other engagements. He states he served a full term of seven months and returned home in the winter, or he can say it was cold weather.

The first report of the attack came on September 14. The event was recorded in a diary of one of the soldiers stationed at Fort Allen:

> Lieutenant Myers, from Fort Allen, came into the Fort, and said he had made his escape from the Indians the night before, and that he had been taken in the Scotch Valley, and that he had thirty three men with him, which he commanded. He was surrounded by the Indians, and thirteen of his men killed, and three taken.[27]

Samuel Rea wrote to President Reed on September 17 with the news:

> [Van Etten's men] were attacked on the Eleventh at the Nusquepeck by a party of whitemen and Indians who had the advantage of first fire on our men which obliged them to retreat. The Enemies loss we cannot ascertain but the wounded & missing of ours, amount to twentythree, four of former [wounded] and Nineteen of the latter [missing]. On the fifteenth a Number of Militia and Volunteers to the amount of one-hundred or upwards marched with a Design of burying the Dead & making such observations as might lead to a Discovery of the Enemies Number or Design.[28]

The situation was so confused that no one had a good grasp of how many were killed, wounded, or missing. A few days later, on September 20, Lt. Col. Stephen Balliet gave his account of the burial detail and what he had discovered:

> Sir, I take the earliest opportunity to acquaint your Excelency of the . . . Misfortune Happened to our Volunteers stationed at the Gnaden Hutts. They having Rec'd Intelligence that a Number of Disaffected Persons lived near the Susquehannah at a place called the Scotch valley, who have been suspected to hold up a correspondence with the Indians, and the Tories in the country. They sat out on the 8th Ins't for that Place to see whether they might be able to find out anything of that nature, but were attacked on the 10th at noon about 8 miles from that settlement by a large Body of Indians & Torys (as one had Rid hair,) Supposed by some forty &

---

27. The diary entry was reproduced in William L. Stone, *The Poetry and History of Wyoming* (Wyoming: Wiley and Putnam, 1841), 230.
28. *Pennsylvania Archives* Ser. 1, Vol. 8, 561.

by others twice that number they totally Dispersed our People, Twenty two out of forty one have since come in several of whom are wounded. It is also Reported that Lieu't Jn's Moyer had been made Prisoner & made his escape from them again & Returned at Wyoming. On the first notice of this unfortuned event the officers of the militia have Exerted themselfs to get Volunteers out of their Respective Divissions to go up & Burry the Dead, their Labour Proved not in Vain we collected about 150 men & officers Included from the Colonels Kern, Giger & my own Batallions who would undergo the fatique & Danger to go their & pay that Respect to their slautered Brethren, Due to men who fell in support of the freedom of their Country. On the 15th we took up our line of march (want of amunation prevented us from going Sooner) on the 17th we arrived at the place of action, where we found Ten of our Soldiers Dead, Scalped, Striped Naked, & in a most cruel & Barborous manner Tomehawked, their throads Cut, &c. &c. whom we Buried & Returned without even seeing any of these Black alies, & Bloody executors of British Tirany . . . . We also have great Reason to beleve that several of the Indians have been killed by our men, in Particular one by Col. Kern & an other by Capt. Moyer both of whome went Volunteers with this partie.[29]

First, note that while many were wounded, Balliet—a man who oversaw the burial detail of the dead—counted only *ten* bodies. Second, Lieutenant Moyer was captured, but escaped. Third, Captain Moyer—undoubtedly William Moyer, father of Lieutenant John Moyer, who served as captain in the militia during this period—went as a volunteer to the area to help bury the dead. All of this is important because as we move forward, we will be referencing these details.[30]

So now for the million dollar question: Just who *led* the expedition? This is where our primary source data becomes scarce and where we really start to get the most bizarre instances of mythological contam-

---

29. *Pennsylvania Archives* Ser. 1, Vol. 8, 564-565.

30. These details were reinforced by Samuel Rea on October 24 in a follow-up letter to Reed: "Col. Baliort [Balliet] informs me that he had Given Council a relation of the killed and wounded he had found Burned near Neskipeki as he was at the place of action his Accts must be as near the truth as any I could procure, tho since that Time Lieut. Myers, who was taken by the enemy in that unhappy action hath made his escape from the savages & reports that ensign Scoby and one Private was taken with him and that the party consisted of 30 Indians and one white savage, that they had 13 Scalps along with them that several of them were wounded & supposes some killed." *Pennsylvania Archives* Ser. 1, Vol. 8, 592.

ination in the narrative. Returning to our most recent historical interpretation by Mr. Moore, as quoted above, it was Daniel Klader. There
is, after all, a headstone and a monument with Daniel Klader's name
on it. So it must be true, right? Right?! Well, here's the thing about
assumptions—don't ever make them.

Truth be told, there is absolutely no record that Daniel Klader ever
existed. Full stop. Say *what*? You read that correctly. No birth records,
no death records, no service records of any kind. In the six pension
records of the survivors of Van Etten's company, not a single mention
of a Daniel Klader can be found. This is quite astonishing because the
individuals mention Lieutenant John Moyer, Captain William Moyer,
Captain Van Etten, and even some of the members of the company
taken prisoner (John Moyer among them), but no one felt it was
worth mentioning a Daniel Klader.

You wouldn't know this from reading Moore's book, as he feels the
need to elaborately detail tons of Klader family history. He lists lots
and lots of information about Daniel Klader's supposed parents and
siblings, but it is hard to determine how Moore arrived at these details
without birth records linking a Daniel Klader (of any sort) to any of
these individuals—a fact Moore must have recognized as he has no
other facts about Daniel Klader*himself* except his age (twenty-five) and
that he was "a powerful physical specimen with a fine record of military service behind him." He lists no evidence for how he arrived at
that information.[31]

So where did this idea come from that a Capt. Daniel Klader led
the detachment? I have a few theories, though it is impossible to know
with any certainty. At the time of the massacre, in the company was
one Pvt. Abraham Clader. At the same time, a Capt. Jacob Clader was
commanding a company of militia along the frontier (and would do
so for three years, under the militia law). Some of the very same men
serving under Van Etten in 1780–1781 would serve under Capt. Jacob
Clader between 1781 and 1783, at various times, for two month tours.
It seems most likely that some old timer in his advanced age combined his service under Van Etten with service under Jacob Clader,
and failed to recall his first name properly.

31. Moore, *The Bloodstained Field*, 35; no pension files name his service, no Permanent
Billet Roll or Active Duty Roll lists his name, and the Pennsylvania Historic and
Museum Commission have no militia abstract card for him—not as a private nor as
an officer—despite having abstract cards for Jacob Clader and Abraham Clader. It's
all very suspicious how Moore can draw these conclusions without any evidence
whatsoever.

This isn't a stretch at all. Pension files are filled with this sort of confusion—remember, these men were into their late seventies and early eighties or older when giving their pension depositions in 1833. Of course, no pension file exists with the name Daniel Klader (or any variant spelling), which is why I believe it was likely developed during interviews with elderly veterans during the mid-nineteenth century.

Even while reading through existing pension files to write this article, I saw veterans of Van Etten's company conflate Van Etten with William Moyer, even though Moyer was not at the battle (many of the men who served under Van Etten also served under William Moyer on their next tour). Uriah Tippie, one such veteran of the volunteers, mistook his service year in the Seven Months Men as 1778 instead of 1780 and also misremembered Lt. John Fish's first name as "Robert."

There is no mention of a Daniel Klader until the mid-1860's, when a newspaper, the *Hazleton Sentinel,* ran an article on the atrocities of the Sugarloaf Massacre written by John C. Stokes. This article, thankfully, was reprinted in 1880 and again in 1888 (the original I cannot track down). This was clearly one of Moore's sources, as it contains all sorts of folklorist notions (like men hiding in the Nescopeck Creek to avoid being killed, or one man hiding behind a tree with his faithful dog companion whose unfortunately timed barks led to his demise, and so forth). The article, however, also contains this interesting tidbit about a dispute among local historians:

> Both Miner and Pearce say that the company was commanded by Capt. [John] Myers, while Chapman . . . says that Wm. Moyer was in command; but the oldest living descendants of the early settlers, with a number of whom we have conversed, agree in asserting that the company was under the command of Capt. Klader, who [performed] deeds of prodigy and valor that caused his name afterwards to inspire feelings akin to veneration.[32]

So much veneration was felt by his men, apparently, that they couldn't even get enough courage to write about him in their pension files. Of course, after this paper was published, almost everyone decid-

---

32. First found in the volume (no author) *History of Luzerne, Lackawanna, and Wyoming Counties, PA: With Illustrations and Biographical Sketches of Some of Their Prominent Men and Pioneers* (Lackawanna: W.W. Munsell & Company, 1880), 404; these were reprinted again in Frederick Charles Johnson, ed., *The Historical Record: Vols. 2-3* (Wilkes-Barre, 1888), 125.

ed it was the truth and so it was republished in local histories from the twentieth century onward, finally landing in Moore's book on the massacre.

The notion that William Moyers led the company was discussed and rejected above, but the thought of John Moyer, the lieutenant of the company, is an interesting one. It seems likely that as a company officer, he could have very well been given command of the detachment while Van Etten remained in garrison with the remainder of the company (not at Fort Allen).[33] It seems likely that John Moyer was indeed left in charge—or perhaps was even in joint command with John Fish (1st Lieutenant) whose pension file also indicates that he was present at the ambush.

I have a copy of a return made on January 15, 1781, produced by Captain Van Etten at Fort Penn at the end of the enlistment of the volunteers. This return is an important piece of the puzzle that was the Sugarloaf Massacre. It indicates that *fourteen* men were killed, despite the fact that the monument lists fifteen men (Daniel Klader doesn't show up on the return), whereas early reports by those who buried the dead say only ten were killed. Lieutenant Moyer twice recounted that thirteen scalps were taken by the Indians (once at Fort Allen and again in his report to Samuel Rea). So what was it: ten or fourteen?

Those individuals responsible for the monument at the site clearly went by the return, because fifteen names are listed (fourteen from the return, plus Daniel Klader). But when doing research for this article, I stumbled on *active duty* returns from Captain Moyer's company in November and December 1781 (over a year after the massacre) with the names of some individuals supposedly killed on September 11, 1780. So what gives?

One example is Peter Krum, whose pension deposition is presented above. Krum is listed on both Van Etten's 1781 return and on the monument (listed as Peter Croom) as having been killed on September 11, 1780. So how could Peter Krum, who supposedly died in 1780, give a deposition in 1833 for his pension hearing? Krum also shows up as a substitute (in other words, he was hired by the county lieutenant) for another man in Captain Moyer's company in 1781 and 1782 (spelled "Krum" or "Crum" on returns). Either Krum performed a miracle and rose from the dead, or, more likely, after the ambush he made his own way back to his farm and never returned to Fort Allen or Penn until just before or shortly after his tour expired (which would account for the lapse in his recollection of service after the massacre).

33. Van Etten is never discussed as being a member of the detachment.

Krum and his family moved to Jackson County, Tennessee (where the national pension was filed), sometime after the war so he would not have had any descendants around Luzerne County in 1933 when the monument was erected. No one was there to dispute his death.[34] His was not the only name to raise red flags.

George Shellhammer is also listed on the monument and the returns as having been killed,[35] but shows up on active duty returns in 1781 and 1782.[36] Most importantly, he has a pension file in which he states that he "marched . . . to Buckhill Luzerne County, where they had an engagement with the Indians & lost twenty one men out of forty one." He lists Baltzar Snyder, William Supple, and "two brothers by the name of Rough."[37] After the battle "he then returned home (or to his residence in Linton Township, Montgomery County)." He did not return to his post, which might have led to the belief that he had perished. George's brother, Philip, also filed for a pension, and deposed "That he . . . was marched with about thirty others by Lieutenant Moyer . . . and that they there fought the Indians. That they lost about fifteen or sixteen men, killed, wounded, or taken prisoner. . . ."

Both George and Philip indicate that Moyer led the company. It's also clear that George Shellhammer and Peter Krum survived the engagement. Philip indicates that perhaps as many as sixteen men were killed, wounded, and captured, while acknowledging that three were taken prisoner, contradicting the fourteen indicated on Van Etten's returns. Balliet's original statement that *ten* men were killed, *not* fourteen, is more likely. That means that there are two more names on the monument that don't belong there. While no pension file exists for him, Paul Neely seems to have survived; according to returns he appears on active service between May 23 and July 21, 1782, at Towamensing under Capt. John Gregory (with Uriah Tippie,

---

34. It may seem like they might be two different people, but the pension file recalls fairly vividly his service in Northampton County, Pennsylvania, listing officers he served under (which are easily verified), including having served in Van Etten's company in 1780. It seems like other people were called to testify to the truth of the return, and all those who did testify confirmed he lived in Northampton County—some claimed to have served with him in the militia (though not Van Etten's volunteers).

35. Moore also suggests Shellhammer was killed; *The Bloodstained Field*, 28.

36. For the active duty returns of Moyer's company, April 18, 1782, see *Pennsylvania Archives* Ser. 5, Vol. 8, 489-492.

37. George Shellhammer further states, rather amusingly, "that he had a discharge which was destroyed by the rats. . . ." The "Rough" brothers might be Jacob and Philip Rouch who are listed as losing a rifle and "appertainances" during the battle. See n.38.

no less), and a militia loan certificate–money owed to those who gave certain items for use of the militia–was issued to him in 1792.

So how could this have happened? How is it that Van Etten didn't notice that his own men were alive after the fighting? For one, the return was taken in January, four months after the action in September. Even by late October, Samuel Rea had not yet known of all the killed and wounded. Van Etten wasn't at the battle so he didn't see which men were killed. Balliet is clear that the bodies were heavily mutilated, possibly making it difficult to identify the remains. Scalping distorts the face (depending upon where one begins to cut) and there were no dental records to match. All accounts indicate that the battle was a chaotic rout; men were running for their lives. Several lost their guns and equipment, either throwing them off to lighten their burden while retreating or having stacked them while they were eating dinner.[38] These men could have simply returned home, rather than risking their lives for the remainder of their enlistments. Or, just as likely, maybe they were on assignment at another location (as stated earlier, men from Van Etten's command were stationed at various places along the frontier) and Van Etten just made his best guess. It could also have been just a paperwork error.

A lot has changed in 235 years. A once sprawling wilderness is now a suburban neighborhood nestled up against a golf course. The Little Nescopeck Creek, where the militiamen who patrolled the area stopped to rest, fill their canteens, and eat, still runs nearby, used as an obstacle for golfers at the scenic site. The golf course and the encroachment of modern housing on the battlefield is a good metaphor for this particular synchronic point in history. After all, this article demonstrates how easily myth and folklore can envelope historical events to create a narrative which can be deceptively realistic, to the point where all traces of what actually happened are replaced by contemporary fiction.

---

38. A return of arms and equipment lost by the detachment can be found in *Pennsylvania Archives* Ser. 5, Vol. 8, 574. Given the amount of times it has been documented that the Pennsylvania militia threw away their arms to lighten their loads to run faster, it seems that this scenario was more likely.

Light Infantry Never Surrender

✿ TODD W. BRAISTED ✿

In August 1780, Lt. Col. Abraham Van Buskirk of the 4th Battalion, New Jersey Volunteers, received orders to form a light infantry company.[1] The commanding officers of five other Provincial battalions around New York City also were directed to form light infantry companies composed of men drawn from the rest of their battalions. It was typical in all British regiments of the time, and many other Provincial ones as well, to have one company of particularly agile, reliable men, trained to fight in open order and move quickly. Light infantry could both cover ground rapidly and, as picked troops, fight tenaciously when called upon.

Van Buskirk was not pleased at the order as this new company was destined to be detached from his regiment, thus depriving him of the service of these men.[2] The 4th Battalion, New Jersey Volunteers had already sent forty officers and men to serve under Maj. Patrick Ferguson in the American Volunteers the previous winter, and they had yet to return. Now he was being called upon to detach even more men for an unknown service and duration.[3]

1. Maj. John André to colonels Beverley Robinson, Gabriel G. Ludow, Edmund Fanning, lieutenant colonels Abraham Van Buskirk, Joseph Barton, and Maj. John Colden, New York, August 15, 1780. Sir Henry Clinton Papers, Volume 275, John André Letterbook, William L. Clements Library, University of Michigan. Hereafter cited as CL.
2. Van Buskirk to Deputy Adjutant General Frederick Mackenzie, New York, August 19, 1780. Sir Henry Clinton Papers, Volume 118, item 2, CL.
3. The American Volunteers was a composite corps of 175 officers and men drawn from eight Provincial battalions at New York City that were not part of the original expedition to take Charleston, South Carolina. After the capture of that city, the corps was to return to New York and the men returned to their various units. Ferguson however lobbied successfully to keep the corps in South Carolina, where it was used to help train newly raised militia units, eventually being destroyed with Ferguson at King's Mountain.

The new light infantry company would be commanded by Captain Jacob Van Buskirk, son of the lieutenant colonel. It would have amongst its ranks representatives of some of Bergen County, New Jersey's most notable families, including those of Van Housen, Christie, Wannamaker, Westervelt, Ackerman, and Zabriskie. The lieutenant of the company would be John Van Norden, and its ensign Richard Cooper. Cooper was an interesting choice, as the twenty-four year old was promoted up from the ranks, having served as his battalion's sergeant major. The company was joined to the other five light companies created, those of the 1st and 2nd Battalions of New Jersey Volunteers, the 3rd Battalion of DeLancey's Brigade, the King's American Regiment, and the Loyal American Regiment, all under the command of Lt. Col. John Watson Tadswell Watson.[4]

Watson was not a Loyalist, but the commanding officer of one of the light infantry companies in the elite Brigade of Guards, a British unit formed of men from the three regiments of Foot Guards in Great Britain. Like Ferguson, John Graves Simcoe, Banastre Tarleton, and Francis, Lord Rawdon before him, Watson was a young officer striving for an independent command, but unable to advance within his own corps through the traditional method of preferment based upon date of commission rather than purely on merit. In these situations, aspiring officers such as those named were given Provincials to command, much to the anger of deserving Provincial officers who saw their corps weakened and neglected for the benefit of favored regular army officers.

After being joined together, the new corps was named the Provincial Light Infantry. The service they were intended for was not local, but rather part of Gen. Alexander Leslie's expedition to Virginia which sailed from New York in early October 1780. After a month or so of raids to capture stores and supplies, Leslie's expedition was re-embarked and stood off for Charleston, South Carolina, to reinforce the British Army under Lord Cornwallis. Watson, Van Buskirk, and the rest of the light infantry, however, did not join Cornwallis' main force, but rather were sent off into the High Hills of Santee to chase down and eliminate partisans under the famous Thomas Sumter.

Sumter had served for years as a field officer in the South Carolina Continentals, but after the fall of Charleston in May 1780 had led bands of militia and irregulars in harassing Cornwallis. In February 1781, however, Sumter ran into a succession of defeats, culminating on

4. The King's American Regiment, raised in December 1776, had actually had a light company since its first formation.

the 27th when he ran across Ens. Richard Cooper and twenty of his light infantry. The story of the ensuing engagement is told by four of the participants.

Lt. Col. John Watson, commander of the Provincial Light Infantry, wrote the following:

> Returning one day from a foraging Party, one of the Waggons, which was bringing a Mill, to grind the Corn, broke down, as it was not above one mile and a half from home, I left an Ensign, whose name was Cooper, with 20 Men, to repair, & bring it on—our Men were but just in and began to dress their dinners; when we heard a centinal firing towards the Line in which he had been left; every Man was instantly in Arms. Suspecting the cause, which was confirmed by the Horses galloping home by themselves. We were soon up to the Spot which was but about a mile for having repaired the Cart, they were proceeding home; when Sumpter wholly surrounded them, & called to him to surrender; but forming his Men in a Circle, round the Trees nearest him, he replied Light Infantry never Surrender, and began firing as hard as they could—seeing us approach, they quitted our Gallant Ensign, & formed to receive us. This business did not last long before they fled, leaving what killed and wounded may be seen by the returns. We took some Prisoners and 30 Horses. Lord Rawdon came the next day, & flattered his young Corps much, by his manner of thanking them, & took that particular notice of Mr. Cooper, he so well deserved. Sumpter was himself said to be wounded, which was probably the case, as he never afterwards appeared in that Quarter, & I believe not very long after died. His Lordship [General Cornwallis] too, much approved the Post, we had taken, and the manner in which we had strengthen'd it.[5]

A New York newspaper published an extract of a letter from Charlestown, South Carolina, dated March 4, 1781; the writer is not identified, but appears to be Surgeon Uzal Johnson:

> General Sumpter with the South Carolina Militia being high up in the country when Lord Cornwallis passed through North-Carolina, was left behind, he has made bold to attack a Post of ours at the Congaree Stores, he met with their usual success, and only lost a few men and all his baggage; since that Colonel Watson has

---

5. Undated, un-addressed letter from Lt. Col. John Watson, Sir Henry Clinton Papers, Volume 232, item 21, CL.

had him hem'd up in a large swamp; news was yesterday brought to town that they had had an action, Sumpter got off with eighteen men killed and five wounded made prisoners; Lieutenant Cowper, of Buskirk's battalion, has gained immortal honour, he was sent with twenty men to a mill for grain, some accident happened [to] his wagon, and before he got fit to proceed to camp, found himself entirely surrounded by Sumpter's whole army, he charged through the whole of them, finding it still impossible to prevent being again surrounded, he ordered his men to form the hollow square, and defended himself upwards of an hour against Sumpter's whole army, until Colonel Watson came up and drove off Sumpter.[6]

Lt. Col. Nesbitt Balfour, commandant of Charleston, sent the following description to Sir Henry Clinton:

In my letter of the 24th Ultimo, I had the honor to communicate to your Excellency, the situation of the Congarees, & of its being invested by a Force under Colo. Sumpter. I have now the honor to inform you, that by the good Conduct of [Brevet] Major [Andrew] Maxwell of the Prince of Wales's [American] Regiment, the Rebels were repulsed in their attempts on that Post. They next turn'd their views to Thompson's & were there likewise Defeated, with some loss. Sumpter, then reconnoitred Nelson's; but finding it too Strong, pass'd the Santee five Miles above that, where he was opposed by some Provincial Light Infantry under Lieut. Colonel Watson, & obliged to Retreat with the loss of Eighteen Killed, a few taken, & many Horses.

This Action was brought on by Sumpter's having surrounded Lieut. Cooper with a Small Party of the Light Infantry,–on which occasion, Colonel Watson mentions, with high Applause, the meritorious Conduct, & Gallant Resistance of that Officer, & which I therefore think it my Duty to communicate to your Excellency.[7]

Col. Francis, Lord Rawdon, commanding at Camden, penned his own brief account from there on March 7, 1781:

Sumter, finding his rear was not pressed, undertook to cross the Santee by swimming his Horses, & passing his Men in two Canoes which he found by accident at Fludd's Plantation. He effected his

6. *The Royal Gazette* (New York), March 21, 1781.
7. Nesbitt Balfour to Sir Henry Clinton, March 3, 1781, Colonial Office, Class 5, Volume 184, folio 155, Great Britain, The National Archives. Hereafter cited as TNA.

purpose on the 27th, & the same evening, fell in with Lt. Col. Watson. An action ensued, in which the Enemy were forced to fly, leaving 18 dead on the field, several wounded, & about forty Horses. Our loss was only a Subaltern & Seven Privates wounded. Harrison's people, mounted & armed with Swords behaved very gallantly routing the Enemy's Cavalry regularly formed & thrice their number.[8]

Following the anti-partisan campaigns, the Provincial Light Infantry was but a fraction of its original strength. Losses by desertion, death, and capture lessened its numbers and effectiveness, which was only made worse by Lieutenant Colonel Watson's return home that summer on leave, the command then devolving on Maj. Thomas Barclay of the Loyal American Regiment. Its last large engagement was its biggest and bloodiest, serving in Brig. Gen. Alexander Stewart's force at the Battle of Eutaw Springs on September 8, 1781, losing forty-eight officers and men out of one hundred and eight engaged, including Captain Van Buskirk seriously wounded.[9]

Ensign Cooper however had done well that day in February, and was promoted to lieutenant the following year. Much hard fighting would continue until the company returned to the New York area in the summer of 1782. Cooper and Van Norden on their return joined other officers of the battalion in forming what would become the St. George's Masonic Lodge, serving in garrison duty until the end of the war.[10]

8. Francis, Lord Rawdon to Charles, Earl Cornwallis, March 7, 1781, Cornwallis Papers, PRO 30/11/69, folios 7-11, TNA.

9. "Return of Killed, Wounded, and Missing in the Army Commanded by Lieut. Colonel Alexander Stewart in the Action at Eutaws September 8th 1781." Colonial Office, Class 5, Volume 104, Page 271, TNA.

10. William Silas Whitehead, *Origin of Masonry in the State of New Jersey: and the Entire Proceedings of the Grand Lodge from its First Organization, A.L. 5786.* (Trenton: Published by Joseph H. Hough, Murphy & Bechtel, Printers, 1870), xxvii.

A Yorktown Footnote:
The Last Days of Colonel
Alexander Scammell

❧ WILLIAM W. REYNOLDS ☙

The highest-ranking Continental army officer to die as a result of wounds received during the Siege of Yorktown in 1781 was Col. Alexander Scammell, 34-year-old commander of the New Hampshire Regiment.[1] The descriptions of his capture and wounding in the many published accounts of the siege contain inconsistencies about where he was captured and associated events. In addition, they are silent as to how he was transported from Yorktown, where he was wounded, over twelve miles to the Continental army hospital at Williamsburg, where he died.[2] Recently discovered evidence of the latter prompted the author to study contemporary reports of the events leading to his death with the objective of resolving those inconsistencies.

The combined Continental army-French army (Allied Army) under Gen. George Washington marched from Williamsburg to Yorktown on September 28, 1781, to complete the isolation of the British army begun when the French navy blockaded the Chesapeake Bay. During the night of September 29–30, the British commander, Lt. Gen. Charles, Lord Cornwallis, ordered the withdrawal of his

1. Henry P. Johnston, *The Yorktown Campaign and the Surrender of Cornwallis 1781* (New York: Harper & Brothers, 1881), 192.
2. "Narrative of Ada Redington," typescript in the library of the Colonial Williamsburg Foundation, 12, contains an ambiguous statement concerning Scammell's return to the Continental army. That statement could be interpreted to mean that the British returned Scammell to the Continental army at Yorktown. The direct testimony by Pvt. Erasmus Chapman below proves that Redington did not know precisely how Scammell was returned to American lines, and kept his account vague on purpose. Redington's original manuscript is owned by Stanford University whose on-line catalog states that it was written in 1838.

forces from its outer defensive works based on his expectation that the British Fleet could break the naval blockade and bring him reinforcements. Early on September 30 American pickets, scouting in advance of the Continental army camps near the center of the Allied Army line, determined there were no British forces in the earthworks they faced and began to probe cautiously towards Yorktown. Col. Alexander Scammell, field officer of the day that began early on September 29 and ended early on September 30, led the pickets in their probing as soon as dawn provided sufficient light, i.e., soon after 5:35 a.m.[3]

A small British cavalry patrol under Lt. Allan Cameron left cavalry headquarters at the Moore House east of Yorktown at dawn in a search for isolated Allied soldiers to capture. They probably reached the position in front of Scammell and his men, northwest of the earthwork called Poplar Tree Fort by the Americans, well before the 6:01 a.m. sunrise, i.e., during the twilight period.[4] Colonel Scammell's account of what happened next was recorded a few days later by a visitor:

> . . . he mistook a few of the enemy's light horse for [Col. Stephen] Moylan's; he thought he knew the officer in front, and was therefore not alarmed. Two of them rode up to him, one of which seized his bridle, while the other pointed a pistol at him. Being thus in their power, and enquiring who they were, a third rode up and shot him in the back, at so near a distance as to burn his coat with the powder; another soldier then made a pass at him with his sword, but being weakened with his wound, and his horse starting at the

3. Jerome A. Greene, *The Guns of Independence: The Siege of Yorktown, 1781* (New York: Savas Beatie LLC, 2005), 114-118; John C. Fitzpatrick, ed., *The Writings of George Washington* 23 (Washington: Government Printing Office, 1937), 148; calculation of dawn ("Civil Twilight" or "when there is enough light for objects to be distinguishable, so that outdoor activities can commence") based on "Spectral Calc.Com" site, www.spectralcalc.com/solar_calculator/solar_position.php for September 30, 1781, and the latitude and longitude of Yorktown.

4. Banastre Tarleton, *A History of the Campaigns of 1780 and 1781 in the Southern Provinces of North America* (Dublin: Colles, Exshaw, White, H. Whitestone, Burton, Byrne, Moore, Jones, and Dornin, 1787), 382-383, 386; *A List of the Officers of the Army and Marines, with an Index* (Thirty-Ninth Edition) (London, 1791), 366; calculation of sunrise based on "Spectral Calc.Com" site.

report of the pistol, he happily fell to the ground and avoided the stroke. He was then plundered, taken to York.[5]

Some of Scammell's men were close enough to witness this episode but unable to act in time to rescue their commander. They reported what they had seen to Col. Philip Van Cortlandt who, as field officer of the day beginning September 30, had just arrived with his men to relieve Scammell.[6] Van Cortlandt described the situation thus:

> I found [Scammell's] men and relieved them; but the Colonel had, before my arrival, observed that [the British] had retired from the poplar-tree redoubt to the road in front, and mistook a British patrol of horse for our men, was under the necessity of surrendering, when one of their dragoons coming up, fired, and wounded the Colonel after his surrender, but whether the dragoon knew of the surrender, being behind him, I cannot say, but from all the information I could obtain, it was after his surrender.[7]

His report or that of Scammell's men spread throughout the Continental camp and within a few days made its way into several journals and letters.[8]

---

5. Letter of October 4, 1781, published in *Freeman's Journal* (Philadelphia) for October 24, 1781, Issue XXVII, 2-3, found on the website GenealogyBank.com. This letter was "written by a gentleman in Williamsburg" who also stated "I have seen his wound, and think he may recover." Clearly he had visited Scammell in the hospital and heard from him the account of his capture. Col. Stephen Moylan commanded the 4th Regiment of Continental Light Dragoons.

6. Philip Van Cortlandt, "Autobiography of Philip Van Cortlandt, Brigadier General in the Continental Army," *Magazine of American History* 2 (May 1978), 293; Fitzpatrick, *Writings of George Washington*, 152. Van Cortlandt placed the capture near the Poplar Tree Fort, which Tarleton described as a "field work . . . on the left [facing south] of the center, to command the Hampton road." Washington's October 2, 1781, letter in Fitzpatrick, *Writings of George Washington*, 157, says "Scammell . . . was wounded . . . as he was reconnoitering One of the Works, which had just been evacuated" which was true of the Poplar Tree Fort. Benson J. Lossing, *Pictorial Field Book of the Revolution* 2 (New York: Harper & Brothers, 1852), 515, places the capture near the Fusiliers' redoubt, on the far left of the Allied line. However, that redoubt, which had not been evacuated, was in front of the French portion of the line and was not likely to have been picketed by Continentals. Tarleton, who was not present at Scammell's capture, later wrote that the colonel was wounded while trying to escape, an account not supported by Scammell or the witnesses who described the action to Van Cortlandt.

7. Philip Van Cortlandt, "Autobiography of Philip Van Cortlandt," 293. Colonel Van Cortlandt clearly arrived within minutes of Scammell's capture.

8. "Journal of the Siege of York in Virginia by a Chaplain of the American Army," *Collections of the Massachusetts Historical Society* 9 (Boston: Hall & Hiller, 1804), 105; Lloyd A. Brown and Howard H. Peckham, eds., *Revolutionary War Journals of Henry*

The surviving British record of Scammell's capture is limited to brief mention in several private journals.[9] However the substance of subsequent events in Yorktown can be surmised with a reasonable degree of confidence. During the morning British army doctors realized that the colonel was seriously wounded and concluded that they had inadequate resources to care for him, especially in the face of the coming Allied attack or siege. Scammell knew that the Continental army had established a hospital in the empty governor's mansion in Williamsburg to provide care beyond that available in a field hospital, and requested parole in order to transfer to that facility. The British agreed to the parole and on the afternoon of September 30 sent under flag to the Allied lines a letter from Scammell to his next-in-command, Lt. Col. Ebenezer Huntington, asking him to send Scammell's personal baggage and servant to Williamsburg. Huntington complied with that request and also dispatched the regimental surgeon's mate, Dr. Eneas Munson, to Williamsburg to care for him.[10]

Dearborn 1775-1783 (Chicago: Caxton Club, 1939), 218 (erroneously dated October 1 instead of September 30); John Austin Stevens, "The Allies at Yorktown, 1781," *Magazine of American History* 6 (New York: A.S. Barnes & Company, 1881), 20-21.

9. Robert J. Tilden, "The Doehla Journal," *William and Mary Quarterly*, Second Series, 22 (July 1942), 247; Stephan Popp and Joseph G. Rosengarten, "Popp's Journal, 1777-1783," *Pennsylvania Magazine of History and Biography* 26 (1902), 40.

10. William Feltman, *The Journal of Lieut. William Feltman, of the First Pennsylvania Regiment, 1781-1782* (Philadelphia: Henry Carey Baird, 1853), 16; John Bell Tilden, "Extracts from the Journal of Lieutenant John Bell Tilden, Second Pennsylvania Line, 1781-1782," *Pennsylvania Magazine of History and Biography* 19, No. 1(1895), 59; Benson J. Lossing, *Reflections of Rebellion: Hours with the Living Men and Women of The Revolution* (London: History Press, 2007), 118; James D. Thacher, *A Military Journal during the American Revolutionary War, from 1775 to 1783* (Boston: Richardson and Lord, 1823), 319-320, 337. Feltman's journal contains the statement that Scammell's clothing was to be sent "to Williamsburg, where he would be sent on parole as soon as his wound was dressed" indicating that the British planned to send Scammell to Williamsburg that day rather than turn him over to the Americans to transport to Williamsburg; as will be seen, that is what occurred. Some accounts state that Scammell was paroled on September 30 and others say October 1. Since he was seriously wounded and the British agreed to parole him on the afternoon of September 30, there would have been no reason to keep him in Yorktown for another day; hence the statement in the text that he was sent to Williamsburg on September 30. Dr. Thacher seems to be the authority for the statement that Washington requested the parole of Scammell; however, no documentation of such a request, which would probably have been made on September 30, has been found.

The British then placed Scammell in one of their boats, possibly from one of the Royal Navy vessels supporting Cornwallis, sailed it up the York River to the mouth of Queen's Creek,[11] then sailed and rowed it up that creek to Capitol Landing, a voyage of twelve miles requiring up to six hours.[12] Virginia militiaman Pvt. Erasmus Chapman was on guard there:

> [W]hile the army continued [at Williamsburg] I frequently stood sentry at a place called the stone bridge which was made over a creek that emtied into York river not far distant[.] [W]hile on duty one night a boat sailed or was rowed up the creek to the bridge, I hailed it, and deterred the boat till a file of men and an officer from our camp came; the boat proved to be a British one, and came with a flag bearing an American colonel who had been taken prisoner by them and was dangerously wounded. I may have forgotten his name but I now think the colo's name was either Scamel or Campbell. He was immediately sent to the Doctors at Williamsburg on a litter[.] [T]he British boat was suffered to return.[13]

11. "Carte des Environs de Williamsburg en Virginie ou les Amees Francoise et Americaine ont Campe's en Septembre 1781. Armee de Rochambeau, 1782." Map Division, Library of Congress; National Oceanic and Atmospheric Administration Chart 12243, "York River-Yorktown to West Point." The former names this stream "Queen's Creek" while the latter calls it "Queen Creek."

12. Jack Coggins, *Ships and Seamen of the American Revolution* (Harrisburg: Promontory Press, 1969), 41-42; Andrew Norris emails to Bill Reynolds, March 29, 2015, March 30, 2015, April 26, 2015, and April 27, 2015 re: York River and Queen's Creek; Log of *HMS Fowey*, September 29–October 1, 1781, ADM 52/1748, UK National Archives, Kew. The boat used could have been the launch or cutter from the frigate *Chalon*. Andrew Norris of the York River Yacht Club provided insight as to the range of time required to sail (supplemented by rowing) from Yorktown to Capitol Landing, based on wind direction from *Fowey*'s log. Assuming the journey began soon after Scammell's letter was delivered to the American army on the afternoon of September 30, arrival at Capitol Landing should have been during the early evening. Based on "Spectral Calc.Com" sunset was at 5:50 p.m. so arrival would have been in darkness lit by a nearly full moon, which rose about 5:30 p.m.

13. Revolutionary War Pension Application (RWPA) R1867 for Erasmus Chapman, filed in 1832, National Archives and Records Administration, Washington, DC, Record Group 15, "Records of the Veterans Administration," microfilm publication M804. A copy of the original document was accessed via the website fold3.com. Chapman served in Capt. John Tankersley's Company of militia from Spotsylvania County, Virginia. RWPA S30457 for Nathan Hawkins states that this company moved from Williamsburg to Yorktown around October 9. On September 30 it was acting as a rear guard for the Allied Army that had marched to Yorktown two days earlier. According to RWPA S48512 for John Tankard, the "Doctors at Williamsburg" included Tankard, Matthew Pope, and John M. Galt. The "stone bridge lately erected at the

The wounded colonel had just over a mile to travel to the hospital in Williamsburg where he probably arrived late in the evening of September 30.[14]

The early visitor mentioned above thought Scammell would recover from the wound. Dr. Munson later reported that he remained with the colonel during the following days and initially he also thought that he would recover. Scammell told Munson and several visitors the details of his capture and wounding, confirming the account given to Van Cortlandt. On October 6 the colonel's condition worsened and he died about 5:00 p.m.[15] He was buried with full military honors, presumably in Williamsburg though the specific location of his burial is unknown.[16] Lt. Col. David Humphreys of Washington's staff, a friend of Scammell's, wrote this fine epitaph:

Capitol Landing" is mentioned in the *Virginia Gazette*, March 24, 1777. According to Cara Harbecke and John Metz, *Phase I Archaeological Testing at Capitol Landing* (Williamsburg: Colonial Williamsburg Foundation, 2005), 2, remains of the stone bridge could still be seen in 1977.

14. This mode of returning Scammell to the Continental army requires comment. While it was more comfortable for him than a wagon ride from Yorktown to Williamsburg, it required far more effort by the British. A generous view is that they realized he was badly wounded and wished to get him to a hospital which could treat him as rapidly as possible.

15. Lossing, *Reflections of Rebellion*, 118; "Open letter to Earl Cornwallis from An American Soldier," dated at Annapolis October 30, 1781, in *Pennsylvania Gazette*, November 14, 1781, 1; Letter of October 4, 1781, published in *Freeman's Journal* (Philadelphia) for October 24, 1781, Issue XXVII, 2-3; Stevens, "The Allies at Yorktown, 20-21; Johnston, *The Yorktown Campaign*, 175; Octavius Pickering and Charles Wentworth, *The Life of Timothy Pickering* 1 (Boston: Little, Brown, and Company, 1867), 303. The writer of the October 30 letter stated that "the circumstances are precisely as related by the Colonel himself." Charles Coffin, compiler, *The Lives and Services of Major General John Thomas, Colonel Thomas Knowlton, Colonel Alexander Scammell, Major General Henry Dearborn* (New York: Egbert, Hovey & King, 1845), 100, gives Dr. Thacher as the authority for the statement that Scammell was wounded after surrendering. Thacher, who remained at Yorktown throughout the siege, must have obtained that information from Dr. Munson when the latter returned to Yorktown after Scammell's death.

16. Philip Van Cortlandt, "Autobiography of Philip Van Cortlandt," 293-294; William O. Clough, "Colonel Alexander Scammell," *Granite Monthly: A New Hampshire Magazine*, Vol. 14, No. 9 (September 1892), 273; Meredith Poole email to Bill Reynolds, April 3, 2015, re: Burials in the Garden of Governor's Palace; Coffin, *Lives and Services*, 100. Find-A-Grave Memorial #51790804 says that Scammell is "reportedly buried among the Revolutionary War graves located in the garden of the Governor's Palace" but Meredith Poole, Staff Archeologist, Colonial Williamsburg Foundation, notes that there is no record of names of the 158 burials in the garden of the Governor's Palace and that efforts to identify them have not been successful. Since records cited below indicate a marker was placed over the colonel's grave, he may have been buried in the Bruton Parish cemetery. No marker is extant.

To the Immortal Memory
of
Alexander Scammell, Esq;
Colonel of the first Regiment of New-Hampshire
(formerly Adjutant-General of the American Army)
who commanded a Regiment of Light-Infantry
at the
Siege of York in Virginia;
Where, in performing his Duty gallantly,
He was unfortunately captured,
And
Afterwards mortally wounded,
He expired 6th October 1781.
Anno Aetatis 34.[17]

17. Stevens, "The Allies at Yorktown," 21; *Boston Evening Post* (Boston), November 24, 1781, Vol. I, Issue 6, 3; Frederic Kidder, *History of the First New Hampshire Regiment in the War of the Revolution* (Albany: Joel Munsell, 1868), 104. The full epitaph was on "a Stone erected by the Army" (or a "monumental tablet") and included a poem that is omitted here. Frank Landon Humphreys, *Life and Times of David Humphreys* 1 (New York: G.P. Putnam's Sons, 1917), 224, contains a slightly different version of the epitaph and poem.

Propaganda Warfare:
Benjamin Franklin Fakes a Newspaper

❧ HUGH T. HARRINGTON ☙

"The press, Watson, is a most valuable institution, if you only know how to use it," said the fictional detective Sherlock Holmes.[1] Benjamin Franklin had a lifetime of experience with the press and knew well how to use it.

In the spring of 1782, five months after Yorktown, Franklin was in Paris working on the complex diplomatic problems involved in negotiating a peace treaty among Britain, France, Spain, the Netherlands, and the United States. Franklin was seeking, among other things, reparations to the United States citizens who had lost their lives and property. Appealing to the British government would likely prove unsuccessful. So Franklin aimed at reaching the British citizens.

Franklin's weapon used in this propaganda warfare operation was the *Boston Independent Chronicle* newspaper. With great skill Franklin created a counterfeit issue of the newspaper,[2] carrying articles written by himself. He intended to have this fake newspaper very discreetly put into the hands of British newspaper editors who he hoped would reprint the articles in their papers. Reprinting articles was common at the time. If successful, his phony articles would then be read by huge numbers of British citizens.[3]

The hoax newspaper purported to be a *Supplement to the Boston Independent Chronicle*, dated "Boston, March 12." The supplement, spu-

---

1. This quotation appears in the short story *The Adventure of the Six Napoleons*, published April 1904.
2. Franklin had a complete printing shop as his position required that he print passports, forms, and official documents.
3. The best authority on the Supplement hoax is Carla Mulford, "Benjamin Franklin's Savage Eloquence: Hoaxes from the Press at Passy, 1782," *Proceedings of the American Philosophical Society*, vol. 152, No. 4 (December 2008), 490-530.

riously identified as "Numb. 705," consisted of one sheet of paper with two articles plus advertisements making it appear in all respects to be a true supplement to the legitimate newspaper.

The primary article in the hoax supplement concerned wartime atrocities by Indians at the behest of the British. The secondary article purported to be a letter from John Paul Jones and was also aimed at the British public. The "Jones" letter denounces the British policies that put captured American sailors in prisons under deplorable conditions with little hope of exchange. This letter did not have the gory fascination of the Indian atrocities letter and received little attention.

The Indian atrocity article appeared to be a legitimate letter from an American militia officer, Captain Samuel Gerrish, to his commanding officer describing a captured letter and packages which had been intended for the British governor of Canada. The officer wrote that he was "struck with Horror to find among the Packages, 8 large ones containing SCALPS of our unhappy County-folks, taken in the three last Years by the Senneka Indians from the Inhabitants of the Frontiers of New York, New Jersey, Pennsylvania, and Virginia, and sent by them as a Present to Col. Haldimand, Governor of Canada, in order to be by him transmitted to England."

The article continued with an alleged letter from a British agent accompanying the eight packages which described their contents in grisly detail:

> At the Request of the Senneka Chiefs I sent herewith to your Excellency, under the Care of James Boyd, eight Packs of Scalps, cured, dried, hooped and painted, with all the Indian triumphal Marks, of which the following is Invoice and Explanation.
>
> No. 1. 43 Scalps of Congress Soldiers killed in different Skirmishes; these are stretched on black Hoops, 4 Inches diameter; the inside of the Skin painted red, with a small black Spot to note their being killed with Bullets. Also 62 of Farmers, killed in their houses; the Hoops red; the Skin painted brown, and marked with a Hoe; a black Circle all round, to denote their being surprised in the Night; and a black hatchet in the Middle, signifying their being killed with that Weapon.
>
> No. 2. Containing 98 of Farmers killed in their Houses . . .
>
> No 3. Containing 97 of Farmers, killed in their fields . . . .
>
> No. 4. Containing 102 of Farmers . . . 18 marked with a little yellow flame, to denote their being of Prisoners burnt alive, after being

scalped, and their Nails pulled out by the roots and other Torments: one of these latter supposed to be of a rebel clergyman, his Band being fixed to the Hoop of his Scalp. Most of the Farmers appear by the hair to be young or middle-aged Men; there being but 67 very grey Heads among them all . . .

No. 5. Containing 88 scalps of Women; hair long, braided in the Indian Fashion, to shew they were Mothers; . . . 17 others, hair very grey . . . no other Mark but the short Club . . . to shew they were knocked down dead, or had their Brains beat out.

No. 6. Containing 193 Boys' Scalps of various Ages . . .

No. 7. 211 Girls Scalps, big and little . . .

No. 8. This package is a Mixture of all the Varieties above mention'd, to the number of 122; with a box of Birch Bark, containing 29 little infants Scalps of various sizes; . . . a little black Knife in the middle to shew they were ript out of their Mothers' Bellies.

Included along with the packages was a "Speech" from the chiefs directed to the British governor of Canada requesting that he "send these Scalps over the Water to the great King, that he may regard them and be refreshed; and that he may see our faithfulness in destroying his Enemies, and be convinced that his Presents have not been made to ungrateful people." In addition the chiefs wrote that, "we are poor, and you have Plenty of every Thing. We know you will send us Powder and Guns, and Knives and Hatchets: but we also want Shirts and Blankets."[4]

Of course, the use of Indian allies was commonplace in past wars. However, Franklin wanted the horrors of war, and especially the horrors of war against the civilian population, brought home to the British citizens. In addition, he wanted to show that the British government did not care about their Indian allies. It was their purpose to use the Indians to kill colonial Britons and in addition to make the Indians dependent upon the British for their supplies, even to the point of "Shirts and Blankets." This state of dependency was something that the colonists had claimed that the British were trying to do to the colonies.

In order to get the supplement into the hands of British printers Franklin sent copies to several correspondents. One he sent to John

---

4. The complete transcription of the Supplement is available at: Founders.archives. gov/documents/Franklin/01-37-02-0132.

Adams, in Amsterdam, admitting that the supplement might be untrustworthy but that the scalping issue was very real. He also sent copies to Charles Dumas, the American agent in the Netherlands, John Jay in Madrid, and James Hutton, a Moravian in England. His letters gently suggested that it would be useful if the supplement was printed in England.[5]

The "scalping" letter from the supplement was published in the *London General Advertiser and Morning Intelligencer*, June 29, 1782.[6] Much of it was also published in *The Remembrancer; or, Impartial Repository of Public Events* (London: J. Almon) in 1782.[7]

In North America the "scalping" letter was published dozens of times beginning with the *New Jersey Gazette* (Trenton, NJ) on December 18, 1782. The *Gazette* noted that it received the piece from the *London General Advertiser and Morning Intelligencer* of June 29, 1782, which cited the *Boston Independent Chronicle*. Clearly, the *New Jersey Gazette* assumed it was publishing a news event. In fact, it wasn't until over 70 years had passed before the October 4, 1854, *The State Gazette* (Trenton, NJ) described the scalping letter as a Benjamin Franklin hoax.[8]

The repulsive and gruesome hoax perpetrated by Franklin was propaganda skillfully designed and executed to demonize the former British ministry in the eyes of the British public. The current ministry would find it hard, facing such images, not to give in to American claims at the peace negotiations.[9]

5. Mulford, *Hoaxes*, 502, 516.
6. *London General Advertiser and Morning Intelligencer*, June 29, 1782.
7. Mulford, *Hoaxes*, 525.
8. Mulford, *Hoaxes*, 529.
9. Carl Van Doren, *Benjamin Franklin* (New York: Viking, 1938), 673.

India: The Last Battle of the American Revolutionary War

❦ JOHN L. SMITH, JR. ❦

The next time you're in a trivia contest and the question comes up, "What was the last battle of the American Revolutionary War?" the judges will probably be looking for the predictable answer of "Yorktown."[1]

That's the neat and tidy answer, but it's not true. After the defeat at Yorktown, King George III brushed it off as a minor stumbling block and decreed that the war in America should continue. He wrote to the prime minister avowing that he would "do what I can to save the Empire."[2] Gen. George Washington, not having read twenty-first century schoolbooks, never knew Yorktown would be considered the end of the war, or famously as the "last battle of the American Revolutionary War." He smartly assumed the British were certainly wounded with Lord Cornwallis' surrender, but that they wouldn't quit. The war would continue. Washington felt it was his absolute duty to keep the Continental army together until there was a final peace treaty signed *and* approved.

A preliminary treaty finally came on November 30, 1782, a year after Yorktown . . . but there was still no formal treaty. Washington remembered what Benjamin Franklin had said, "The British Nation seems . . . unable to carry on the War and too proud to make peace."[3]

1. Actually Yorktown wasn't even a battle. It was a siege. Two different things. You can correct the judges on that also, aside from what you learn in this article.
2. George III to Lord North, February 26, 1782, in Sir John Fortescue, ed., *The Correspondence of King George the Third from 1760 to December 1783* (London: Macmillan, 1927-1928), 5:326.
3. George Washington to Nathanael Greene, September 23, 1782, in John C. Fitzpatrick, ed, *The Writings of George Washington from the Original Manuscript Sources*, Vol. 25 (Washington, DC: Government Printing Office, 1939), 195.

The politicians were all still talking in Paris. Washington instinctively didn't trust the British and knew it could be a mistake to lower his guard of them, even while talks were going on. As late as January 1783, from Newburgh, New York, he wrote to Maj. John Armstrong that he suspected Parliament would still "provide vigorously for the prosecution of the war."[4]

But in the meantime, between Yorktown and the preliminary peace treaty, there were at least forty-four more documented world-wide battles, sieges, actions, incidents, and skirmishes of the American Revolutionary War.[5]

France officially entered the war in 1778, followed eventually by Spain and the Netherlands. What was once a provincial police action by the British in their American colonies soon became a world war. Britain essentially abandoned fighting the Continental army in the stalemated northern states and switched to a southern strategy. Thinking that the population in the southernmost states was more Loyalist friendly, the strategy also allowed Britain to keep its fleet and armies closer to their real economic strong box of the Caribbean (and Jamaica, in particular). Great Britain began to focus on protecting its world-wide economic interests from French and Spanish plunder.[6] Some of these global hotspots included the West Indies, Gibraltar and the Mediterranean, Africa, and India.

India, long the profitable domain of the British East India Company, was literally a world away from Great Britain and from any means of speedy communication in the late eighteenth century. Word of the signing of the Revolutionary War preliminary peace treaty in Paris didn't arrive in India for quite a while after the ink was dry.

---

4. George Washington to Major Armstrong, January 10, 1783, at memory .loc. gov/ cgi-bin/query/r?ammem/mgw:@field(DOCID +@lit(gw260041)) (accessed May 13, 2015); The Writings of George Washington from the Original Manuscript Sources, 1745-1799. John C. Fitzpatrick, Editor.

5. en.wikipedia.org/wiki/List_of_American_Revolutionary_War_battles. The exact number is unknown. The brutal partisan fighting in the southern states continued and is not counted in this cited listing. One particular battle in April 1783 may have been the last battle fought on American shores. It was between British and Spanish forces and fought in Louisiana, although the location would now be considered Arkansas. It was called the Battle of Arkansas Post. A Smithsonian publication lists the final battle of the American Revolutionary War on American soil as happening in November 1782 "between American, Loyalist, and Shawnee forces in the Ohio territory." Stuart A. P. Murray, *Smithsonian Q&A: The American Revolution* (Irvington, NY: HarperCollins Publishers, 2006), 103.

6. This is in addition to the fact that Britain had to keep some of its naval fleet near its own shores to protect itself from a perceived Franco-Spanish invasion. The threat of a copy-cat revolution in Ireland was also a concern in Parliament.

Thus, your correct answer to the trivia question should be, "the last battle of the American Revolutionary War was fought in India."[7]

THE BACK STORY

Since the 1600s, both Great Britain and France had colonies in India. But when France declared war against Britain in 1778 and entered into the American Revolutionary War, the British East India Company (which actually had *its own soldiers!*) decided to attack the other French colonies in India. To help out, the British government told the company that they would also send some British army regulars to India, along with some hired Hanoverians.

For history book labeling, this started the Second Anglo-Mysore War lasting from 1780 to 1784 (you can think of it as a war within a war). It was also the second of four Anglo-Mysorean wars, but there's no need to get hung up on the numbers. The only thing you have to remember is that our indirect ally in this off-shoot war was a guy named Hyder Ali, the Sultan of Mysore. Ali had allied himself with our friends, the French, early on and because of his ferocity and military expertise, he became a real pain for Great Britain until his death[8] in December 1782. From 1780 to 1783, the Franco-Mysorean forces fought the British all over western and eastern India in far-off-sounding places like Mahé and Mangalore.

By early 1783 and now that Hyder Ali was dead, the British decided to retake the important and ancient seaport city of Cuddalore, on India's eastern shore of the Bay of Bengal. British Gen. James Stuart left Madras with his army bound for the French-Mysorean garrison quartered in the fortress of Cuddalore. It's not like they were all strangers there—the British and French had already battled in Cuddalore during the earlier Seven Years' War. But this time, General Stuart came equipped to besiege Cuddalore into surrender. British command was also sending a warship fleet to reinforce Stuart's siege

7. Andrew Jackson O'Shaughnessy, *The Men Who Lost America: British Leadership, the American Revolution, and the Fate of the Empire* (New Haven, CT: Yale University Press, 2013), 14.

8. Hyder Ali (Khan) did not die in battle, but rather from a cancerous growth on his back in December 1782. His son, Tipu Sultan, took over his father's command of Mysorean forces in 1783. The Third and Fourth Anglo-Mysorean Wars were then fought. With the death of Tipu Sultan, Mysore finally fell in 1799 to the British East India Company forces. Incidentally, Hyder Ali was illiterate, but spoke six languages. He also invented Mysorean rockets which he used against British East India Company soldiers. These were the first rockets to be enclosed in iron casings. After the wars, the British did technical innovations to Ali's rockets and developed the Congreve rockets . . . which they used against Americans in the War of 1812.

Siege of Cuddalore, June 1783 by Richard Simkin, 1890. (*Anne S. K. Brown Military Collection, Brown University Library*)

through a naval blockade of Cuddalore. The French heard about it and readied their own fleet of battleships to reinforce their loyal soldiers and to battle the slightly superior British fleet.

The last battle of the American Revolutionary War in the summer of 1783 was shaping up to be a major engagement—halfway around the world from America.

THE SIEGE OF CUDDALORE (JUNE 7–JUNE 25, 1783)

Under the steamy summer sun of east India, the British forces arrived outside the fortress of Cuddalore on June 7. The British army had bolstered the troops owned by the British East India Company, and had added assistance with Bengal sepoys and Carnatic battalions of the Bengal army. "The next five days were spent in landing guns, tools, ammunition, and a detachment of the 16th Hanoverians."[9] The British formed initial siege lines facing the Cuddalore fort, stretching from the seashore to the hills. The French-Mysoreans themselves, under Marquis de Bussy-Castelnau and Sayed Sahib, formed up facing the British lines and began the construction of trenches and redoubts as protection against the expected siege and assault. To support the siege, eighteen British ships of the line (the battleships of the time)

9. Lieutenant-Colonel W. J. Wilson, *History of the Madras Army* (Madras: E. Keys, Government Press, 1882), 2:76.

under Sir Edward Hughes, had arrived and anchored off of Cuddalore creating a naval blockade.

Just one week later, on June 13, the British decided to attack a Franco-Mysorean redoubt to put them into a better position for the coming siege. But an unplanned, all-out skirmish began with attacks and counterattacks by both sides. The ferocious fighting (each side is said to have committed about 11,000 soldiers) lasted until the two warring factions counted about a thousand casualties each. Both sides retired to lick their wounds, and the French-Mysoreans fled back behind the fortress walls. General Stuart then began the siege bombardment of Cuddalore.

THE (NAVAL) BATTLE OF CUDDALORE (JUNE 20, 1783)

But, surprise, the French fleet under Adm. Pierre Andre de Suffren sailed up on the evening of June 16. The fifteen French ships of the line also carried 1,200 reinforcements.

"Suffren sailed to contest the blockade, though his ships were in poor shape, undermanned, and outnumbered. He cleverly maneuvered to draw the British out of the Cuddalore roadstead and occupied it himself."[10]

Admiral Suffren asked the Cuddalore commanders if he could keep the 1,200 reinforcement troops he had transported onboard ship, so that the ship gunnery crews would be well manned. With those extra personnel aboard, "he boldly went out to attack the superior British force."[11]

The two fleets aligned themselves in the wind on June 20 and began cannonading each other. The three-hour long naval battle unfolded in the late afternoon, amazingly with light casualties on both sides and without a lot of damage to either fleet. Although basically a draw, the Battle of Cuddalore goes down in history books as a French victory because the British disengaged and then both fleets sailed away from each other. Soon after though, Sir Edward and his ships set sail back to Madras since they were very short of drinking water and were experiencing a "severe outbreak of scurvy, from which nearly 2,000 men were in hospital."[12]

That left the French fleet to be able to sail up to Cuddalore again, and Admiral Suffren was able to disembark his promised 1,200 soldiers that he had borrowed earlier from the fortress defenders, along

---

10. R.G. Grant, *Battle at Sea: 3,000 Years of Naval Warfare* (New York: DK Publishing, 2011), 169.
11. Ibid., 169.
12. Wilson, *History of the Madras Army*, 80.

with an additional 2,400 reinforcement troops. "Upon the departure of the British squadron to Madras, M. de Suffrein immediately proceeded to Cuddalore, where he not only returned the 1,200 land forces which had been lent by the Marquis de Bussy, but he landed 2,400 of his own men from the fleet, as a most powerful aid to the defence."[13]

THE FRENCH COUNTER-SIEGE ATTACK (JUNE 25, 1783)

With the additional soldiers and replenished supplies, the French-Mysoreans inside Cuddalore decided to strike out again against the besieging British. On June 25, they repeatedly made attacks against the British lines and repeatedly were driven back, sustaining heavy losses each time. The French attacks were a disaster. Many French officers were taken prisoner, including the assault commander Chevalier de Dumas, a very high-ranking officer. Also taken prisoner was a sergeant in the Régiment de Royal-Marine, Jean Bernadotte, who survived his capture and lived through the Cuddalore expedition. In an example of a great career path, he eventually was named Marshal of the Empire by Napoléon, which led him to becoming the King of Sweden.

THE DISINTEGRATION OF THE SIEGE AND WORD OF THE TREATY (JUNE 29, 1783)

After nearly a month of fighting, both on land and in the Bay of Bengal, the British along with the French-Mysoreans were becoming weary and disillusioned. Both sides were racked with disease and thirst. The sick and wounded on both sides were dying at an alarming rate.

General Stuart felt like he'd been abandoned by British command and fired off angry letters from Cuddalore to the Madras government. He was soon fired and sent back to England in disgrace where he had to fight a duel to defend his honor; he was severely wounded.

Marquis de Bussy was also dealing with disheartened defenders because of the many failed attempts to break out of the siege. But unlike the treatment of Stuart, de Bussy was soon honored for holding out during the British siege. He was made the governor general of

13. Edmund Burke, *The Annual Register, or a View of the History, Politics, and Literature for the Year 1783* (London: J. Dodsley, Pall-Mall, 1785), 112; books.google.com/ books? id=Mr0vAAAAYAAJ&pg=PA112&dq=Cuddalore+1,200+reinforcements&hl=en&s a=X&ei=CghZVd37KILdsAWVy4GgBg&ved=0CCMQ6AEwAQ#v=onepage&q= Cuddalore%201%2C200%20reinforcements&f=false (accessed May 17, 2015).

Pondicherry, another important port city in India, but died in 1785, just two years after the siege.

On June 29, with both sides of the Cuddalore siege disintegrating in the oppressive heat of late June, a British vessel flying a white truce flag sailed up to Cuddalore. Sir Edward wrote, "on June 27, I dispatched his Majesty's ship *Medea*, as a flag of truce, with letters to M. Suffrein and the Marquis de Bussy."[14] The letters carried news that the American Revolutionary War was over. An initial peace treaty had been signed on November 30, 1782, seven months *before* the siege and the Battle of Cuddalore. But there was no way to get the news to eastern India any faster. The final Treaty of Paris was signed on September 3, 1783, and ratified by Congress a few months later. Under the terms of the treaty with the French, ironically, a curious game of India musical chairs happened. Britain gave Pondicherry back to the French, and (after all that) Cuddalore was awarded back to the British.

The final battle of the American Revolutionary War had happened. It hadn't been fought in a New England meadow, in a forested wilderness, or in a southern swamp. It had been fought in the Bay of Bengal and outside the fortress of Cuddalore, India.

You'll really win the trivia contest with *that* one!

14. James Boswell, "Affairs in the East Indies—App 1783; Extract of a Letter from Vice-Adm. Sir Edward Hughes to Mr. Stephens," *Scots Magazine*, Vol. 45 (1783), 685, 688; books.google.com/books?id=Tt8RAAAAYAAJ&pg=PA682&hl=en #v= one page&q=Cuddalore&f=false (accessed May 13, 2015).

A Spy Wins a Purple Heart

☙ TODD W. BRAISTED ❧

On June 8, 1783, Gen. George Washington issued the following orders to the Continental army from his headquarters in Newburgh, New York:

> Serjeant Bissel of the 2d Connecticut regt. having performed some important services, within the immediate knowledge of the Commander in chief, in which the fidelity, perseverence, and good sense of the said serjeant Bissel were conspicuously manifested; it is therefore ordered that he be honored with the badge of merit; he will call at Head Quarters on tuesday next for the insignia and certificate to which he is hereby entitled.[1]

The badge of merit had been recently instituted; although the design inspired the Purple Heart medal, at this time it was awarded for distinguished service. "Serjeant Bissel" was the third and final recipient of this prestigious mark of recognition. Who was he and what were the "important services?"

Daniel Bissell enlisted in the spring of 1777 in Windsor, Hartford County into Capt. Abner Prior's Company of the 5th Connecticut Regiment, commanded by Col. Philip B. Bradley. In this corps he served until the Connecticut Line was reorganized in 1781, when he became a sergeant in Col. Heman Swift's 2nd Connecticut Regiment. On August 14 of that year he was dispatched on a secret mission by Lt. Col. Robert Harrison, one of Washington's aides-de-camp. The mission was to pose as a deserter and gather intelligence on British

---

1. John C. Fitzpatrick, ed. The Writings of George Washington from the Original Manuscript Sources, 1745–1799, Vol. 26 (Washington, DC: Government Printing Office, 1939), 481.

military strength in New York City, presumably with a view of utilizing it in formulating an attack on the city.

The following day, Bissell arrived in New York City. To effect his mission he took the extraordinary step of immediately enlisting in a Provincial regiment of the British army. He joined the American Legion, the combined infantry and cavalry unit commanded by none other than Brig. Gen. Benedict Arnold. Bissell later explained his enlistment as a measure to avoid being pressed into the Royal Navy,[2] but there is no evidence to corroborate that claim. While presses were sometimes made in the city they were usually chronicled by Maj. Frederick Mackenzie of the Adjutant General's Department, but Mackenzie noted none at that time. Bissell may have been warned by others that he was liable to be seized should a press occur, but he also may have simply recognized that American deserters frequently joined Loyalist regiments and saw it as a relatively easy way to accomplish his task.

Bissell pointed out "that he never bore arms against America, having been confined in the hospital or employed in the Quarter Master's department the whole time."[3] There is no evidence of the latter, but the Legion's muster of November 1781 does record that he was confined in the hospital. The Legion was part of the expedition to Connecticut under General Arnold that led to the burning of New London and the storming of Fort Griswold on September 6; for Bissell not to have participated, and therefore served against his country, he must have gone into the hospital within two weeks of his enlistment or been assigned to some sort of detached duty. He served constantly thereafter with the Legion garrisoning of posts around New York City, first at Ireland Heights, then Fresh Meadows, Harlem Lane, and finally being ordered to Staten Island on May 27, 1782.[4] Here he served at the Flag Staff post until deserting back to the Continental army on the night of September 26, 1782. Four others, including two sergeants, deserted from the Legion at the same time.

Upon his arrival back into the Continental army, Bissell made a very detailed report of British troop strength and the state of their fortifications. The information would have been invaluable if an attack on New York had gone forward. However, events had long since overtaken the importance of his original mission. Almost immediately after

---

2. Pension deposition of Daniel Bissell, US National Archives, Collection M-804, Pension and Bounty Land Application Files, No. W23604, Daniel Bissell (Theoda), Connecticut.
3. Ibid.
4. Benjamin Craven Orderly Book, Newberry Library, Vault Case MSF 8326.2.

Bissell's entry into British lines Washington had determined against attacking New York, opting instead to concentrate his efforts against British forces in Virginia. It is a mystery why Bissell waited thirteen months to return to the Americans. There were frequent desertions of British, German, and Provincial soldiers from Staten Island, and indeed all the New York posts, throughout Bissell's time with them. Yet his report states that he "frequently" made efforts to return, but could not until September of 1782. Regardless, his account provides an interesting glimpse of intelligence gathering as seen through the eyes of a non-commissioned officer. Of particular interest is the level of detail given the fortifications around New York. He probably had the best knowledge of those on Staten Island, given that they were the freshest in his mind when he made his report and that he spent the most time around them.

Bissell's original account is in Series 4 of the George Washington Papers at the Library of Congress. It appears below in its entirety:

Substance of Information given by Sergt. Bissel of the 2nd Connecticut Regt., who was sent into N.Y. for the purpose of obtaining Intelligence in the month of Augt. 1781 by Col. H—— and made his Escape from Staten Island on the 27th of Septr. 1781.

He reports, that on his arrival in the City, there being a hot press to man the Kings Ships & finding no other means to avoid it, or escape, he enter but by entering into the land Service; he enlisted in Arnolds Corps, and never has had an opportunity of getting off until Thursday last, tho he has frequently made efforts to effect it[5]—in the mean time he has exerted his utmost care & ability in obtaining information of the strength & state of the Enemy's Force, which from his own knowledge & observation as well as the Information of others he believes to be nearly as follows viz.

	No. of men
{22nd Regt. British	340
On Staten Island {57 Regt. Do.	320
{2 Compys. British Grenads.	100
{Arnold's Corps	125
	885

NB The strength of these Corps he knows positively from his own observation having drawn provisions & done duty with them.

---

5. Daniel Bissell enlisted in Capt. Samuel Wogan's Company of the American Legion on August 15, 1781. He deserted from the post at the Flagstaff on Staten Island, along with four others, on September 29, 1782. National Archives of Canada, RG 8, "C" Series, Volume 1871, Page 29 & Volume 1872, 29.

	{7th Regt. British	300
	{37th Regt. Do.	360
	{40th Regt. Do.	300
On York Island	{42nd (two Battalions)	600
	{British Grenadiers not	
	{ joined their Corps	400[6]
	{17th Light Dragoons	260
		2220

NB This is the most accurate account he could obtain from Sergts. & others with whom he conversed—he cannot be positive as to the 7th Regt. which has lately arrived from Savannah,[7]

	{38th Regt.	300
On Long Island	{54th Regt. Do.	350
		650
Total		3755
Deduct Arnolds		125
Total British		3630[8]
Battalions of Delanceys Brigade		600
Skinners Brigade		700[9]
Kings American Dragoons		300
Pensylvania Loyalists		160[10]
Arnolds Corps		125
Total New raised Corps		1885[11]

6. These were the grenadier companies for corps that were not at New York or that had been taken prisoner at Yorktown, namely, the 17th, 23rd, 33rd, 43rd, 63rd, 64th, 70th, 74th & 76th regiments of foot.

7. The 7th Regiment had evacuated Savannah, Georgia, that July. They arrived in New York with about 260 officers and men. Great Britain, The National Archives, Colonial Office, Class 5, Volume 106, 333 (hereafter cited as TNA, CO 5).

8. The total British rank & file present and fit for duty on September 1, 1782, was actually 4,563. Some of the numbers Bissell reported exactly corresponded to the British troop return; he only neglected mentioning the very under-strength 3rd Battalion of the 60th Regiment. TNA, CO 5/107/220–221.

9. The 1st and 3rd (late 4th) Battalions, New Jersey Volunteers, commanded by Brig. Gen. Cortland Skinner.

10. This was about the combined strength of both the Maryland and Pennsylvania Loyalists. These units had been taken prisoner by the Spanish in May of 1781. They arrived in New York on parole the following July and were exchanged about a year later.

11. This number is amazingly close to the actual number of present and fit for duty on September 1, 1782: 1,846; however, there were more corps than he listed, including the Queen's Rangers and British Legion.

German Troops to the best of his knowledge   4000[12]
three hundred & fifty of which at Pawlis Hook

The method he took to obtain a knowledge of the strength of the several Corps, was by enquiring of the Sergts. & others with whom he was
acquainted and by comparing repeatedly the force at different Posts, from
the fuel Returns &c. He has also overheard Major Menzies (commandant
of Arnolds Corps) say that there were about 10,000 Troops in all this
Department exclusive of Militia, 4000 of which were Germans. He has
himself very frequently upon collecting intelligence, made memoran-
dums, & compared the several Reports together, but after Sir Guy
Carletons arrival & intimation being given that any Persons being discovered to have written Information would be treated as Spies; he was forced
to destroy his Papers & Estimates.

Sergt. Bissel further says, there are 24 sail of the Line now lying in
New York Harbour, that they are all of them refitting or have been
repaired since they came into Port. That a fleet sailed last Week, consisting of two Ships of the Line, one Frigate & twenty five Transports, said
to be bound to Charles Town, to effect the evacuation of that Garrison.[13]

That when he left Staten Island, four Ships had just come too, against
the Light House, one of which was a Prize under Jury Masts. He adds, all
Vessels (Private Property or not) which have been stript of their sails, &
laid up for a long time are now refitting for Sea. He believes there are
more than 100 Transports in the Harbour. Notwithstanding the preparations, &* a Certainty that the Heavy Artillery has been removed from the
Park, as to the amount of Twenty Peices of Brass Cannon (24 & 18
Pounders) which were supposed to be put on Board Transports in the
East River near the Ship Yards. Yet it is not the opinion of the Officers or
Citizens in general, that New York will be evacuated until next Spring. In
the mean time a number of Refugees are preparing to go to Halifax, the
number is reported to be 200,[14] but he did not hear of any British that
were to sail except the Officers & Non Commissd. Officers of Lord

12. This was the only number in which he was significantly off, there being over 7,000
Germans present with their corps and doing duty at the time. The troops at Paulus
Hook consisted primarily of a detachment of the Anhalt-Zerbst Regiment.
13. Charlestown, South Carolina, was indeed evacuated on December 14, 1782. 126
vessels carried troops and Loyalists to New York, St. Lucia, Jamaica, England, East
Florida, and Nova Scotia.
14. This was the garrison of Fort DeLancey on Bergen Point, New Jersey. The
Refugees were commanded by Major Thomas Ward. 471 men, women and children
embarked in early October for Digby, rather than Halifax. TNA, Headquarters Papers
of the British Army in America, TNA 30/55/5663.

Rawdons Corps, who are to go to Ireland.[15] As to magazines of Fuel & Forage he observes, tho considerable, they are not sufficiently large, but that the Enemy are daily encreasing them. It is expected whenever the British abandon New York, the New Corps will be sent to Canada. Annexed is a plan of the Enemy's works.

*This fact he knows from his own observation.

The Main fort on Staten Island is from East to West is about one Hundred & Forty feet Through and about one Hundred feet from the North Side to the South. The Intrenchmt. is About Ten feet Wide & Six Deep With a Row of pickquets[16] Set Up in the Senter of the Intrenchment, the Tops of the piquets About Level With the Surface of the Earth.[17] A Row of Abattis[18] about Two Rod, in front of the Intrenchment and About one Rod Through & about Breast High.

Their is a Row of piquets all Around the Breastwork Upon the Top of the Timber Which is Level With the Ground.

The fort Will Contain fifteen Hundred men the Heigth of the Breastwork is a Bout Five feet High and about 18 feet Through.

The Gate is on the South Side of the Fort Next to the Warter. The Door of the Bumproof[19] is facing that. Their is Fourteen Ambrasures[20] in the fort & Twelve Twenty four pounders Mounted in it, four pointed against the Warter Two Upon the North Side Two Upon the South Side Four Upon the West Side. If the fort was to be atacked it Would be Best Upon the South Side of it Next to the Warter by the Gate.

As you Enter the Gate Upon your Rite hand their is mounted Two Twenty four pounders Within fifthteen Rod South of the Gate their is a three Gun battery With Three Twenty four pounders.

About Twenty Rod Below that Their is a Nother Two Gun Battery With one Twenty four & one Eighteen pounder. One Nine pounder their Not mounted.

About Forty Rods below that is a Nother 3 Gun Battery With 2 Twenty Four pounders & one Thirty Two.

---

15. Lord Rawdon's corps was the Volunteers of Ireland. British General Orders for August 3, 1782, announced that the regiment in America would be drafted, with the commissioned and non-commissioned officers being sent to Ireland.

16. Piquets (or pickets), poles driven into the ground and standing straight up, at close intervals.

17. That is, the trench was six feet deep, and had a six-foot high wall of picquets in the middle of it.

18. Abbatis, an obstruction formed by felling trees so that the branches face the enemy.

19. Bombproof, an underground chamber covered with enough earth that mortar bombs cannot penetrate it.

20. Embrasures, cutouts in the parapet for cannon to fire through.

The Other fort Lies Southwest of the former it is four Squair With Much Such an Intrenchment[21] Picketed Abatiss With Two peses in the fort one 24 one 12 pounder. The Gait is Upon the East Side of the fort the platform the peses Stands Upon is on the West Side of the fort.

The Ditch or Coral[22] Runs in front of Byards Hill is a bout 14 Feet Wide and Ten Deep it Runs along Just in front of old fort Bunker Hill from the North River to the East River from the Top of the Hill at the East River it Runs a Long South Upon the East River Bank.

There is a Nother Coral Runs from What was Call'd Cobble Hill at Brookline along Upon the Edge of the Hill Till it Comes Down to the Water Up against the Old Ship Jersey in A Direct Line With that on York Island.

The Grand Battery at New York is of Late Ben Repair'd, it is Ben Drawn in Less Compers[23] but in the Same manner they have Now Mounted On the Grand battery In New York. Sixty Three peses of Cannon the Most part of them are Twenty Four pounders the Rest Eighteens & Nines.

21. That is, a trench much like the one of the other fort.
22. Bissell appears to use the word Corral to mean a ditch connecting a series of fortifications, but we have not found this term in any period military dictionary.
23. That is, encompassing a smaller area.

The Impact of Capt. Jonathan Carver's Journal and Maps on the 1782–1783 British-American Peace

❦ MERV O. AHRENS ❦

Captain Jonathan Carver was hired in August 1766 as a surveyor and draughtsman by Major Robert Rogers, the newly appointed governor-commandant of British Fort Michilimackinac. Rogers instructed Carver to familiarize himself with the northern Mississippi River basin and western Lake Superior region's geography, prepare a map of the area, and then, if directed, join an exploration team on a westward trek to discover a route to the Pacific Ocean.

Shortly after Carver's return to Michilimackinac in late August 1767, Rogers was arrested on a charge of treason and taken to Montreal. Although Carver was left unpaid for his year's work, he spent the ensuing winter and early spring at the fort working on his journal and survey plans before returning to his home near Boston, Massachusetts. Carver's explorations were recorded in his travel journal and on his manuscript map, compiled during and shortly after his travels in the region.[1] His geographic details were derived from personal surveys, reconnaissance, and from information shared by fellow traders, voyagers, and Native Americans he met during his twelve month mission of good will and discovery.

After his early September 1768 arrival in Boston, Carver offered its citizens an opportunity to subscribe to a publication of his journal and map. Because of insufficient local interest in his explorations and being desperate for money, he sailed for England in February 1769. His itin-

---

1. Jonathan Parker, ed., *The Journals of Jonathan Carver and Related Documents 1766-1770* (St. Paul: Minnesota Historical Society Press, 1976), 25-44 (hereinafter Parker, *The Journals*). Parker did a comparative analysis of Carver's published travel narrative and the versions of his MS journal and maps held by the British Library.

erary included collecting his overdue wages from the Crown and securing a publisher. Using a letter of introduction written by Reverend Samuel Cooper in Boston, Carver met face-to-face in London with Benjamin Franklin. As part of their meeting Carver likely enthusiastically shared his personal exploits, manuscript journal, and map. After conferencing with Carver, Franklin wrote to Cooper thanking him "for giving me an Opportunity of being acquainted with so great a Traveller. I shall be glad if I can render him any Service here."[2]

Carver finally self-published his journal-based book, *Travels through the Interior Parts of North-America in the Years 1766, 1767 and 1768* in London in 1778. It was an immediate best seller, being reprinted by publishers in London and Dublin in 1779, again in London in 1781, and many further editions in the following decades; in 1780, a German translation was published in Hamburg.[3] A first edition copy was almost immediately acquired by Franklin, who in 1778, was America's ambassador stationed in Paris, France.[4] Profits were not sufficient, however, to spare Carver from dying in poverty in early 1780.

The book contained a small engraving of his manuscript map.[5] His published map, titled *A PLAN of Captain Carver's Travels in the interior Parts of NORTH AMERICA in 1766 and 1767*, was first engraved by Thomas Kitchin and subsequently less professionally re-engraved before being included in *Travels*. It shows White Bear Lake (47^0 N 95^0 W) as the main northern source of the Mississippi River. The source is correctly positioned relative to the continental drainage divides, Red Lake and Lake du Bois (hereinafter Lake of the Woods). Carver's White Bear Lake might be any of the smaller lakes (Itasca, Winnibigoshish, Turtle, Bemidji, etc.) in north central Minnesota. A note on the map reads "The Head Branches of the Mississippi are little known Indians seldom travel this way except War Parties." The regional hydrology is shown with considerable accuracy.

2. National Historical Publications and Records Commission—Founders Online (hereinafter NHPRC-FO), founders.archives.gov/documents/Franklin/01-16-02-0056. Part of Franklin's 27 April 1769 letter to Rev'd Samuel Cooper, a Congregational minister in Boston.
3. Jonathan Carver, *Travels through the Interior Parts of North-America in the Years 1766, 1767 and 1768* (London: Printed for the Author; and Sold by J. Walter, at Charing-cross, 1778) (hereinafter *Travels*). This edition of Carver's book is available online at Internet Archive, static.torontopubliclibrary.ca/da/pdfs/37131055399208d.pdf.
4. NHPRC-FO, founders.archives.gov/documents/Franklin/01-28-02-0135. *Travels* is recorded on Franklin's November 1778 list of loaned books.
5. Parker, *The Journals*, 35. Carver's 1767-68 manuscript map is part of the Collection of the British Library, catalogue number Add.8949.f.41.

Carver's manuscript map coordinates were adjusted on his published map. For example, he placed the easternmost part of Lake of the Woods at 105 degrees West on his manuscript map whereas it is re-positioned at 96°30′ West on his published map (actual is approximately 94°W). Almost all geographic and text details from Carver's manuscript map were accurately transposed to his published map with little alteration or addition.

Carver's portrait is the frontispiece in *Travels*, 1781 London edition.

Dr. J. C. Lettsom, who likely sponsored the 1781 edition of Carver's *Travels*, sent Benjamin Franklin a letter along with a copy of the new release. Lettsom wrote,

> Sept. 13. 1781 . . . May I request Dr. Franklin's acceptance of the publications herewith sent. The octavo volume by Captn. Carver is more interesting, on acct. of the importance of a Country whose back settlements it describes, and which is one day destined, I hope to form the hemisphere of freedom.[6]

Carver investigated and collected considerable data on the source of the Mississippi River. This information appears on his maps and is expanded upon in *Travels*. His book relates,

> Not far from this Lake [Red Lake], a little to the south-west, is another called White Bear Lake, which is nearly about the size of the last mentioned. The waters that compose this Lake are the most northern of any that supply the Mississippi, and may be called with propriety its most remote source. It is fed by two or three small rivers or rather large brooks.[7] There are an infinite number of small lakes, on the westward parts of western head-branches of the Mississippi.[8]

---

6. NHPRC-FO founders.archives.gov/documents/Franklin/01-35-02-0357. The letter is from Franklin's acquaintance and Royal Society fellow in London. The copy of *Travels* sent to Franklin was a re-issue of Carver's book sponsored by Lettsom in 1781 (see Parker, *The Journals*, 41-42). A 1781 edition of *Travels* was part of Franklin's library; it is Volume 542 in Wolf and Hayes' inventory of his books.
7. Carver, *Travels*, 116.
8. Ibid., 93. Carver's interest in the northwesternmost branches of the Mississippi reflected his possible need to cross from the Mississippi to the Red River system en route to his intended 1767-68 wintering place near Fort des Praires on the Saskatchewan River. The latter route was known to the local natives and was later used by fur traders.

STEPS TOWARD PEACE

Britain's resolve to continue war in America diminished by early 1782. British peace emissary Richard Oswald met the United States' plenipotentiary Benjamin Franklin to determine grounds for securing an end to the war. Franklin, in Paris since 1776, responded with a list that included the voluntary surrender of Canada. American commissioner John Jay, previously on assignment in Madrid, emphasized their new country's claim to lands extending west to the Mississippi River, from its northwestern source southward towards its mouth. By September 1782, beginning peace talks in Paris were replaced with productive negotiations.

The first British-American draft accord, concluded in Paris, established among many requirements a boundary for the new United States.[9] Although no official map was part of any preliminary peace agreement, several editions of John Mitchell's famous 1755 map of North America served as drawing boards from which the boundary of the United States slowly emerged.[10]

FIRST DRAFT PEACE TREATY (EARLY OCTOBER 1782)

Oswald and Jay successfully concluded the first draft peace agreement that in part defined the northwest portion of the divide between their two nations.[11] They agreed the boundary would run from the intersection of the 45th North parallel and the St. Lawrence River "thence

9. Mary A. Giunta, et al., ed., *The Emerging nation, a documentary history of the foreign relations of the United States under the Articles of Confederation, 1780-1789* (Washington, DC: National Historical Publications and Records Commission, 1996), 598-599 (reference hereinafter Giunta, *Emerging Nation*).

10. *A Map of the British and French Dominions in North America WITH THE Roads, Distances, limits, and Extent of the SETTLEMENTS, Humbly Inscribed to the Right Honourable The Earl of Halifax And the other Right Honourables, The Lords Commissioners for Trade & Plantations, By their Lordships Most Obliged and very humble servant Jno Mitchell, Published by the author Febry13th 1755.* The 3rd and 4th editions of the map were printed for Jefferys and Faden, Geographers to the King. The 4th edition, released circa 1775, omitted '*and French*' from the title. For detailed information on the multiple editions of Mitchell's 1755 map see the following by Matthew H. Edney: "John Mitchell's Map of North America (1755); A Study of the Use and Publication of Official Maps in Eighteenth-Century Britain," *Imago Mundi* 63 (2001): 63-85; "A Publishing History of John Mitchell's Map of North America, 1755-1775," *Cartographic Perspectives* 58 (Fall 2007): 4-27; "The Most Important Map in U.S. History," Online publication at: Osher Map Center, Smith Center for Cartographic Education, University of Southern Maine, oshermaps.org/exhibitions/map-commentaries/most-important-map-us-history.

11. Giunta, *Emerging Nation*, 597. The first draft peace treaty was formalized in Paris on 5th-8th October 1782.

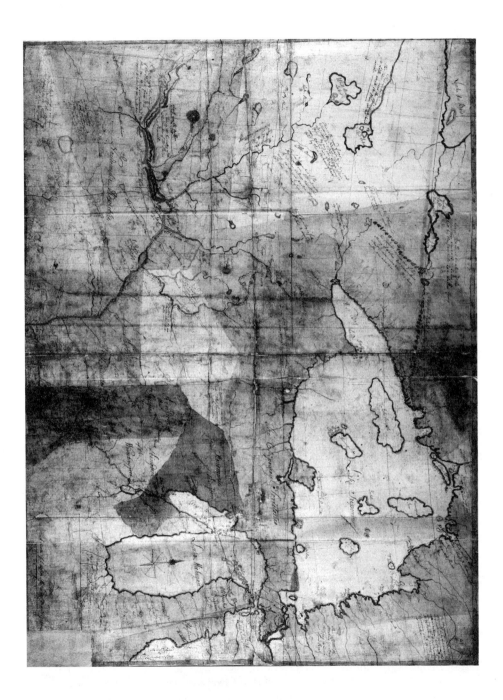

Carver's manuscript map (c. 1767-68) of the western Great Lakes and northern Mississippi River basin. (*British Library*)

Streight to the South end of Lake Nipissing and then Streight to the Source of the River Missisippi."[12] (This line later became known as the Nipissing Line.[13]) Both commissioners plotted their version of the line on separate Mitchell maps. They expected their respective governments to ratify the agreement.[14]

Because of illness, Franklin had limited involvement in finalizing the first draft treaty.[15] However, Lettsom's gifted copy of Carver's *Travels*, received in late September 1781, renewed Franklin's opportunity to acquaint himself with Carver's work. The explorer's geographic and cartographic details provided Franklin with much needed, credible information about the extreme northwestern reaches of the Mississippi that now greatly interested the United States. Carver's details on the river appear to have influenced how the draft boundary was plotted on both Jay's and Oswald's maps.

Once agreement was reached on the Nipissing Line, Oswald added his version of the line to his fourth edition Mitchell map.[16] Franklin must have shared his knowledge about the Mississippi headwaters with Oswald before the latter's Nipissing Line was plotted.[17] The most northwestern portion of Oswald's line roughly parallels Jay's but it

12. Ibid., 598. The section of the Nipissing Line from the St. Lawrence River to Lake Nipissing was designated by King George III's Royal Proclamation of 1763 as the southwest boundary of the new province of Quebec. The agreed upon line from the St. Lawrence River to Lake Nipissing and straight to the source of the Mississippi River was in accordance to Congress's boundary objectives per Adams' 1779 peace commissioner appointment and instructions. See NHPRC-FO founders.archives.gov/documents/Adams/01-04-02-0002-0001.

13. Walter Nugent, *Habits of Empire: A History of American Expansionism* (New York and Toronto: Knopf Doubleday Publishing Group, Random House, 2008): 33-35. Andrew Stockley, *Britain and France at the Birth of America* (Exeter, UK: University of Exeter Press, 2001), 64.

14. Jay's 3rd edition Mitchell map is held by the New-York Historical Society, Call No. NS4 M32.2.1A. Oswald's 4th edition Mitchell map (also known as King George III's *Red-Lined Map*) is held by the British Library, catalogue number K.Top (118.49.b).

15. NHPRC-FO founders.archives.gov/documents/Franklin/01-38-02-0090. Franklin's chronic problem with gout and kidney stones limited his participation in September–early October 1782 peace negotiations.

16. Only faint red traces of Oswald's Nipissing Line remain on his Mitchell map. His map eventually became part of George III's extensive map collection. For further details on Oswald's map see: J.P.D. Dunbabin, "Red Lines on Maps: The Impact of Cartographical Errors on the Border between the United States and British North America, 1782-1842," *Imago Mundi* 50 (1998) and "Red Lines on Maps' Revisited: The Role of Maps in Negotiating and Defending the 1842 Webster-Ashburton Treaty," *Imago Mundi* 63 Part 1 (2011): 39-61.

17. Because of illness, it is unlikely Franklin was present when Oswald plotted his Nipissing Line to the source of the Mississippi.

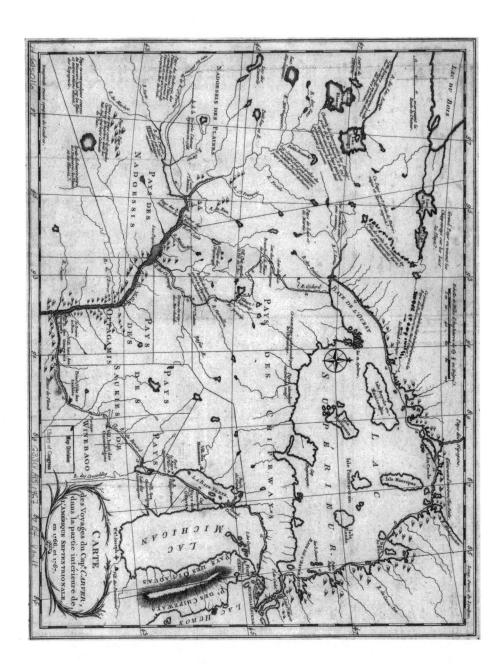

A Plan of Captain Carver's Travels in the Interior of North Ameica in 1766 and 1767 was first published in Jonathan Carver's 1778 self-published book, *Travels.* (*Library of Congress*)

ends abruptly at the lower right edge of Mitchell's inset map *A NEW MAP of HUDSON'S BAY*. . . . Oswald's (Franklin's) location for the source of the Mississippi closely approximates that shown on *A Plan of Captain Carver's*.

The Nipissing Line on both maps lacked geographic distinctiveness; i.e., it wasn't a natural boundary like a mountain ridge, river, or lake, etc., and it angled tangentially across several degrees of latitude.

NEGOTIATIONS CONTINUE

Before the end of October 1782 peace negotiators in Paris were aware Britain had rejected the proposed boundary in the first draft treaty.[18] To negotiate, among other matters, a more acceptable northwestern boundary, the British Cabinet ordered Henry Strachey to Paris to assist Oswald.[19]

After discussions on the boundary were re-opened, Strachey likely soon sharpened the Americans' focus on Dr. John Mitchell's authoritative Mississippi map note,[20]

> The Heads of the Missisipi is not yet known; It is supposed to arise about the 50th degree of Latitude, and Western Bounds of this Map; beyond which Nth America extends nigh as far Westward as it does to the Eastward by all accounts.[21]

18. Giunta, *Emerging Nation*, 623. News of Britain's rejection of the first draft treaty was known to Oswald and Jay on October 24, 1782.
19. Ibid., 631. British Under-Secretary of State for the Home Department, Henry Strachey, assisted Oswald to conclude the preliminary peace treaty. Adams and Franklin had previously met Strachey during a 1776 failed peace initiative on Staten Island.
20. Ibid., 628. Shortly after his Paris arrival Strachey made known through Oswald he hoped the Americans would accept a line of longitude east of the Mississippi as their western boundary. The Americans (Jay) refused to consider this option and warned Oswald they would break off negotiations if it was insisted upon. Strachey and commissioners from both nations spent considerable time studying earlier North American boundaries on a variety of maps as well as acts, laws, and proclamations that might bear on establishing a revised boundary.
21. Mitchell's map note about the source of the Mississippi is located under the inset map *A New Map of Hudson's Bay* at latitude 46°30′ N. His text is similar to Henry Popple's 1733 note on his gigantic map *A map of the British Empire in America with the French and Spanish settlement adjacent thereto*. Franklin was long acquainted with both of these early maps. French cartographer Philippe Buache's 1754 map *Carte physique des terreins les plus eleves de la partie occidentale du Canada* has remarks in French about the source of the Mississippi. Based on French army officers' regional reconnaissance starting in the 1730s, the French concluded the source of the Mississippi lay south and nearby their trading route from Lake Superior to their forts on Rainy Lake, Lake of the Woods, and Assiniboine River. Buache's map can be viewed at McGill University's digital map library digital.library.mcgill.ca/pugsley/IMAGES/3%20-%20300%20D PI%20 JPGs/Pugs31.jpg.

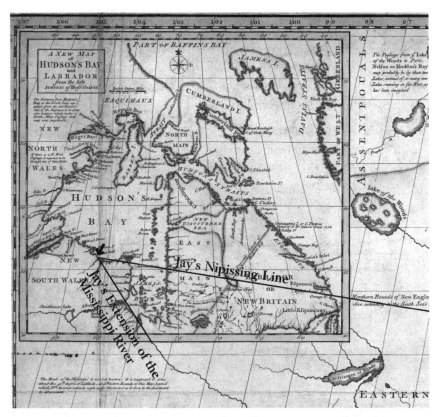

Portion of Jay's MS Nipissing Line and northern extension of the Mississippi River (enhanced) on his 3rd ed. *Mitchell* (1755). His MS lines overlap Mitchell's inset corner map. (*Library of Congress*)

The ensuing second brief, intense round of negotiations afforded the Americans an opportunity to revise their northwestern boundary. Both Jay and Franklin (the latter via Oswald) had earlier disclosed their desired course for the boundary on two different Mitchell maps thereby making known their best estimates for the Mississippi's source. Newly arrived peace commissioner John Adams along with Jay and Franklin likely quietly and quickly responded to Strachey's geographic directives and admonitions concerning the rejected north-western boundary.[22] Adams recorded in his peace journal on

22. NHPRC-FO founders.archives.gov/documents/Adams/01-02-02-0001-0004-0009. As early as 1771 Adams was cognizant of Carver's Mississippi basin explorations.

Relying on the correctness of Carver's personal surveys and reconnaissance in the northern Mississippi region, Franklin, Adams, and likely Jay may have immediately

November 2, "We have made two Propositions. One the Line of forty five degrees. The other a Line thro the Middles of the Lakes."[23] Their simplest proposal was an extension of the existing New York— Canada 45th degree North latitude boundary starting at the St. Lawrence River and running westward to the Mississippi. The second "Middles of the Lakes" option was a line running, in part,

> . . . between that Lake [Huron] and Lake Superior, thence through Lake Superior Northward of the Isles Royal and Philipeaux to the Long Lake [actually a river inlet to Lake Superior], thence through the middle of said Long Lake and the water communication between it and the Lake of the Woods, to the said Lake of the Woods, thence through the said Lake to the most north- western point thereof, and from thence on a due western Course to the River Mississippi.[24]

Most of the geography for the Americans' new proposed boundary, from the intersection of the St. Lawrence and the 45th parallel through the Great Lakes to Lake of the Woods, was detailed in Carver's *Travels* and on *A Plan of Captain Carver's*. For example, Carver did a masterful job of describing and illustrating the passageway from Lake Superior to Lake of the Woods using information gleaned during his 1767 summer stay at Grand Portage.[25] The water communication route to Lake of the Woods, in Carver's time, was

recognized the vast NW territory to be gained by accepting Strachey's input. NHPRC-FO founders.archives.gov/documents/Franklin/01-38-02-0205. The American commissioners likely remained silent as Strachey possibly encouraged them to accept the correctness of Mitchell's information about the Mississippi. Adams described Strachey as "artfull and insinuating a Man as they could send. He pushes and presses every Point as far as it can possibly go. He is the most eager, earnest, pointed Spirit."

23. Giunta, *Emerging Nation*, 631. An interval of only three days elapsed between the joint commissioners' beginning review of Strachey's maps and documents and the Americans' presentation of their "Middles of the Lakes" proposal. NHPRC-FO founders.archives.gov/documents/Adams/01-03-02-0001-0004-0002. See Adams's diary note for the Americans' revised NW boundary line.

24. Ibid., 650-652. The Americans' "Middles of the Lakes" proposal was recorded on a separate folio and marked on the map Strachey carried back to London. Strachey's map could have been Oswald's 4th ed. Mitchell map (later known as King George III's *Red-Lined Map*).

25. Parker, *The Journals*, 180-191. Using information from Carver's *Travels* and James Goddard's journal Carver was at Grand Portage landing from 19 July to 8 August 1767.

NW portion of Oswald's MS Nipissing Line terminated at Carver's transposed source of the Mississippi (both enhanced) on 4th ed. *Mitchell* (1755). (*British Library*)

known only to area natives, a few British fur traders, and veteran French voyageur-traders.[26] In Carver's words, he arrived

> at the Grand Portage, which lies on the north-west borders of Lake Superior. Here those who go on the north-west trade, to the Lakes De Pluye [Lac de la Pluie or Rainy Lake], Dubois [Lake du Bois or Lake of the Woods], &c. carry over their canoes and baggage about nine miles, till they come to a number of small lakes, the waters of some of which descend into Lake Superior, and others into the River Bourbon [Carver used this composite name to identify the southeastern arm of the river systems draining into Hudson Bay via Lake Winnipeg and the Nelson River].[27]

> [Lake of the Woods] lies still higher up a branch of the River Bourbon, and nearly east from the south end of Lake Winnepeek

26. Veteran French voyageur-trader, Charles Boyer, traded for furs in the Rainy Lake / Lake of the Woods area in the 1740's. He is likely 'Mr. Boyce' referenced in Major Robert Rogers' letter dated 10 June 1767 (Parker, *The Journals*, 197). James Goddard's journal reference to 'Monsr. Boyiz,' was likely the same Charles Boyer (Parker, *The Journals*, 191). Boyer, who was in a partnership with Forrest Oakes in 1767, and later with his brother Michel Boyer, established a trading settlement at Rainy Lake. For the Rainy Lake 1771 Boyer settlement, see Glyndwr Williams, ed., *Andrew Graham's Observations on Hudson's Bay 1767-1791* (Hudson's Bay Record Society, London, 1969), 289. See also Denis Combet, et al., ed., *From Pierre-Esprit Radisson to Louis Riel: Voyageurs and Metis* (Presses Universitaires De Saint-Boniface, Winnipeg, MB, 2014): 59-70.

27. Carver, *Travels*, 106.

[Winnipeg]. It is of great depth in some places. Its length from east to west about seventy miles, and its greatest breadth about forty miles.[28]

[Rainy Lake] appears to be divided by an Isthmus, near the middle into two parts: the west part is called Great Rainy Lake, and east, the Little Rainy Lake, as being the least division. It lies a few miles farther to the eastward, on the same branch of the Bourbon, than the last-mentioned lake [Lake of the Woods].[29]

Eastward from [Rainy Lake] lie several small ones, which extend in a string to the great carrying place [Grand Portage], and from thence into Lake Superior. Between these little lakes are several carrying places, which renders the trade to the north-west difficult to accomplish, and exceedingly tedious.[30]

The northwest corner of *A Plan of Captain Carver's* has additional information about the water–land route to Lake of the Woods. Carver replaced Mitchell's erroneous inlet immediately west of Isle Royale with an accurate rendering of a small, short stream entering Lake Superior northeast of Grand Portage Bay.[31] Shown above "The Grand Portage" label are two small opposing arrows marking the Atlantic—Arctic drainage divide.[32] The map scale included near the top of his

28. Ibid., 113.
29. Ibid., 114.
30. Ibid., 115.
31. The inlet/bay shown on *Travels'* second map, *A New Map of North America from the Latest Discoveries 1778,* is likely Long Lake shown on Mitchell's 1755 map. There is no such massive shoreline indent; its existence can be traced to Mitchell's erroneous interpretation of regional features shown on earlier French maps (e.g., see footnote 22—Buache's "Lac Long").
32. Carver, *Travels,* 106. Carver expanded on the meaning of the two opposing arrows on his map. He states:
    "[traders] carry over their canoes and baggage about nine miles, till they come to a number of small lakes, the waters of some of which descend into Lake Superior, and others into the River Bourbon." This continental drainage divide is between North and South Lake on the Ontario–Minnesota international boundary.
    Water features between Lake Superior and Lake of the Woods on Mitchell's map promote Lake of the Woods as the source waters of the St. Lawrence drainage complex. The Americans' faith in Carver's hydrological details bolstered their conviction to their new NW boundary proposal. For details on the former drainage theory see William E. Lass, *Minnesota's Boundary with Canada: Its Evolution since 1783* (St. Paul: Minnesota Historical Society Press, 1980): 15, 17 & 18. See also Dunbabin, *Imago Mundi* 50 (1998), 109 (footnote 17).

map permitted reasonable estimates for distances west of Lake Superior.[33] Coordinates for the south-eastern part of Lake of the Woods are very close to modern values.

In Paris, on November 30, 1782, the Preliminary Articles of Peace was endorsed by commissioners from both nations. For the north-western boundary Britain chose the "Middles of the Lakes" option.[34] The details of boundary Article 2 were much influenced by Mitchell's faulty map. The revised boundary awarded America an extensive tract of both real and "not-so-real" land in the northwest.[35] Article 2 states

> . . . thence along the middle of said Water Communication into Lake Huron, thence through the middle of said Lake to the Water Communication between that Lake and Lake Superior; thence through Lake Superior northward of the Isles Royal and Phelipeaux to the Long Lake; thence through the middle of said Long Lake and the water Communication between it and the Lake of the Woods, to the said Lake of the Woods; thence through the said Lake to the most Northwestern point thereof, and from thence on a due west Course to the river Missisippi.[36]

The American commissioners' mid-December 1782 homeward communication emphasized their northwestern boundary negotiating successes. The line "divides the Lake Superior, and gives us Access to its Western & Southern Waters."[37]

---

33. Using Carver's map scale of "69.5 British Miles to a Degree," America's commissioners could approximate the distance from Lake Superior to Lake of the Woods and westward to "Mitchell's Mississippi."

34. Prime Minister Shelburne's cabinet may have opted for the "Middles of the Lakes" boundary because it appeared "geographically distinct" and provided a "boundary of certainty." The latter expressions were used in the British House of Commons when the New York–Canada boundary was debated before enacting the Quebec Act of 1774.

35. If coordinates 50°N and 106°W, implied by Mitchell's Mississippi map note, were applied to a modern map, boundary Article 2 would have entitled America to territory extending north of the international boundary (49°N) and west to near Moose Jaw, SK, Canada. Thus the real and not-so-real territory gained by the American commissioners' acceptance of Mitchell's faulty NW geography was the triangle-like territory extending from Carver's source of the Mississippi to that of Mitchell's and back to Lake Superior (Isle Royale and fictitious Isle Phelipeaux were also within the new proposed American territory).

36. Avalon Project, avalon.law.yale.edu/18th_century/prel1782.asp#art2. Part of Article 2, Preliminary Articles of Peace, 30 November 1782.

37. NHPRC-FO founders.archives.gov/documents/Adams/06-14-02-0076. American Peace Commissioners to Robert R. Livingston, Paris, 14 December 1782.

Because the source of the Mississippi, according to Mitchell, was near the western edge of his map and about 50°N, Britain needed the latitude of the due west treaty line from Lake of the Woods to be less than fifty degrees.[38] Article 2 stated the divide line was to proceed due west from the most northwestern corner of Lake of the Woods to the Mississippi River (not its source).[39] Strachey was likely mindful of Mitchell's latitude for the lake's northwest corner, although not numerically quantified in the treaty, because he recognized his nation's need to retain land abutting the Mississippi to preserve his country's navigational rights to the river.[40]

About two months after signing the preliminary treaty, Franklin's January 20, 1783, letter book entry revealed his knowledge about the "ground truth" of the Mississippi. He recorded

> The Limits of the thirteen United States, acknowledged by England, shall be formed . . . by a Line continued from Lake Superior through Long Lake, until the Lake of the Woods, by a Line tending towards the South and connecting the Lake with the River Missisippi.[41]

38. Although the NW corner of Lake of the Woods is not shown on Carver's published map, it's likely about 51°N.

39. The northwest corner of Lake of the Woods extends to 49°30ʹN on Mitchell's map. British astronomer-surveyor David Thompson initially reported in 1797 an on-site measurement for the northwest corner of Lake of the Woods (outlet of the lake) to be 49°37ʹ N. Today's geopolitical actual is at the NW end of Angle Inlet (Lake of the Woods) at 49°23ʹ 55ʹ N.

The Hudson's Bay Co.'s (HBC) southern limit is boldly marked on Oswald's map using a contrasting color wash and a labelled bicolored red and blue MS line coincident with the 49th degree North parallel. Its MS annotation reads "Boundary between the Lands granted to the Hudson's Bay Company and the Province of Quebec." The HBC MS line continues westward across the southern end of Lake of the Woods to the right edge of the inset *A New Map of Hudson's Bay*. Shelburne had earlier in 1763 considered the company's desired 49°N (southern) limit when he was First Lord of Trade but no document has been located that formally granted the HBC their long standing request.

40. NHPRC-FO founders.archives.gov/documents/Franklin/01-38-02-0334. American Commissioners to R. Livingston, 14 December 1782, "Their possessing the Country on the River, North of the Line from the Lake of the Woods, affords a foundation for their claiming such Navigation; . . . The Map used in the Course of our Negotiations was Mitchells."

41. Giunta, *Emerging Nation*, 755-756.

Opposite: Annotated NW corner of *Mitchell* (1755) showing a portion of the 1783 treaty line running due west from the northwest corner of Lake of the Woods to Mitchell's Mississippi. Also shown are Oswald's and Jay's Nipissing lines and Carver's transposed river source. (*Library of Congress*)

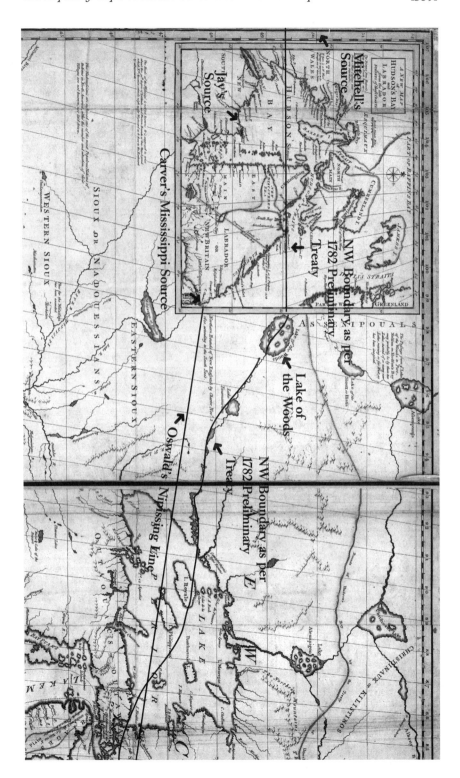

Benjamin Vaughan, a close friend of Franklin's and Britain's intermediary between the Paris negotiators and Prime Minister Shelburne
and his cabinet in London, offered Shelburne some background information regarding Article 2. His letter to the first minister, dated
February 21, 1783, advised

> The line to be drawn from the last boundary lakes [Lake of the
> Woods] to the Mississippi, probably should go South, and is by
> mistake said to go West. . . . It ought to stand in the definitive treaty
> perhaps to the nearest part of the Mississippi in a direct line; [or]
> from thence [Lake of the Woods], on a due South course to the
> Mississippi.[42]

During the British parliamentarians' debate focused on the preliminary treaty, Lord North, then Opposition Leader, sharply criticized
the geography on which Article 2 was predicated. He orated

> The second article of the Provisional Treaty contained some very
> remarkable things; it states that a line drawn through the Lake of
> the Woods, through the said Lake, to the most N. W. point there-
> of; and from thence on a due west course to the River Mississippi.
> Now this being duly considered, would be found to be absolute-
> ly impossible; for this line would run far beyond the source of the
> Mississippi: thus [First Minister Shelburne] would agree as to the
> reciprocity; the mouth of this river is in the hands of the Spaniards;
> its source in the possession of the Americans; one side of it is with-
> in the boundaries ceded to the Colonies; the other is in the hand
> of the Spaniards; thus the river, the half of which is given to us by
> the treaty, belongs wholly to other powers, and not an inch of it,
> either at north or south, at west or east, belongs to us. This, no
> doubt, would establish the reciprocity beyond a cavil.[43]

Terms of the November 1782 preliminary peace settlement were
unknown in America when James Madison's list of recommended reference books to be acquired and made available to Congress was read

42. Benjamin Vaughan Papers, American Philosophical Society, Mss.V46P, TLS Cy
Vaughan to Lansdowne, William Petty, Marquis of, 21 February 1783.
43. *Full and Faithful Report of Debates in Both Houses of Parliament, Monday the 17th of
February, and Friday the 21st of February, 1783 on the Articles of Peace* (Printed for S.
Bladon, London, England, 1783), Numb. 13, 19 D2. Available online at Internet
Archive, archive.org/details/cihm_36137. Lord North may have based his knowledge
on William Faden's maps of the British colonies in North America (1777 & 1783) that
displayed much of Carver's northern Mississippi River details. Faden became King
George III's Royal Geographer in summer 1783.

in Independence Hall in Philadelphia. Carver's *Travels* was on Madison's list.[44]

Official communication of peace with Britain reached Philadelphia on March 12, 1783.[45] Anne-Cesar, Chevalier de la Luzerne, the French diplomat stationed in Philadelphia since 1779, reflected to Charles Gravier, Comte de Vergennes, senior French statesman in Paris, his thoughts on the new United States' northwest boundary in a letter on March 19, 1783:

> They [the United States] seem to have availed themselves chiefly of a journal *printed by a Traveller*, for in fixing the boundaries from Lake Superior to the sources of the Mississippi, one has no hope of obtaining a boundary so extensive in that area; One thinks that the Plenipotentiaries, by extending their possessions to the Lake of the Woods inclusively, are preparing for their posterity, in times still very distant, a communication with the Pacific Ocean.[46]

The traveller mentioned by Luzerne could be none other than Captain Jonathan Carver. Carver's geographic information and maps and their influence on America's boundary-defining goals appears to have been known for some time in Philadelphia and beyond, and to have preceded the arrival of news of the peace settlement.

Within a few months after the signing of the 1782 Preliminary Articles of Peace, cartographers on both sides of the Atlantic were busy drafting maps of the new United States of America. William McMurray first offered his map to Philadelphians by subscription in early August 1783.[47] McMurray, a former Assistant Geographer to the United States, acknowledges using *in toto* the northwest quadrant of *A Plan of Captain Carver's* to complete his map *The United States*

44. NHPRC-FO http://founders.archives.gov/documents/Madison/01-06-02-0031. During the second half of 1782 James Madison, Virginia's delegate to the Second Continental Congress, identified Carver's 3rd edition of *Travels* printed in London in 1781, as a recommended book to be acquired for Congress. His book list was reviewed by Congress on 24 January 1783.

45. Giunta, *Emerging Nation*, 767. Luzerne, in his 9 February 1783 letter to Vergennes, indicated the peace terms with Britain were common news in America. NHPRC-FO http://founders.archives.gov/documents/Adams/06-14-02-0076, fn 2. Official notice from the American commissioners of the 30 November 1782 preliminary treaty, along with a copy of the latter, were received in Philadelphia on 12 March 1783.

46. Giunta, *Emerging Nation*, 801-802; italics are as per Guinta.

47. http://loc.gov/exhibits/mapping-a-new-nation/online-exhibition.html. McMurray's map would have been America's first map of the new nation had it not experienced publication difficulties. (Post-treaty details would not have been part of the map

According to the Definitive Treaty of Peace signed at Paris, Sept.r 3.d 1783.[48] In the lower right his inset map of North America exhibits an enticing open gateway to the West between Lake of the Woods and the source of the Mississippi.

John Cary's plan, *An Accurate Map of the United States of America*,[49] was published in London in early August 1783. He borrowed numerous details from *A Plan of Captain Carver's*. Cary labelled the traveller's 1766 wintering locale on a westward tributary of the Mississippi and he illustrated Carver's entire 1766–67 circle exploration route departing from and returning to Michilimackinac.

CONCLUSIONS

The Preliminary Articles of Peace was jointly signed by commissioners from the United States and Britain on November 30, 1782. Article 2 called for the extreme northwestern portion of the line of separation between their two nations to extend due west from the northwest corner of Lake of the Woods to the Mississippi River. The boundary defined in the preliminary treaty was confirmed verbatim in the Definitive Treaty of Peace signed in Paris on September 3, 1783.

Based on knowledge of Captain Jonathan Carver's maps, surveys, and travel narrative, at least one American commissioner knew the westward extension of the boundary from Lake of the Woods to the Mississippi was geographically impossible. Benjamin Franklin was most aware of the implications of Carver's observations. By shrewdly acquiescing to Mitchell's erroneous cartography, the Americans demonstrated their willingness to trade significant territorial interests along the Atlantic coast and "Nipissing country" for a vast additional tract of interior North America.

Numerous experts have postulated the Americans plotted the northwest boundary to Lake of the Woods because they considered it the source of a continuous water connection supplying the St. Lawrence River. Franklin's knowledge of the continental drainage divide immediately west of John Mitchell's Long Lake should dispel the mythology associated with the Lake Superior—Lake of the Woods water communication route. Shortly after signing the 1782 preliminary treaty, the American commissioners wrote,

offered to the public by subscription as per McMurray's receipt issued 13 August 1783.) See Harvard Map Collection, 2011 *Toward a National Cartography: American Mapmaking 1782-1800*, guest curator Michael Buehler, at: www.americanmapmaking.com/nation.php.

48. Library of Congress map collection: www.loc.gov/item/gm71005423/.
49. Library of Congress map collection: www.loc.gov/item/gm71005488/.

and having no Reason to think Lines more favourable could ever have been obtained, we finally agreed to those described in this Article: indeed they appear to leave us little to complain of, and not much to desire.[50]

By 1807, the gambit on the due west line from Lake of the Woods to the Mississippi, although not free from controversy, compromise, and re-definition, netted for the United States of America all the territory visited and mapped by Capt. Jonathan Carver, envisioned by Lettsom, and secured by Franklin, Adams, and Jay in 1782.[51]

50. NHPRC-FO founders.archives.gov/documents/Adams/06-14-02-0076. American Peace Commissioners' letter to Robert Livingston, Paris, 14 December 1782.
51. Negotiators from United States and Britain reached in March 1807 an agreement recognizing the 49th North parallel as the boundary between their territories from Lake of the Woods west to the Rocky Mountains. This agreement was officially adopted by the Convention of 1818. Boundary particulars of the section from Lake Superior west to Lake of the Woods were finalized by the 1842 Webster-Ashburton Treaty. The latter portion of the international divide line follows the land-water communication route investigated and described by Carver in 1767. Ancillary details on setting this portion of the U.S.–Canada boundary were summarized by U.S. Agent Major Joseph Delafield in Robert McElroy and Thomas Riggs, ed., *The Unfortified Boundary* (New York, 1943): 403-465. See also William E. Lass, *Minnesota's Boundary with Canada*, footnote 33.

Drilling Holes in George Washington's Wooden Teeth Myth

JOHN L. SMITH, JR.

George Washington did not chop down a cherry tree and carve wooden teeth from it.

Maybe one of the most enduring myths in American history is that George Washington had wooden teeth. It seems to never go away, generation after generation. Well, not only did the first president not have wooden teeth, you could also honestly say that Washington's bad teeth helped the young United States win the American Revolution. How? You'll see . . .

Sometimes described as cold, aloof, unsmiling, and formal, George Washington was largely driven in his adult life by his teeth, or lack of them and the resulting pain. As a twenty-first century dentist's dream, young George had his first tooth pulled at the age of 24 and his life-long battle with tooth decay, gum disease, and tooth pain started from there. Only a few years later, in 1760, Washington's friend George Mercer noted, "His mouth is large and generally firmly closed, but which from time to time discloses some defective teeth."[1] By the time Washington became president nearly three decades later, he had one bicuspid tooth remaining on the lower left of his jaw.

1. Graeme Mercer Adam, et al., *George Washington: a character sketch* (Milwaukee, WI: H.G. Campbell Publishing Co., 1903), 37; George Mercer to a friend, 1760, quoted in *The Papers of George Washington, Colonial Series*, Volume 1, edited by W.W. Abbot, Dorothy Twohig, and others (Charlottesville: University Press of Virginia, 1988), 192n-193n; also in Henry Wiencek, *An Imperfect God: George Washington, His Slaves, and the Creation of America* (New York: Farrar, Straus and Giroux, 2003), 65-66.

How did Washington lose his teeth? In his autobiography, John Adams said George himself "attributed his misfortune to cracking of Walnuts in his Youth."[2] Sure, that didn't help any, but Mount Vernon associate curator Laura Simo thinks George Washington's family genetics was half to blame for his tooth problems. The other half was the dental hygiene of the time.[3]

It's not that George Washington was sloppy about dental hygiene; it's just that dental hygiene was practically non-existent in the late eighteenth century. In fact, in some social groups, taking care of your teeth was even considered effeminate or vain. But Washington was very wise about the message an image can send, and knew that in the Continental Congress, and as commander-in-chief and president, he had to look the part of a leader . . . which meant at least having teeth. Aside from the possible constant pain Washington endured from his bad teeth, he stayed on a constant life quest to (simply said)—have teeth in his mouth. And he paid a lot for professional dental care all through his lifetime. "Payments to dentists and purchases of tooth-brushes, teeth scrapers, denture files, toothache medication, and cleaning solutions are also regularly present in Washington's communications throughout his life."[4]

WASHINGTON'S MOST NOTABLE DENTISTS

DR. JOHN BAKER was the first noteworthy dentist that Washington employed. Baker was an English-trained dentist who set up shop in Williamsburg in 1772 and in fact, "Mr. Baker Surgeon Dentist"[5] (as Washington called him in his diary) may have been the first professionally trained dentist in America.

Baker's services, however, did not come cheap and Washington's ledger shows Baker's charges for the "period between March 1772 and

---

2. John Adams, *Diary and Autobiography of John Adams*, 4 volumes, edited by L. H. Butterfield, and others (Cambridge, MA: Belknap Press of Harvard University Press, 1961), 3:280; my thanks to Mary V. Thompson, Mount Vernon, for this citation source.

3. Colonial Williamsburg: audio podcast between Harmony Hunter and Laura Simo, February 20, 2012, "The Wooden Teeth That Weren't"; podcast.history. org/2012/ 02/20/the-wooden-teeth/ (accessed October 22, 2014).

4. Mount Vernon Estate and Gardens: online article: www.mountvernon.org/ george-washington/the-man-the-myth/the-trouble-with-teeth/ (accessed October 21, 2014).

5. "[Diary entry: 13 October 1773]," Founders Online, National Archives (founders. archives.gov/documents/Washington/01-03-02-0003-0020-0013 [last update: 2014-09-30]). Source: *The Diaries of George Washington*, vol. 3, 1 January 1771–5 November 1781, ed. Donald Jackson. Charlottesville: University Press of Virginia, 1978, 209 (accessed October 26, 2014).

November 1773 amounted to £14.6."[6] That of course included a pro-
longed house call to Mount Vernon from Dr. Baker starting on
October 13, 1773, and you know how expensive that can be. Baker
apparently fitted Washington with a partial denture made of ivory and
wired parts of the denture to Washington's existing teeth. Then, like
dominoes, the rubbing of the wire helped to loosen Washington's
other existing teeth and so on and so on. Either way, it was not comfortable at all. It appears, then, Baker moved to Philadelphia and
became Washington's sometimes-dentist during much of the
Revolutionary War.

How Did Washington's Bad Teeth Help Win the Revolutionary
War?

Washington always tried to keep his tooth problems private. But in
1781, he was informed that a packet of mail and documents had
been intercepted by the British. Washington knew that one of the
letters inside that packet was a confidential letter Washington had
written to Dr. John Baker, his personal dentist at that time, who
was in Philadelphia. In the letter Washington was asking if Baker
would send a tooth scraper to his headquarters in New Windsor,
New York, saying he had "little prospect of being in Philadelph.
soon."[7] After verifying that the intercepted mail was real and not a
set-up, the British Army commander in America, Sir Henry
Clinton, became convinced that Washington and his army was
going to stay put the Hudson Highlands north of New York City.
Clinton let his guard down.

Little did Clinton know that just after Washington had written
the tooth-scraping letter, both Washington and Rochambeau
began planning the Franco-American armies' movement down to
Virginia – down to meet General Cornwallis at Yorktown for the
siege that basically ended the Revolutionary War.

DR. JEAN-PIERRE LE MAYEUR, although French-born, had been Sir
Henry Clinton's dentist in 1781, when they were both in New York.
But one day, Le Mayeur overheard some rude things said about the
French alliance with the Americans, so Le Mayeur packed his dental

6. Frank E. Grizzard Jr., *George Washington: A Biographical Companion* (Santa Barbara,
CA: ABC-CLIO, Inc., 2002), 103.
7 George Washington to Dr. Baker, May 29, 1781, New Windsor; from the Gold Star
Collection of the Clements Library; clements.umich.edu/exhibits/online/ spies/let-
ter-1781may29.html (accessed October 24, 2014).

bags and in a snit snuck over to the enemy camp. In this case, he offered his dental services to General George Washington, and Washington accepted. But first, in a move that would seem very contemporary, Washington had a secret background check done on Le Mayeur, "a private investigation of this man's character and knowledge of his profession."[8] After passing with flying French colors, it was the start of a long relationship between Washington and Le Mayeur, which also promised the possibility of transplanting real teeth into Washington's mouth.

Washington's Attempt at Transplanting Teeth

Washington had heard that Dr. Le Mayeur had some success at transplanting teeth, a technique best described as taking purchased human teeth (usually from poor people) and jamming the tooth down inside the open socket on a jaw, and then wiring it to the neighboring teeth. Then I think it's just hoped that the tooth grows in place without benefit of a nerve or root blood supply.

In 1784, Le Mayeur sent Washington a letter touting his success at transplanting teeth into the mouth of Washington's private secretary, Richard Varick, and a few others who were indebted to him, "by furnishing them with good living teeth in the Room of those which were broken or otherwise decayed," and that the transplanted teeth "are in a promising state and will be perfectly ferm [firm]."[9] After hearing positive things from Varick himself, Washington became very interested in the transplanting procedure. Washington excitedly wrote back to Varick, "I received great pleasure from the Acct which you have given me of Doctr La Moyeur's operations on you; and congratulate you very sincerely on the success."[10]

---

8. Ron Chernow, *Washington: A Life* (New York: Penguin Press, 2010), 438; also James Thomas Flexner, *George Washington* (New York: Little, Brown and Company, 1965), 2:500.

9. "To George Washington from Jean Le Mayeur, 20 January 1784," Founders Online, National Archives (founders.archives.gov/documents/Washington/04-01-02-0044 [last update: 2014-09-30]). Source: *The Papers of George Washington, Confederation Series*, vol. 1, 1 January 1784–17 July 1784, ed. W. W. Abbot (Charlottesville: University Press of Virginia, 1992), 63–64 (accessed October 26, 2014).

10. "From George Washington to Richard Varick, 22 February 1784," Founders Online, National Archives (ounders.archives.gov/documents/Washington/ 04-01-02-0110 [last update: 2014-09-30]). Source: *The Papers of George Washington, Confederation Series*, vol. 1, 1 January 1784–17 July 1784, ed. W. W. Abbot (Charlottesville: University Press of Virginia, 1992), 148–149 (accessed October 26, 2014).

Following the Revolutionary War, "Doctr. L'Moyer"[11] became a frequent visitor to Mount Vernon through the years 1785–1788. During his stays, he may have been attempting tooth transplants on the retired General George. Washington kept some of his own teeth in a locked drawer of his Mount Vernon desk and had also just spent 13 shillings apiece to buy nine teeth from "Negroes."[12]

Conclusion? "Whether he wanted the teeth implanted directly in his mouth or incorporated into dentures, we cannot say… we can deduce that Washington's dental transplant miscarried, since by the time of his presidential inauguration in 1789, he had only a single working tooth remaining."[13]

DR. JOHN GREENWOOD had a dental office in New York City, and that's where newly inaugurated President Washington apparently started employing Greenwood to create and repair his dentures. Greenwood had fought in the Revolutionary War and had studied dentistry under none other than Paul Revere—it was a part-time profession for the renowned silversmith. Washington continued to use Greenwood when the new national capital was moved to Philadelphia and the relationship continued into Washington's retirement. Greenwood is perhaps the best known of Washington's dentists, but the long-distance relationship made it really hard for Greenwood to get a right fit for Washington's false teeth. Because of that, apparently Washington sometimes tinkered with his own dentures out of necessity.

Occasionally he sent a letter to Greenwood asking for replacement parts: "Send me some spiral spring, about a foot long, without cutting them, and join to this nearly double that length of gold wire, (little breaking) of a diameter that you judge suitable for me to attach them as customary, to my tooth."[14] It sounds like in messing with his

11. "September [1785]," Founders Online, National Archives (founders. archives.gov/documents/Washington/01-04-02-0002-0009 [last update: 2014-09-30]). Source: *The Diaries of George Washington*, vol. 4, 1 September 1784–30 June 1786, ed. Donald Jackson and Dorothy Twohig (Charlottesville: University Press of Virginia, 1978), 189–200 (accessed October 26, 2014).
12. Selling of teeth by the poor and "Negroes" back then was akin to homeless people selling their blood today. Chernow, *Washington: A Life*, 438; also from Peter R. Henriques, *Realistic Visionary: A Portrait of George Washington* (Charlottesville: University Press of Virginia, 2006), 154.
13. Chernow, *Washington: A Life*, 438-439.
14. George Washington to John Greenwood, January 20, 1797, Philadelphia; *The writings of George Washington, from the original manuscript sources*, vol. 35, John C. Fitzpatrick, ed., etext.lib.virginia.edu/washington/; also from *George Washington, Writings*, John Rodehamel, ed. (New York: Library of America, 1997), 986.

uncomfortable dentures, Washington would file them down to ease the pain but sometimes wreck them in doing so. Washington wrote Greenwood in a letter dated January 25, 1797, "By filing these parts away (to remedy that evil) it has been one cause of the teeth giving way, having been weakened thereby."[15] The president complained to Greenwood in the same letter that the existing denture contraption, "causes both upper, & under lip to bulge out, as if swelled."[16] That "swelled" mouth look is very evident in the famous Gilbert Stuart portrait of the same year. Stuart, however, also might have accented the swelled look of Washington's mouth in the painting because of their volatile relationship.[17] Exaggerated or not, the look of Washington's lower lip being pushed out by the dentures was (as Washington's stepgrandson George Washington Parke Custis said in the 1790s) Washington's most obvious facial feature. But either way, you could see where Washington was coming from if you, too, had to clench your jaws tightly shut to keep a spring-loaded contraption down that didn't fit inside your mouth.

Earlier Dr. Greenwood had created a lower partial denture[18] and an upper denture[19] for Washington. But the most famous of Washington's dentures, also created by Greenwood, is the only full set

15. "From George Washington to John Greenwood, 25 January 1797," Founders Online, National Archives (founders.archives.gov/documents/Washington/ 99-01-02-00220 [last update: 2014-09-30]). Source: "this is an Early Access document from The Papers of George Washington. It is not an authoritative final version" (accessed October 26, 2014).
16. Ibid.
17. To say it mildly, Stuart and Washington did not get along. Washington did not like to sit still and be stared at for hours at a time by *any* painter. But Stuart, who felt painters were superior to everyone else, engaged his subjects with "showy and outrageous talk." Washington hated that even more and the two aimed barbed words at each other during their sittings. "But it may well be that Stuart, who angrily used General Knox's portrait as the door of his pigsty, was motivated in his relationship with Washington also by rage. No other man's rage did Washington's historical image more harm." James Thomas Flexner, *Washington—The Indispensable Man* (New York: Little, Brown and Company, 1974), 339-340.
18. This lower denture is in the National Museum of Dentistry, Baltimore, MD; another lower jaw denture is at the New York Academy of Medicine.
19. This upper denture is on display at the National Museum of American History, Smithsonian Institution.

that exists today and is at Mount Vernon Estate and Gardens.[20] In the photo of the famous false teeth, one can see an open spot in the lower left. That accommodated Washington's only remaining real tooth in his head by the time he was inaugurated president in 1789. But eventually the tooth decay that plagued Washington so much through his life (along with probably the chafing of the tooth by the denture's lead base) made even saving that single tooth impossible. So Dr. Greenwood pulled George's final remaining tooth in 1796 and in a nice gesture, Washington gave the tooth to Greenwood as a gift. We don't know if it was in lieu of payment, but Greenwood put the tooth inside of a glass locket that hung from his watch chain.[21]

WASHINGTON SPEAKING AND EATING IN PUBLIC

George Washington never really liked speaking in public. Thomas Jefferson, far from being an extroverted public speaker himself, slammed Washington, saying he "had neither copiousness of ideas, nor fluency of words."[22] Although Washington didn't have the classical education that Jefferson had, Jefferson also didn't have a spring-loaded gadget in his mouth that Washington had. Public speaking for Washington was many times awkward, especially in saying words that had a "hiss" or "sh" in them (called "sibilant sound" in phonetic talk).

But possibly Washington's greatest speaking fear was of a spontaneous, hearty laugh where his unanchored dentures would go flying out of his mouth. "Opening his mouth relaxed the pressure on the curved metal springs connecting the upper and lower dentures, which might cause them to slip out."[23] Not the type of image and presence that Washington always strove for as a wealthy landowner, general, president, or statesman.

His dentures also began to dictate what foods Washington could eat. He naturally began to go towards soft foods, which could be chewed delicately by whatever front teeth he had. "Nelly" Custis Lewis, Martha Washington's granddaughter, confirmed that George

20. This famous full denture set came to light in approximately 1820, according to Mount Vernon associate curator Laura Simo. The dentures were inside a studded packing crate (marked #34) along with other clothing worn by George and Martha Washington. The packing crate and materials were donated by Martha Washington's oldest granddaughter, Eliza Parke Custis Law (1776-1831). www.c-span.org/video/?295393-1/mount-vernon-collections-storage-area (accessed October 24, 2014).
21. Dr. Greenwood's locket of Washington's last tooth is at the Fraunces Tavern Museum of the New York State Sons of the Revolution in New York City.
22. *Thomas Jefferson, Political Writings*, ed., Joyce Appleby and Terence Ball (London: Cambridge University Press, 1999), 40.
23. Chernow, *Washington: A Life*, 609.

Washington's favorite breakfast was sort of mushy pancakes, "hoecakes swimming in butter and honey."[24] A visitor to Mount Vernon also wrote much the same thing, but this time directly tied Washington's breakfast in with his dental problems: "Since his retirement he has led a quiet and regular life. He gets up at 5 o'clock in the morning, reads or writes until seven. He breakfasts on tea and caks [cakes] made from maize; because of his teeth he makes slices spread with butter and honey . . . "[25]

For the whole last decade of Washington's life, from 1790 to 1799, letters show that Washington and Dr. Greenwood sent boxes of false teeth and dentures back and forth through the mail, somewhat like a modern day amazon.com relationship. A sad example of Washington's chronic pain early in his final decade was from his diary entry of January 18, 1790: "Monday 18th. Still indisposed with an Aching tooth, and swelled and inflamed Gum."[26] And the discomfort and embarrassment of bad-fitting dentures still continued eight years after that diary entry, until nearly Washington's death. In a late December 1798 letter to Greenwood, Washington complained about the new set of false teeth sent to him, saying that they "shoot beyond the gums" and "forces the lip out just under the nose."[27]

HOW DID THE "WOODEN TEETH" MYTH GET STARTED?

George Washington never had wooden teeth, nor did anybody of his time. It would have been kind of dumb to make teeth out of wood when better materials were available. Washington's dentures over the course of his lifetime used materials like human teeth along with bone

24. "Nelly" Custis (Lewis), quoted in *Dining With the Washingtons: Historic Recipes, Entertainment, and Hospitality From Mount Vernon* (Chapel Hill: UNC Press Books, 2011), 38, also in www.mountvernon.org/research-collections/digital-encyclopedia/article/hoecakes-and-honey/ (accessed October 24, 2014).

25. Julian Ursyn Niemcewicz, entry for June 5, 1798, in *Under Their Vine and Fig Tree: Travels Through America in 1797-1799, 1805, with some further account of life in New Jersey*, translated and edited by Metchie J. E. Budka (Elizabeth, NJ: Published as Volume XIV in the *Collections of The New Jersey Historical Society* at Newark by the Grassman Publishing Company, 1965), 102-103; my thanks to Mary V. Thompson, Mount Vernon, for this citation source.

26. "[Diary entry: 18 January 1790]," Founders Online, National Archives (founders.archives.gov/documents/Washington/01-06-02-0001-0001-0018 [last update: 2014-09-30]). Source: *The Diaries of George Washington*, vol. 6, 1 January 1790–13 December 1799, ed. Donald Jackson and Dorothy Twohig (Charlottesville: University Press of Virginia, 1979), 9 (accessed October 26, 2014).

27 George Washington to John Greenwood, December 7, 1798, W.W. Abbot and Dorothy Twohig, eds. *The Papers of George Washington: Retirement Series*, 4 vols. (Charlottesville: University Press of Virginia, 1998-1999), 3:245.

and ivory from hippopotamus, or "sea horse"[28] as it was called in its day. Ivory from walrus and elephant may also have been used, along with lead, gold metal wire and springs, and brass screws. None of that sounds very comfortable.

It's hard to say when the wooden teeth myth got started, but historians and forensic dentists possibly know how it got started. Ivory and bone both have hairline fractures in them, which normally can't be seen. With Washington's fondness for Madeira wine, a very dark wine, over time the darkness of the wine started to darken the false teeth of the dentures. Then the thin fractures in the bone started to darken even more than the rest of the tooth, making the lines look like the grain in a piece of wood "that misled later observers."[29]

In fact (just as would happen today with the dentist scolding the patient), in a December 1798 letter to Washington, Dr. Greenwood scolded Washington: " . . . the sett you sent me from Philadelphia which when I received was very black, occasioned either by your soaking them in port wine, or by your drinking it."[30]

But also, just like today, one finds when reading the same original letter from Dr. Greenwood, he has added a "P.S." at the very bottom of the page that says, "Sir, the additional charge is fifteen dollars."[31]

Thanks to Melissa Wood, Laura Simo, and Mary V. Thompson, research historians at The Fred W. Smith National Library for the Study of George Washington at Mount Vernon Estate and Gardens, for their research assistance, guidance, and source material on this article.

28. "It was finally necessary to have them extracted from one jaw and replaced with a set of artificial teeth made of 'seahorse' (hippopotamus) ivory." New York, March 1790; Stephen Decatur Jr., *Private Affairs of George Washington from the Records and Accounts of Tobias Lear Esquire, His Secretary* (Boston: HoughtonMifflin, 1933), 124.
29. www.mountvernon.org/research-collections/digital-encyclopedia/article/wooden-teeth-myth/ (accessed October 24, 2014).
30. John Greenwood to George Washington, New York, December 28, 1798; from the Collection of Mr. William Alexander Smith; *Magazine of American History with Notes and Queries*, vol. XVI, ed. Martha J. Lamb (New York: Historical Publication Company, 1886), 294.
31. John Greenwood to George Washington, New York, December 28, 1798; from the Collection of Mr. William Alexander Smith; *Magazine of American History with Notes and Queries*, vol. XVI, ed. Martha J. Lamb (New York: Historical Publication Company, 1886), 295.

AUTHOR BIOGRAPHIES

MERV O. AHRENS

Merv O. Ahrens is an independent researcher from Canada who lives immediately adjacent to the Minnesota–Ontario boundary that traces the historic waterway into the Northwest. Following his retirement as an educator he has focused on studying the early history of this region. The development of the local fur trade and the geopolitics surrounding the establishment of the Canadian–American 49th North boundary are his current interests. He has presented his findings at a number of conferences and has authored several journal articles on these topics.

TODD ANDRLIK

Todd Andrlik, founder and editor of the *Journal of the American Revolution*, is author of *Reporting the Revolutionary War: Before It Was History, It Was News* (Sourcebooks, 2012), named one of the Best Books of 2012 by Barnes & Noble and Best American Revolution Book of the Year by the New York American Revolution Round Table. A full-time marketing and media professional, Andrlik has written or ghost-written thousands of published articles on various business topics. His history-related work has been featured by *Slate, Huffington Post, Boston Globe, Smithsonian, TIME,* NPR, C-SPAN, CNN, MSNBC, Mount Vernon, the American Revolution Center, Fraunces Tavern Museum, and more.

MICHAEL BARBIERI

A life-long Vermonter, Michael has spent forty years researching and interpreting the Revolution with a concentration on the northern theater. He has taught history at high school and college levels and has given numerous presentations on eighteenth century history and culture. In 1974, Michael helped form Whitcomb's Rangers and subsequently based his master's thesis on the original unit. He worked for a number of years at the Lake Champlain Maritime Museum and is currently an active supporter of historic sites in the region, particularly Hubbardton and Mount Independence.

J. L. BELL

J. L. Bell, associate editor of the *Journal of the American Revolution*, is the proprietor of boston1775.net, a popular website dedicated to the history of the American Revolution in New England. A Fellow of the Massachusetts Historical Society and American Antiquarian Society, he is author of the National Park Service's study of George Washington's work in Cambridge, and has delivered papers to the Massachusetts Historical Society, the Organization of American Historians, and historic sites around greater Boston. He is the author of *The Road to Concord: How Four Stolen Cannon Ingnited the Revolutionary War* (Westholme, 2016), an inaugural volume in the *Journal of the American Revolution Books* series.

TODD W. BRAISTED

Todd Braisted is an author and researcher of Loyalist military studies. His primary focus is on Loyalist military personnel, infrastructure, and campaigns throughout North America. Since 1979, Braisted has amassed and transcribed over 40,000 pages of Loyalist and related material from archives and private collections around the world. His website, royalprovincial.com, is a leading source for Loyalist information. A past president of the Bergen County Historical Society, an honorary vice-president of the United Empire Loyalist Association of Canada, and a Fellow of the Company of Military Historians, he has authored numerous articles and books on the American Revolution, and has appeared on such shows as PBS's *History Detectives*. His book, *Grand Forage 1778: The Battleground Around New York City* (Westholme, 2016), is an inaugural volume in the *Journal of the American Revolution Books* series.

KIM BURDICK

Kim Burdick is the founder and chairperson of the American Revolution Round Table of Northern Delaware. As 2003–2009 National Project Director of the Washington-Rochambeau Revolutionary Route (now W3R-NHT), Kim coordinated a nine-state and DC effort celebrating the 225th Anniversary of the Yorktown Campaign. Advisor Emeritus to the National Trust for Historic Preservation and former Chairman of the Delaware Humanities Council, she has served as project director for some of Delaware's most innovative public history programs including the nationally recognized June 2014 symposium entitled *George Washington: Man and Myth*; the Delaware Memorial at Gettysburg; and a one-act traveling play, entitled "Delaware Ghosts."

ALEXANDER CAIN

Alexander Cain graduated from Merrimack College in 1993 with a degree in economics and the New England School of Law with a juris doctrate. In addition to being a litigation attorney, Alex is a professor at Merrimack College and Northeastern University. He frequently lectures on constitutional, criminal, and historical issues and developments in the United States. Alex has published several research articles relevant to New England militias and Loyalists during the American Revolution. He has published two books: *We Stood Our Ground: Lexington in the First Year of the American Revolution* (2nd Edition) and *I See Nothing but the Horrors of a Civil War*. Alex resides in Massachusetts with his wife, Paula, and his children John and Abigail.

JETT CONNER

Jett Conner is a retired political science professor, college administrator, and academic policy officer for the Colorado Department of Higher Education. Conner received his PhD in political science from the University of Colorado, Boulder. He studied the political thought of the American founding period during a National Endowment for the Humanities summer fellowship at Princeton University, and contributed "Tom Paine and the Genesis of American Federalism," to *The Embattled Constitution: Vital Framework or Convenient Symbol*, Adolph Grundman, ed. (Malabar, Florida, Krieger Publishing Co., 1986).

KEN DAIGLER

Ken Daigler is a retired CIA operations officer. He earned a B.A in history from Centre College of Kentucky and an M.A. from the Maxwell School at Syracuse University, and served in the U.S. Marine Corps during the Vietnam War. His numerous articles have appeared in various journals within the US intelligence community, including *Studies in Intelligence* and *The Intelligencer*. His latest book is *Spies, Patriots and Traitors* (Georgetown University Press, 2014), which describes American intelligence activities during the Revolutionary period both within the colonies and abroad.

NORMAN DESMARAIS

Norman Desmarais, professor emeritus at Providence College, is editor-in-chief of *The Brigade Dispatch*, the journal the Brigade of the American Revolution. He is the author of *Battlegrounds of Freedom*, *The Guide to the American Revolutionary War* and *The Guide to the American Revolutionary War at Sea and Overseas* (in preparation). He has also translated the *Gazette Française*, the French newspaper published in Newport, Rhode Island, by the French fleet that brought the Count de Rochambeau and French troops to America in July 1780. It is the first known service newspaper published by an expeditionary force.

THOMAS FLEMING

Thomas Fleming is a distinguished historian and novelist. He is the author of many bestselling books, including *The Great Divide: The Conflict between Washington and Jefferson that Defined a Nation* (Da Capo, 2015), *A Disease of the Public Mind: A New Understanding of Why We Fought the Civil War* (Da Capo, 2014), *The Intimate Lives of the Founding Fathers* (Harper Perennial, 2010), *One Small Candle: The Pilgrims' First Year in America* (W. W. Norton,

1980), *Washington's Secret War: The Hidden History of Valley Forge* (Smithsonian, 2005), and *Beat the Last Drum: The Siege of Yorktown* (St. Martin's, 1963). He has written frequently for *American Heritage* and other magazines and is often a guest on C-Span, the History Channel, and PBS.

NORMAN FUSS

Norman Fuss is an avocational historian and living history interpreter who for the past forty years has focused on the history of the period of the American War for Independence. After retiring from a career as a chemical engineer and management consultant, he moved to Williamsburg, Virginia, where he conducts guided tours for the Jamestown–Yorktown Foundation and acts as a volunteer consultant for the American Revolution Museum at Yorktown, opening in late 2016. He also serves as a subject matter expert for Colonial Williamsburg's Electronic Field Trips. A frequent writer and speaker, he has published over three dozen articles on a variety of topics related to the Revolutionary War period.

DON N. HAGIST

Don N. Hagist, editor of the *Journal of the American Revolution*, is an independent researcher specializing in the demographics and material culture of the British army in the American Revolution. He maintains a blog about British common soldiers (http://redcoat76.blogspot.com) and has published a number of articles in academic journals. His books include *The Revolution's Last Men: the Soldiers Behind the Photographs* (Westholme, 2015), *British Soldiers, American War* (Westholme, 2012), *A British Soldier's Story: Roger Lamb's Narrative of the American Revolution* (Ballindalloch Press, 2004), *General Orders: Rhode Island* (Heritage Books, 2001) and *Wives, Slaves, and Servant Girls* (Westholme, 2016). Don works as an engineering consultant in Rhode Island, and also writes for several well-known syndicated and freelance cartoonists.

HUGH T. HARRINGTON

Hugh T. Harrington, editor emeritus of the *Journal of the American Revolution*, is an independent researcher and author whose books include *Remembering Milledgeville* (History Press, 2005), *More Milledgeville Memories* (History Press, 2006), *Civil War Milledgeville* (History Press, 2005), and a biography of the Gilded Age magician *Annie Abbott, "The Little Georgia Magnet"* (Createspace, 2010). His articles have appeared in a number of magazines and journals, including *Journal of Military History, Georgia Historical Quarterly, America's Civil War, Southern Campaigns of the American Revolution, American Revolution,* and *Muzzle Blasts*. He has written extensively on Sherlock Holmes and is a member of the Baker Street Irregulars. He lives in Gainesville, Georgia.

STUART HATFIELD

Stuart Hatfield lives in Muskegon, Michigan. He earned his masters in Military History from AMU (focused on the American Revolution). He currently works in IT and has published three novels and currently curates an American Military History blog at historiamilitaris.org. He is currently researching the relationship between the Continental Congress and the Continental army.

ALLISON K. LANGE

Allison K. Lange is an assistant professor of history at the Wentworth Institute of Technology, Boston. She helped curate the Norman B. Leventhal Map Center at the Boston Public Library's "We Are One" exhibition. Lange received her PhD in American history from Brandeis University. Currently she is completing a manuscript on the visual culture of the woman's rights and woman suffrage movements in the United States. Her work has appeared in *Imprint* and *The Atlantic*. She also works with the National Women's History Museum. Learn more about her research at allisonklange.com.

CHRISTIAN M. McBURNEY

Christian McBurney is an independent historian based in Washington D. C. He is author of *Spies in Revolutionary Rhode Island* (History Press, 2014), *Kidnapping the Enemy: The Special Operations to Capture Generals Charles Lee and Richard Prescott* (Westholme, 2014), and *The Rhode Island Campaign: The First French and American Operation of the Revolutionary War* (Westholme, 2011). He has a book on kidnapping attempts against Revolutionary War Military and government leaders to be published in 2016 by McFarland. For more information on these books, see christianmcburney.com.

LOUIS ARTHUR NORTON

Louis Arthur Norton, a professor emeritus at the University of Connecticut, has published extensively on maritime history topics that include *Joshua Barney: Hero of the Revolutionary War* (Naval Institute, 2000) and *Captains Contentious: The Dysfunctional Sons of the Brine* (University of South Carolina Press, 2009). Two of his articles were awarded the 2002 and 2006 Gerald E. Morris Prize for maritime historiography in the Mystic Seaport Museum's LOG, and he received the Connecticut Authors and Publishers Association's 2009/2010 and 2010/2011 awards for fiction and essay writing respectively.

GENE PROCKNOW

Gene Procknow is a frequent contributor to the *Journal of the American Revolution*. His research concentrations include interpreting the Revolution from a non-American perspective, better understanding the Revolution's global aspects, and Ethan Allen and the creation of Vermont. He is the author of the *Mad River Gazetteer* (Lulu, 2011), which traces the naming of prominent Vermont place names to Revolutionary War patriots. Procknow authors a multidisciplinary writers blog on leadership development, poetry, and additional articles on the Revolution and Vermont at geneprock.com.

RAY RAPHAEL

Ray Raphael in an award-winning historian. An associate editor of the *Journal of the American Revolution,* he coauthored with Marie Raphael *The Spirit of '74: How the American Revolution Began* (New Press, 2015), and is author of *Founding Myths: Stories that Hide Our Patriotic Past* (New Press, 2004, 2014), *Constitutional Myths: What We Get Wrong and What We Get Right* (New Press, 2013), *Mr. President: How and Why the Founders Created a Chief Executive* (Knopf, 2012), *Founders: The People Who Brought You a Nation* (New Press, 2009), and *A People's History of the American Revolution* (New Press, 2001, and Harper Perennial, 2016). A complete list of his books and articles, as well as some key historical documents not published elsewhere, can be found at rayraphael.com.

MATTHEW REARDON

Matthew Reardon earned his BA in history and an MA in education from Sacred Heart University in Fairfield, Connecticut. His research interests include Connecticut during both the American Revolution and the Civil War. He currently serves as the executive director of the New England Civil War Museum and is a middle school teacher in Vernon, Connecticut. His new military study on the New London Raid of 1781 is forthcoming.

WILLIAM W. REYNOLDS

William W. Reynolds, a native of Virginia, received engineering degrees from Virginia Tech and Southern Methodist University and was a registered Professional Engineer before retiring from the consulting field. His interest in the American Revolution has resulted in several articles on that subject, the most recent of which, concerning the history of the 9th Virginia Regiment and the contribution of the Virginia militia to the Siege of Yorktown, were published in *Military Collector & Historian.* Mr. Reynolds lives in Sarasota, Florida.

BRYAN RINDFLEISCH

Bryan Rindfleisch earned his Ph.D. in history from the University of Oklahoma, and is currently an assistant professor at Marquette University, where he teaches courses in Colonial American and Native American history. He has written a number of articles which have been published in a variety of journals and magazines, including *Ethnohistory, History Compass, Native South,* and *Wisconsin Magazine of History.*

BOB RUPPERT

Bob Ruppert is a retired high school administrator from the greater Chicagoland area. He received his undergraduate degree from Loyola University and his graduate degree from the University of Illinois. He has been researching the American Revolution, the War for Independence, and the Federal period for more than fifteen years. His interest began in 1963 when his parents took the whole family to Newport Beach, Virginia, and a small town that was slowly being restored to its eighteenh-century prominence: Williamsburg.

MICHAEL SCHELLHAMMER

Michael Schellhammer is a former U.S. Army infantry, intelligence, and civil affairs officer. He served in the Persian Gulf War, Haiti, Bosnia, and Iraq. His work has appeared in the *Washington Post*, the *Washington Times*, and the *Military Intelligence Professional Bulletin*. He is the author of *The 83rd Pennsylvania Volunteers in the Civil War* (McFarland, 2003), and *George Washington and the Final British Campaign for the Hudson River, 1779* (McFarland, 2012).

GARY SHATTUCK

Gary Shattuck served over three decades in the Vermont law enforcement community as a supervising officer with the Vermont State Police, an assistant attorney general, and as an assistant United States attorney with the U.S. Department of Justice. He has also served as a legal advisor to governments in Kosovo and Iraq during their recent conflicts. An alumnus of the University of Colorado and magna cum laude graduate of the Vermont Law School, Gary is currently completing a master's degree in military history, concentrating on the Revolutionary War. He is a member of the Fort Ticonderoga National Council and is the author of *Artful and Designing Men: The Trials of Job Shattuck and the Regulation of 1786–1787* (Tate Publishing, 2013) and *Insurrection, Corruption and Murder in Early Vermont: Life on the Wild Northern Frontier* (History Press, 2014).

MICHAEL J. F. SHEEHAN

Michael J. F. Sheehan holds a bachelor's degree in history from Ramapo College of New Jersey. A historical interpreter at the Stony Point Battlefield State Historic Site, Michael has spent most of his time studying the American Revolution with a focus on the role of the Hudson Highlands and Lower Hudson Valley, where he has lived his whole life. He also studies artillery, uniforms, and Highland regiments. Deeply involved in the Brigade of the American Revolution since 2008, Michael has reenacted and spoken at many historic sites and societies in New York and New Jersey, and is currently serving as a board member for Lamb's Artillery Company.

JOSHUA SHEPHERD

Joshua Shepherd, a sculptor and freelance writer, has created over twenty public monuments. His articles–with a special focus on revolutionary and frontier America–have appeared in *MHQ: The Quarterly Journal of Military History*, *Military Heritage*, *Muzzle Blasts*, *The Artilleryman*, and other publications. He lives in rural Indiana with his wife and three children.

JOHN L. SMITH, JR.

John L. Smith, Jr., is a retired corporate communications manager for a Florida energy company. He is a state certified social sciences instructor and a former board member of the Tampa Bay History Center. Smith is a

Vietnam-era veteran and holds honorable discharges from the U.S. Air Force Reserve and the U.S. Army Reserve. He graduated with a BS degree from the University of South Florida in 1989 and received an MBA from the University of Tampa. Listed in the Internet Movie Data Base (IMDB), Smith is an active SAG-AFTRA member, having appeared in many films, television shows, commercials, and corporate training videos. He is currently writing a book about the American Revolution and his historical work has been featured by *Knowledge Quest*, *National Review*, and *Smithsonian Magazine*.

DANIEL J. TORTORA

Daniel J. Tortora is assistant professor of history at Colby College in Waterville, Maine, where he teaches courses in American and Native American history. He is author of *Fort Halifax: Winslow's Historic Outpost* (History Press, 2014) and *Carolina in Crisis: Cherokees, Colonists, and Slaves in the American Southeast, 1756–1763* (University of North Carolina Press, 2015). He speaks extensively on the French and Indian War and Revolutionary War eras, leads battlefield and historic tours, and has contributed to films, archaeological projects, exhibits, and research projects. He is part of the movement to rebuild and interpret Fort Halifax in Winslow, Maine.

THOMAS VERENNA

Thomas Verenna is a member of the Valley Forge Chapter, Sons of the American Revolution, an associate board member of the Moore Township Historical Commission, and a history student at Columbia College, Missouri. He is an alumnus of the Valley Forge Military Academy, located about five miles from the site of the 1777–1778 encampment. Thomas's research focuses on Pennsylvania's military and political role in the War for American Independence.

INDEX